Praise for *The Good and the Right*

"In this clear and creative introduction, Clanton and Martin map otherwise confusing moral terrain with a distinctively Christian GPS. An excellent resource for teaching moral philosophy with faith in mind."

—**Rebecca DeYoung,** Professor of Philosophy, Calvin University

"*The Good and the Right* is a guide to the major theories that philosophers have devised about morality. Clanton and Martin ably illuminate the theories with memorable examples and comparisons with competing theories, and they assess them in the light of an ecumenical Christianity."

—**Robert C. Roberts,** Distinguished Professor Emeritus of Ethics, Baylor University

"*The Good and the Right* is the best introduction to ethics available, period."

—**Logan Paul Gage,** Professor of Philosophy and Director of Catholic Studies, Franciscan University of Steubenville

"This book offers a wonderful introduction to the landscape of moral philosophy, while putting this discussion in conversation with particular presuppositions, commitments, and perspectives of the Christian faith. The chapters provide a nuanced but accessible overview and evaluation of the major normative moral theories. The range of coverage is diverse, exemplary, and fitting. The tone of the book is appreciative and critical in its analysis, ecumenical in its engagement with different theories, and constructive in the development of its own proposal. The book's appeal to divine revelation is not an invitation to a confessional retreat but rather reflects a deeply integrative project!"

—**Frederick Aquino,** Professor of Systematic Theology, Southern Methodist University

"J. Caleb Clanton and Kraig Martin give sympathetic and charitable accounts of the leading moral theories; yet for each theory, they offer as well an honest overall assessment from the standpoint of both philosophical reflection and Christian faith. Add to these virtues an unusuallyclear writing style, and *The Good and the Right* stands as an exemplary approach to Christian philosophical ethics."

—**Christopher Tollefsen,** Professor of Philosophy, University of South Carolina

"In my two decades teaching introductory ethics courses to undergraduate and seminary students, I've long sought a textbook that is accessible, philosophically rich, and committed to exploring the import of Christian faith to our moral lives. With the publication of *The Good and the Right*, my search is over. Clanton and Martin offer a captivating, readable introduction to the major categories and language of philosophical ethics. The concrete illustrations they employ throughout the book well illustrate the connection between philosophy and everyday moral questions. Most importantly, Clanton and Martin make a constructive case for the relevance of Christian faith to these questions. I am thrilled that my ethics students will benefit from the work of these authors."

—**Dr. Vic McCracken,** Professor of Ethics and Theology, Abilene Christian University

"Finally, an introduction to moral philosophy that takes seriously the claims and ethical commitments of Christianity! Clanton and Martin offer fresh insight into ancient debates in order to help every student of philosophy not only understand but practice moral philosophy from a distinctly Christian perspective. Advocating a combination theory, this book encourages students to appeal to both reason and revelation in assessing moral truths and ethical obligations. This book fills a lacuna in the philosophy textbook world, allowing the best of moral theory to be presented through a decidedly Christian lens in a way that is both accessible and scholarly."

—**Nathan Guy,** Associate Professor of Philosophy, Theology, and Ethics, Harding University

"It seems to have escaped popular consciousness that moral choices need be (or even *can* be) based on anything beyond feelings. So clear a volume as this one that alerts its readers to major ethical theories can help move those uncritical choices into the realm of thoughtful and intentional behaviors. For Christians in a post-Christian culture, this sort of thoughtful move—with the historic philosophical theories critiqued from a perspective of orthodox faith by two competent scholars—is especially critical."

—**Rubel Shelly,** PhD, Professor of Philosophy and Religion (retired), Lipscomb University

"*The Good and the Right* examines the dominant theories in moral philosophy at an introductory level. On every level of examination, whether description, analysis, or critique, the authors deal with each theory's strengths and weaknesses thoroughly, clearly, and fairly. As the subtitle makes clear, the book reads the history of moral philosophy through Christian eyes. This feature makes the book especially attractive to Christian readers, though anyone can read it with profit. After getting a grasp on the eight main attempts to philosophical theories treated by the authors, readers will appreciate the last chapter, which attempts to construct a 'Non-Reductive Combination Theory' of morality useful for Christians. I recommend this book highly for college and graduate students or to anyone who wishes to understand the basic categories within which modern Western people approach moral issues. The book is intelligent, lucid, well-researched, thorough, well-written, and appropriately illustrated with examples from daily life."

—**Ron Highfield,** Professor of Religion and Philosophy, Pepperdine University

A CHRISTIAN
INTRODUCTION TO
MORAL PHILOSOPHY

THE GOOD AND THE RIGHT

J. CALEB CLANTON
KRAIG MARTIN

THE GOOD AND THE RIGHT

A Christian Introduction to Moral Philosophy

ACU
PRESS

ISBN 978-1-68426-122-2 | LCCN 2024049269

Printed in the United States of America

LIBRARY OF CONGRESS CATALOGING-IN-PUBLICATION DATA
Names: Clanton, J. Caleb, 1978- author. | Martin, Kraig, Ph.D. author.
Title: The good & the right : a Christian introduction to moral philosophy / J. Caleb Clanton and Kraig Martin.
Other titles: Good and the right
Description: Abilene, Texas : Abilene Christian University Press, [2025] | Includes bibliographical references and index. |
Identifiers: LCCN 2024049269 (print) | LCCN 2024049270 (ebook) | ISBN 9781684261222 (paperback) | ISBN 9781684268368 (ebook)
Subjects: LCSH: Ethics.
Classification: LCC BJ1012 .C57 2025 (print) | LCC BJ1012 (ebook) | DDC 170—dc23/eng/20250209
LC record available at https://lccn.loc.gov/2024049269
LC ebook record available at https://lccn.loc.gov/2024049270

Cover design by Outerwear
Interior text design by Sandy Armstrong, Strong Design

For information contact:
Abilene Christian University Press
ACU Box 29138
Abilene, Texas 79699

1-877-816-4455
www.acupressbooks.com

25 26 27 28 29 30 31 // 7 6 5 4 3 2 1

For Shepherd and Annabelle

—J. C. C.

For Lela and Jed

—K. M.

CONTENTS

ACKNOWLEDGMENTS

Our work together as coauthors has benefited immensely from the input of several friends and interlocutors that we have each enjoyed over the years, and we both owe them a debt of gratitude. For helpful comments, insights, or input related to different points connected to this book, we thank Richard Goode, Lee Mayo, Josh Strahan, Lauren White, Scott Sager, Leonard Allen, Lee Camp, John Mark Hicks, Marc Schwerdt, David Holmes, Paul Begin, Chris Metress, Michael Hodges, Aaron Simmons, Chris Shrock, Christopher Tollefsen, Steve Evans, John Hare, Janine Marie Idziak, Tom Olbricht, Fred Aquino, Derek Estes, Jim Baird, David Mafhood, Peter Rice, Mac Sandlin, Nathan Guy, Matt Love, and Scott Adair. We are grateful also to Jason Fikes, Mary Hardegree, and the other reviewers and editors at Abilene Christian University Press for their input on the manuscript.

We gratefully acknowledge the editors and publishers of the following articles for permission to rework and reuse material that originally appeared in their publications. Parts of Chapter Eight derive from "Understanding Aquinas on Natural Law," *Journal of Faith and the Academy* 12, no. 2 (Fall 2019): 37–56, as well as "Aquinas and Scotus on the Metaphysical Foundations of Morality," *Religions* 10, no. 2, art. 107 (2019):

1–14. Parts of Chapter Nine derive from "William of Ockham, Andrew of Neufchateau, and the Origins of Divine Command Theory," *American Catholic Philosophical Quarterly* 94, no. 3 (2020): 405–29, as well as "On Moral-Natural and Moral-Positive Duties: A Combination Metaethical Theory in the Restoration Tradition," *Studies in Christian Ethics* 30, no. 4 (2017): 429–48. Parts of several chapters derive from "Virtue Depends on Natural Law and Divine Commands," *Religions* 16, no. 1, art. 34 (2025): 1–14.

Lastly, Kraig would like to thank Marty Spears, provost of Harding University, as well as Dean Monte Cox and the faculty of the College of Bible and Ministry at Harding—and the Amigos—for their support of his research. Caleb would like to thank Jennifer Shewmaker, provost of Lipscomb University, for her support of his research. And a special word of heartfelt gratitude to Candice McQueen, president of Lipscomb University, for an act of grace in leadership that will never be forgotten.

chapter one

INTRODUCTION

Day in and day out, people wrestle with questions of moral philosophy—and not just in college classrooms but in coffee shops, at baseball games, in online discussions, at the grocery store or barber shop, around the kitchen table, or in front of the TV. They debate whether their schools or churches should require vaccines or face masks, or whether the latest presidential candidate should have said that, or whether the police should have done that, or whether the Supreme Court should have handed down that ruling, or whether the public library should make a certain book available to schoolkids. They wonder whether it is right or wrong for someone to take a particular job offer, carry a gun, have sex, move in with one's boyfriend, invite one's mother-in-law to move in with the family, claim a deduction on one's taxes, eat genetically modified foods, smoke pot, get an abortion, play first-person shooter video games, buy petroleum products from Russia, support Israel or Palestine, recycle, water the lawn, drive an electric car, invest in a certain company, or pursue transgender hormone therapy. They argue with their spouses about how to spend money and what to think about artificial intelligence. They lose sleep over how to raise their children and about where to send them to school and whether to let them have a smart phone or use social media. They confide in their friends about their destructive habits, or about their anger issues, or their loneliness and fears—or about their loves or joys or hopes for the future. Either directly or indirectly, all of this connects up with basic questions in ethics or, as we will call it, *moral philosophy*.[1]

This is a book about moral philosophy. More to the point, this is a *Christian* introduction to moral philosophy. What that means is that this book is intended to offer a lucid survey of the major normative moral theories in the history of philosophy, and do so in a way that engages with the presuppositions, affirmations, and implications of the Christian faith—and specifically in a way that takes them seriously.

Unfortunately, there is no precise and illuminating way at the outset to state what moral philosophy is, in part because there is no simple and uncontroversial way to define what *morality* is in the first place. Plainly enough, morality is connected to our goals, motivations, decisions, actions, habits, and character traits as human beings. But any effort to define morality in crisper terms beyond that almost invariably implicates us in one side of this or that controversial philosophical issue. We will come to many of those very controversies in the pages ahead. Ideally, though, we would like to minimize the extent to which we decide the issues before we have even had a chance to explain them. So, for now, we will need to make do with a fairly loose working definition of what morality is and, hence, of what moral philosophy is. Broadly speaking, moral philosophy is the study of important questions pertaining to human goals, motivations, decisions, actions, habits, and character traits.

We can sometimes get a better handle on what a thing is by paying some attention to what it is *not*. Along those lines, it might help to reflect briefly on what morality is not. The study of morality is not merely a study of what is required by the law or a company policy or the codes of this or that guild or professional association or what is customary in this or that society or tradition. That's because morality is ultimately prescriptive in nature and not merely descriptive. That is to say, morality is about how things *should* be—about how the world *ought* to be—not simply about how things are, or used to be, or even will be one day. Similarly, the study of morality is not simply a study of human feelings or emotions or tastes or preferences. And morality is not simply about etiquette or even about what would be proper or rational in this or that setting. Admittedly, emotions, preferences, and self-interests can be connected in important ways to moral philosophy, but morality is not reducible to them. Instead, moral philosophy is the endeavor to understand what sorts of things are valuable, how we should behave toward ourselves and others, and how we should strive to live our lives and shape our characters. In attempting to identify those things, moral philosophy attempts to articulate standards for evaluating persons, rules, policies, laws, institutions, societies, and organizations—as well as standards for justifying decisions and actions and explaining them to others.

This endeavor inevitably ropes us into the process of considering different proposals, reasons, and arguments about the nature of morality. John Locke (1632–1704) famously held that on any occasion a particular rule of morality is proposed, we should expect some sort of reason to be offered in support of the rule—which is in part why Locke thought that we do not *innately* know any moral rules in the first place.[2] After all, why should we expect that the proposer would need to pony up if the rules of morality were somehow already within us? If the rules of morality *were* simply innate, then we really wouldn't need to ask the one who proposes a moral rule to justify it, since we would already know the answer innately.

We need not go as far as Locke in rejecting the theory of innate ideas in order to appreciate his point about the connection between theorizing about the nature of morality and the practice of considering and exchanging reasons. When someone asserts "we have a moral obligation to ______," or "it's morally wrong to ______," that person is assuming that something holds true for all of us—or, at the very least, that at least *some* of the rules in question are universally applicable in scope. But if such a rule were true and universally applicable, it would (or should) overrule other considerations we might have in mind. And so it is fitting that we know how and why the proposed rule of morality is correct in the first place. In other words, it is fitting that we know how and why these claims about the nature of morality are true. And what we are seeking in this book is an account of morality that, all things considered, seems correct.

Of course, moral philosophy is not done in a vacuum. We inevitably bring our background beliefs with us into the inquiry. That is, we bring with us our most fundamental assumptions and hard-fought convictions about the underlying nature of reality, as well as the hunches, intuitions, and experiences shaped by those assumptions and convictions. Some people are convinced, for example, that there is no such being as God and, furthermore, that any viable explanation of this or that feature of reality must appeal only to natural or scientific facts. So those folks bring their own preconceptions into the inquiry. Similarly, people who believe that God *does* exist also bring their own preconceptions into the inquiry in question. The same goes for us, too: We bring our most fundamental assumptions about the underlying nature of reality with us into the inquiry at hand. And we—the authors of this book—are Christians. We have no desire to disguise that fact, to make apologies for it, or to bracket that fact out of our inquiry into the nature of morality. In fact, our aim in this book is to try to identify an account of morality that, all things considered, seems correct to us *as Christians*. First, though, we need to set the stage by saying a bit about what we take moral philosophy to involve before speaking to some of the distinctive features of this book.

1.1. The Branches of Moral Philosophy

Part of the challenge in formulating a precise definition of moral philosophy is the simple fact that questions about human goals, motivations, decisions, behaviors, habits, and character traits can take a variety of different forms. Put differently, there is a persistent, though subtle, ambiguity in what is meant by the term "moral philosophy": It is sometimes used in reference to the tasks of applied ethics, at other times it is used in reference to the tasks of normative moral theory, and sometimes it is used in reference to metaethics. Consider each of those three branches of moral philosophy in turn.

People sometimes ask very specific questions about whether we ought to be this way as opposed to that way, or whether we ought to do this action as opposed to that action. For example, we might wonder which character traits would best equip us to flourish, and what these traits look like in different contexts. Is the generous man or the tight-fisted fellow more likely to lead the kind of life to which we should aspire? What does courage look like in the midst of a pandemic? How does temperance apply to one's relationship to, say, the use of plastic or eating meat? Or we might wonder whether it is morally wrong to use a friend's Netflix password or take the morning-after pill or genetically enhance a baby or torture a terrorist or assassinate a genocidal dictator. Those sorts of inquiries fall within the domain of *applied* (or *practical*) *ethics*.

Answering the questions of applied ethics eventually requires us to weigh in on other philosophical questions. We might start out by asking, "Is it morally permissible to assassinate a dictator who is killing thousands of innocent people?"; but we might soon find ourselves asking, "What is the general principle that, when applied to the situation at hand, yields the proper verdict about whether assassinating bloodthirsty dictators is morally permissible?" Those two questions are importantly connected, of course. And that's because, when doing applied ethics, we often presume a broader theoretical framework in the background. Take a different example. Suppose we can all agree that it would be morally wrong for a parent to kill a newborn baby simply because she was born female. This is a judgment of applied ethics. But what is the proper theory or principle or rule that, if true, would explain *why* infanticide of female babies is immoral? Because it discriminates on the basis of sex? But what makes *that* wrong? Perhaps female infanticide is wrong because it would result in more suffering in the world than would otherwise exist. Or perhaps such a practice is wrong because it is contrary to how we wish everyone would behave in similar circumstances. Or maybe it is wrong because God commands us not to do stuff like that, or because a virtuous person would refrain from such an act. And so on. Notice how agreement at the level of applied ethics hardly guarantees agreement about the general principle. In other words, everyone might agree female infanticide is wrong but still disagree when it comes to the deeper explanation of *why* it is wrong. Applied ethics is done at a level of particularity and with highly contextual and specific moral judgments, while the broader theories or general principles in question fall within the territory of *normative moral theory*. Competing normative moral theories try to identify the more general standards or principles according to which we should make specific evaluative judgments and direct our actions. In other words, normative moral theories try to identify the conditions under which something could be said to be good or bad or the conditions under which an action can be said to be right or wrong.

There is yet a third area within moral philosophy—what often goes under the heading of *metaethics*. Metaethics deals with questions that are less about the substantive content of morality and more about surrounding semantic, metaphysical, epistemological, and psychological issues that arise in connection to morality. For example, metaethics deals with such questions as "What are we actually saying when we claim something is right or wrong?"; "What do moral claims really mean at the end of the day?"; "Are there objective moral facts in the first place?"; "How can we come to have moral knowledge?"; or "What is the fundamental source or grounding of morality in the first place?" Admittedly, the questions of metaethics and the questions of normative moral theory are at times intimately connected. For that reason, it can be difficult to delineate a clear boundary between these two branches of moral philosophy. But one relatively standard way of characterizing the difference is simply to stress their different foci.

Normative moral theories focus on articulating principles that yield correct, applied ethical judgments, while metaethical theories focus on, say, the source of morality itself, how we come to know about morality, and so on. For example, classical utilitarianism (which is one of the major normative moral theories we discuss in Chapter Four) asserts that the following principle, when correctly applied, yields the proper verdict of applied ethics: *act in a way that promotes the greatest net sum of happiness for the greatest number*. But the question of *what makes it true* that we have such a requirement is not per se a central feature of the normative moral theory itself. Normative moral theories generally seek to get the proper results with respect to the judgments of applied ethics. In other words, they try to articulate a principle that, plausibly, explains the general structure of the correct judgments of applied ethics by identifying the conditions under which something is good (or bad) or under which an action is right (or wrong). In some respects, then, it is fair to say that normative moral theories simply do not directly endeavor to answer the questions of metaethics, though they may sometimes have implications on metaethical questions.

To be sure, we will sometimes touch on matters of applied ethics and metaethics in this book. But for the most part, we mean to focus primarily on the tasks of normative moral theory. And that's because we are chiefly concerned with explaining and evaluating various historically influential attempts to explain the basic conditions under which something is good or bad, right or wrong. Simply put, we want to explore different positions on the nature of the good and the right.

1.2. The Good versus the Right

There is a distinction we have been hinting at so far, but we have yet to address it directly. We should pause here to make things as clear as we can. The distinction we have in mind is the distinction between what is valuable—what is good—and what we morally ought to do—what is right. Philosophers sometimes describe this as a distinction between *axiological* (root word: value) categories and *deontic* (root word: duty) categories. Commonly enough, though, philosophers talk about this as the distinction between *the good* and *the right.*

Start with the former. One vital task for any moral theory is to explain what makes something valuable, disvaluable, or value-neutral. Put differently, one task of any moral theory is to articulate (a) the conditions under which something is good, (b) the conditions under which something is bad (or evil), and (c) the conditions under which something is value-neutral (that is, neither good nor bad). Throughout this book, we will refer to all of this as moral theory's *account of the good.*

When reflecting on an account of the good, we will sometimes want to know what the theory says is *intrinsically* good, as well what the theory says is *extrinsically* or *instrumentally* good. To say that something is intrinsically good is to say it is valuable in and of itself—that is, its goodness is in no way dependent on or borrowed from something else. By contrast, something is extrinsically or instrumentally good when its goodness is reliant on something other than itself. We can clarify this distinction by way of example. Some philosophers think happiness is intrinsically good because they regard happiness as something that is valuable in and of itself—full stop. Meanwhile, in their view, money is only ever extrinsically or instrumentally good: It can help buy the things that might bring about happiness. In other words, money is valuable only as a means to procure what is intrinsically valuable, so its goodness is reliant on what is bought with it. In and of itself, money is not valuable; its value is derived from something else.

Now, sometimes we say something is good or bad or value-neutral in a morally benign sense. For example, we might talk about a good car or a bad cell phone or a classroom chair that is neither particularly good nor bad. In these cases, we aren't praising or blaming the car or phone or chair in any morally significant sense (as though these things would somehow be contemptible or shameful if they lacked the value that might be said to belong to a good car, phone, or chair). Instead, we are reflecting on their *nonmoral* value. By contrast, though, we sometimes say that something is good or bad in a morally significant sense. That is, we sometimes reflect on something's or someone's *moral* value. For example, when we say that the man who risks his own life to help others is a good man, we are praising this person for being morally good.

In addition to those things, a normative moral theory also endeavors to explain when and under what circumstances an action is right or wrong. More specifically, such a theory attempts to explain: (a) the conditions under which an action is morally obligatory or required or dutiful, (b) the conditions under which an action is morally wrong or illicit or impermissible or forbidden, and (c) the conditions under which an action is optional or okay or permissible (but not required). To be clear, there are plenty of synonyms for each of those three categories. The key thing here, though, is that each of those three deontic categories designates an action either as something we *should* do, as something we *should not* do, or as something we *may* do. Throughout this book, we will refer to all this as moral theory's *account of the right.*

A quick cautionary note about the word "right" before moving on. When we say something is right, we are effectively saying it is *not wrong.* For that reason, the word "right" is ambiguous because there are two ways an action can be not wrong—that is, there are two deontic categories beyond the morally forbidden. As it turns out, we sometimes use the word "right" to refer to actions that are morally *optional.* For example, we might say, "It is perfectly right for us to eat sushi from time to time." In this case, we are saying it is simply morally permissible for us to sushi—not that it is morally required. (After all, surely it is permissible to eat something other than raw fish!) But the word "right" can also be used to refer to actions that are morally *obligatory*. For example, we might say, "It is right to take care of your kids." In this case, we are saying that taking care of one's children is morally required, a duty, something we morally ought to perform, and so on. Notice, then, that the term "right" can be used in reference to two distinct deontic categories: the obligatory and the optional.

There are two additional items to note about the distinction between the good and the right before we move on. First off, notice that an action could be morally good and praiseworthy but nonetheless not be morally obligatory, which is part of why the good and the right are not identical concepts. Suppose someone were to volunteer at the soup kitchen every single weekend—as well as every single night of the work week. It seems fair to say that this person's behavior is morally good, but perhaps it is not actually morally obligatory, at least not to the extent in question. After all, there would seem to be no guilt if one failed to keep up such a schedule. In moral philosophy, such behavior is commonly labeled *supererogatory*. Saying an action is supererogatory is to say that it is morally good but not morally required—typically because the action goes above and beyond the call of duty, as it were. Along similar lines (but moving in the opposite direction), one might be tempted to think that an action could be morally bad but not morally forbidden—a *suberogatory* action, as it is sometimes called. Perhaps, for example, it would be morally bad for a professor to make one's students write long and tedious essay assignments that one has absolutely no intention of actually reading—but perhaps it is not morally *impermissible* for one to do so. Of course, we might wonder whether there are such things as suberogatory actions or whether it is always morally wrong to do what is morally bad, but we need not settle the matter here.

The second point about the distinction between the good and the right is that people often fail to keep this distinction in plain view, which can create unnecessary confusion. In everyday conversations, people often talk about moral issues in ways that simply elide between axiological terms (good, bad/evil, value-neutral) and deontic terms (obligatory or right, wrong, and optional). For example, people will say things like "You ought not cheat on your taxes—doing so is *bad*." On the one hand, this elision is understandable enough. But on the other hand, at least when we are doing moral philosophy, we should try to keep the distinction between axiological categories and deontic categories in mind. We encourage the reader to keep the terminology of the good separate from the terminology of the right. For one thing, doing so can help one better appreciate some of the important structural features of the different moral theories surveyed in this book. For another thing, doing so can help one better evaluate this or that moral theory in a more charitable light.

1.3. Why This Book?

There are lots of introductory books about moral philosophy out there, so one might naturally wonder why the world needs yet another. What is the point of *this* book? What makes this book distinctive from all the rest? We happily acknowledge that there are indeed plenty of excellent and widely read introductions to moral philosophy that provide, in their own way, wonderful resources for thinking about ethics. However—and this point is key—only a small handful of contemporary introductions to moral philosophy attempt to engage explicitly and systematically with the Christian faith in a way that takes it seriously.[3] But that is precisely our goal here. So one of the key distinctive features of this book is that we aim to be transparent and explicit in our consideration of the presuppositions, affirmations, and implications of the Christian tradition in dealing with the basic questions of moral philosophy.

What we have insinuated here—that there is something of a gap in the literature—may strike some as hard to believe, and for at least two reasons. After all, isn't it safe to assume that virtually every introduction to ethics has at least *something* to say about God in relation to morality? And isn't there a whole field out there known as "Christian ethics"? Surely *that* field has produced a slew of books that introduce moral philosophy in a way that takes the Christian faith seriously!

We will consider both of those questions in turn, starting with the first. While one might naturally assume nearly every introduction to ethics would have something of substance to say about God in relation to morality, this isn't true in every case. As it turns out, many of the most prominent and widely read introductions to moral philosophy (produced by professional philosophers, at least) can seem dismissive of the claims of

Christianity, or they simply overlook religiously salient considerations altogether. For example, in many of the books in question, some of the moral theories that traditionally have been associated with religious worldviews—natural law theory and divine command theory in particular—receive a fairly short, hasty discussion, *if any*. And what little discussion one does find in such books—or of other considerations pertinent to Christianity in particular—is not always especially charitable.

While it is possible that this lack of charity is intentional in some cases, we suspect that in most cases it is not intentional at all. In fact, our working assumption is that the authors in question are sincerely aiming to be fair-minded and even-handed in their inquiries. The root of the problem may be the simple fact that one's perspective on different theories of morality is shaped, at least in part, by one's own background assumptions. And whether or not one affirms or adheres to a religious faith can affect *how* one approaches the inquiries of moral philosophy.

An analogy can help illustrate the point here. A house will inevitably look different to a real estate agent than to the person who lives in it and calls it home. What the homeowner sees as a cozy living space chock-full of family memories, the real estate agent may see as a lack of curb appeal needing neutral paint colors. Of course, it can be important for the homeowner to consider the real estate agent's perspective when assessing the fair market value of the property, but the homeowner is in a better position to know whether and when the house's market value is sufficient motivation for selling it. Similarly, moral theories that traditionally have been associated with a religious tradition can look less plausible to those who stand outside of—and are critical of—that religious tradition. Those same theories can seem considerably more plausible, though, when viewed under a different light. In general, surveys of moral philosophy often have the feel of having been authored from the perspective of someone who lives outside of the Christian faith, as it were. We seek to flip that perspective in the chapters ahead.

We recognize the need to be mindful of the potential dangers associated with doing so. One potential danger we face is that the religious commitments we bring to the inquiry at hand might cloud our thinking. Like a homeowner who is unable to fairly evaluate the market value of her own home because of her sentimental attachments to it, we run the risk of our commitments to the Christian tradition impairing our ability to fairly evaluate the arguments involved in moral philosophy. Philosophers often try to control for such intellectual biases, which may explain why most introductions to moral philosophy are written in a way that methodologically occludes religiously salient considerations—and, by extension, explicitly *Christian* considerations. The idea seems to be that if one wants to be *purely* "philosophical" in approach, one should stick with trying to glean moral insight by means of natural human reasoning and arguments alone—and hence without any appeal or accountability to any alleged *super*natural revelation. The motivation behind this approach is perfectly understandable: By sticking with religiously neutral, publicly accessible secular reasons and arguments, one can avoid unnecessarily parochial and seemingly interminable theological disputes, and one can better justify one's positions in terms of considerations that *everyone* can endorse as their own, despite their various walks of life.[4] So to return to the analogy above, just as the real estate agent can better evaluate the actual market value of the home precisely *because* he does not live in it, the purebred philosopher can better evaluate the arguments of moral philosophy precisely *because* she doesn't occupy the perspective of a religious tradition.

Naturally enough, then, the worry is that approaching moral philosophy by engaging with the Christian faith and tradition might hinder our ability to fairly evaluate the arguments and theories. On the one hand, we have no desire to simply dismiss this worry. In fact, we concede that this worry ought to be kept in mind. On the other hand, we have no desire to *over*correct, as it were. After all, it is not as though those who operate *without* Christian background assumptions are somehow magically devoid of their own background assumptions and biases. Real estate agents live in houses too—just like the rest of us. Similarly, non-Christians bring their own background assumptions into their moral theorizing too. And a common background assumption of many moral philosophers is that only natural facts are properly called on to offer the kinds of explanations sought in moral philosophy. But what if *that* particular background assumption is just mistaken? If God exists, and if the central tenets of Christianity are true, then surely approaching moral theory from *within* a Christian perspective puts us in an even better starting position than approaching moral theory *without* those assumptions in place—or (even worse) with *false* assumptions about God and Christianity in place.

The Christian tradition presumes that God has revealed certain truths connected to the nature of morality, among other things. If we take the idea of having divine revelation seriously, then the parameters of what counts as "philosophical" will inevitably shift, in part because we would believe that our access to the truth has been supernaturally improved. And if we take ourselves to have some sort of access to divinely revealed truths—whether through Scripture or tradition or conscience or whatever—we will naturally want to make use of those resources in addition to the resources of natural human reasoning and argument. This is hardly a novel insight or method. Plenty of serious thinkers throughout history have understood this point, including Augustine of Hippo, Anselm of Canterbury, Thomas Aquinas, John Duns Scotus, and John Locke, just to name a few. These towering figures would routinely cite biblical texts or other respected thinkers within the Christian tradition to provide data on which to reflect and from which to develop larger theories.[5] In other words, plenty of serious philosophers throughout history have approached philosophical questions from a decidedly Christian perspective. We mean to work in this vein.

To be clear, this book is not meant to be an apologetic case for Christian beliefs; that is simply not our task here. But nor do we expect that the reader will share all our Christian assumptions on the front end. Many—perhaps most—of the considerations we raise in evaluating the various moral theories considered in this book will not require the reader to have a position one way or another about whether Christianity is true. However, we recognize that at least some of our considerations will indeed pivot on whether this or that Christian claim is actually true. At those junctures, we can only invite non-Christian readers to reflect on how the argument under consideration might appear if one were to take the presuppositions, affirmations, and implications of the Christian religion seriously. How might doing so affect one's evaluation of this or that theory? In other words, we invite the reader to consider the Christian position *charitably*—to try it on for size, so to speak.

We should be clear here: There is indeed a vast literature on moral philosophy produced by theistic or Christian philosophers, and that literature can be immensely helpful in taking a Christian position charitably.[6] However, much of that scholarly literature would not be particularly helpful as an *introductory survey* to moral philosophy—and for two main reasons. First, much of the literature in question is so derivative and argumentatively dense that it can be difficult for nonspecialists to process and engage. This isn't a criticism, to be sure; it is just a recognition that much of that literature is not geared toward the nonspecialist. Second, much of that literature is focused on arguing for or defending one singular moral theory in particular (e.g., natural law theory or divine command theory) rather than giving an overview and evaluation of the major players in the history of normative moral theory. Our goal is wider in scope since we seek to introduce a wide range of the major players in moral philosophy in a way that takes the Christian position charitably.

But perhaps it is still hard to believe that there are not already many such Christian introductions to moral philosophy in existence. Remember our second question above: Is there not a whole field within academia called "Christian ethics"? Hasn't *that* field produced a slew of such introductions to moral philosophy?

The answer here is, well, not exactly in the sense we mean. While the field of Christian ethics has produced lots of important and exciting work pertinent to the moral life—work that of course relates to, and at times overlaps with, the tasks of moral philosophy—those works tend to ask different questions than the ones *philosophers* tend to ask. Although there are of course some exceptions, the field of Christian ethics tends to be focused on cultural criticism, relatively specific issues in applied ethics, and how the Christian church, in general, ought to be involved in bringing about justice in the world.[7] For example, Christian ethics is often focused on how Scripture, tradition, or theological reflection bears on how Christians should live in the world with respect to, say, war, political engagement, certain economic policies, sexuality, marriage and divorce, adoption, abortion, euthanasia, the environment, nonhuman animals, and so on. Along similar lines, the field of Christian ethics often features critical reflections by theologians on broader cultural trends. And the field of Christian ethics tends to take up the task of applied ethics and cultural critique by engaging with a certain tradition of theories and thinkers—only some of which overlap with the theories and thinkers pertinent to an introduction to moral philosophy. In this book, though, we are interested in the questions of normative moral theory in particular, as opposed to the questions of applied ethics. What makes something good as opposed to bad? When and under what circumstances is an action right versus wrong? What is the connection between the good and the right? What makes a person virtuous or vicious? There is a rich history of philosophical reflections on those questions—reflections that have evolved and matured into reasonably identifiable schools of thought or theoretical frameworks for answering those questions. The work done in the field of Christian ethics often has less to say about those *philosophical* frameworks and traditions, just as philosophers often have little or no serious engagement with decidedly *Christian* commitments and tradition.

So we return to the point with which we started above—namely, that there is something of a gap in the literature. Despite the multitude of introductions to moral philosophy in existence, and despite the vast contributions within the field of Christian ethics, there are really only a handful of introductions to normative moral theory written from a Christian perspective.[8] What explains that fact? We don't pretend to know the full answer, but one point that may help explain this fact is that some Christians are simply suspicious of what philosophers have to offer to the study of morality in the first place—particularly Christians among low-church, evangelical, or evangelical-adjacent Protestant denominations that place a high value on the normative authority of Scripture. The underlying thought for some is that if we simply study Scripture and apply the teachings of Jesus to our daily lives, philosophy and philosophers are unnecessary at best and downright harmful at worst. (Isn't the Bible enough? Best trust the theologians or biblical scholars!) We come from such a denomination whose representative thinkers have, on occasion, come quite close to saying this sort of thing. But we think such a view is deeply mistaken, in part because the work philosophers do can enhance the moral life of those who accept the Lordship of Jesus and the authority of Scripture in a variety of ways. Several points seem relevant here.[9]

For starters, philosophizing can help us better interpret and draw out the implications of what Scripture teaches about moral issues in the first place. Second, even if we take Scripture to be perfectly perspicacious in what it teaches (and hence in no special need of further interpretation), Scripture simply does not speak to every issue of concern to the moral life. For example, Scripture is largely silent with respect to marijuana, genetic engineering, hacking, speeding, social media use, whether to vote for this or that candidate, how much TV to watch, and so on. Philosophizing can help us connect the dots, so to speak, by contemplating a broader systematic moral framework—one that is capable of addressing issues that extend beyond what is explicitly addressed in the biblical cannon.

Third, the view that philosophy does not have anything to offer to the study of morality is not itself a scriptural position in any straightforward sense. In fact, any serious defense of such a position would likely require one to make use of the very philosophical tools the view itself eschews. And, as it turns out, Christian Scripture actually seems to *approve* of the endeavor of moral philosophy. How so? In some ways, attempting to discern the correct moral theory can be contemplated as an expression of, or an accompaniment to, natural theology. Natural theology is simply the effort to discern truth about God by means of natural human reason without relying on divinely revealed sources of information. And the apostle Paul seems to authorize the project of natural theology pretty explicitly in the first two chapters of his letter to the Romans.

Fourth, philosophizing can help Christians engage faithfully in dialogue with non-Christian approaches to thinking about morality, which may have an important apologetic dimension in its own right: In helping Christians better understand their own positions, moral philosophers can also help Christians better represent or defend their own positions to others. Done well, then, moral philosophy can help Christians understand and articulate not only why Christianity is reasonable but also how Christians might best respond to non-Christian positions in an apologetic fashion.

Finally, we think John Locke was right when he said, "God, when he makes the prophet, does not unmake the man."[10] In other words, even when God graces us with divine revelation of moral truths, that doesn't somehow nullify or undo our capacity for reasoning about those revealed truths. Nor does it nullify the other truths accessible to us through reason. God made us, at least in part, as creatures who can reason and philosophize about how best to live. To abnegate that capacity or to christen it as "unnecessary" is to look too cheaply upon how and by whom we were made. Faith and reason need not, and ought not, be pitted against one another.

This book endeavors to take both sides of the equation seriously—that is, the Christian faith *and* philosophical reasoning. We want to introduce the major theories of normative ethics most often discussed by philosophers, and we want to take their arguments and reasons seriously. And we want to do that in a way that takes the presuppositions, affirmations, and implications of the Christian faith seriously, too. Importantly, though, we do not want to take the Christian faith seriously in the *wrong* sort of way—for example, in a dogmatic fashion where we present theistic or Christian claims as though they are somehow beyond the scope of intellectual critique. Nor do we want to be narrow in our engagement with the Christian faith. Rather, our goal is to practice ecumenically minded intellectual engagement with the Christian faith and tradition and do so with the appropriate measure of humility. And we hope to exhibit an open-minded, reason-responsive engagement with moral philosophy from the perspective of the Christian faith.

To do all this, though, we should start with an honest acknowledgment. We can't help but recognize that, along with the very best examples of intellectual work done in the Christian tradition, one can also find perfectly toxic appeals to Scripture and tradition that have been used to support a shamefully long list of atrocities carried out in the name of Christ—from mistreatment of women to the enslavement of dark-skinned peoples to genocide. We think the appropriate response to this sin—and any sin—is confession, repentance, and humility. So while we want to engage with the presuppositions, affirmations, and implications of the Christian faith, we want to do so in a way that appropriately acknowledges the sinful *mis*uses of Christian ideas and Scripture that have stained the history of the global church. May we not repeat the sins of the past.

1.4. What Lies Ahead

It remains for us to look ahead. The following chapters are dedicated to a curated overview and evaluation of the major normative moral theories in the history of philosophy. Readers will notice that each chapter conforms to a certain pattern. At the outset of each chapter, we explain, in fairly broad strokes, the moral theory under consideration and what it says. This section will include a reconstruction of the theory's account of the good and the theory's account of the right, as well as the theory's procedure for making moral decisions. Once we have a clear view of what the given moral theory says, we then turn to a consideration of the case for the moral theory in question. What reasons, intuitions, and arguments have been or can be offered in support of this particular moral theory? What might be said by way of evaluation of that case? Finally, each chapter closes with a discussion of the case against the moral theory under consideration, along with relevant replies to those objections where applicable. Along the way, both in discussing the arguments for and the arguments against each view, we consider the theory in light of the intellectual resources and commitments of the Christian tradition. How does the theory in question resonate with the presuppositions, affirmations, and implications of Christianity? How might this theory find itself at odds with Christian commitments? Our attempt to answer those questions will mean we engage not only with Hebrew and Christian Scripture but with other intellectual resources in the Christian tradition, like important creeds or historically prominent Christian thinkers and ideas.

We do not pretend that our reconstruction or critical assessment of the various moral theories covered in this book is novel at every point. In fact, much of what we offer by way of analysis and evaluation is fairly standard among contemporary introductions to moral philosophy. Our agenda, however, is to organize this inquiry in a way that is clear and easy enough to understand for those who are willing to spend some time sorting through the arguments, even if they happen to be new to the discipline of philosophy. Additionally, we do not intend to have the final and definitive word on every theory we consider in this book, though some of our discussions will prove to be more conclusive than others. Nonetheless, in the final chapter, we try to tie up some loose ends and make explicit some of the conclusions that seem to us most reasonable to draw. We fully expect that this will, of course, invite some dispute. But moral philosophy is fraught with controversy and debates—that simply comes with the territory. Our agenda here is to set the stage for further reflection at least as much as it is to settle the score once and for all.

chapter two

RELATIVISM

Thomas E. Huggins of Tampa, Florida, did something in the summer of 2013 that few Americans could ever dream of doing: He ate the family dog.[1] One warm June morning, Huggins strangled his puppy pitbull Bandit with a grocery bag, skinned and quartered the carcass, cooked and ate some of the ribs, and stored the rest of the meat in the freezer. After discovering Bandit's remains later that evening, a concerned family member notified the local authorities. According to the police report, Huggins explained that "they needed something to eat," so he decided to butcher and cook the dog in the same way his mother had taught him to prepare small game animals such as rabbits and squirrels, which the impoverished Florida family had sometimes relied on for protein. The twenty-five-year-old Huggins was charged and eventually convicted of animal cruelty, though his prison sentence was suspended after a court psychologist persuaded the judge that the perpetrator suffered from schizoaffective disorder. Huggins agreed to submit to mental health treatment and was banned from owning pets and living with nonhuman animals.

Now suppose this situation had been less gruesome. Suppose, for example, that Huggins had employed gentler methods for harvesting the dog's meat. Would this change your perspective?

For many people, it can seem that Huggins acted inappropriately when he ate Bandit, regardless of how he killed the dog and harvested its meat. After all, dogs aren't like wild game animals—or so one might say. But imagine this event had taken place not in Tampa, Florida, but in, say, China, Vietnam, or South Korea, where an estimated sixteen to twenty-six million dogs are slaughtered each year for human consumption.[2] Could it be that Huggins was wrong to kill and eat Bandit in Florida whereas other folks in some Asian cultures *aren't* wrong to kill and eat *their* dogs? Admittedly, in Huggins's culture, people commonly contemplate dogs as pets: They name them, feed them, care for them, and become emotionally connected to them in ways they don't with most other animals. But this is less common in other cultures. Meanwhile, some cultures strictly forbid eating cows or pigs, which is of course commonplace in Florida. Is it hypocritical for a culture that eats massive quantities of beef and pork to frown on the consumption of dog meat? Is it simply ethnocentric to suppose that the animals designated for special protection in *one* culture should be similarly protected in *every* culture? Is this all simply a matter of taste?

Different societies, religious traditions, people groups, and cultures throughout human history and across the globe today have held differing assumptions and beliefs about what is morally obligatory or permissible or forbidden. This diversity of opinion is reflected in the myriad practices and customs that have evolved over time in various settings. Some of these practices can strike us as not just distasteful but also deeply disconcerting. Consider, for example, the following:

- In Iran, as in several other Muslim-majority societies, women are expected or legally required to wear hijabs in public settings. In some cases, failure to do so has resulted in severe forms of punishment, including flogging and imprisonment.[3]
- While no longer technically legal, it is not uncommon for men in Kyrgyzstan to select wives by kidnapping women off the street—often violently and without consent. This traditional practice is called *ala kachuu*, which roughly translates as "grab and run."[4]

- Polygamy has been practiced in a variety of cultural settings, including among the ancient Israelites. To this day, significant percentages of several sub-Saharan African countries live in polygamous households, including in Burkina Faso (36 percent), Mali (34 percent), and Nigeria (28 percent), among several others.[5]
- In at least thirty countries in Africa, the Middle East, and Asia, young girls are often expected to undergo a painful procedure thought to have religious significance where the external female genitalia are either partially or wholly removed, fused, or exposed to other nonmedicinal forms of cutting and mutilation. Affecting more than 230 million girls and women worldwide, this procedure is commonly performed without anesthesia and outside of a hospital setting.[6]
- Various cultural groups throughout history have practiced cannibalism, including the Korowai tribe in West Papua, who are among the last known to continue doing so today.[7]
- Chattel slavery was socially accepted—and legally protected—in many jurisdictions within the United States for more than two centuries.
- In various historical settings, including within ancient Greek and Roman contexts, pederasty was an acknowledged form of sexual and romantic expression.

Naturally enough, we might ask about the moral status of these practices. But does the answer inevitably vary on *who* is asking the question—and *where*? Are we simply stepping out of line in some way when we make judgments about the practices of cultures beyond our own? Is there something about the fact that certain practices are endorsed, accepted, or tolerated within a given culture that makes them morally permissible, at least for folks within that particular context? Or are certain practices simply beyond the pale everywhere and for everyone, regardless of whether they align with the beliefs of any particular cultural group?

As it turns out, some people seem to presume that all moral judgments—that is, all of our judgments about what is good and evil or what is right and wrong—are more or less akin to matters of taste. The idea goes roughly as follows: Whereas scientific questions have objective answers, moral questions just aren't like that, in large part because the whole enterprise of morality is inextricably tethered to cultural mores or something even more localized, like an individual's feelings, preferences, or other subjective states. Accordingly, moral standards simply vary from culture to culture or even from person to person. That sort of presumption goes to the heart of a way of thinking about the moral universe commonly known as relativism. This chapter is dedicated to a consideration of several different versions of this theory, namely cultural relativism and more individualized versions of relativism.

We begin with a consideration of cultural relativism.

2.1. What Cultural Relativism Says

Cultural relativism depicts morality as being anchored at its most basic level to the culture in which one lives. Most centrally, cultural relativism holds that what is good and what is right ultimately depend on the culture to which a person belongs. Animating the view here is the thought that there are simply no objective standards for morality waiting out there to be discovered by us. Instead, the different cultures throughout time and space do all the heavy lifting, so to speak. Accordingly, what a certain culture takes to be right *just is* right for the members of that particular culture. After all, cultural relativism holds that matters of good and evil or right and wrong are *relative* to—and hence determined by—a culture's prevailing set of beliefs and assumptions about morality, together with the various customs and practices that embed these beliefs and assumptions. Notice that this isn't to say morality is some sort of grand illusion or that all moral claims are somehow false or meaningless. In fact, cultural relativism doesn't try to deny that moral judgments can be true in some more modest or restricted sense. Instead, cultural relativism holds that moral judgments, if and when they are true, are true *for* or *relative to* this or that cultural group.

One way of getting a better handle on any moral theory, including cultural relativism, is to analyze it into its constituent parts. And cultural relativism is less of a unified theory and more of a cluster of five distinct but loosely related affirmations. Namely, cultural relativism holds the following:

- i. There are no universally applicable, culturally transcendent, objective standards of morality.
- ii. The moral status of one's actions depends on the moral code of the culture to which one belongs.
- iii. Different cultures have different moral codes.
- iv. The moral code of one culture is in no way superior to the moral code of any other culture.
- v. To say an action has this or that moral status is simply to say the action in question has this or that moral status for members of the culture in question.

The first element of cultural relativism to note here can be thought of as a *nonuniversality thesis*: There are simply no universally applicable, objective standards for good and evil or right and wrong—that is, no standards that somehow hover over all the cultural groups in the world and in turn stand in judgment of those cultural groups. In one way, this is a perfectly pessimistic thesis insofar as it simply denies the existence of moral standards beyond or above those embedded in local cultures. And if so, there would be little sense in trying to discern or articulate what those standards are.

The second affirmation of cultural relativism is more positive in nature. What we might call the *culture-dependency thesis* affirms that morality ultimately depends at its most fundamental level on the culture to which one belongs. In other words, whether something is good or bad or whether one's action is right or wrong is somehow grounded in or determined by the particular culture to which one belongs. In effect, descriptive facts about each culture (e.g., what a culture happens to endorse or accept as good or bad or right or wrong) double as the root source of normativity for that culture (that is, what *ought* to be the case within that culture).

The third element of cultural relativism—call it the *diversity thesis*—is simply the recognition that different cultural groups have different moral codes. By the phrase "moral code," we simply mean to refer to a culture's prevailing set of assumptions and beliefs about what is good and evil and/or what is right and wrong, together with the various customs and practices that reflect those assumptions and beliefs. The moral code of one culture differs from another when it includes beliefs, assumptions, and practices that conflict with those of another culture. As it turns out, the fact that there are a variety of differing moral codes is simply an empirically verifiable observation, and the study of history, international affairs, sociology, and anthropology serves only to put this diversity in high relief.

Fourth, cultural relativism affirms an *equality thesis* according to which the various moral codes of the various cultures throughout time and space are fundamentally on a par with one another. In other words, the moral code of one culture is in no way superior or inferior to that of any other culture—they are all on equal footing. This equality stems in part from the simple fact that, according to cultural relativism, there are no culturally transcendent, objective moral standards on the basis of which any culture could gain such a superior status in the first place.

Fifth, and lastly, cultural relativism presupposes what we can think of as a *restricted-scope thesis*. Assuming there are no culturally transcendent moral standards, if and when a moral judgment is true, the scope of that judgment's truth would be restricted to members of the culture in question. Accordingly, when one makes a pronouncement about the moral status of an action, one is merely making an assertion that pertains *only for members of the culture in question*. For example, a cultural relativist might claim that headscarf requirements are wrong for those living *in Paris*, even if they are permissible or obligatory for folks *in Tehran*.

Now, in the effort to comprehend cultural relativism, it helps to understand not only what the theory says but also what the theory does *not* say. Cultural relativism is not identical to the more modest assertion that the moral status of an action partially depends on facts about the situation in which one finds oneself. This is a subtle but important point that is perhaps best illustrated by way of example. Suppose you are at the movie theatre with your friends and you see an overweight, middle-aged man collapse to the ground. And suppose it soon becomes apparent to you that this fellow needs CPR right away or else he will surely die. Do you have a moral obligation to administer CPR in this particular situation?

Perhaps. But notice how the answer at least *partially* hinges on facts about the situation you find yourself in, including whether you actually know how to administer CPR in the first place, whether you have (or the man in question has) an infectious disease, whether there is a physician or nurse nearby, and so on. If you do not know how to administer CPR, it could be dangerous, and hence problematic, for you to try to learn in this moment—especially if the man's life is at stake. (You might ought to focus on finding someone who can do CPR, and quickly.)

Notice how claiming that the moral status of an action at least partially depends on the facts of the situation at hand is *not* equivalent to denying that there is a universally applicable, culturally transcendent, objective moral truth at play here. In fact, it might very well be objectively true that everyone everywhere (including you!) has a moral obligation to help others when one can do so without making things worse. Yet, in this case, what *your* specific moral obligation is—and is not—at least partly hinges on details of the situation at hand. After all, those details include facts about whether you would actually make things worse if you tried to administer CPR. And *those* details can surely help determine whether and how the putative universal moral truth in question would apply.

Remember, however, that cultural relativism claims far more than this. Cultural relativism does not say merely that facts about one's context partly affect what is right and wrong in a given situation. Rather, given the nonuniversality thesis, it denies that there are any such culturally transcendent, objective moral truths in the first place. And, furthermore, cultural relativism says one's culture is itself the root source, and indeed the only source, of what is good or evil and right or wrong within that cultural context. So, on this view, whatever is *accepted* as good or right within a particular cultural group simply *is* good or right for members of that cultural group. Culture is itself the value-making or right-making mechanism, so to speak—at least for members of the culture in question.

Now, when analyzing a moral theory into its constituent parts, it is important to keep in mind the distinction between the theory's account of what is good and the theory's account of what is right. A moral theory's *account of the good*, as we are calling it, is simply the theory's underlying explanation of the conditions under which something is good, evil, or value-neutral. And a moral theory's *account of the right*, as we are calling it, is just the theory's explanation of the conditions under which an action is morally obligatory, wrong, or optional (that is, morally permissible but not required). Obviously enough, a theory's account of the good and its account of the right are importantly and perhaps even intimately connected to one another. At any rate, it will be helpful to keep this distinction in plain view moving forward.[8]

So notice, first, how cultural relativism's account of the good would run. According to cultural relativism, something can be said to be good for a person if and only if and just because it is valued by the culture to which the person belongs. Similarly, something can be said to be bad for a person if and only if and just because it is contrary to what is valued by the culture to which the person belongs. And something can be said to be value-neutral for a person if and only if and just because it is neither valued nor contrary to what is valued by the culture to which the person belongs.

By contrast, consider cultural relativism's account of the right. According to cultural relativism, an action is morally obligatory for a person if and only if and just because that action is required by the moral code of the culture to which the person belongs. An action is morally wrong for a person if and only if and just because that action is forbidden by the moral code of the culture to which the person belongs. And an action is optional for a person if and only if and just because that action is neither required nor forbidden by the moral code of the culture to which the person belongs.

A final point: At least part of what we should expect of any moral theory is that it offers some sort of guidance—a procedure of sorts—for making decisions about how to act and how to live. In other words, we should expect that a moral theory offers, either explicitly or implicitly, what we can think of as a *moral decision procedure*. And it is easy enough to see what the decision procedure for cultural relativism might look like.

> STEP 1: Take note of the moral code of the culture to which one belongs.

STEP 2: Determine whether the action in question accords or conflicts with the norms of that moral code.
STEP 3: Act accordingly.

2.2. The Case for Cultural Relativism

Why might one be tempted to think cultural relativism is the correct view of morality in the first place? Two of the most commonplace arguments in favor of cultural relativism rest on considerations about the immense array of conflicting moral codes, as well as on considerations about the importance of tolerance in a diverse and multicultural world. We will consider each argument in turn.

The argument from diversity

The first argument for cultural relativism leverages the diversity thesis as a way of motivating the nonuniversality thesis and, hence, the culture-dependency thesis. The argument goes roughly as follows:

(1) Different cultures have different moral codes in the sense that each moral code includes beliefs, assumptions, and practices that conflict with those of other cultures.
(2) If there is a diversity of moral codes across cultures, then there are no universally applicable, culturally transcendent, objective standards for morality.
(3) If there are no universally applicable, culturally transcendent, objective standards for morality, then the moral status of one's action depends on the moral code of the culture to which one belongs.
(4) Thus, cultural relativism is the correct theory of morality.

How should we go about evaluating this argument? First off, notice that this argument is deductively *valid*—that is, *if* the premises are all true, then the conclusion must be true. So the salient question is whether this argument is *sound*—that is, whether, in addition to being valid, this argument has true premises.

Start with premise 1. Proponents of cultural relativism typically place a good deal of emphasis on the facts of diversity. On one level, that is a perfectly understandable place to begin. It is an empirically verifiable fact that different cultures indeed have (and have long had) differing moral codes in at least some respect. But we are right to ask about the *range* and the *depth* of the differences between and among those moral codes. Take the question about range first. Just how wide or narrow is the disagreement among cultures supposed to be? Should we understand the diversity thesis in premise 1 to be saying that there are *absolutely no shared* moral beliefs, assumptions, and practices across all cultural groups?

Surely that would be a stretch. After all, it seems perfectly plausible to imagine that at least *some* very basic moral norms are needed for a society—any society—to survive for any significant length of time. Minimally, for example, a society would need to have some sort of restriction on indiscriminate killing in place, together with some sort of expectation that, say, children ought to be cared for. (Just imagine if a society had no such moral norms.) And perhaps other basic moral norms and expectations would need to be in place, too.

As it turns out, there is at least some preliminary evidence that the different cultures throughout history have indeed shared some moral norms and expectations. The literary scholar and Christian writer C. S. Lewis (1898–1963) compiled a fairly extensive list of such shared norms affirmed in the historical-literary record. Lewis's list of shared cross-cultural norms includes, among other things, nonmaleficence toward others, duties to one's parents and children, certain restrictions on sex, and prohibitions on dishonesty.[9] Similar claims have also been made in more recent decades by prominent anthropologists such as Donald E. Brown, who identifies hundreds of "human universals" found in every culture. Among these universals, according to Brown, are a plethora of decidedly *moral* universals, such as prohibitions on murder, rape, and incest; restrictions on violence; concepts of fairness, turn-taking, property; and resistance to abuse of power and dominance, among others.[10]

So if we take the literary and anthropological data seriously, it seems profoundly mistaken to interpret the diversity thesis as saying that the moral codes of the different cultures across space and time are in conflict about absolutely everything. What about a *weaker* interpretation of the diversity thesis? Suppose, in other words, that the claim on offer in premise 1 above is simply that while there might be *some* shared moral assumptions and beliefs, there remains at least a *subset* of beliefs, assumptions, and practices about which there is conflict. Such an interpretation of the diversity thesis would seem to square better with the data.

Turn now to the question about the *depth*. Granted, different moral codes indeed disagree with respect to at least a subset of beliefs, assumptions, and practices. But just how deep or shallow is that disagreement? Is it deep enough that the various moral codes in question should be regarded as *drastically* different? Or is the disagreement in question simply about how to interpret, specify, or apply otherwise commonly held moral norms, rules, and principles? And is it possible that the disagreements in question are less about *moral* norms, rules, and principles than about surrounding *nonmoral* facts? Return to the disagreement we mentioned at the outset of this chapter, for example—whether it is morally permissible to eat one's dog. Perhaps this disagreement is not fundamentally a *moral* disagreement in the first place. It might instead be more of a disagreement about whether dogs are more cognitively and emotionally advanced in comparison to small game animals like squirrels or rabbits. Or take abortion as another example. One group strongly opposes it. Another group holds that it should be safe, legal, and widely accessible. Admittedly, these two groups might seem to be in deep *moral* disagreement with each other. But what if the disagreement here is less of a disagreement about the underlying moral norm (e.g., that it's immoral to kill innocent humans) and more of a disagreement about when life or personhood begins? Imagine, for example, that the two groups somehow eventually came to agree about when life or personhood begins. Perhaps the two groups would then actually come to consensus on the moral question at that juncture, too. If so, then the real disagreement in this particular case was mostly a disagreement on the nonmoral facts of the issue—not about the shared, underlying moral norm that it is wrong to kill innocent human persons.

For now, though, put questions about the diversity thesis to one side. There is a bigger problem for the argument above: Premise 2 is clearly on shaky grounds. The simple fact that different cultures have competing moral codes does not mean that there are no universally applicable, culturally transcendent, objective standards for morality. After all, there very well could be such a set of objective moral standards even if this or that culture—or even every culture—failed to recognize or accept them. After all, a culture—or even every culture—could simply be mistaken. So the simple fact that a diversity of beliefs about morality exists does not necessitate that there is *not* an objectively correct belief on the matter. Put differently: The nonuniversality thesis simply does not follow from the diversity thesis.

An analogy can help illustrate this point here. The famous Christian evangelist Billy Graham (1918–2018) and the atheist evolutionary biologist Richard Dawkins (1941–) clearly disagreed with each other about whether there is such a being as God. But the simple fact that these two men disagreed about the issue hardly counts as evidence that there isn't an objective truth of the matter—one way or the other. Either God exists, or God does not exist. The fact that Graham and Dawkins disagreed does not affect whether God actually exists. Why should things be any different when it comes to disagreement about moral issues? One culture disagreeing with another culture about the permissibility of, say, cannibalism provides absolutely no evidence that there isn't a universally applicable, culturally transcendent, objective answer to the question of whether cannibalism is morally permissible. In other words, the diversity thesis simply does not entail the nonuniversality thesis. So premise 2 is false.

Premise 3 is false, too. And here's why: Even if there were absolutely no universally applicable, culturally transcendent, objective standards for morality, that fact alone wouldn't be enough to entail that good and evil and right and wrong are somehow determined by one's culture (as though *that* were the only alternative). After all, if there were no universally applicable, culturally transcendent, objective standards for morality, one possibility would be that nihilism is true such that the whole enterprise of morality is a grand farce. Of course, our point here isn't that nihilism needs to be taken seriously; the point here is that the nonuniversality thesis, even if it were true, would not necessitate the culture-dependency thesis. So the argument from diversity for cultural relativism is clearly unsound.

The argument from tolerance

There is a second consideration in favor of cultural relativism that we should consider. Part of what makes cultural relativism enticing is that it can seem to support a more tolerant and open-minded outlook in a multicultural and pluralistic world fraught with cultural differences and nuance. The thought here is that if one accepts the nonuniversality thesis along with the culture-dependency thesis and the restricted-scope thesis, then one will inevitably come to embrace the equality thesis, as well. And once one comes to embrace the equality thesis, one is naturally poised for greater understanding of cultural differences, for greater broad-mindedness, and ultimately for more forbearance. Some proponents of cultural relativism seem to gesture in this sort of direction. The early twentieth-century anthropologist and folklorist Ruth Benedict (1887–1948), for example, offered much of the groundwork for this very line of reasoning. She argues:

> We do not any longer make the mistake of deriving the morality of our locality and decade from the inevitable constitution of human nature. We do not elevate it to the dignity of a first principle. We recognize that morality differs in every society, and is a convenient term for socially approved habits. Mankind has always preferred to say, "It is morally good," rather than "It is habitual". . . . But historically the two phrases are synonymous.[11]

Notice how Benedict's line of thinking could be extended: Once we come to see that the moral code of our own culture is on an equal footing with that of other cultures—and that *neither* reflects some culturally transcendent standard—then we will have grown more tolerant in our attitudes toward the differing beliefs, assumptions, practices, and customs of other cultures. And this tolerant posture makes us less arrogant, less ethnocentric, less imperialistic, more empathetic and peace-seeking global citizens. The argument at play here can be summarized as follows:

(1) We should embrace a tolerant posture toward other cultures.
(2) Accepting cultural relativism will make us more tolerant.
(3) Thus, we ought to accept cultural relativism.

There are at least three problems with this sort of argument. First off, notice how this argument assumes from the get-go that tolerance is something that would be good for everyone to embrace. But, ironically, that very understandable assumption turns out to be a rather strange bedfellow to one of the central affirmations of cultural relativism, namely the nonuniversality thesis. Notice how premise 1 assumes tolerance is something we—presumably all of us—should embrace. In other words, given premise 1, tolerance seems to be something akin to a universally applicable, culturally transcendent, objective standard for morality! But if premise 1 is true in any nontrivial sense, then the nonuniversality thesis would be false.

A second problem haunts this argument. Consider premise 2. Accepting the nonuniversality thesis, the cultural-dependency thesis, and the equality thesis does not necessarily provide a formula for tolerance—as opposed to imperialism and violence. Suppose, for example, that we indeed came to sincerely believe that there are no universally applicable, culturally transcendent, objective standards for morality and, hence, that our own culture's moral code is no better or worse than those of other cultures. If we were truly convinced of this particular point—that there are no universally applicable standards to which our own culture is accountable—what is to stop us from thinking we should just *conquer* other cultures as opposed to tolerate them? (After all, even if those cultures are morally equal to our own, they are still not *ours*.) Why, in other words, should we suppose that tolerance—as opposed to imperialism—would be the default response to an acceptance of the equality thesis? The point here is simply that premise 2 seems debatable at best.

A final problem with the argument from tolerance: It is logically invalid. That is, *even if* it is true that we should embrace a tolerant posture toward other cultures, and *even if* it is true that accepting cultural relativism *would* make us more tolerant, it simply doesn't follow that we ought to accept cultural relativism. Why? Because there are considerations other than tolerance that matter. An analogy can illustrate the point here. Perhaps it is true that we should strive to empathize with the parents of severely disabled children. One way of becoming more empathetic in this regard is by plucking out the eyes of one's own kids. But it surely doesn't follow that we should pluck out our own kids' eyes so that we can become more empathetic of parents with severely disabled children.

So both arguments in favor of cultural relativism leave quite a bit to be desired. Both are unsound. And so cultural relativism remains a conclusion in search of a good argument. Still, admittedly, one of the most attractive features of cultural relativism is that it *seems* to provide something of an intellectual antidote to narrow-minded dogmatism, bigotry, and intolerance. But it is worth noting that while the desire to find such an antidote is praiseworthy enough, the promise of cultural relativism remains illusory in this regard. After all, the opposite of dogmatism is not actually relativism. The opposite of dogmatism is something more akin to *fallibilism* or *epistemic humility*—that is, the willingness to change one's mind in light of new considerations and evidence. Fortunately, we don't need to take on board the vastly more controversial elements of cultural relativism in order to embrace humility and open-mindedness when evaluating our beliefs and assumptions about good and evil and right and wrong.

2.3. The Case against Cultural Relativism

We should be careful at this juncture. So far, our inquiry has shown only that the case *for* cultural relativism remains unmade. But that point doesn't somehow show that cultural relativism is false or otherwise defeated as a moral theory. Is there a positive case *against* it? Consider the following objections to cultural relativism, the fifth of which is of special concern for Christians.

Cultural relativism conflicts with our deep-seated convictions about the moral status of certain practices

If cultural relativism is true, then any action or practice is permissible or even obligatory within a culture as long as it is endorsed or required by the moral code of the culture in question. Unfortunately, such a view could be used to rationalize virtually any form of abuse or evildoing. This is hardly an abstract, philosophical point unconnected to real events. In 2015, the *New York Times* published a gut-wrenching story about Lance Cpl. George Buckley Jr., who had been serving in the US military in southern Afghanistan. In his last phone call home before he was shot to death, Buckley complained to his father that he had been overhearing Afghan police officers sexually abusing young boys who were brought to the military base where he was stationed. When his father admonished Buckley to report the matter to his superior officers, Buckley assured him that he had already done so. His father told reporters: "My son said that his officers told him to look the other way *because it's their culture*."[12]

Pay attention to the problem here: As long as the action in question reflects the prevailing mores of the culture in which it occurs, then *any* action—including practices such as the honor-killing of unwed mothers, discrimination against women and minorities, violent political oppression of dissidents, genocide, and child abuse—would be permissible *in those cultural contexts*. But surely those practices are morally problematic anywhere and everywhere they occur, even in those cultural contexts where they are accepted as perfectly normal. So cultural relativism conflicts with our considered moral convictions about the status of certain actions.

Cultural relativism eliminates the basis for moral evaluation and moral improvement

If cultural relativism is true, then there are no universally applicable, culturally transcendent, objective standards to which one could ever appeal in order to criticize the practices that are accepted within another culture. After all, cultural relativism holds that the moral status of one's action depends wholly on the culture to which one belongs in the first place. But notice the problem: If cultural relativism is true, then there is simply no basis on which anyone could ever negatively evaluate, say, female genital mutilation or chattel slavery—as long as the culture in which it was practiced happened to endorse or condone it. And this conundrum would hold true both for the one who *belongs* to the culture in question and for the one who stands *outside* of that culture. Why is that? If cultural relativism is true, there are no culturally transcendent, objective standards to which one could ever appeal, which means there wouldn't be any rational basis upon which to evaluate the accepted practices of a given cultural group. But surely this is a problematic implication of cultural relativism.

Yet things get worse. If there is no rational basis on which to critique—and hence to try to improve—the accepted practices of a given cultural group, then there could also be no moral progress. Notice the oddity of this. Consider the practice of slavery within US history. Slavery was a widely accepted and legally protected practice within the newly admitted state of Alabama in the early nineteenth century. So given cultural relativism, slavery would have been morally permissible *for Alabamians* in, say, 1825. Fast forward to the present. Slavery is neither culturally accepted nor legally protected in Alabama now. Accordingly, it is certainly tempting to suppose that, at least with respect to slavery, there has been some significant moral progress in Alabama over the past two centuries. But notice how cultural relativism must deny this very claim about moral progress. Why? According to cultural relativism, whatever the culture accepts at that moment simply *is* morally permissible or obligatory for members of that culture *at that moment*. And if that point were true, then no moral progress would have occurred in Alabama: Things were just fine in 1825, and they would be just fine now, too. But that's surely false.

Cultural relativism invites contradictions

The culture-dependency thesis holds that the moral status of an action depends on the moral code of the culture to which one belongs. But there is a serious problem facing this thesis, even if it is true: One's culture is not always internally consistent, especially during periods of social change and legal transition. Take, for example, the predicament within Kyrgyzstan over the last few decades. While the practice of *ala kachuu* has been traditionally condoned within that society, and while the practice still remains somewhat commonplace there today, it was legally banned in 1994. This simple point invites a question that can be difficult to answer with precision: Is *ala kachuu* endorsed or condemned by the moral code of Kyrgyzstan?

In some sense, the answer seems to be "both." But notice the problem this point poses for cultural relativism. If indeed the culture in question condemns the practice in one (legal) sense and accepts the practice in some other (nonlegal) sense, then, given cultural relativism, *ala kachuu* is both wrong *and* right for members of this society. The contradiction can be hard to ignore.

Cultural relativism suffers from a vagueness problem

A related problem stems from the difficulties of specifying what is meant by the terms "culture" or "cultural group" in the first place. To what exactly are we referring here? How specific do we need to be? What or who should count, exactly? Westerners? Americans? Southerners? Texans? Christians? Catholics? Protestants? White people? Black people? People who have a certain sexual orientation? Members of one's fraternity? Members of one's extended family?

Notice the problem this line of questioning produces for cultural relativism. If we cannot clearly delineate what or who should count as a culture or cultural group, then there is no way for us to clearly identify what the moral code of a given culture is supposed to be. In turn, we have no way of specifying what is right or wrong for members of that culture. And if that is the case, then we are left with no way of following cultural relativism's moral decision procedure. Vagueness is built into the theory's very account of the good and the right.

This problem is only amplified when we factor in the complexities of living in a modern pluralistic, multicultural society such as the United States. Many of us, perhaps all of us, belong to more than one cultural group at any given time—depending on how the terms "culture" or "cultural group" get defined. The opportunity for contradictory moral verdicts to arise given cultural relativism only increases proportionately.

Cultural relativism conflicts with the presuppositions of Hebrew and Christian Scriptures

A final objection to cultural relativism is of special significance to Christians. If the nonuniversality thesis and the cultural-dependency thesis were true, then we would have no way of making sense of the various moral evaluations and the divine warnings voiced by the Old Testament prophets, especially those directed at societies *beyond* Yahweh's chosen people, Israel and Judah. For example, if cultural relativism were true, then the practices of ancient Damascus, Gaza, Tyre, and Edom would have been morally permissible *for members of those various societies*, assuming those practices were actually accepted within the respective cultures in question. But if so, then there would have been no legitimate basis for the prophet Amos to have declared God's moral condemnation of them.[13]

Or consider the case of the prophet Jonah, who was sent (begrudgingly) to warn Nineveh to repent of its evil ways lest it be destroyed by God within forty days. Notice how the Jonah story clearly presupposes that there were culturally transcendent moral standards that the Ninevites had indeed violated. Furthermore, notice also how the Jonah story clearly affirms the possibility of moral progress—a possibility that cultural relativism must deny—precisely because the Ninevites ultimately repented and were thus spared. If cultural relativism were true, then no such moral progress would have been possible for the Ninevites whom Jonah warned. And for similar reasons, if cultural relativism were true, we wouldn't be able to make any sense out of the foretelling of God's righteous judgment upon *all nations*, as conveyed variously in Joel 3:2, Matthew 25, and Revelation 20:11–15.

Lastly, consider the so-called Great Commission passage toward the end of the Gospel of Matthew. In it Jesus explains, "All authority in heaven and on earth has been given to me. Therefore go and make disciples of all nations, baptizing them in the name of the Father and of the Son and of the Holy Spirit, and teaching them to obey everything that I have commanded you" (Matt. 28:18–20 NIV). Two observations are relevant here. First, the assumption here is that Jesus's commands are valid for *all nations*—all humans everywhere. And clearly some (if not all) of Jesus's commands are moral in nature. Thus, Jesus seems to presuppose that there are at least some universally applicable, culturally transcendent, objective standards for morality.

Second, the context of this passage seems to suggest that what makes Jesus's commands morally binding is that the commands originate from him *in whom all authority resides*. Minimally, this point squarely conflicts with the culture-dependency thesis. After all, cultural relativism holds that *culture* is that in which all authority resides—that is, *culture alone* somehow has the capacity to make something good or right merely by accepting it as good or right. But it cannot be both ways: *All* authority cannot reside both in Christ alone *and* in culture alone.

2.4. Subjectivism

In light of the difficulties facing cultural relativism, we might wonder whether a modified version of relativism would fare any better. And there is indeed a more extreme version of relativism that we should consider at this juncture—what we might simply call *individual relativism*. Like cultural relativism, individual relativism denies that there are universally applicable, culturally transcendent, objective standards of morality waiting out there to be discovered. In fact, the individual relativist denies that there are standards of morality that even transcend individual persons. Instead of claiming that morality is dependent on culture, individual relativism holds that morality depends on an individual's own subjective states—that is, one's own beliefs, attitudes, feelings, and so on. In this view, what is good and what is right are basically in the eye of the beholder, so to speak. That is, whatever one sincerely holds to be morally acceptable for oneself simply *is* morally acceptable *for oneself*. There are two different expressions of individual relativism worth attending to: subjectivism and emotivism. We will consider each in turn.

Take subjectivism first. In this view, moral judgments are effectively reports about the subjective states of the person who believes or asserts them. Accordingly, when one asserts that a given action is right or wrong, one is merely articulating a claim about one's own approval (or disapproval) of that action. Suppose, for example, that someone says, "Late-term abortions are morally vile." According to subjectivism, this particular claim is true *for the individual in question* if and only if and just because the claim accurately conveys the individual's own subjective state toward late-term abortions.

Two things are worth noting here. First, notice how subjectivism, if true, effectively becomes a way of translating moral language into descriptions of the subjective states of the individual in question. Suppose someone, S, says, "X is good" (or "X is right"). Given subjectivism, S's assertion here ultimately translates into something like "S feels approvingly about X." Similarly, when S says, "X is bad" (or "X is wrong"), this claim ultimately reduces to something on the order of "S feels disapprovingly toward X."

Second, notice how, given subjectivism, one effectively serves as the truth-maker (or falsity-maker) of one's own moral claims. That is, an individual's moral assertions are made true or false simply by virtue of one's own subjective states. The right-making (or wrong-making) mechanism is simply the individual's own feelings or attitudes—as opposed to the moral code of one's culture or the commands of Christ or something else altogether. Thus, if S has positive feelings about X, then S's moral claim that "X is morally obligatory" is true.

There are lots of objections facing this view. We will briefly mention four.

Subjectivism invites contradictions

One objection to subjectivism stems from the fact that it attaches morality to the subjective states of individuals. But one's subjective states—especially one's feelings—can be fickle, tricky, and unstable things. After all, it is perfectly psychologically possible for a person to have conflicting feelings about a singular action—that is, approval *and* disproval states directed toward the same thing at the same time. For example, a person might simultaneously feel positively *and* negatively about, say, the prospect of taking a new job, or remaining with an abusive spouse, or taking care of one's aging parents. Given subjectivism, these actions (or inactions) would be both right *and* wrong for the conflicted individual in question, which seems contradictory.

Subjectivism entails that there is no real moral disagreement

If subjectivism is true, an individual's subjective states determine the truth of a moral judgment *for that individual*. Notice the peculiar ramification. Suppose two individuals were to utter what might seem to be conflicting statements concerning whether one has a moral duty to be vaccinated against COVID-19, which was a point of considerable public debate during the height of the pandemic.[14] Admittedly, it might sound as though these individuals morally disagree with one another. But according to subjectivism, they don't actually disagree in any significant sense.

To illustrate the point here, imagine a fictitious conversation between the former director of the National Institute of Allergy and Infectious Diseases, Dr. Anthony Fauci, and the anti-vaccine activist and presidential hopeful Robert F. Kennedy Jr. (who later became the US Secretary of Health and Human Services during the second Trump Administration). Suppose Dr. Fauci were to say, "It's a moral duty to get vaccinated in order to protect people who are immunocompromised." According to subjectivism, Fauci's claim would translate roughly to something on the order of "I, Fauci, feel positively toward vaccination." Meanwhile, imagine Kennedy were to say, "It's immoral to require or encourage people to be vaccinated." Given subjectivism, Kennedy's claim would reduce to something akin to "I, Kennedy, feel negatively about vaccination requirements." Now, notice that when these seemingly conflicting statements are translated into descriptive reports about their respective subjective states, there is actually no *real* disagreement about the issue at hand—no matter how things may have sounded initially. In this imaginary case, Fauci feels positively about vaccination efforts while Kennedy feels negatively about them. So Fauci and Kennedy would not actually disagree with one another. That's because Kennedy could fully agree that Fauci feels positively about getting the jab; and Fauci could surely accept that Kennedy feels negatively. There would be no real disagreement between these two. In fact, given subjectivism, Fauci and Kennedy could never have *any* moral disagreement whatsoever!

Here's the problem, though: Disagreement is a perfectly salient feature of our experience as human beings. Disagreement is not an illusion. Disagreement is real. So something about subjectivism seems off base.

Subjectivism entails infallibility

There is a related problem in the neighborhood: Subjectivism implies that we humans are morally infallible. After all, if it is actually true that one's own subjective states determine whether one's moral claims are true or false, then one could never be wrong in one's moral judgments, at least as long as one's assertions *sincerely* report one's feelings on the matter. Imagine a Parisian woman who feels negatively about hijab requirements and says, "It's wrong to force a woman to wear head coverings in public." Given subjectivism, this statement is true *for the individual who uttered it* as long as it accurately conveys her subjective states. But suppose this woman converts to Islam and has a change of heart with respect to hijab requirements. In turn, imagine that she says, "It's *not* wrong to force a woman to wear head coverings in public." Given subjectivism, this woman's moral judgment was true in the first instance, and it was also true in the second instance. Why is that? One can never be wrong in making a moral assertion according to subjectivism as long as one's assertion accurately conveys one's subjective states at the time of uttering it. Notice how this effectively makes moral truth reducible to the mere sincerity of assertion. And as long as one is being sincere, one's moral assertions or judgments are true, so one is never wrong as long as one is being sincere.

But surely sincerity isn't equivalent to truth. Like disagreement, *fallibility* is also a salient feature of human experience. To err is human, after all. Furthermore, a central teaching of the Christian faith is that *all* have sinned (Rom. 3:23), and, hence, all of us are morally fallible in some respect. So subjectivism is clearly at odds with the Christian faith on this point.

Accepting subjectivism as true gives one license to perpetrate evil

If one serves as the truth-maker of one's own moral judgments, notice the brutal implication. Any action a person might choose to undertake—no matter how heinous—would be morally justifiable, as long as the individual in question simply approves of what one is doing and sincerely believes that one is acting rightly.

The problem here is plain to see. History is replete with evildoers who perhaps *sincerely* approved of their own actions. But they are no less morally blameworthy. Adolf Hitler comes quickly to mind here, as do other more recent world-stage actors, such as the henchmen of the Islamic State of Iraq and the Levant (ISIL) or Russian President Vladimir Putin. Yet surely, if we know anything about the nature of morality, we know that Hitler was profoundly mistaken in his beliefs about the moral permissibility of the atrocities he orchestrated against Jews and other targeted groups. Surely, the ISIL executioners were grossly mistaken in their apparently sincere beliefs about the righteousness of broadcasting the beheadings of twenty-one innocent, orange-clad Coptic Christians on a beach in Libya in 2015.[15] And surely Putin was gravely mistaken in his perhaps sincere stance about the moral righteousness of invading Ukraine in 2022 in order to "de-Nazify" the Ukrainian people.

Sincerity on the part of the responsible evildoer does nothing to justify the heinous actions in question. And if that is so, then subjectivism must be wrong.

2.5. Emotivism

In light of the problems facing subjectivism, the would-be individual relativist might try to seek refuge in an even more nuanced and extreme view in the vicinity of subjectivism: emotivism. Like subjectivism, emotivism holds that moral claims are rooted in and connected to an individual's own subjective states. But, unlike subjectivism, emotivism holds that moral claims are merely *expressions* of one's subjective states, not *reports* about one's subjective states. *Expressions* and not reports—that's the key point here. This is a subtle nuance that makes quite a bit of difference to the moral theory in question. *Reports* about one's subjective states can be either true or false, depending on one's actual subjective states. But things are different when dealing with the mere *expressions* of one's emotional states.

To illustrate this point, return to the person who says, "Late-term abortion is morally vile." According to emotivism, this utterance simply *expresses* the speaker's emotional disgust with late-term abortion in the way that booing or hissing during the big game might express a sports fan's disdain for the rival team. Notice the comparison: booing and hissing are *neither* true *nor* false. Like swearing or grunting or moaning, those utterances are not actually propositional in nature; instead, they are simply audible ways of venting one's negative emotion toward something or someone. Given emotivism, moral claims aren't even truth claims about morality at all; they are simply ways of venting one's emotional states in a way that serves rhetorically as invitations to others to *feel* the same way.

Proponents of emotivism will likely want to explain how the subtleties of emotivism allow it to skirt at least some of the problems facing subjectivism that we raised above. We will not try to settle the score of whether emotivism can be successfully defended against the problems enumerated above. Instead, we will highlight three separate problems facing emotivism.

Emotivism encourages deception

Suppose emotivism is true and, hence, that our moral judgments really are nothing more than mere expressions of our emotional states—expressions that are neither true nor false. If so, then there is a significant sense in which we were deceived all along in using moral language. While we may have *thought* we were doing one thing—for example, asserting that X is indeed wrong—according to emotivism we were really just doing another thing altogether, that is, venting our negative feelings about X. We may have thought our moral language was *really* about objective moral truths, but the truth of emotivism implies that it was not *really* about that after all.

Notice, however, that a proponent of emotivism who uses moral language to motivate others to take on his own preferred views effectively banks on this very subtle sort of deception. After all, the emotivist here would need to rely on the listener believing that moral language is really about objective moral facts, even while emotivism itself explicitly denies that it could be. Alasdair MacIntyre (1929–2025) captures the problem nicely in his reflection on C. L. Stevenson (1908–79), who was an early proponent of emotivism:

> Stevenson . . . understood very clearly that saying "I disapprove of this; do so as well!" does not have the same force as saying "That is bad." He noted that a kind of prestige attaches to the latter, which does not attach to the former. What he did not note however—precisely because he viewed emotivism as a theory of meaning—is that the prestige derives from the fact that the use of "That is bad!" implies an appeal to an objective and impersonal standard in a way in which "I disapprove of this; do so as well" does not. That is, if and insofar as emotivism is true, moral language is seriously misleading and, if and insofar as emotivism is justifiably believed, presumably the use of traditional and inherited moral language ought to be abandoned. This conclusion none of the emotivists drew.[16]

If an emotivist were to come out and say what the emotivist takes his own moral assertions to mean, then his utterance would lose much of its rhetorical punch in dialogue with others. Alternatively, if an emotivist wants his moral claims to carry much rhetorical force in dialogue with others, then the emotivist will need to say what the emotivist himself does not actually mean. If MacIntyre is correct in his criticism, then notice how emotivism clashes with a rather intuitively appealing belief about the nature of morality: that moral language ought not be misleading.

Emotivism lacks explanatory power

A second problem follows closely on the heels of the first. Namely, emotivism fails to explain some rather intuitively appealing convictions we tend to have: that moral language appeals to something *objective* in nature; that moral claims are more than mere expressions of one's emotional states aimed at nudging others to feel the same way; and that moral claims are intended by us, and at least sometimes understood by us, to be fact-tracing and fact-stating in some significant sense.

Emotivism squarely conflicts with the affirmations of the Christian faith

A third and final problem for emotivism—and for any other form of relativism mentioned in this chapter—is this: The Christian faith plainly affirms that at least some acts are, objectively speaking, right or wrong. In other words, Christianity firmly presupposes some form of moral realism. Put loosely, moral realism is the metaethical view that at least some of our assertions about what we morally ought (or ought not) do are indeed *true*—and that they are true not merely in virtue of subjective states but in virtue of objective facts.

Why should we think the Christian faith is committed to some form of moral realism? In part because the Christian faith, like the other major Abrahamic faiths, affirms the objective reality of *sin*. In fact, the concept of sin plays a central role in the Christian religion, as evidenced by the simple fact that the objective reality of sin is affirmed by the Apostles' Creed, the Nicene Creed, the Lord's Prayer, and repeatedly throughout the arc of the biblical narrative.[17] And there is clearly a tight connection between the notion of sin and the notion of an objective moral wrongdoing (and hence objective moral obligation)—even if it can be difficult to specify the precise nature of that particular connection. But whatever that relationship might actually be, the important point for our purpose is that the concept of sin is at least *inclusive* of the concept of objective moral wrongdoing (and hence moral obligation), even if sin is not identical to it. And this point puts a central affirmation of the Christian faith in direct conflict with the assertions of emotivism, as well as those of subjectivism and cultural relativism.

chapter three

ETHICAL EGOISM

September 11, 2001, was a day that can be hard for many people to forget. In a surprise attack masterminded by the Saudi Arabian Islamic militant Osama bin Laden, nineteen al-Qaeda terrorists hijacked four passenger airplanes and turned them into hand-guided missiles. At approximately 8:46 a.m., American Airlines Flight 11, carrying twenty thousand gallons of jet fuel, slammed into the North Tower of the World Trade Center. Just eighteen minutes later, United Airlines Flight 175 crashed into the South Tower. Both skyscrapers fell within a matter of hours, blanketing Manhattan with dust and ash. As those events were unfolding in New York, at 9:45 a.m., American Airlines Flight 77 plowed into the western wing of the Pentagon building in Arlington, Virginia. The fourth plane—United Airlines Flight 93—was being flown toward its target in Washington, DC, when several passengers fought back against the hijackers, crashing the plane into a field near Shanksville, Pennsylvania. Everyone aboard died. By the end of the day, nearly three thousand lives were lost in the deadliest attack ever carried out on American soil.

That day, 9/11, is remembered not only for ushering in the so-called War on Terror but also for many acts of bravery and personal sacrifice—not only by the passengers of Flight 93 but also by the many first responders at the Twin Towers and elsewhere throughout the United States. Among the first on the scene was the British-born Rick Rescorla. A former soldier and police officer, Rescorla had served for many years as the director of security for Morgan Stanley, a financial company that occupied nearly two dozen floors of the South Tower. He had long worried about the possibility of a terrorist attack on the building, and he had even anticipated many of the details of a bombing that had occurred there eight years prior. Following that particular tragedy in 1993, Rescorla had grown determined to prepare Morgan Stanley employees for any such future emergencies, stubbornly insisting on routine drills. So on the morning of 9/11, Rescorla was ready to jump into action. He ignored intercom announcements that instructed everyone to remain at their desks and instead evacuated nearly all of his company's employees out of the building. According to several eyewitnesses, Rescorla had every opportunity to escape that day, but he refused to do so until he could get everyone else out first. He clearly recognized the stakes involved, as he even called his wife to say his last goodbyes. Rescorla was in the South Tower when it collapsed. His body was never recovered. According to some estimates, his actions in the minutes before he died helped save more than two thousand lives that day.[1]

Contrast Rescorla with Matt and Noah Colvin, two brothers from Chattanooga, Tennessee, who at the outset of the COVID-19 pandemic in the summer of 2020 allegedly stockpiled more than seventeen thousand bottles of hand sanitizer in order to sell them at a profit on Amazon's online marketplace. According to one report, Matt was able to peddle a small container of sanitizer for as much as seventy dollars—about ten times more than its typical price—precisely because of the sudden supply-chain shortage combined with a dramatic increase in demand because folks were desperate to stave off the spread of the novel coronavirus.[2] Ultimately, the Colvin brothers were investigated by state officials for violating Tennessee's price-gouging laws. To dodge legal charges and fines, the Colvin brothers eventually agreed to donate their stockpile of hand sanitizer to others through their local church congregation.

Who provides the better model of the moral life—Rescorla or the Colvin brothers? Could one ever have a moral obligation to do the sort of thing Rescorla did on 9/11? If laying down one's life seems too extreme, then suppose the stakes were lower. What if one could save others without risking one's own life but instead by risking, say, an arm or a leg? Or what if one could save others not by risking life or limb but simply by foregoing the opportunity to boost one's profits on Amazon? Or even less?

The underlying question at play here is whether we ever have a moral obligation to prioritize the interests of others at the expense of our own. And at least one theory of morality says we do *not*. In fact, according to this particular theory of morality, those whom we might be tempted to regard as heroic for their self-sacrifice—folks like Rescorla, for example—might actually be acting *immorally*, while others—those like the Colvin brothers—are perhaps more in line with the requirements of morality. This chapter is focused on a consideration of such a moral theory, namely ethical egoism.

3.1. What Ethical Egoism Says

Ethical egoism is a theory of morality according to which each individual ought to pursue what is, ultimately, to one's own advantage. More specifically, in this view, an individual's fundamental moral duty is to do that which promotes one's own self-interests. There are three central affirmations of ethical egoism:

i. The moral status of one's action depends on the consequences of the action in question.
ii. The only consequences that matter are those affecting a person's own genuine self-interests.
iii. The only self-interests that matter are those of the individual in question.

Consider each point in turn. First, notice that ethical egoism is a *consequentialist* theory of ethics. That is, ethical egoism holds that the moral status of one's action depends on the result of one's action. In other words, ethical egoism judges actions by their fruits, not by the intentions, aspirations, or motives of the individual in question. And that's because, for ethical egoism, whether one is acting for the sake of some noble ideal or with some particular intention in mind simply doesn't matter. Rather, the consequences of one's behavior are what determines whether an action is right or wrong.

Second, ethical egoism holds that the sort of consequences that are pertinent with respect to the moral status of one's action are those pertaining to a person's welfare or self-interests—that is, whatever improves one's well-being or might make one's life better off. Importantly, ethical egoism does not assume people are somehow infallible in discerning their own self-interests. After all, one's *actual* interests do not always align with what one previously *thought* they were. We are sometimes mistaken, in other words. For example, one could sincerely believe that taking out a massive student loan to pay for an expensive graduate degree will make one's life better, only to find oneself years later crippled with debt that one cannot repay. Ethical egoism holds that one's moral obligation is to pursue what is *really* and objectively in one's best interest—not just what one *perceives* or *believes* to be one's own self-interest. In this respect, ethical egoism is at odds with subjectivism.

Additionally, ethical egoism is not committed to saying individuals should act on any and every pleasure-seeking impulse one might have. Rather, ethical egoism holds that one has a moral duty to promote what is genuinely in one's self-interest for the long haul. In this sense, ethical egoism is clearly at odds with what we might think of as *spring break hedonism*. After all, notice how the very concept of one's own genuine self-interest could include things like one's overall health, wellness, financial security, a quality social life, family stability, and so on. Accordingly, the various ingredients that comprise one's genuine self-interest might, in turn, entail obligations to exercise, eat well, do one's job with excellence, be sociable and return favors, spend time with family, and the like.

Third, ethical egoism is agent-centered in scope. That is, ethical egoism holds that the full extent or scope of the consequences that are morally relevant for an individual are those—and *only* those—of the individual in question. In other words, the individual has no moral obligation to promote the interests of others *in addition to* or *at the expense of* one's own—except perhaps in those cases when doing so ultimately enhances one's own self-interests. Truly altruistic behavior, then, is neither required nor even morally permissible according to ethical egoism.

Now, while ethical egoism is probably most often contemplated as an account of the right, we can nonetheless construe it also as an account of the good. For example, ethical egoism says that for each individual, one's own genuine self-interest—that is, one's own objective well-being—is what is intrinsically good. Accordingly, something is extrinsically good for that individual if and only if and just because it facilitates one's own genuine self-interest. Something is extrinsically bad for an individual if and only if and just because it thwarts one's own genuine self-interest. And something is value-neutral for an individual if and only if and just because it neither facilitates nor thwarts one's own genuine self-interest.

In turn, ethical egoism's account of the right can be summarized as follows. An action is morally obligatory for an individual if and only if and just because that action best promotes one's own genuine self-interest. An action is wrong for an individual if and only if and just because it does not best promote one's own genuine self-interest. And an action is optional if and only if and just because it is tied for first place, as it were, with what best promotes one's own genuine self-interest.

Notice how ethical egoism's account of the right implies a fairly straightforward decision procedure:

STEP 1: Determine which actions are available.
STEP 2: For each action, determine what the likely consequences would be.
STEP 3: Determine which set of consequences would best promote your genuine self-interest.
STEP 4: Do the action that best promotes your genuine self-interest (or, in the case of a tie, do one of the actions that is tied for first place in best promoting your genuine self-interest).

3.2. The Case for Ethical Egoism

One of the noteworthy advantages of ethical egoism as a moral theory is that it provides a clear and forceful answer to the question of why one should concern oneself with being moral in the first place. The answer here, according to ethical egoism, is simple: It is in your self-interest to be moral precisely because pursuing your self-interest *is* your moral duty! Of course, this hardly amounts to a full-blown case for ethical egoism. Below, we consider four different arguments for ethical egoism.

The argument from psychological egoism

One argument for ethical egoism is premised on a key assumption about human psychology, namely that one is always and only ever *motivated* by the perception of one's own self-interests. This is a view known as *psychological egoism*. More specifically, this theory says that the only thing an individual is psychologically capable of being motivated by is, ultimately, a consideration about one's own self-interest. Notice that psychological egoism is a descriptive theory of *psychology*, and so it is distinct from ethical egoism, which is a normative theory about how we *ought* to behave. So taken by itself, psychological egoism does not even attempt to specify an account of the good or an account of the right. Instead, psychological egoism is simply a theory about how humans are psychologically hardwired, so to speak. And on this theory, humans are motivated solely by their own self-interest. So if psychological egoism is true, then anytime someone appears to be acting altruistically—that is, anytime one might seem to be pursuing another's interests instead of one's own—it is really just an illusion. That's because, according to psychological egoism, one can only ever be motivated by one's own self-interest.

Notice how such a theory of human psychology could be leveraged into an argument for ethical egoism. The argument would go roughly as follows:

(1) If psychological egoism is true, then we are psychologically unable to act altruistically—that is, we are psychologically unable to act in ways that are motivated by the interests of others over those of ourselves.

(2) Psychological egoism is true.

(3) So, we are psychologically unable at act altruistically.

(4) Since we are psychologically unable to act altruistically, then it is not possible for us to act altruistically.

(5) Ought-implies-can principle: If we are morally obligated to X, then it is possible for us to X.

(6) Thus, we are not morally obligated to act altruistically.
(7) Thus, by elimination, ethical egoism is the correct theory of morality.

This sort of argument is hardly without its problems. For starters, premise 2 is either plainly false or simply unsupported by the total evidence available to us. Take Rick Rescorla, for example. Rescorla's choice to sacrifice himself on 9/11 for the people in the World Trade Center certainly *seems* like a pretty clear counterexample to psychological egoism and hence to premise 2. Of course, proponents of psychological egoism will inevitably seek to redescribe examples of this sort (where people *seem* to be acting altruistically) as cases where, in fact, the individuals in question are simply pursuing their own self-interests (as they understood them) all along.

But how exactly was Rescorla motivated by his own self-interest when he refused to leave the South Tower, knowing full well that the building would in all likelihood collapse on him? The psychological egoist says: Rescorla still sought to satisfy his own desire, which happened to be a desire to evacuate as many people as possible before the skyscraper collapsed. Perhaps Rescorla knew he would feel immense guilt if he hadn't done everything he could have done that day. Or perhaps Rescorla believed he would receive a reward in the afterlife if he died in the process of saving others. Or perhaps Rescorla judged that the lasting honor of dying a hero's death was, ultimately, of greater gain than surviving. Whatever it may have been, says the psychological egoist, there was *something* Rescorla took to be in his own interest that Rescorla obtained in satisfying his desire to evacuate others out of the South Tower. So Rescorla—like everyone else—was most fundamentally motivated by his own self-interest, namely the satisfaction of his desire, whatever it may have been. Or so says the psychological egoist.

Notice, though, two very subtle conflations at the heart of the psychological egoist's redescription of the Rescorla case.[3] First, psychological egoism confuses the *possession* of a desire to help the people of the South Tower with the ultimate *aim* of having that desire in the first place. True, the desire to vacate the South Tower was indeed possessed by Rescorla—it was indeed *his* desire after all. No one denies that. But the *aim* of Rescorla's desire surely was not to help himself—he died, after all—but to help those *other* than himself (the more than two thousand people who lived as a result of his actions that day). And simply because Rescorla had a desire to accomplish this hardly entails that his desire was self-serving. As it turns out, the fact that Rescorla had a desire aimed at the good of others—and at his own expense—would seem to illustrate that his desire was not egocentric in the least.

A second conflation: Psychological egoism confuses the side-effects of fulfilling one's own desire with the agent's underlying *motive*. Perhaps Rescorla indeed felt an immense sense of gratification in helping thousands of people escape certain death on 9/11. But that sense of gratification—if Rescorla indeed ever took a moment to soak it in—does not somehow entail that his underlying motive was to enjoy such a sense of gratification. In fact, it is tempting to suppose that no such gratification ever crossed Rescorla's mind, and if it did, it was simply a side-effect of acting on his actual motive to help others.

So the case for psychological egoism's redescription of the Rescorla case remains unmade. Of course, the psychological egoist might simply continue to claim that Rescorla—like all *seemingly* altruistic agents—was ultimately motivated at some deep, unseen level by his own perceived self-interest, whatever that may have been. But if so, then the proponent of psychological egoism advocates for a theory of human psychology that would appear to be resistant to, and hence untestable by, the testimony of history, the testimony of witnesses, and—what is worse—the testimony of individual human actors themselves.[4] But theories that insist that we ignore the evidence staring us in the face are probably not theories we should be eager to bet our lives on. Yes, we are of course sometimes deceived about the root motives of others, and even sometimes about our own motives. But not always.

At any rate, even if psychological egoism were true, there is a second problem facing the argument for ethical egoism above: *It is logically invalid.* To see the point here, just pretend that premises 1–5 were true. Notice how, strictly speaking, the only thing that follows from those premises is that altruistic behavior is not morally obligatory. And, unfortunately, ethical egoism isn't the only moral theory compatible with such a conclusion. For example, nihilism—the view that morality is just a farce—fits with that. To be clear, our point here is *not* that nihilism is somehow on better footing than ethical egoism. The point is just that the argument above doesn't succeed in making the case for ethical egoism in particular.

The invisible hand argument

A different approach to arguing for ethical egoism proceeds by emphasizing the public good that comes about when each individual focuses on one's own self-interest. This sort of strategy is plausibly attributable to Adam Smith (1723–90), who is something of an iconic figure in the discipline of economics and in the history of free market capitalism.[5] In his famous book *Wealth of Nations*, for example, Smith contends that "by pursuing his *own* interest," an individual can thereby "promote that of society more effectually than when he really intends to promote it."[6] (In fact, continues Smith, "I have never known much good done by those who affected to trade for the public good.") The basic idea here seems to be that when each individual attends to one's own self-interests—which one knows intimately "in his local situation" and which one cares about most enthusiastically—this engenders a maximally competitive marketplace wherein each individual is compelled to both improve the quality of one's own contribution to society while also doing so with the greatest efficiency. By contrast, one is never in a good position to discern, nor to be motivated to attend to, the interests of others with comparable insight, motivation, or efficacy. Ultimately, then, by intending "only his own gain," the egoist is "led by an invisible hand to promote an end which was no part of his intention," namely the public good.[7]

Following Smith's reasoning, notice how we might formulate an invisible hand argument for ethical egoism:

(1) When individuals focus on promoting their own self-interests, the public good is served with the greatest efficiency.

(2) When individuals focus on promoting the interests of others (in addition to their own), the public good is served with less efficiency.

(3) We have a moral duty to promote the public good with the greatest efficiency.

(4) Thus, individuals ought to focus on promoting their own self-interests.
(5) Thus, ethical egoism is the correct theory of morality.

Unfortunately for advocates of ethical egoism, this argument suffers from a simple, though fatal, flaw. Even if it is true that self-serving competition would result in a better overall economy for everyone (which is an empirical claim that's at least debatable, if not simply false), the problem is that this argument relies on a premise that conflicts with ethical egoism itself. After all, if ethical egoism is true, then premise 3 can certainly seem peculiar. Premise 3 stipulates that we have a moral duty to promote the *public* good. But that sort of claim is at odds with the core assertion of ethical egoism, namely that an individual's sole moral duty is to do that which promotes one's *own* self-interests. What could possibly explain the fact that one has a duty to promote the public good in the first place according to the ethical egoist? And what should the ethical egoist do when one's own self-interests conflict with the public good? Ultimately, the problem here is that for premise 3 to be true, the core assertion of ethical egoism would have to be false. So this argument for ethical egoism clearly won't work.

Ayn Rand's "objectivist" argument

A third sort of argument for ethical egoism hails from the popular twentieth-century Russian American author Ayn Rand (1905–82), who is perhaps best known for her novels *Atlas Shrugged* and *The Fountainhead*. Rand's case for ethical egoism hinges on what she regards as a plain but crucial metaphysical fact about humanity together with a criticism of alternative moral theories in light of that key metaphysical fact. In her book *The Virtue of Selfishness*, for example, Rand contends that what makes living organisms distinct from inanimate matter is simply that there is no real question of whether inanimate matter (as such) will continue to exist—it will (think: the law of conservation). But the same point simply isn't true of living organisms: They can, and will, cease to exist *if they are not properly supported*. This point provides the root basis for all valuation, according to Rand: Inanimate objects are neither *for* nor *against* anything, whereas living creatures are inherently *for* their own survival and *against* their own demise. Meanwhile, the necessary conditions for a living creature to survive are fixed by facts concerning the kind of creature it is. And that is just an inescapably objective matter.

All this has a vital implication, according to Rand. For each living person, one's own life is the supreme and intrinsic good: It is both the standard of value (whatever promotes one's life is good; whatever opposes or destroys one's life is evil) *and* one's chief purpose. What does (and does not) promote this supreme good is determined by nature—it is not a matter of mere social convention or subjective preference or whim. Accordingly, Rand understands her ethical view to be fully *objectivist*: What genuinely promotes the individual's life is, for that individual, the true objective standard for morality. Accordingly, that which would compromise or impair one's life is evil precisely insofar as it is opposed to what is, for that individual, the supreme intrinsic good. Importantly, in Rand's view, all non-egoist theories of morality—what Rand subsumes under the heading of "altruism"—force the individual to contemplate one's own supreme intrinsic good as something one must be willing, at least in principle, to sacrifice either for some alleged *greater* good or for the good of *some other* individual, whether that's the will of some deity or the betterment of society or, worst of all, some subjective whim of another person. The basic thought here is that non-egoist (i.e., altruistic) theories of morality hold that individuals must be willing to forego their own self-interests if doing so is necessary to, say, do the will of God or improve society at large or whatever else is propped up as a supposedly "greater" good. But such a willingness is the height of irrationality, according to Rand, since there is nothing of greater value to an individual than one's own life.[8] Thus, in Rand's view, altruistic conceptions of ethics are in principle, if not in fact, opposed to what is supremely valuable to the individual, namely, the individual's own life.[9]

Rand's case for ethical egoism can be summarized as follows:

(1) For each individual, one's own life is intrinsically—and supremely—valuable.

(2) Non-egoist (i.e., altruistic) theories of ethics require that an individual be willing, at least in principle, to sacrifice one's

own life for something other than what is, for that individual, supremely and intrinsically valuable.

(3) Ethical egoism, by contrast, requires that an individual uphold the value of the individual's own life.

(4) Thus, ethical egoism is the correct theory of morality.

Rand's argument is questionable for at least one reason, if no other. Focus on premise 1. Even if we agree with Rand that human life is intrinsically valuable, it is certainly debatable that for each individual, the individual's *own* life is *supremely* valuable. Perhaps it is fair to say that human life simpliciter is intrinsically valuable and, hence, that all human lives should be appropriately respected and protected. But that's much different from saying that, for me, *my* life is supremely valuable. And if Rand is wrong about that particular claim, then premise 1 is false, in which case her argument fails to get off the ground.

So is it true that, for each individual, one's own life is the *summum bonum*—the supreme good? Christians can be forgiven if they balk at such an idea. After all, since at least the days of Anselm of Canterbury (ca. 1033–1109), the Christian tradition has contemplated God as *that than which nothing greater can be conceived*—that is, as the supremely perfect and maximally great being. Rand seems to suggest that, for each individual, that than which nothing greater can be conceived would really just be one's own life. But that is of course problematic because, surely, each individual can imagine something greater than oneself, namely that which does not lack any perfection and which is at no risk of going out of existence in the first place precisely because it exists with necessity. If so, then premise 1 is false, and the case for ethical egoism remains unmade.

An argument from Christianity?

There is perhaps yet another case for ethical egoism that we should consider—one that turns explicitly on the truth of Christianity. Roughly put, the basic idea is that if one accepts some of the central teachings of the Christian tradition, then one should accept ethical egoism too.

How might such an argument proceed? Return to a point made at the outset of this chapter: Ethical egoism doesn't assume that people are infallible in discerning their self-interests. In other words, ethical egoism can readily acknowledge that there is sometimes a rather serious gap between what a person *perceives* to be in one's self-interest and what is *genuinely* in that person's self-interest. And on this point, ethical egoism and the Christian tradition are in alignment. Consider the simple fact that people commonly believe they are indeed pursuing their own best interests by obtaining the pleasures and treasures of this earthly life—whether that be through education, wealth, professional accomplishment, travel, social status, physical health, sexual gratification, and so on. Yet Jesus suggests that these folks are shortsighted about what is *really* in their ultimate best interest; their genuine self-interests are not going to be found *on earth*, as it were. In fact, one of the central teachings of the Christian faith is that the *most* valuable and important thing an individual can attain is a loving relationship *with God* (both now and in the life to come). So it is hardly surprising that Jesus exhorts us to play the long game, as it were. After all, Jesus teaches in the Sermon on the Mount that we shouldn't strive to store up earthly riches but instead store up for ourselves "treasures in heaven, where moths and vermin do not destroy, and where thieves do not break in and steal" (Matt. 6:20 NIV). Notice how Jesus seems to be presuming here that, in the long run, one's genuine self-interest is intimately connected to having an everlasting, loving relationship with God in heaven—and Jesus seems to be encouraging us to pursue that above all else! In other words, it can seem like Jesus is effectively saying that one ought to pursue one's own *genuine* self-interest above all else. But that's what the ethical egoist says, too—or so the argument might go. We can summarize this case for ethical egoism in the following way:

(1) Christianity holds that we should pursue a loving relationship with God above all else.

(2) Having a loving relationship with God is ultimately in one's genuine self-interest.

(3) So, effectively, Christianity teaches that one should pursue one's own genuine self-interest above all else.

(4) If Christianity teaches that one should pursue one's own genuine self-interest above all else, then accepting Christianity

entails accepting ethical egoism as the correct theory of morality.

(5) Thus, accepting Christianity entails accepting ethical egoism as the correct theory of morality.

The problem with this line of reasoning is that premise 4 is false. And that's because merely affirming that one should pursue one's own genuine self-interest above all else isn't actually enough to entail ethical egoism—at least, not given what *Christianity* understands one's genuine self-interest to be. To say that it is in one's genuine interest to be in a loving relationship with another person—in this case, God—is to say that the one's genuine self-interest *coalesces* with the self-interest of one's beloved. However, ethical egoism presumes that the *only* self-interest that actually matters is that of the individual person in question. Consider a human analogy here. If a wife's genuine self-interest is bound up in a loving relationship with her husband, then her husband's self-interest becomes inextricably bound up with her own—and vice versa. Their interests become united, in other words. After all, if the wife were to think of her own self-interest as being fundamentally in competition with the self-interest of her husband, then the love between them would be thereby diminished. So notice how true love between a wife and a husband stands in tension with the agent-centered scope of ethical egoism. And if that's correct, then premise 4 is false, in which case the argument above is unsound.

3.3. The Case against Ethical Egoism

Even if the arguments for ethical egoism are unsound, that does not entail that ethical egoism is false. So we are right to wonder whether there is a positive case *against* ethical egoism. And, in fact, there are a host of objections facing ethical egoism. We will highlight five.

Ethical egoism licenses wicked behavior

If ethical egoism were true, then the following sort of question would become especially difficult to ignore: What happens if and when it is in the best interest of an individual to run roughshod over the interests of others? Imagine a scenario wherein it becomes necessary for an elected official to perpetrate voter fraud and mass deception in order to promote his own self-interest of being reelected to political office. Or imagine a situation in which a king who, in pursuit of his own self-interests (viz., sleeping with his neighbor's wife), has his neighbor killed in an effort to cover up his indiscretions. In both cases, ethical egoism would seem to give the green light to wickedness.[10]

Of course, the dedicated ethical egoist will likely push back here by saying that this sort of objection simply begs the question against ethical egoism—precisely because it antecedently judges that certain actions are immoral (e.g., deception, fraud, adultery, murder, etc.) and in turn judges that ethical egoism must be false, insofar as it condones those actions in cases where the pursuit of one's genuine self-interest might require them. However (says the ethical egoist), if ethical egoism is in fact true, then those actions—while perhaps unpopular and controversial—would in fact be morally permissible or even obligatory for the individual in question, that is, *if* they truly advance the individual's own genuine self-interest.

In response: Even if the objection begs the question against ethical egoism, we are right to wonder whether we should be inclined to trust a *theory* over our own intuitions that tell us that mass deception and fraud and adultery and murder are wrong. Theories (and people) that trample our attentiveness to what can seem morally obvious should be handled with caution.

Ethical egoism lacks integrity

A second problem facing ethical egoism runs as follows: If ethical egoism were true, then ethical egoists would be morally forbidden from publicly advocating for ethical egoism.[11] Why? To see the point at hand here, imagine that a proponent of ethical egoism lets others know that she accepts the theory and, in turn, explains her case for doing so. One of two things will happen: She will either convince others to become ethical egoists, or she won't. Suppose she remains unconvincing. Those who aren't compelled by her advocacy will now know her for what she truly is: an ethical egoist. And in outing herself in this way, the ethical egoist has now let the world know that she is committed to pursuing her own self-interests, no matter what. In response, non-egoists will rightly regard the out-of-the-closet egoist with suspicion—especially in cases where the ethical egoist might be lying about or dissembling her ulterior motives in a situation. This is surely contrary to the self-interest of the egoist in question.

Suppose, however, that the public advocate of ethical egoism is winsome, persuasive, and convincing. If the ethical egoist is successful in getting others to accept her preferred moral theory, there will now be fewer altruistic suckers around to help the ethical egoist advance her own self-interests! This predicament is surely contrary to the egoist's self-interests, too. So, in either case, publicizing one's belief in ethical egoism runs counter to the self-interest of the dedicated ethical egoist. Thus, if ethical egoism is true, then the dedicated ethical egoist morally ought to remain silent about the truth of it. That would seem to mean that the dedicated proponent of ethical egoism invariably lacks *integrity* because there is inconsistency between one's inner convictions and one's outward presentation.

Admittedly, this objection hardly demonstrates that ethical egoism is false. After all, perhaps proponents of ethical egoism might rather enjoy life in the closet, so to speak. But even if this objection doesn't exactly defeat ethical egoism, it does cast the theory in a rather shady light. And it can seem intuitive to think that a moral theory ought to have nothing to hide.

Ethical egoism is arbitrary in the same way racism is

An altogether different case against ethical egoism hinges on the complaint that this moral theory is unacceptably arbitrary in the very same way that racism is. James Rachels and Stuart Rachels level this sort of objection against ethical egoism. They reason roughly as follows:[12]

(1) Principle of equal treatment: We should treat people equally, unless there is a relevant difference between them that justifies treating them unequally.

(2) Racism divides people into groups and then discriminates against members of one group in a way that is not justified by any relevant difference between the groups.

(3) So, racism is immoral because it violates the principle of equal treatment.

(4) Like racism, ethical egoism divides people into groups—namely, *oneself* and *everyone else*—and gives preference to the

one group (oneself) in a way that is not justified by any relevant difference between the groups.

(5) Thus, ethical egoism is problematic for the same reason racism is—it violates the principle of equal treatment.

Does this argument constitute a definitive refutation of ethical egoism? For the sake of testing Rachels and Rachels's argument, consider the following thought experiment. Suppose a sinister terrorist has taken you captive and offers you the following dilemma at gunpoint. You must decide whether you or the stranger standing next to you will be shot in the head and killed. One of you is going to be killed no matter what—and *you* must decide who survives. Assume the stranger standing next to you is your equal in every morally relevant sense. Under these terrible circumstances, would you be justified in picking yourself to be the one who gets to survive?

If the answer to this question is "yes," then there is a problem with Rachels and Rachels's argument against ethical egoism. After all, in the thought experiment at hand, you and the stranger are equals. Accordingly, there cannot be a principled, nonarbitrary basis for privileging yourself over the stranger (the two of you are equals, after all). So if you think you are indeed justified in choosing yourself to live, then you thereby hold that one can be justified in treating equal parties unequally. But that's to deny premise 1 of Rachels and Rachels's argument. And if premise 1 is false, then the argument is unsound.

But suppose premise 1 *is* true. And suppose that, believing premise 1 is true, you conclude that you aren't justified in choosing yourself to live over the stranger. (After all, you are no better or worse than the stranger standing next to you—and she deserves to die no more or less than you do.) So given premise 1, perhaps you should just resort to a coin toss.

But what *should* you choose in this sort of dilemma? It can be tempting to think that you would indeed be justified in choosing yourself to live. (And if you *didn't* choose yourself to live, wouldn't Ayn Rand be right to say you didn't properly value your own life?) This has led some philosophers to wonder whether we have just stumbled upon a basic—and unexplainable—axiom of morality: That an individual is morally warranted in prioritizing one's own self-interest over that of others *in circumstances like the one described above* (wherein each person is equal but only one can win), even if one is not warranted in prioritizing one's own self-interest on every occasion.[13]

Whether this is a settled matter for Christians is perhaps another story. Jesus summarizes the moral law, in part, by saying that you should love your neighbor *as yourself*, where your neighbor includes the stranger (at least according to the Parable of the Good Samaritan in Luke 10). It is less clear, though, what Jesus's teaching might imply in circumstances of equality wherein there is both a winner *and a loser*, so to speak—like in the thought experiment just imagined. In that kind of scenario, there is a lingering curiosity: How do you both (a) love your neighbor in the same way that you love yourself, and (b) still love *yourself*? We leave this question as homework for the reader.

Ethical egoism is incompatible with robust friendship, Christian marriage, and responsible parenthood

In his famous discussion of friendship in *Nicomachean Ethics*, Aristotle points out that one of the prerequisites for true, complete friendship is not only that one has goodwill toward another but that one wishes for good things *for the other's sake*—and not merely because those good things might have a spillover effect back to oneself.[14] The thought here is, roughly, that A wants what is in B's genuine best interest, regardless of how that affects A. But if ethical egoism were true, the model of friendship Aristotle has in mind here isn't just naïve, it is downright immoral. Why? On at least some occasions, A's willing and pursuing B's self-interest could require A to compromise on pursuing what is in A's own self-interest. And ethical egoism holds that this kind of compromise is fundamentally contrary to A's ultimate moral duty to advance A's own self-interest. Yet if A wishes good for B only to the extent that doing so advances (or at least is consistent with) A's own self-interest, then A is a fair-weather friend indeed—A isn't wishing for good things *for B's own sake*! Thus, ethical egoism is at odds with real friendship, at least as Aristotle describes it.

But suppose a less robust model of friendship (whatever that might be) is enough for the otherwise lonely egoist. There is a related problem: Ethical egoism is incompatible with the Christian understanding of marriage, at least as it is depicted in the traditional wedding vow wherein a couple solemnly agrees to be faithful to one another in sickness and in health, for richer or for poorer, and *for better or for worse.*[15] Although the exact language used in wedding ceremonies has of course evolved over time and across different denominations, the underlying covenant remains the same: A will be faithful to B, regardless of whether doing so is in A's own self-interest. And this faithfulness isn't simply about, say, sexual fidelity. The apostle Paul writes, "Husbands should *love* their wives as they do their own bodies" (Eph. 5:28 NRSV—emphasis added). That is, husbands should care for and attend to the interests of their wives as if their wives were themselves. In other words, the interests of the wife should be adopted as the interests of the husband. But that runs contrary to what ethical egoism requires.

For similar reasons, ethical egoism also conflicts with what it takes to be a good mother or father. A good parent nurtures and cares for one's child and does so for the *child's* sake—not for the *parent's* sake. In fact, sometimes caring for one's child comes at the expense of the parent's financial, professional, physical, and psychological well-being. To be perfectly clear, this hardly makes the parent heroic—that's just part of being a loving and responsible parent. And to the extent that proper parenting inevitably calls for personal sacrifice from time to time, ethical egoism must condemn it.

Admittedly, the ethical egoist might try to deflect the objection on offer here by pointing out that the underlying reason *Christians* value sacrificial love (whether in friendship, marriage, or parenthood) is precisely because they see it as part of what is needed to become the kind of person who can ultimately attain one's genuine self-interest in the long run (i.e., storing up treasures in heaven). Thus, according to the ethical egoist, while it might appear that sacrificial friends, spouses, and parents are acting in ways that are contrary to their own self-interests, they are really only acting in ways that are contrary to their short-term interests in the pursuit of their long-term or ultimate self-interests.

Unfortunately for ethical egoism, this defensive strategy fails. The underlying problem is that ethical egoism requires us to delineate between an *ego's* self-interests and the *other's* self-interests. In other words, ethical egoism forces us contemplate the self-interests of an ego—say, a mother—as discrete from the self-interests of another—say, the child. If the ethical egoist *were* willing to stretch the concept of an ego to the point at which it actually includes the *other*, then perhaps this moral theory could be salvaged. But notice, if we stretch the concept of the ego in the way that would be required to deflect the objection on offer, then the very concept of self-interest becomes unstable and problematic. And that concept is fundamental to the theory.

Ethical egoism conflicts with affirmations of the Christian faith

Suppose that the objections mentioned so far aren't enough to defeat ethical egoism. There is one final point to consider: Ethical egoism squarely conflicts with several affirmations of the Christian faith.

Return to Jesus's emphasis on the commandment to love your neighbor as yourself. While loving one's neighbor might not be reducible to merely promoting the neighbor's interests, the former surely *includes* the latter. In other words, at least part of what is implied by Jesus's commandment is that one should promote the genuine interests of one's neighbors in the same way that one promotes one's own self-interests. So, minimally, a clear implication of Jesus's summary of the moral law is that we are *not* licensed to value and promote our own personal self-interests *at the exclusion of all other considerations*. We should love others *equally* to how we love ourselves.

It might seem that the apostle Paul goes even further than Jesus in his letter to the Romans when he says to "honor one another *above* yourselves" (Rom. 12:10 NIV—emphasis added). Such an exhortation can seem to suggest that there are at least some occasions wherein Christians are morally required to allow the interests of others to *overrule* their own self-interests. Ultimately, though, Jesus goes even further than Paul in commanding his followers to love one another in the same manner that Jesus loved his own friends: by laying down his life for them (John 15:12). Notice how Jesus's model is to promote the interests of others *even at the expense of one's own life*, which will of course seem absolutely bananas to any self-respecting ethical egoist. Self-sacrifice isn't impressive or praiseworthy or heroic according to ethical egoism; it is idiotic, irrational, and immoral. Jesus, so it seems, could never make a good ethical egoist.

A final point is relevant here. Jesus makes it crystal clear that the *greatest* commandment of all—even greater than the commandment to love your neighbor as yourself—is captured in the ancient Jewish confession of faith known as the Shema: "Hear, O Israel: The Lord our God, the Lord is one. Love the Lord your God with all your heart and with all your soul and with all your mind and with all your strength" (Mark 12:29–30 NIV). In other words, if Jesus is right, you should love God with everything you have, and thus you should love God *above all else*. As humans, the tendency to love oneself comes naturally, we might say. Ethical egoism gets that point well enough. Jesus's command to love your neighbor as yourself puts the love of others on par with your own self-love. Yet the greatest command according to Jesus is to love God *even more than you love yourself*, which is perfectly incompatible with ethical egoism.

How might we make sense out of the thought that loving God is *even more obligatory* than loving oneself—especially given just how natural loving oneself can seem and given just how difficult it can be to love someone else equal to how one loves oneself (let alone *more* than oneself)? The medieval Christian philosopher John Duns Scotus (ca. 1265–1308) can be helpful here. Scotus reasons roughly as follows.[16] Suppose God actually exists. If so, then there is a supremely perfect being that exists and exists with necessity (that is, this perfectly good being cannot not exist—anything less would be a lack of perfection). The term "good" simply refers to that which is to be loved. Accordingly, that which is *perfectly* good is to be loved *above all else*. Thus, if God actually exists, then God is to be loved above all else. And if God exists with necessity, it is *necessary* that God is to be loved above all else. Pay attention to the implication here. Whereas the obligation to love others, or even oneself, might be conditional upon, say, facts about the sorts of creatures we are by nature or facts about what would maximize happiness or facts about what would show respect to persons or facts about what God commands (or some other such account), the obligation to love God above all else is contingent upon nothing other than God's divine nature, which is itself necessary. So the obligation to love God above all else—*even above oneself*—is necessarily obligatory. And if that is true, ethical egoism isn't just problematic, it is patently and necessarily false.

chapter four

UTILITARIANISM

Suppose you control a massive drawbridge not unlike the historic Tower Bridge in London or the many famous bascule bridges that span across the river in downtown Chicago. Your one and only job is to make sure the bridge is drawn up when ships need to pass through the waterway and lowered down when passenger trains need to cross over it. A train is coming around the bend, and you face a terrible dilemma. If you don't lower the bridge right now, hundreds of people aboard the train will die. However, if you lower the bridge at this particular moment, an innocent child who is playing near the hinge gears of the drawbridge will be crushed to death.

What would *you* do? More important: What *should* you do? What is the right thing in this situation?

For many, the answer can seem obvious, if gut-wrenching: You should save as many lives as possible and minimize the harm done along the way. Sadly, the child will have to suffer and die. But—so the thought goes—there is simply no other way to prevent a far worse calamity from occurring. The decision at hand is not about what would be in the interest of just one person or even a few privileged people but about what might minimize the harm for the greatest number possible.

Thought experiments of this sort can seem as far-fetched as they are distressing. But people do sometimes face relevantly similar dilemmas—and with far more frequency than one would wish. Consider what happened to Jim and Diane Houpt of Greenwood, Indiana—and many others—during the height of the COVID-19 pandemic, when there was still great uncertainty and fear about the full societal effects of the highly transmissible novel coronavirus that originated in Wuhan, China. As a seventy-three-year-old who suffered from pulmonary fibrosis, Jim was hospitalized when he contracted COVID. Because the hospital had been enforcing a policy that was relatively commonplace throughout the United States at the time, Diane was prohibited from visiting her husband in his hospital room. Jim passed away two weeks later on May 2, 2021, just five days before the couple's thirty-third wedding anniversary. He died alone. Diane was never allowed to say her goodbyes, despite the fact that Indiana Governor Eric Holcomb had only three days prior signed into law a bill that required medical facilities to allow just such visitations.[1]

Notice the parallels to the drawbridge case. We can perhaps understand why the hospital staff refused to allow Diane to visit Jim, despite the heartbreaking consequence: They were simply trying to prevent the spread of COVID-19 in conditions of immense uncertainty at the time. Surely the hospital staff took no delight in denying a distraught wife the chance to say goodbye to her dying husband any more than any sane drawbridge controller would enjoy lowering the bridge on an innocent child. But like the drawbridge controller, the hospital staff judged that the harm that could have befallen the well-being of others necessitated the terrible decision.

These kinds of scenarios pump an intuition that many if not most people find especially forceful, if not just plain inescapable: We ought to do that which will bring about the greatest amount of good or the least amount of harm for the greatest number of people. In fact, many regard this particular intuition to be absolutely central to the nature of morality, which helps explain some of the widespread appeal of the moral theory known as utilitarianism, which is the focus of this chapter.

4.1. What Utilitarianism Says

In some ways, the conceptual roots of utilitarianism date back to antiquity. Certain elements of it can be seen in thinkers as far back as Epicurus (341–270 BC) and perhaps even further back to the Chinese philosopher Mozi from the fifth century BC.[2] Still, in other ways, utilitarianism is very much a product of the modern era. Key components of the theory feature prominently in the work of such Enlightenment thinkers as Francis Hutcheson (1694–1746) and David Hume (1711–1776). But its most influential and culminating expression is found in the work of two nineteenth-century English philosophers, Jeremy Bentham (1748–1832) and his protégé John Stuart Mill (1806–1873). The version of utilitarianism that emerges from Bentham and Mill in particular is often referred to as *classical* utilitarianism.

Bentham was optimistic that moral decision-making could be seen as a science of sorts. In his view, we simply need to determine the consequences that would follow from various courses of actions one might take and then calculate the respective pleasures and pains involved. From there, the path forward would be simple enough: Take the course of action that produces the greatest amount of pleasure (or the least amount of pain) for all parties involved. The underlying thought is that pleasure is intrinsically good while pain is intrinsically evil, and so the right course of action is the one that maximizes what is good and minimizes what is evil.

Of course, the tricky part of the equation is calculating the net *utility* of an action with precision. (The term "utility" is just a shorthand way of referring to the net sum of pleasure minus the net sum of pain that an action's consequences would produce.) To calculate an action's utility properly in Bentham's view, we need to consider the following items:

INTENSITY: How intense are the pleasures (and pains) involved?
DURATION: How long will they last?
CERTAINTY: How certain (or uncertain) are we that they will occur?
PROXIMITY: How soon after the action will those pleasures (or pains) occur?
FECUNDITY: Will those pleasures (or pains) give rise to additional pleasures (or pains) down the road?
PURITY: Will those pleasures (or pains) be mixed with pains (or pleasures)?
EXTENT: Whom will those pleasures (or pains) affect? How many parties will be affected?

Think of it this way. By attending to these seven questions, we can better quantify the utility in question. Imagine, for example, that we were to stipulate (on a scale from one to one hundred) that eating a pepperoni pizza with one's friend produces a total of five units of pleasure. By comparison, we might then judge that the pursuit and completion of a college education—together with its attendant pleasures, career opportunities, and long-term positive social effects—produces ninety units of pleasure (though with, perhaps, fifteen units of pain along the way). The idea is that by following such a process of stipulation and comparison, we would then be able to calculate an action's overall net utility, whereupon we could then better determine whether a given action is right or wrong. That's because, in Bentham's view, the ultimate goal of human behavior is, and ought to be, to produce the greatest amount of happiness for the greatest number. Here is Bentham's somewhat tedious description of how an individual can determine whether an action is right or wrong:

> Sum up all the values of all the *pleasures* on the one side, and those of all the pains on the other. The balance, if it be on the side of pleasure, will give the *good* tendency of the act upon the whole, with respect to the interests of that *individual* person; if on the side of pain, the *bad* tendency of it upon the whole. . . . Take an account of the *number* of persons whose interests appear to be concerned; and repeat the above process with respect to each. *Sum up* the numbers expressive of the degrees of *good* tendency, which the act has, with respect to each individual, in regard to whom the tendency of it is *good* upon the whole: do this again with respect to each individual, in regard to whom the tendency of it is *good* upon the whole: do this again with respect to each individual, in regard to whom the tendency of it is *bad* upon the whole. Take the *balance*; which, if on the side of *pleasure*, will give the general *good tendency* of the act, with respect to the total number or community of individuals concerned; if on the side of pain, the general *evil tendency* with respect to the same community.[3]

Bentham's optimism, as well as his method, can seem naïve, in no small part because it seems like a stretch to say we can quantify the value of this or that pleasure or pain with any accuracy or consistency across time and circumstances—especially when multiple individuals are involved. After all, even if one could stipulate that eating pizza would produce five units of pleasure, and even if one could judge that, by comparison, pursing and completing a college education would bring ninety units, difficult questions remain. How is one supposed to make those sorts of comparisons across different persons? How could one quantify the units of pleasure (or pain) that an action would have on someone else? And how is *someone else* supposed to determine the units of pleasure or pain an action might bring about *for you*? The answers to those questions remain unclear, and so Bentham's hedonistic calculus can seem ambitious, if not simply unrealistic.

At any rate, a deeper problem for this version of utilitarianism comes to the surface when we reflect on the fact that, for Bentham, pleasure is pleasure is pleasure. That is, in his view, there are no *qualitative* differences between various instances of pleasure. Still in other words, no one kind of pleasure is of an inherently superior or inferior quality than any other kind. Accordingly, pleasures vary only with respect to their *quantity*—that is, in *how much* pleasure is present, as it were. But thought experiments of the following sort illustrate the problem facing Bentham's view here.

Imagine that right before you were born, you were given a choice between living the life of either an immortal jellyfish or the late, great Steve Irwin (1962–2006), popularly known as "the Crocodile Hunter."[4] Irwin was a famous and widely adored Australian zookeeper, wildlife expert, and TV personality who traveled the globe, met all kinds of interesting people, received all manner of accolades, and of course handled all kinds of neat animals—especially crocodiles—before dying at the young age of forty-four. By contrast, immortal jellyfish are about the size of a human fingernail and are thought to be the only animal species capable of continuous endurance, in part because of their special capacity for effectively reverting to earlier stages of the lifecycle development process.[5] Now, take a moment and consider your options. Which life would *you* choose to live? (And which life would *Bentham* recommend?) Keep in mind that—precisely because it can live such a *long*, if somewhat dull, life—the immortal jellyfish would plausibly ultimately rack up a greater *quantity* of strictly sensual, low-grade pleasures than Irwin's shorter life.

Let's face it: If we are being honest, most of us would prefer to live Irwin's life, which suggests that we actually prefer the thing about Irwin's life that makes it superior in *quality* to the mere *quantity* of pleasures afforded to the immortal jellyfish.

Mill, for his part, recognized this concern and, as a result, offered a subtle but important modification to the theory handed down to him from Bentham. In Mill's view, we have to appreciate the distinction between the pleasures associated with the use of our intellectual capacities and those associated with the use merely of our sensual capacities. And, for Mill, the pleasures of the intellect are of a *different and superior quality* to the pleasures of the senses.

Why should we think such a thing? Mill answers this question by appealing to competent judges: Just ask those who are familiar with both types of pleasure. Assuming they haven't allowed their capacities to wilt and die on the vine, so to speak, competent judges will inevitably recognize that intellectual pleasures are superior to sensual pleasures, which is precisely why, for Mill, the life of a *dissatisfied Socrates* would on the whole be better than the life a *satisfied pig*. So whereas Bentham's quantitative version of utilitarianism might tip us in the direction of choosing the life of an immortal jellyfish, Mill's version of utilitarianism would likely lead us toward choosing the exciting, if shorter, life of the Crocodile Hunter. And that's because, for Mill, when calculating the utility of an action, we have to take into account not only the *quantity* of the pleasures and pains involved but also the *quality* of those pleasures and pains as well. Mill summarizes his version of utilitarianism as follows:

> The creed which accepts as the foundation of morals "utility" or the "greatest happiness principle" holds that actions are right in proportion as they tend to promote happiness; wrong as they tend to produce the reverse of happiness. By happiness is intended pleasure and the absence of pain; by unhappiness, pain and the privation of pleasure. . . . [P]leasure and freedom from pain are the *only* things desirable as ends; and . . . all

> desirable things . . . are desirable either for pleasure inherent in themselves or as means to the promotion of pleasure and the prevention of pain.[6]

To better appreciate the component parts of classical utilitarianism, we will emphasize five of its key affirmations:

i. The good is prior to the right.
ii. The proper account of the good is hedonistic in nature.
iii. The moral status of an action depends on the consequences of the action in question.
iv. We should maximize good and minimize evil.
v. Everyone's happiness matters, and it matters equally.

First, notice that utilitarianism defines right (or wrong) action in terms of what is good (or bad)—and not the other way around. That is, whether an action is morally obligatory, optional, or wrong depends on how much value (i.e., happiness understood as pleasure and privation of pain) or disvalue (i.e., unhappiness understood as pain and the privation of pleasure) it brings about. What that means is, for utilitarianism, the account of the good is more fundamental than—and hence logically prior to—the account of the right. Put differently, utilitarianism's account of what is right and wrong relies on the theory's underlying account of what is good and evil.

Second, as Mill makes clear, utilitarianism assumes a hedonistic account of the good. That is, according to utilitarianism, the *only* intrinsically good thing is happiness understood as pleasure and the absence of pain. (The Greek root word in "hedonism" (*hēdonē*) means "pleasure.") Thus, anything else we might come to regard as good is good only in some instrumental sense—that is, because it somehow promotes pleasure (or the absence of pain), either now or later. Furthermore, the only intrinsically bad or evil thing is pain and the privation of pleasure. Accordingly, in this hedonistic account of the good, something is value-neutral when it neither promotes nor detracts from happiness understood as pleasure and the privation of pain.

Third, utilitarianism, like ethical egoism, is a consequentialist theory of morality. Recall that consequentialist theories hold that the moral status of an action hinges on what comes *after* the action takes place—that is, the consequences—and *not* on the reasons or intentions or motives of the one who performs the action. What this means then is that an action is never inherently right or wrong all by itself. Instead, an action becomes right or wrong by virtue of the consequences it produces. While the motives or intentions of the agent might say something significant about the person who performs the action, they do nothing to affect whether the action itself is right or wrong. In this respect, utilitarianism is a results-focused, bottom-line account of right and wrong, and the underlying value or disvalue that an action produces serves as the right-making or wrong-making mechanism.

Fourth, utilitarianism holds that the only reasonable and appropriate response to what is intrinsically good—namely, happiness understood as pleasure and the privation of pain—is to bring about as much of it as possible. That is, utilitarianism holds that we should *maximize* the good and minimize evil.

Lastly, when it comes to the question of *whose* happiness and unhappiness matters, utilitarianism is universal in scope and impartial and egalitarian in outlook. That is, *everyone's* happiness and unhappiness matter—not just that of the individual who is acting. Accordingly, we must pay attention to how our actions bear on any and all parties involved. This point is precisely what distinguishes utilitarianism from ethical egoism, which is decidedly agent-centered in scope. But according to classical utilitarianism, no one individual's happiness and unhappiness should count for more than anyone else's. So not only does everyone's happiness and unhappiness matter; everyone's happiness and unhappiness matter *equally*. So utilitarianism is ultimately impartial in how it weighs the happiness and unhappiness of all parties involved.

We are now in a position to summarize classical utilitarianism's account of the right, as well as the moral decision procedure that it implies. (Since utilitarianism's account of the good has already been articulated—it is encapsulated by the hedonistic account of the good—we will simply focus here on stating utilitarianism's account of the right.) According to classical utilitarianism, an action is morally obligatory if and only if and just because the action produces the greatest net sum of pleasure minus pain. An action is wrong if and only if and just because it fails to do that. And an action is morally optional if and only if and just because the action produces a net sum of pleasure minus pain equal to that of the best alternative(s) available. It is worth stressing here one of the key implications of utilitarianism's account of the right: No action is right or wrong all by itself. Instead, the moral status of an action is determined by its consequences. What this means is that, in principle at least, *any* action could be morally justified *as long as it produces enough happiness*. As we will see, this is both one of the most seductive and one of the most controversial components of utilitarianism.

If classical utilitarianism succeeds as a moral theory, then the following decision procedure would identify the morally correct action:

> STEP 1: Determine which actions are available.
> STEP 2: For each action, determine the likely consequences and calculate how much pleasure and pain would result for all parties involved.
> STEP 3: Determine which set of consequences would result in the greatest utility.
> STEP 4: Do the action that produces the greatest utility (or, in the case of a tie, do one of the actions that is tied in producing the greatest utility).

4.2. The Case for Utilitarianism

There are plenty of reasons why utilitarianism can seem like an attractive theory of morality. For starters, it is relatively straightforward and easy to apply: One doesn't have to be a rocket scientist to understand, remember, or make use of the central principle of utilitarianism—or so it can seem. And, along similar lines, utilitarianism can seem intuitive in lots of ways. For example, it seems obvious that the consequences of our actions matter, just as it seems natural enough to think that increasing happiness and reducing unhappiness in the world is connected to the enterprise of morality. Furthermore, utilitarianism captures nicely something that ethical egoism flatly misses—that morality requires us to be attentive to the interests of everyone, not just our own.

Another advantage to utilitarianism is that it seems to set forth a fairly simple, publicly accessible, and empirically verifiable process for evaluating actions, institutions, and policies: Utilitarianism instructs us to pay close attention to *all* of the consequences for *all* parties involved. In that sense, it offers lucid and practical guidance, which we are right to ask of a theory of morality. Not only that, but utilitarianism seems capable of explaining why lots of our widely held moral beliefs would be justified. Take, for example, our conviction that it is wrong to kill indiscriminately, that we ought not cheat, that we ought to care for our young, and so on—such actions would alter the net utility for all parties involved. And, for many people, one of the most seductive features of utilitarianism is that it seems to be nimble where other moral theories can seem rigid and wooden. What should we do in circumstances where our moral obligations appear to conflict with one another? For utilitarianism, the answer is obvious: Do what promotes the greatest net sum of happiness.

Yet while those features might make utilitarianism seem attractive, they do not somehow entail that utilitarianism is the *correct* account of morality. So what argument might be offered on behalf of utilitarianism?

Bentham's argument

Bentham contends that utilitarianism is not the sort of thing that could be proven by means of an argument, in part because he thinks the principle of utility is itself assumed in *any* moral argument one might try to make, including any moral argument *against* the principle of utility. So in his view, it is just not possible to give a non-question-begging argument for utilitarianism. "That which is used to prove every thing else," Bentham says, "cannot itself be proved: a chain of proofs must have their commencement somewhere."[7] And in his view, the principle of utility is effectively a basic feature of any moral argument in the sense that there is no moral principle that is more fundamental—it is the rock bottom starting point. That said, Bentham does suggest that any *rejection* of the principle of utility would involve a contradiction, which provides an indirect case for utilitarianism. He writes, for example:

> When a man attempts to combat the principle of utility, it is with reasons drawn, without his being aware of it, from the very principle itself. His arguments, if they prove any thing, prove not that the principle is *wrong*, but that, according to the applications he supposes to be made of it, it is *misapplied*.[8]

Unfortunately, Bentham's case here, such as it is, leaves us wanting to hear more, to say the very least.

Mill's argument for hedonism

Fortunately, Mill goes the extra mile and puts forth a case for accepting the hedonistic account of the good, which he clearly regards as the key, linchpin claim of the whole theory of utilitarianism. The idea seems to go roughly as follows. If it is indeed true that happiness (understood as pleasure and the privation of pain) is the *only* intrinsically good thing, then the rest of utilitarianism would seem to follow: We clearly ought to promote what is intrinsically good by maximizing it everywhere and for anyone to whom it pertains. Here's how Mill articulates the first leg of his argument for hedonism:

> To be incapable of proof by reasoning is common to all first principles, to the first premises of our knowledge, as well as to those of our conduct. But the former, being matters of fact, may be the subject of a direct appeal to the faculties which judge of fact—namely, our senses and our internal consciousness. Can an appeal be made to the same faculties on questions of practical ends? Or by what other faculty is cognizance taken of them?
>
> Questions about ends are, in other words, questions [about] what things are desirable. The utilitarian doctrine is that happiness is desirable, and the only thing desirable, as an end; all other things being only desirable as means to that end. What ought to be required of this doctrine . . . to make good its claim to be believed?
>
> The only proof capable of being given that an object is visible is that people actually see it. The only proof that a sound is audible is that people hear it; and so of the other sources of

> our experience. In like manner, I apprehend, the sole evidence it is possible to produce that anything is desirable is that people do actually desire it. If the end which the utilitarian doctrine proposes to itself were not, in theory and in practice, acknowledged to be an end, nothing could ever convince any person that it was so. No reason can be given why the general happiness is desirable, except that each person, so far as he believes it to be attainable, desires his own happiness. This, however, being a fact, we have not only all the proof which the case admits of, but all which it is possible to require, that happiness is a good: that each person's happiness is a good to that person, and the general happiness, therefore, is a good to the aggregate of all persons.[9]

Plausibly, the case for hedonism that Mill seems to have in mind can be reconstructed in the following way:[10]

(1) The sole evidence that X is desirable as an end is that people actually desire X for its own sake and not as a means to something else.
(2) Each person desires one's own happiness for its own sake.
(3) So, for each person, one's own happiness is indeed desirable as an end.
(4) If, for each person, one's own happiness is desirable as an end, then general happiness is desirable as an end for the aggregate of all persons.
(5) If X is desirable as an end, then X is intrinsically good.
(6) Thus, for each person, one's own happiness is intrinsically good.
(7) Thus, for the aggregate of all persons, general happiness is intrinsically good.

Now, suppose we just grant that each person desires one's own happiness for its own sake in the way Mill asserts. Is that the *only* thing people desire for its own sake? To his credit, Mill acknowledges that people sometimes appear to desire things *other than* happiness too—and that they even seem to desire those things for their own sake and not for any other reason. For example, some people appear to desire virtue, knowledge, money, power, and fame *for their own sake*. So given the line of reasoning above, wouldn't this simple fact constitute evidence that there are multiple intrinsically valuable goods and thus that Mill's hedonism is either false or profoundly incomplete?

Not according to Mill. In his view, all those other things beyond happiness that are desired for their own sake are desired only because they are effectively *part of*—that is, constitutive of—happiness. So on final analysis, in his view, there is really only one ultimate end, namely happiness.

Unfortunately, there are at least three problems facing Mill's argument for hedonism—and hence his overall case for utilitarianism. First, notice how this argument above subtly shifts the meaning of the term "desirable." In premise 1, the term "desirable" would seem to mean nothing more than "able to be desired." However, in premises 3, 4, and 5, "desirable" appears to mean something more akin to "worthy of being desired." But if so, Mill's argument equivocates and, as such, is invalid.

Second, aside from that worry, though, premise 4 is certainly questionable. Why should we assume that general happiness is desirable to the aggregate of persons simply because, for each of the parts of the aggregate in question, one's own happiness is desirable? The worry here is that premise 4 commits the composition fallacy insofar as it assumes that what pertains to a part (an individual person) also pertains to the whole (aggregate of all persons). To add to the problem, it is hardly clear what it means to say that *general happiness* is good for the aggregate of all persons in the first place. Admittedly, we know what it means to say, for example, that Barak Obama's happiness is desirable as an end *to Barak Obama*. But what does it mean to say that general happiness is desirable as an end to the *aggregate* of all persons? We know there is a person who is Barak Obama who, we can assume, desires Barak Obama's happiness. But are we to suppose there is some actual corporate entity that is "The *Aggregate* of All Individual Persons" who has intentions, beliefs, and desires? Is there such a thing as "The American Public," for example, that desires general happiness for itself? This is hardly obvious, in any case.

Third, even if we ignore the first two problems facing Mill's argument, it seems dubious to say that everything that is desired for its own sake (beyond happiness) is merely *part* of what constitutes happiness (understood as pleasure and the privation of pain). After all, people appear to desire lots of things that are neither pleasure nor pleasure-producing nor even *part* of pleasure—no matter how broadly Mill wants to construe the concept of happiness or pleasure. Isn't it at least possible that we might desire something even though, and even when, it does not bring us happiness (qua pleasure) but suffering? Why should we assume those things are merely part of happiness or pleasure for the person who so desires them? Why not just entertain the possibility that there might be *multiple* intrinsically valuable goods at stake? And if we follow Mill in stretching the definition of happiness or pleasure to simply subsume those other goods, shouldn't we wonder whether we have simply stretched the term beyond all recognition—or that we have simply changed the subject altogether?

A Millian argument from Christianity?

There is perhaps another argument for utilitarianism that one might advance on Mill's behalf—one premised on Christian theism. In effect, one might try to argue that, if we accept Christianity as true, then we should also accept utilitarianism. To be perfectly clear, Mill himself does not develop or defend such an argument. But we can still imagine it on his behalf by drawing inspiration from two of his reflections on the compatibility of utilitarianism and Christianity.

First, Mill contends that utilitarianism is perfectly harmonious with the belief in the existence of a good deity, and Christianity of course affirms that God is *perfectly good*, in addition to being omniscient and omnipotent. As Mill sees it, a *good* deity would inevitably "desire, above all things, the happiness of his creatures."[11] So imagine how one might extend Mill's line of reasoning on this point. One might reason that, since God is perfectly good, and since God would know how to maximize human happiness, it must be the case that any and all of God's commands would be aimed at promoting human happiness. Accordingly, or so one might reason, utilitarianism fits neatly with the Christian worldview. Of course, one might wonder whether Mill is right to assume that a perfect God would necessarily desire the happiness of his creatures *above all things*. But suppose we set that worry to one side for now.

Mill's second reflection on the compatibility between Christianity and utilitarianism centers on the so-called Golden Rule—do unto others as you would have them do unto you—as well as Jesus's command to love your neighbor as yourself. In Mill's view, these two important teachings of Christ are effectively "the complete spirit of the ethics of utility" and "constitute the ideal perfection of utilitarian morality."[12] How so? Think of it like this: If you really followed the Golden Rule and abided by Jesus's command to love your neighbor as yourself, you would inevitably maximize the net sum of happiness in the world—and vice versa. Extending Mill's reflections, then, one might formulate an argument for utilitarianism that goes like this:

(1) The culminating expression of Jesus's ethics includes the Golden Rule and the command to love your neighbor as yourself.
(2) Christians should accept the culminating expression of Jesus's ethics.
(3) So, Christians should accept the Golden Rule and the command to love their neighbors as themselves.
(4) Each individual desires one's own happiness.
(5) So, by extension, each individual desires that others act in ways that maximize one's own happiness.
(6) Since Christians should accept the Golden Rule and the command to love their neighbors as themselves, and since each individual desires that others act in ways that maximize one's own happiness, Christians should also accept that one should act in ways that maximize others' happiness too.
(7) Utilitarianism holds that one should act in ways that maximize others' happiness too.
(8) So, Christians should accept utilitarianism.

Does this argument hold water? Would Jesus actually embrace the claim that we should act in ways to maximize the net sum of happiness *understood as pleasure and the privation of pain*? Perhaps not. In his Sermon on the Mount (from which the Golden Rule is derived), Jesus appears to be working with a different account of what is intrinsically good than the one presupposed by Bentham or Mill. He says, for example, "Blessed are those who mourn," and "Blessed are those who are persecuted because of righteousness," and "Blessed are you when people insult you, persecute you and falsely say all kinds of evil against you because of me" (Matt. 5:4–11 NIV). Here, and in general, Jesus seems less interested in the utilitarian concept of happiness and more in the concept of *blessedness*. Blessedness can be contemplated as a state of the soul that is consistent with total flourishing, a concept that is perhaps more expansive than what can be captured in the utilitarian calculation of pleasure minus pain. If this is correct, then perhaps premise 6 is wrong: Accepting the Golden Rule might entail acting for the blessedness of others but not necessarily for their happiness, at least as utilitarianism understands happiness.

There is a second worry in the neighborhood. In some cases, utilitarianism might recommend actions that run contrary to what the Golden Rule would require. Return to the predicament faced by Diane and Jim Houpt during the COVID-19 pandemic. Suppose we ignore issues about what was or wasn't legally permitted in this case. Should the head nurse have allowed Diane to visit her dying husband in the hospital? Plausibly, following the Golden Rule might lead the nurse to let Diane in, since (in all likelihood) the nurse would want to visit her own spouse if she were in Diane's shoes. And yet, plausibly, utilitarianism would advise the nurse to refuse to let Diane in, since doing so could jeopardize the health of many others. The important point here is that there is sunlight between what utilitarianism requires and what the Golden Rule requires. The Golden Rule is focused on a particular person within a particular context—this or that nurse should be thinking about what she herself would want done to *her* were *she* in Diane's shoes. Utilitarianism intentionally brackets out those kinds of particularized considerations and instead holds that everyone's happiness and unhappiness should be accounted for impartially—including those who could be infected by COVID-19—and that everyone's interests in the matter count *equally*.

Lastly, in reference to premises 1 and 2, we should wonder whether the Golden Rule or the commandment to love your neighbor as yourself actually constitutes the *complete* culminating expression of Jesus's own ethics, as Mill suggests. When Jesus was specifically asked about the matter, he replied that the *greatest* commandment is to "Love the Lord your God with all your heart and with all your soul and with all your mind and with all your strength" (Mark 12:28–32; Matt. 22:34–40). Notice that the *most* crucial thing for Jesus is the love of *God*—not the love of oneself or one's neighbors or even the net sum of happiness for all parties. This is an important point because the Christian tradition has long held that getting one's loves out of order, so to speak, is serious business indeed. Augustine of Hippo (354–430), for example, described the fundamental nature of sin as the misdirected and inordinate love of non-divine things—things inferior to the God who created them. In failing to order and prioritize one's loves properly, the will turns away from God.[13] In the process, the sinful will does not appropriately love and thus does not properly pursue that which is supremely worthy of one's affection—namely, God. In other words, in Augustine's depiction, sin is where one turns toward and inordinately loves God-inferior things as though they were actually worthy of the love that is appropriate only for what is supremely good (i.e., God). This same sort of point appears to be on display in the first chapter of the apostle Paul's letter to the Romans, where Paul appears to pin the root source of sin on *idolatry*—the love of something *other* than God in place of, or above, the love of God.

4.3. The Case against Utilitarianism

There is something of a cottage industry among philosophers for producing objections to utilitarianism. In fact, given utilitarianism's initial plausibility as a theory of morality, it can be somewhat surprising to learn how many objections there are. We cannot possibly canvas them all here, so we will limit ourselves to discussing only a representative sample of the objections facing the most central components of utilitarianism. More specifically, we will consider objections directed at utilitarianism's moral decision procedure, the hedonistic account of the good, the consequentialist account of the right, and impartialism.

Utilitarianism's moral decision procedure cannot be followed

One of the initially attractive features of utilitarianism is that it seems to set forth a fairly straightforward, publicly accessible, and empirically verifiable process for making moral decisions and thinking about public policy. Recall the utilitarian's moral decision procedure:

> STEP 1: Determine which actions are available.
> STEP 2: For each action, determine the likely consequences and calculate how much pleasure and pain would result for all parties involved.
> STEP 3: Determine which set of consequences would result in the greatest utility.
> STEP 4: Do the action that produces the greatest utility (or, in the case of a tie, do one of the actions that is tied in producing the greatest utility).

Notice how STEP 2 requires us to predict the various consequences of a given action, and to do so with at least a passing degree of accuracy. An abiding worry is that the consequences of an action only come *after—not before*—the point of acting. So unless we have a fairly reliable crystal ball, we have no way of knowing for certain what we need to know to make use of utilitarianism's decision procedure. We cannot make it past STEP 2—or so goes a common complaint.

Proponents of utilitarianism may not feel overly concerned about this since they can draw a distinction between the *expected* consequences and the *actual* consequences of the actions in question. Accordingly, even if we cannot predict an action's actual consequences, we can nonetheless—through the study of history, human psychology and so on—make some solid enough predictions about what would *likely* occur if we did this or that. And, realistically, that's about the best anyone could hope for in the first place. Thus, so the utilitarian might contend, the moral decision procedure is really about *expected* consequences: We ought to do the action that will result in the best expected consequences.

But what does it mean here to say we *ought* to do what will result in the best expected consequences? If this particular "ought" is a *moral* ought, then a new problem arises for utilitarianism: We appear to be saying both (a) that we morally ought to do one thing—the action with the best *expected* consequences—while at the same time asserting (b) that we have a moral obligation to do what might turn out to be an altogether different thing—the action with the best *actual* consequences. Obviously enough, our expectations are sometimes accurate. But sometimes our expectations are, well, dashed. So which is it—option (a) or (b)? Are we morally obligated to do the action with the best *expected* consequences or the one with the best *actual* consequences?

Unfortunately for utilitarianism, there are problems with either choice. Start with option (b). Suppose, in other words, that utilitarianism is committed to saying we morally ought to do what maximizes *actual* utility. If so, utilitarianism faces problems in cases where someone makes what *seems* to be the correct moral decision on the front end that, sadly, proves incorrect in the end. Imagine, for example, that a firefighter bravely rushes into a burning house to find a small child who is trapped inside. He has time to check only one more room before the walls cave in. There are a bedroom and a hallway closet that have not yet been checked. He decides to check the bedroom with the expectation that the child is most likely to be in a bedroom. But suppose the child was hiding in the closet all along. Given option (b), the firefighter would have acted immorally since his action wouldn't have produced the best actual consequence—the world would have been far happier had he checked the closet instead of the bedroom. But given the information available to him at the point of action, and given that he only had time to check one more room, it can certainly seem odd to think that the firefighter acted immorally. This seems to have just been bad luck.

To circumvent this problem, suppose the utilitarian goes with option (a): We morally ought to do what maximizes *expected* utility. Accordingly, given the odds involved, checking the bedroom had better expected consequences than checking the closet. Thus, assuming (a), we get the verdict that the firefighter acted rightly.

But while this defensive maneuver might vindicate the firefighter in this particular case, unfortunately it robs utilitarianism of one of its most attractive features: the *objective* nature of its moral verdicts. Notice that with option (b), what someone morally ought to do is based solely on objective features about the world, namely what maximizes actual utility. However, given option (a), what someone morally ought to do is based at least partly on subjective features about what one *believes* about the world.

Unfortunately, though, sometimes people believe pretty crazy things. And—given option (a)—if someone sincerely believes those crazy things, then what that person morally ought to do is maximize utility according to those same crazy beliefs. Suppose, for example, that King Herod of Judea sincerely believed utility would be maximized by slaughtering all the babies in Bethlehem under the age of two. According to option (a), Herod had a moral obligation to kill all the babies in Bethlehem, which is plainly nuts. Similarly, if one had sincerely believed vaccines are actually left-wing tracking devices for the federal government, then given option (a), one would have violated one's moral duty by getting the jab. Notice, then, how option (a) strips the objectivity out of utilitarianism's moral verdict.

To keep things interesting, though, just suppose the problems related to the distinction between actual and expected consequences can be mitigated. There is yet another problem facing utilitarianism's moral decision procedure, namely a problem related to the so-called butterfly effect. Suppose the Roman Empress Julia Agrippina (AD 15–59) had shown greater affection to her son Nero (AD 37–68) while he was still a small child. Perhaps then Nero never would have had her assassinated and—what is more—perhaps Rome never would have been set ablaze and, hence, the Christians never would have been scapegoated and the apostles Peter and Paul would not have been executed as a result. (But perhaps then the early Christian martyrs never would have inspired the growth of the new Christian religion?) Or suppose Klara Pölzl Hitler (1860–1907) had slept in a slightly different position on the night Adolf was conceived. The course of human affairs would perhaps have gone very, very differently.[14] (But in which ways? And would the changes have been only for the better?)

Unfortunately, even at our very best, we simply cannot enumerate with certainty or any degree of probability the full range of consequences that even an innocuous-seeming action (like playing with one's kids or sleeping on one's left side) might yield in the future. After all, even if we could predict *some* of the consequences well enough, what about the *remote* consequences we simply have no way of ever knowing about—especially those that might run, say, to the end of human history? And why on strictly utilitarian grounds should we privilege the consideration of consequences that are temporally closest to us? It hardly seems like a committed utilitarian should do that sort of thing, if indeed consequences are the right-making mechanism. Yet if we abide by a strict utilitarian policy of impartial consideration of the full range of consequences across not only geographic distances but also across temporal distances, the task of predicting the full range of consequences seems practically hopeless.

Take note of how this temporal impartiality can lead to some rather counterintuitive conclusions. Consider the tragic killing of Botham Jean (1991–2018), a well-loved twenty-six-year-old Black man from Saint Lucia who had recently graduated from Harding University and had been working as an accountant for PricewaterhouseCoopers in Dallas, Texas. Jean was home alone on the night of September 6, 2018, when a White off-duty police officer, Amber Guyger, entered Jean's apartment after mistaking it for her own. Guyger shot and killed the unarmed Jean. Everyone can agree that Guyger's action was morally grievous. She should not have entered the wrong apartment and recklessly unleashed deadly force on an innocent man in his own home. But suppose this horrible event somehow eventually led to a constructive social movement concerning matters of policing, gun use, and racial prejudice. Suppose, for example, that the news of this atrocity spread far and wide and the horror people felt when learning about it caused culture to be reshaped and institutions to be reconceived—all in ways that bring about greater public safety as well as sustainable racial justice and equality until the very end of human history. In theory (at least according to utilitarianism), the consequences of Jean's murder over time—and across centuries into the future—might produce so much value that the world would be better off than it would have been had the terrible event never occurred in the first place. But notice the counterintuitive conclusion: If that were the case, then not only would Jean's killing have been justified by utilitarianism's decision procedure, but the atrocious act would also have been morally *obligatory*. Yet such a conclusion—that future events could somehow morally justify and even morally require Guyger to kill Jean—is suspicious at best. And there is a related practical problem in any case. Jean's killer would certainly have had no way of knowing what the long-term consequences of her action would be. In fact, no one could ever fully ascertain all the consequences that would follow from one's actions, and hence no one could ever determine whether any action in question would indeed maximize the net sum of happiness for the greatest number *over time*.

Things can get even trickier for utilitarianism's decision procedure, though. What if the world never actually comes to an end? In other words, what if time marches indefinitely into the future? Perhaps this is exactly what the Gospel of John seems to presuppose: "For God so loved the world, that he gave his only begotten Son, that whosoever believeth in him should not perish, but have *everlasting life*" (John 3:16 KJV—emphasis added). If there is indeed a world without end in which such an everlasting life could ever occur, then notice the ramifications for utilitarianism's decision procedure: It becomes literally impossible—not just in practice but also *in principle*—to determine the full set of consequences that would follow from our actions. If so, utilitarianism's decision procedure could never be followed.

Utilitarianism has a flawed account of the good

One of the core features of classical utilitarianism is its hedonistic account of the good: Happiness (understood as pleasure and the privation of pain) is intrinsically good—and indeed the *only* intrinsically good thing. In fact, Mill seems to contemplate hedonism as the linchpin affirmation of utilitarianism. After all, he argues for hedonism as a way of making a case for utilitarianism more generally. But even if we agree that happiness qua pleasure is an intrinsically good thing, we are right to ask whether happiness qua pleasure is the *only* intrinsically good thing. Reflect on the following cases.

Nearly fifty thousand people were lobotomized in the United States during the twentieth century, mostly between 1949 and 1952. Dr. Walter Freeman (1895–1972) was the surgeon who first introduced this procedure in the United States, having performed about 2,500 of them himself. According to Freeman, lobotomized patients become childlike, thereby experiencing less intense emotions and mental anguish. For decades, it was thought that lobotomies could be used to treat such conditions as tension, anxiety, depression, insomnia, suicidal ideation, delusions, hallucinations, crying spells, melancholia, obsessions, panic states, disorientation, psychalgesia, nervous indigestion, and hysterical paralysis.[15] With the rise of psychiatric pharmaceuticals, lobotomies fell into disfavor during the second half of the twentieth century. But imagine that lobotomy procedures were still widely performed today. And suppose also that getting a lobotomy could allow one to lead a worry-free, childlike, happy-go-lucky life, thereby increasing one's overall balance of pleasure to pain. Should one seek to get a lobotomy for oneself? What about for one's emotionally distressed teenager? Surely, most of us think it would be deeply problematic to get a lobotomy when there is no medically necessary reason to do so, which seems to suggest that there is something intrinsically valuable at stake other than pleasure and pain—namely, goods connected to mental and emotional capacities beyond those of a small child.[16]

Would things be any different if there were an increase in *general* happiness? Consider what happened in 2019 to a woman who had been in a persistent vegetative state for nearly a decade at an Arizona nursing facility.[17] The woman became pregnant and ultimately went into labor and delivered a child before anyone at the facility grew aware of her situation. Assuming the woman remained unconscious throughout it all, the hedonist might conclude that she suffered from no decrease in happiness. Meanwhile, the woman's assailant (presumably) experienced pleasure in raping his unconscious victim. And suppose further that the life of the victim's newborn baby brought about a dramatic increase in the total net sum of happiness in the world. Yet *even if* there was an increase in overall happiness in this case, the outrage we feel in reflecting on this situation suggests that happiness understood as pleasure and the privation of pain cannot be the only thing of intrinsic value at play here. After all, it seems like something of tremendous intrinsic value was, in fact, violated: human dignity and justice.

There are other counterexamples to hedonism as well. Consider a thought experiment made famous by Robert Nozick (1938–2002).[18] Suppose you could plug your brain into an extremely advanced virtual reality machine. While you are plugged into the machine, you could enjoy whatever happiness-provoking experience your little heart desires—for example, meeting interesting historical figures, marrying the man or woman of your dreams, conquering the domain of advanced theoretical physics, climbing Mount Everest, or swimming the English Channel with

Donald J. Trump *and* Joseph R. Biden. All the while, you would actually be sitting in an oxygen-rich tube with your brain plugged into a USB port. Importantly, though, while you are plugged into this machine, *it seems to you* that you are actually walking down the red carpet or climbing or swimming or whatever—it feels utterly real, in other words, and you simply cannot tell that you are in a machine.

Now for the million-dollar question: If you could plug into this experience machine for the rest of your biological days, would you?

Nozick contends that we would *not* plug in. But why not? In his view, there are things that we value more than pleasurable, happiness-provoking experiences—namely, *actually doing* certain things (not just having the pleasurable experience of them), *actually being* certain ways (not just having the pleasurable experience of being that way), and having contact with reality. It seems, in other words, that truth and contact with reality are intrinsically valuable, and our experiences in the machine simply are not the real deal.

Less dramatically, consider ordinary, everyday cases where there appears to be something intrinsically valuable at stake that nonetheless runs contrary to one's happiness understood as pleasure and the privation of pain. Take, for example, the good involved in remaining with one's spouse *through thick and thin*—even when doing so comes at the cost of one's own happiness because, say, one's spouse has grown quite ill, cranky, and perhaps quite difficult to be around. Something other than happiness appears to be intrinsically good here: marital fidelity and friendship.

Admittedly, self-respecting hedonists will likely want to push back on these sorts of counterexamples. Return to the lobotomy case, for example. A proponent of hedonism might insist that the person who was supposedly made happier by the lobotomy was not *really* made happier in the truest sense of the word "happiness." Admittedly, the lobotomized person might be spared from certain types of pains, but she is also cut off from certain types of pleasures—namely, higher intellectual pleasures—available only to those with advanced mental and emotional capacities. Accordingly, the hedonist might insist that simply because happiness is understood as pleasure and the privation of pain, this doesn't entail that all pleasures should count the same. (Remember the difference between Mill and Bentham.)

So the Millian hedonist will likely want to stick to her guns and argue that we have not yet identified something of intrinsic value beyond happiness properly understood. And perhaps the hedonist can say something similar in the case of the spouses who have earned hard-fought goods of a long marriage. Isn't this just a higher *pleasure* of sorts? (Admittedly, says the hedonist, attaining the higher pleasure involved in enduring one's cranky spouse can sometimes run contrary to some lower pleasures, but the intelligent pursuer of pleasure readily endures the lower pain in the pursuit of the higher pleasure of a seasoned marriage.) So, again, the Millian hedonist can stick to her guns by appealing to the distinction between higher and lower pleasure.

Unfortunately for the hedonist, this sort of defensive strategy lands hedonism in another ditch. And here's why: If pleasure can be subdivided into higher and lower pleasures, then there must be some evaluative concept that divides the superior from the inferior, and that evaluative concept—whatever it is—cannot itself be reducible to pleasure. To put the point here another way, since there is a goodness attained by higher pleasures that is not attained by the lower pleasures, that goodness cannot itself be reducible to pleasure. After all, the higher pleasures are not thought of as simply being *more pleasurable* but of an altogether different type of goodness. So, it turns out, the effort to defend hedonism from the objection that happiness is not the only pleasure by means of differentiating between higher pleasures and lower pleasures still commits the hedonist to a line of argumentation that entails that pleasure is not the only thing of intrinsic value.[19]

Now, if hedonism is the root of the problem for utilitarianism, one way of hanging on to utilitarianism is simply to let go of hedonism and take on board a different account of what is intrinsically good. One strategy is to move in the direction of something like *desire-satisfaction utilitarianism*. Desire-satisfaction utilitarianism jettisons the hedonistic account of the good and replaces it with the view that the satisfaction of desires is the thing that is intrinsically good. Accordingly, instead of saying that our moral duty is to maximize the net sum of happiness in the world, desire-satisfaction utilitarianism holds that maximizing the satisfaction of desires—whatever those desires may be for—is fundamental to our moral duty.

Unfortunately, though, the desire-satisfaction account of the good is itself deeply flawed. For starters, certain things appear to be good even though they were never desired. Suppose, for example, that you unexpectedly meet a stranger at the grocery store who eventually becomes your soul mate. Or suppose you happen to receive a surprise stimulus check in the mail from the federal government, as many American citizens did during the COVID-19 pandemic. When we get these sorts of surprises in life, we seem to be made better off as a result, which suggests that something can be good without actually being attached to the fact that they had been antecedently desired.[20] Second, we sometimes have desires that, when met, don't actually make us or anyone else better off. Suppose, for example, that you desire to have your ashes spread among the fields of gold behind Gordon Matthew Thomas Sumner's (a.k.a. Sting's) old family home in Ireland (think: "*You'll remember me, when the west wind moves* . . ."). And suppose that desire gets fulfilled. No one is made any better off, which seems to suggest that something could be desired without actually being good. A third and final problem facing desire-satisfaction utilitarianism is that some desires aren't merely neutral but are instead simply degrading or depraved. Suppose, for example, that one desired to be dominated by members of the opposite sex or, say, to become a slave. Or, more disturbingly, consider the case of the forty-three-year-old German software engineer, Bernd-Jurgen Brandes (1958–2001), who responded to an internet advertisement looking for a volunteer to be killed and eaten by Armin Meiwes. Apparently, Brandes had a desire to be cannibalized.[21] But the satisfaction of such a desire seems plainly evil—not a good. So the account of the good according to desire-satisfaction utilitarianism seems false.

In light of the difficulties facing utilitarianism's underlying account of the good, yet another strategy for defending utilitarianism might be to endorse an expanded, non-hedonistic conception of happiness. Aristotle (to take one example) took *eudaimonia* (a term that often gets translated as "happiness") to be something far broader than pleasure and the privation of pain. So suppose the utilitarian were to follow suit and reconceive happiness as being not merely about pleasures and pains but also about, say, the development of one's capacities, human dignity, justice, contact with reality, marital fidelity, and so on. In other words, perhaps the term "happiness" could become something of a catch-all umbrella term for the manifold of things we hold to be intrinsically good. But notice how the hedonist's claim that happiness is the *only* intrinsically good thing starts to seem perfectly laughable, precisely because happiness would now be conceived as a complex of multiple intrinsically valuable goods.

Suppose, then, that the defender of utilitarianism gives in and just concedes that there are actually a *variety* of intrinsically good things. This strategy of modifying its underlying account of the good could help bolster utilitarianism by providing a ready explanation for why, say, opting for a lobotomy would be wrong, or why the man who raped the woman in a vegetative state did something heinous, or why Nozick's experience machine shouldn't be used for the remainder of one's biological life. Opting for the lobotomy fails to maximize goods that require advanced mental capacities. The rapist's actions failed to maximize the goods associated with human dignity and bodily autonomy. And plugging into the experience machine for the rest of your life fails to maximize the good of pursuing the truth and engaging with reality. In each of these cases, there were intrinsically good things at play that weren't maximized. And notice how the fundamental intuition behind utilitarianism—that one ought to maximize what is good in the world—appears to remain intact, precisely because the underlying account of the good on offer does *not* reduce to pleasure and the privation of pain but instead moves in the direction of value pluralism.

The move toward a value pluralism version of utilitarianism might seem to enjoy some compatibility with the Christian faith. After all, there is no obvious reason to think Christianity denies that there are or could be a plurality of intrinsically good things. Still, there is a persistent worry that any Christian ought to have about *any* account of the good, including the one affirmed by a value pluralism version of utilitarianism: Christian theism affirms that *God* is intrinsically and necessarily good—and, indeed, the supreme good. Accordingly, any Christian account of the good would need to countenance this point in particular. And one might worry that the account of the good undergirding even the value pluralism version of utilitarianism simply cannot account for the Christian theist's view about the *distinctive* goodness of God. God is not merely one among a plurality of intrinsically good things. God is indeed intrinsically good. But God also stands in a unique relationship to all other intrinsically good things—a relationship that none of the other goods could possibly share toward the other intrinsic goods. That is, God *explains* the other goods, and not vice versa.

Consequentialism justifies too much

Even if utilitarianism's moral decision procedure and its commitment to hedonism are flawed, perhaps only a partial retreat is needed. After all, the thought that our moral duty is to behave in ways that maximize goodness—whatever goodness actually is—can still seem rather intuitive. And perhaps the true heart of utilitarianism isn't its commitment to a hedonistic account of the good (or any other account of the good, for that matter) but rather its insistence that we ought to act in ways that maximize good consequences, whatever those might actually be. Unfortunately, though, a serious problem still remains because we can imagine cases where something is morally required in the situation *other* than what would maximize good consequences (no matter how the good gets defined). For example, consequentialism holds that we should act in ways that maximize good consequences *even if* doing so requires violating justice or human rights, or doing something intrinsically evil. But surely people should *always* get what justice requires, and we should never ignore human rights, and we are never morally obligated to commit intrinsically evil acts. So insofar as consequentialism entails that the ends justify the means, consequentialism ultimately justifies far too much.

To illustrate the point here, consider the case of Walter "Johnny D." McMillian (1941–2013), an African American man from Monroeville, Alabama, who at the age of forty-five had been married for twenty-five years, was raising nine children, and had a modest woodcutting business.[22] McMillian was arrested in June 1987 and sent immediately to death row by a newly elected sheriff who had been under political pressure to locate the killer of Ronda Morrison, a White teenager who had been murdered eight months prior. It is believed that McMillian was identified as a suspect in no small part because he had engaged in an affair with a White woman in the small, largely segregated Alabama community. After hearing McMillian's alibi—McMillian insisted he had been at a church fish fry at the time—the sheriff reportedly told McMillian: "I don't give a damn what you say or what you do. I don't give a damn what your people say either. I'm going to put twelve people on a jury who are going to find your [expletive] ass guilty."[23] Despite the fact that numerous (Black) witnesses testified under oath that they had indeed seen McMillian at the church fish fry, McMillian was convicted by a nearly all-White jury after only two days of trial, and, ultimately, he was sentenced to death. After serving six years on death row and after multiple unsuccessful appeals, McMillian's conviction was eventually overturned by a unanimous decision of the Alabama Court of Criminal Appeals because of multiple due process violations that, by all appearances, had been racially motivated. The original jury had convicted McMillian largely on the basis of the testimony of four shady characters, two of whom claimed to have seen McMillian's low-rider truck at the scene at the time of the murder. Both of those witnesses later confessed that they had indeed lied. A third witness also admitted to lying under pressure by state officials to do so. Plus, it was discovered that McMillian's truck did not even have its distinctive low-rider conversion until *after* the crime had been committed, and state officials were found to have deliberately withheld exculpatory evidence. McMillian was legally exonerated on March 2, 1993.

But imagine that overturning McMillian's unfair conviction would *not* have maximized good consequences in the world. Suppose, for example, that freeing McMillian would have brought about widespread disillusionment in the judicial system, violent race riots, or worse. Suppose, in other words, that allowing McMillian to be scapegoated for a crime he didn't commit would have maximized good consequences in the world. What should the appellate judges have done under such conditions?

Given consequentialism, so it seems, they should have upheld McMillian's unjust conviction. But surely McMillian should have been released because—and *just because*—he did not actually commit the crime! In one way, the consequences of upholding the conviction are perfectly irrelevant: Justice should have reigned, no matter what. McMillian had a right *not* to be held guilty of a crime he did not commit, and that is true *even if* finding him guilty would have somehow maximized good consequences for society as a whole. After all, if maximizing good consequences is the *only* thing that matters, then all manner of evil would be justified on those occasions when allowing it maximizes good consequences. That point can be seen when reflecting not only on McMillian's case but also when reflecting on other cases that involve, say, group punishment, torturing children, organ transplants involving babies, and peeping tom cases, among others. So we return to the main point above: There are cases where something is morally required *other* than what would actually maximize good consequences (again, no matter how the good might get defined by the consequentialist).

There are at least two ways one might try to defend consequentialism against this objection. The first way is what we might think of as the white-knuckled, hard-nose approach: Just bite the bullet and contend that many of our moral intuitions about what we should or should not do are just mistaken. Hence, on this view, we should simply ignore the intuitions that pull us away from consequentialism and trust the theory instead. Return to the intuition that it would be morally wrong for a judge to uphold McMillian's conviction even if doing so would maximize good consequences. According to the consequentialist, that intuition is simply defective. Instead, says the consequentialist, we should buck up and accept that certain actions that might initially seem wrong to us are actually morally required on those very occasions when doing them would maximize good consequences. Of course, the bullet one has to bite here runs the risk of breaking one's teeth.

Fortunately, there is another way of defending consequentialism that doesn't overrule the intuition that people should get what they deserve and have their basic rights as humans respected. But this alternative strategy for defending consequentialism involves an important shift in the very understanding of consequentialism itself. So far in this chapter, we have been contemplating consequentialism as the view that one should always do the specific *actions* that will maximize good consequences. But imagine instead that consequentialism said one should always abide by the *rules* that, when followed, will maximize good consequences over time. At play here is the distinction between act-consequentialism on one hand and rule-consequentialism on the other.

To see how a shift to rule-consequentialism might help one circumvent the objections above, return to the imaginary appellate judges who would uphold McMillian's unjust conviction simply because doing so would maximize good consequences for the greatest number. The problem here, so the rule-consequentialist insists, is that the hypothetical judges were focusing on the consequences of the specific judgment in question when they should have been asking about which *rules*, when followed, would maximize good consequences for society over time. And according to the rule-consequentialist, the rule that would indeed maximize good consequences over time goes roughly as follows: Judges should only ever convict someone based on evidence that proves the individual in question is guilty. The thought here is that, if such a rule weren't followed, society would eventually come to distrust the verdicts of the courts, which would lead to a breakdown in the public order, which would eventually lead to a far worse state of affairs for everyone. And since rule-consequentialism says we should always follow the rule that will maximize utility, rule-consequentialism says the appellate judge should not uphold the unjust conviction of the innocent McMillan—*even if* doing so would maximize good consequences in this isolated, particular case. (Ultimately, rule-consequentialism would employ a similar strategy for defending consequentialism anytime it would appear to justify an otherwise heinous action if the consequences of doing so are salutary enough.)

Unfortunately for the consequentialist, the shift from act-consequentialism to rule-consequentialism is self-referentially unmotivated. To see the point here, suppose we follow the advice of the rule-consequentialist and abide by a specific rule, R, precisely because R, when followed, would maximize good consequences for the greatest number over the long haul. Notice how we would be motivated to adopt R precisely because we are assuming that, in general, we have a duty to maximize good consequences. But if we base our adoption of R on the claim "R maximizes good consequences," then we should also be unmotivated to follow R on those individual occasions when doing so *fails* to maximize good consequences. After all, if our motivating reason for adopting R was

"R maximizes good consequences," why shouldn't we ignore R when doing so would maximize good consequences?

Remember how we got here in the first place: The objection was that act-consequentialism entails that we ought to ignore justice and human rights and do intrinsically evil acts on those occasions when doing so maximizes good consequences. Consequentialists can either bite the bullet and accept this point or adopt rule-consequentialism. However, any argument for why we should adopt rule-consequentialism over act-consequentialism seems to commit us to the very same principle that undergirds act-consequentialism. So we are right back where we started, which makes the move from act-consequentialism to rule-consequentialism seem ad hoc and hence like a move one should be unwilling to make—except that one is trying to avoid biting down on a rather hard bullet.

Consequentialism demands too much

There is yet another problem for the consequentialist component of utilitarianism. Not only does consequentialism imply that some seemingly horrendous actions are morally permissible or even obligatory, but it also entails that some of our everyday, ordinary actions that seem perfectly innocuous are deeply immoral and, hence, blameworthy. So, bizarrely, the objection on offer here is that in addition to being too permissive, consequentialism is also *too demanding.*

To illustrate the objection, suppose you decide to spend some of your hard-earned money on a special night out on the town with your new fiancé. Or, if that seems too frivolous, suppose you decide to just save that money so you can use it to pay for your college tuition. Of course, you could do lots of other things with your money. Instead of going to a fancy restaurant, you could just eat a very simple meal at home and donate all the remaining money to build wells in places that lack potable water. Or instead of blowing a ton of money on college, you could get a bus ticket and a free library card and donate all the remaining funds to feed hundreds of impoverished children throughout the world. Notice: It seems pretty clear that, of all the options available to you, you did *not* choose the option that would maximize good consequences in the world when you chose to save for college or enjoy a special night out on the town. So if consequentialism is true, you are morally blameworthy in these and similar cases. But of course, many of us think it is perfectly okay to go out to dinner now and then or to pursue a college education. Hence the objection: Consequentialism seems *too* demanding.

Admittedly, Christians might be rather unimpressed with this particular complaint against consequentialism. After all, the Christian tradition has long regarded avarice (i.e., greed) as a vice to be shunned and sacrificial generosity as a virtue to be cultivated. The early church father Basil of Caesarea (329–379) argued that when we provide for ourselves at the expense of addressing others' needs, "it is the *hungry one's* bread that you hoard, the *naked one's* cloak that you retain, the *needy one's* money that you withhold."[24] The thought here seems to be that, as Christians, we really owe others more than sometimes meets the eye. And, along similar lines, when the rich young ruler asked Jesus what one must do to inherit eternal life, Jesus tells him to sell all his belongings and give the proceeds to the poor (Mark 10:17–22). These points might actually seem to align the Christian with the very implication of consequentialism in question: Morality demands that we live very differently than we are perhaps accustomed to meet the demands of justice and for the sake of loving of one's neighbor. Still, few Christians would agree that everyone who has ever paid college tuition or enjoyed a night out was *sinning* in the process. But that is precisely what consequentialism seems to entail.

Consequentialism conflicts with Christian Scripture

In other ways, Christianity seems to be at odds with consequentialism itself. Consider, for example, the apostle Paul's comment in Romans 3:8: "Why not say—as some slanderously claim that we say—'Let us do evil that good may result'? Their condemnation is just!" (NIV). The point Paul makes here seems to indicate that we should not condone or excuse evil acts with the rationalization that they will bring about good consequences. When taken at face value, then, this Pauline principle appears to be a fairly straightforward biblical injunction against consequentialism in general. Notice also how Jesus's teachings in the Sermon on the Mount appear to imply that something *other* than the consequences of one's actions are morally significant. After reciting the ancient commandment prohibiting adultery, Jesus says that "anyone who looks at a woman lustfully has already committed adultery with her in his heart" (Matt. 5:28 NIV). And after reciting the ancient commandment against murder, Jesus says that someone who harbors anger or contempt toward another is, in a sense, guilty of wrongdoing (Matt. 5:21–22). Notice how, in both case, Jesus attaches moral guilt to the offender even in cases where there is no resulting sex or death. Consequentialism holds that the moral status of an action attaches exclusively to the consequences of the action (or to rules that are determined by those consequences). But Jesus indicates that one can be guilty of moral wrongdoing even when the consequences of one's outwardly behavior is the same as that of the one who is morally upright. So at the very least, given Jesus's view here, consequentialism represents an *incomplete* account of the right.

Utilitarianism cannot countenance obligations of loyalty

A final objection to utilitarianism pertains to its impartialism and egalitarianism. At its core, utilitarianism holds that we have a moral duty to maximize net utility in the world. So herein lies the impartialism: No one person's happiness and unhappiness (or whatever else might count as valuable and disvaluable) count for more than anyone else's. And not only does everyone's happiness and unhappiness matter, their happiness and unhappiness count equally. So utilitarianism is impartial in how it weighs the utility of all parties involved, and it insists that one's special connections to other individuals or to one's communities have no legitimate bearing on one's obligations to those individuals or communities except insofar as they affect the net increase or decrease of utility in the world.

Yet it can sometimes seem that one's relationships to family or friends or to one's local community or even to one's nation—the relationships that partially define who one is in the first place—*do* provide unique and morally relevant considerations on occasions. In other words, it can sometimes seem that one has a special set of obligations to those with whom one's own sense of self is deeply intertwined. So, plausibly, one's special connections to people and communities sometimes have a bearing on one's obligations in ways that go beyond impartial and egalitarian utility calculations. That is, plausibly, we seem to have what we might call *obligations of loyalty or solidarity*.[25]

To illustrate this point, consider the unique sorts of obligations parents have toward their children. Parents naturally and rightly should feel the responsibility to provide food, shelter, and clothing for their *own* children—obligations they do not feel (at least not to the same degree) toward *other* children. Yet if some of our moral obligations are imposed on us (or at least intensified) because of our special relationships, then not all our moral obligations can be fully explained by the need to maximize net utility with impartiality and equality. To complicate matters, parents don't just feel the obligation to provide for their own children; they also rightly feel a need to take the heat when their own kids step out of line. Imagine, for example, a young child violently hits another kid at the playground. Parents rightly feel the need to apologize on their child's behalf and attempt to make amends for their child's behavior, even though it is entirely possible that *the parents* did nothing to deserve blame or guilt in this situation.

A curiosity arises here. When our children do things to hurt other people or to damage their property, we appear to have a reason to apologize or make amends. Similarly, when our relatives or congregations or communities or ancestors perpetrate injustice on others, we at least *sometimes* plausibly have a reason to make reparation. And perhaps this is true *even though* one cannot be guilty for the actions of another person. So how can we make sense out of the felt need to apologize or make amends for the actions of *others*—whether of our children or our community or our nation or even our distant ancestors? One answer could be that we can have obligations of loyalty that are placed on us through the actions of those who are closest to us, those who at least partially define who we are. Notice how the existence of obligations of loyalty can explain two things: (1) the intuition that no one can be guilty for the actions of another, *and* (2) the intuition that it sometimes makes sense to apologize or make amends for the actions of others.

Admittedly, there is indeed something compelling about utilitarianism's impartiality requirement, precisely because many forms of partiality can seem deeply problematic. For example, suppose a father coaches his son's basketball team. In some ways, the father has a moral responsibility to treat his son no differently than he treats anyone else on the team. For example, the father would be wrong to make his son the starting point guard simply because the boy is his own son. But at the same time, the father still retains some special obligations to his son that he doesn't have to the other players. After all, the father has the responsibility of providing shoes for his son to wear to the games even if he doesn't have the obligation of doing so for the other players. So while there is *something* correct about the idea that morality should be impartial in outlook, utilitarianism seems to take that outlook too far in insisting that we can have no moral obligations except insofar as they result from our obligation to maximize utility in general.

A Christian has perhaps even more reason to question the impartiality requirement of utilitarianism. Consider the fifth of the Ten Commandments: "Honor your father and your mother, so that you may live long in the land the LORD your God is giving you" (Exod. 20:12 NIV). This commandment explicitly identifies the child–parent relationship as the basis of a moral obligation. A similar theme emerges at the end of the so-called Holiness Code in the book of Leviticus, where the Lord admonishes the reader to confess not only their own sins but the sins of their *ancestors* (Lev. 26:40). Turning to the New Testament, a similar basis of moral obligations can be seen in Paul's first epistle to Timothy: "Anyone who does not provide for their relatives, and especially for their own household, has denied the faith and is worse than an unbeliever" (1 Tim. 5:8 NIV). Notice how Paul appears to assume that Christians in particular have certain obligations to their own relatives and households that they do not have (at least to the same degree) to nonrelatives and those who are not of their own households. In short, special relationships appear to provide a basis for certain moral obligations according to Christian Scripture.

Interestingly, familial relationships are not the only type of special relationship emphasized by the biblical writers: Local community and national bonds—among others, perhaps—can also give rise to special obligations. Consider, for example, how Jesus lamented over his own nation of Israel: "Jerusalem, Jerusalem, you who kill the prophets and stone those sent to you, how often I have longed to gather your children together, as a hen gathers her chicks under her wings, and you were not willing"

(Matt. 23:37 NIV). Here, Jesus seems to have felt a need to aid *his own* particular community, Israel, in a way that went beyond his compulsion to aid all human communities in general—not because his community was better or more just than other communities (it wasn't!) but simply because it was, well, *his*. And consider Paul's letter to the Galatians: "Therefore, as we have opportunity, let us do good to all people, especially to those who belong to the family of believers" (Gal. 6:10 NIV). Here, Paul seems to recognize a special kind of responsibility to help one's community members within the fellowship of the church. In sum, then, there appear to be biblical reasons for thinking that we can incur at least some moral obligations on the basis of our special relationship to others, and in ways that go *beyond* the impartial maximization of utility.

chapter five

KANTIAN DEONTOLOGY

In the aftermath of an FBI investigation dubbed "Operation Varsity Blues," federal prosecutors pressed charges in early 2019 against more than fifty people for their involvement in a nationwide, multimillion-dollar bribery and fraud scheme orchestrated by William "Rick" Singer. The accused had allegedly tried to buy admission into the freshman class of several elite universities across the United States. Among the most famous charged in connection to this racket were actresses Felicity Huffman and Lori Loughlin together with Loughlin's husband, fashion designer Mossimo Giannulli. Huffman was accused of paying $15,000 to a fake charity set up by Singer to bribe an exam proctor to inflate her daughter's SAT scores. The *Desperate Housewives* actress said she wanted to make sure her daughter got "a fair shot."[1] Meanwhile, the *Full House* star Loughlin and her husband Giannulli were accused of paying $500,000 in exchange for Singer's help in getting their daughter into the University of Southern California. Ultimately, Giannulli was ordered to pay a fine of $250,000 and was sentenced to five months in prison. Loughlin had to pay a $150,000 fine and served two months in prison. Meanwhile, Huffman was fined $30,000 and ultimately spent only ten nights in prison. Reflecting on Huffman's punishment, one commentator quipped, "Money talks and privilege walks."[2]

Rewind the clock nearly a century to 1932, when the US Public Health Service (and later the Centers for Disease Control) began working with the Tuskegee Institute in Macon County, Alabama, to study the effects of untreated syphilis, a highly contagious disease that can cause blindness, deafness, insanity, heart disease, and death. Lured by the promise of free medical exams, meals, and burial insurance, and without informed consent, six hundred impoverished men—all of them African American—became subjects in what would eventually become known simply as the "Tuskegee Study." Among these men, 399 had syphilis. Although they were told they were being treated for "bad blood," none of these men were ever actually treated for syphilis, and none of them were ever offered penicillin despite the fact that the antibiotic was known to be effective in treating the disease and was widely available as early as 1943. The study went on for forty years. An Associated Press reporter first broke the news in 1972, which effectively pulled the curtain—and the plug—on the federal government's blatantly racist experiment. The following year, the famed civil rights attorney Fred D. Gray, who had previously represented Rosa Parks and Martin Luther King Jr., filed a $1.8 billion lawsuit against several of the parties involved. The case never went to trial and was ultimately settled out of court. Survivors of the study received $37,500 each; heirs of the deceased victims received $15,000 each. President Bill Clinton issued a formal presidential apology in 1997, some sixty-five years after the study began.[3]

These two episodes in American history may seem to have little in common at first glance. The first is a tale of prestige, status, influence, higher education, corruption, and all the unfair advantages that money and fame can buy. Huffman, Loughlin, and others acted as though they were somehow exempt from the rules that everyone else was expected to follow. The second story is one of disease, poverty, racism, manipulation, and preventable death. Human persons—all of them African Americans—were treated as though they mattered only as instruments in service to someone else's ends, and all in the name of science. So what exactly do these two episodes have in common? Both ended in shame. And both force us to confront powerful convictions at the heart of a moral theory developed by the Prussian philosopher Immanuel Kant (1724–1804)—namely, that we ought always act in ways that we could will everyone would act, and that we ought always respect humans and never treat them as means only. This chapter is dedicated to a consideration of that theory of morality, which is commonly known as Kantian deontology.

5.1. What Kantian Deontology Says

It is fair to say that Kant's theory of morality has been profoundly influential since the time of the Enlightenment. Unfortunately, his written work is notoriously difficult to read and understand. To make matters worse, his view can be hard to encapsulate in one simple summary because there are multiple parts to it. So to get a good handle on what Kantian deontology says, we need to get a bit of a running start. To keep our presentation of it as lucid as possible, we will organize our explanation around the following five key assertions:

i. The only thing that is intrinsically and unqualifiedly good is a good will. All other good things are good in only some qualified sense.
ii. A good will is a will that moves a person to do one's moral duty for the sake of doing one's moral duty.
iii. Because the good will is defined in terms of dutiful action, the right is conceptually prior to the good.
iv. The root source of the moral law is found in reason, and reason issues imperatives about how one should direct one's will and behave.
v. Ultimately, doing one's moral duty centers on reason's categorical imperative to act in ways that one could will to become universal law and, hence, to always respect persons as ends in themselves.

Kant on the good will

Kant organizes his moral theory around a partial presentation of his account of the good. And his account of the good is focused on what he takes to be intrinsically and unqualifiedly good. As Kant sees it, there is only one thing that is unqualifiedly good in and of itself. Here's how he describes it:

> There is no possibility of thinking of anything at all in the world, or even out of it, which can be regarded as good without qualification, except a *good will.* Intelligence, wit, judgment, and whatever talents of the mind one might want to name are doubtless in many respects good and desirable, as are such qualities of temperament as courage, resolution, perseverance. But they can also become extremely bad and harmful if the will, which is to make use of these gifts of nature and which in its special constitution is called character, is not good. The same holds with gifts of fortune; power, riches, honor, even health, and that complete well-being and contentment with one's condition which is called happiness make for pride and often hereby even arrogance, unless there is a good will to correct their influence on the mind and herewith also to rectify the whole principle of action and make it universally conformable to its end. . . . A good will is good not because of what it effects or accomplishes, nor because of its fitness to attain some proposed end; it is good only through its willing, i.e., it is good in itself.[4]

The argument Kant seems to be hinting at runs roughly as follows:

(1) The most plausible candidates for being intrinsically and unqualifiedly good things are either:
   (a) *talents of the mind* (e.g., intelligence, courage, resolution, perseverance, and other character traits and virtues); or
   (b) *gifts of fortune* (e.g., power, riches, honor, health, happiness, and so on); or
   (c) *a good will.*

(2) Talents of the mind, when employed by a bad will, can be used for evil ends.

(3) Gifts of fortune, when employed by a bad will, can be used for evil ends.

(4) By elimination, then, the only thing that is intrinsically and unqualifiedly good is a good will.

Notice how for Kant—contrary to what classical utilitarianism holds—happiness is *not* actually something that is *unqualifiedly* good in and of itself. Why? When coupled with a bad will, happiness can lead a person to pridefulness and arrogance, which are bad. What is more, though, when someone who is *unworthy* of happiness is nonetheless happy, something seems out of place. Hence Kant says that "the sight of a being who is not graced by any touch of a pure and good will but who yet enjoyed uninterrupted prosperity can never delight a rational and impartial spectator." To appreciate Kant's point here, just imagine a genocidal dictator who is genuinely happy. Something seems awry. Whether a person is *worthy* of happiness seems to matter more than whether the person actually *is* happy. And for Kant, "a good will seems to constitute the indispensable condition of being even worthy of happiness."[5]

Now, we might wonder how strong Kant's argument above is supposed to be. Arguments that proceed by way of elimination often pose a similar worry, and Kant's argument is no exception. Take premise 1. Has Kant considered *all* the relevant candidates for being intrinsically and unqualifiedly good? Aside from that particular worry, though, we might wonder whether a good will, too, could be used for bad ends—just like talents of the mind or gifts of fortune can be. Why *couldn't* a good will be used for evil ends? Lastly, even if a good will is indeed intrinsically and unqualifiedly good, why should we suppose that a good will is the *only* such good? Might there be others?

Leave those questions to one side for now and just grant that indeed the only intrinsically and unqualifiedly good thing is a good will. What exactly is a good will supposed to be? For Kant, a good will is a will that moves one to perform one's moral duty. But there's more. A good will moves one to do one's moral duty *for the right reason*—namely, precisely because the action in question is the dutiful action. In other words, a good will is a will that moves one to do one's moral duty simply for the sake of doing one's moral duty. A good will is good precisely because it moves one to act out of deference to and respect for the moral law.

One way of understanding Kant's point here is to notice what doing one's duty for the sake of doing one's duty would have to exclude. Obviously, if you fail to do your duty in the first place, then clearly you have *not* done your duty for the sake of doing your duty. So you do not deserve to be praised. But along similar lines, if you do your moral duty by accident, then you have not done your duty for the sake of doing your duty. Suppose, for example, your moral duty is to lower a massive draw bridge when the train is coming. The big moment has arrived, and you are fast asleep. Alas, while snoring away, you fall face-forward onto the big red button that lowers the bridge. Everyone is spared, thankfully. Have you done your duty? Sure, but *only by accident*, which is precisely why you do not deserve to be praised in this case. You failed to do your duty *for the sake of doing your duty*.

Or suppose your moral duty is to charge a fair market price for batteries, generators, and other such items at the local hardware store you own and manage. A natural disaster strikes the area, and your customers are desperate for energy sources because the power grid is down. Suppose you refuse to price-gouge because you know that, in the long run, you would run the risk of alienating your customers in the future if you do. In other words, you do your duty for the sake of pursuing your own long-term financial gain. Did you do your moral duty? Yes. But notice how you failed to do your moral duty *for the sake of doing your moral duty*, and to that extent you have not exhibited a good will as Kant conceives of it. Similarly, Kant thinks you wouldn't have done your duty for the sake of doing your duty if you did your duty out of, say, natural inclinations or even entrenched habits. In those cases, doing your duty simply requires no will power on your part, so you are not doing anything particularly praiseworthy.

It can be easy to get the wrong impression here, so pay attention to Kant's main point. The point is *not* that, in doing your moral duty by accident or out of self-interest or by habit or out of a prior inclination, you did something morally blameworthy. After all, you still did your duty. Kant's point here is just that, in doing your moral duty for the wrong reasons, your action lacks moral worth—that is, your behavior is not morally praiseworthy, even if it wasn't exactly blameworthy. For the action in question to be morally praiseworthy, you must do your duty *for the sake of doing your duty*. It's then, and only then, that you would be acting out of respect for the moral law. And it's then, and only then, that you would be exhibiting a good will. That's the key point for Kant.

Take stock of the situation so far. For Kant, the only thing that is intrinsically and unqualifiedly good is a good will, which he defines as a will that moves one to do one's duty for the sake of doing one's duty. Notice how the good Kant has in mind—that is, good will—is defined in terms of the right—that is, moral duty. Having a good will requires one to do what is obligatory (right) and to do so for the right reason (for the sake of doing one's duty). In this respect, for Kant, the right is *prior* to the good—that is, the right is logically more fundamental than the good. This is a point that will become relevant later on.

Kant's account of the right: the first formulation of the categorical imperative

If it is true that a good will is a will that moves one to do one's duty for the sake of doing one's duty, then we need to ask: What determines one's duty in the first place? And how can one know what that duty is? Ultimately, Kant contends that reason, and reason alone, is the root source of the moral law, which specifies what one's duty is.

Think of the matter like this. Start by reflecting on the common, everyday notion of the moral law and moral duty. To Kant's mind, if there is such a thing as a valid moral *law* in the first place, then that moral law would have to be binding on all rational creatures in an absolute sense—that is, without exception. Now, admittedly, some of the duties we have in life aren't exactly absolute. And that's because *those* duties aren't really *moral* duties in the first place; they are things like professional or organizational or legal or perhaps familial duties. In other words, we incur certain duties in life simply by taking on this or that job or living in this or that legal jurisdiction or by occupying this or that social role. Accordingly, these duties can be rendered moot or simply get overruled by other considerations. But moral duties aren't like that. That's because moral duties aren't binding merely on the basis of one's location or because one is, say, a schoolteacher or a doctor, or a man or a woman—or, for that matter, even on the basis of being human. Rather, the moral law binds strictly on the basis of the fact that one is *rational*. What this means, then, is that the root source of the moral law, and the moral duties of that law, is reason and reason alone, because reason is the only feature shared by all rational beings.

Notice what Kant's view here effectively *excludes* as the basis for the moral law. The basis or source of the moral law cannot be rooted in facts about human nature—including facts about what humans desire or need or even what might be required for human happiness. After all, it is at least possible that there could be *nonhuman* rational creatures (though Kant doesn't actually think there are any), and the source of the moral law would have to pertain to all rational creatures, human or not. Nor could the source of the moral law be rooted in the differing circumstances humans might face in life, since such circumstances are not shared, in principle or practice, by all rational beings. For those reasons, consequentialist approaches to ethics would be fundamentally misguided. So reason—and reason alone—is the only source of the moral law according to Kant.

But how, exactly, does reason give rise to the moral law according to Kant? To see what he has in mind here, consider the distinction between *theoretical* reason and *practical* reason. (Philosophers dating back to Aristotle have worked with this distinction in mind, and Kant is no exception.) We can think of theoretical reasoning as (roughly) what we are engaged in when we are trying to describe how the world is. And we can think of practical reasoning as (roughly) what we are engaged in when we are trying to discern how the world ought to be. While theoretical reason *describes*, practical reason *prescribes*. That is to say, practical reason tells us how the world *should* be. So the pronouncements of practical reasoning are effectively reason's way of informing us about what needs to happen if, say, we are to reach a certain end or goal. Accordingly, practical reason issues imperatives to us—it commands us to do things, as it were.

Now, some of the imperatives issued by reason are practical in nature, though not moral in nature. For example, suppose you want to lose weight. Practical reason issues you an imperative: Eat less and move more. But notice that reason doesn't *always* and *everywhere* issue this particular imperative. Some people need to eat more and move less. And some people do not really have a desire to lose weight in the first place. So notice how the imperative of practical reason in this case would be fully conditional upon someone's having the end goal of losing weight. In other words, if someone didn't have the end goal of weight loss in mind, then the dictate of practical reason ("eat less and move more") wouldn't be binding for that person. The imperative here is what Kant labels a *hypothetical* imperative.

Importantly, the moral law is not comprised of hypothetical imperatives of practical reason. But why is that? Remember that, in Kant's view, if the moral law is to be valid at all, it must bind absolutely, and hypothetical imperatives are merely *conditional* on an individual's desires or chosen end goals. Morality isn't like that, though. And that's because morality sometimes requires us to do things that run *contrary* to what we desire or wish. For Kant, morality consists of the imperatives issued by practical reason that are in no way hypothetical or conditional upon someone's subjective desires or chosen end goals.

So imagine we could somehow strip practical reason of any and all empirical inputs related to a person's own subjective desires, preferences, or chosen end goals. What, then, would practical reason command of that person? The imperatives of practical reason under these conditions would now be strictly about those ends that are nonsubjective in nature (that is, *objective*) and fully nonparticularistic (that is, *universal*) in the sense that they are ends that *every* rational being would be forced to recognize as ends, simply insofar as they are rational. Such imperatives of practical reason under these conditions are what Kant famously labels *categorical imperatives*. And in his view, there is really only *one* such categorical imperative issued always and everywhere by practical reason (though, to complicate matters, Kant says that this one categorical imperative can be formulated in several different ways). The categorical imperative of practical reason is this: *Act only on those maxims that you could at the same time will to become universal law.*

To understand this categorical imperative in the proper light, we need to get clear what Kant means by the term "maxim," and we also need to get a handle on what it means to ask whether a maxim can be willed as universal law. Start with the term "maxim" first. We can think of a maxim as something like the policy one is following when one does something; it is more or less a formal statement of one's reason for acting, in other words. A complete articulation of one's maxim would at the least need to include a description of one's action, the circumstances in which one would be acting, and the end for which one would be undertaking the action in the first place. Suppose, for example, that you intend to mow your lawn after work because your neighbors have been smirking unhappily at your unruly grass lately. The maxim according to which you would be acting might be stated as follows: "I will mow my lawn when the grass gets unruly in order to improve my relationship with my neighbors."

The question now is whether this maxim could be willed to become a universal law in the way that, say, gravity is a universally applicable law of nature. Could the maxim in question be *universalized*, as it were? To answer this question, suppose we work in reverse and ask when a maxim is *not* universalizable.

There are effectively two ways that a maxim can fail to be universalizable, and these two ways of failing yield two distinct types of duties within Kant's theory of morality.[6] First off, a maxim could be such that even the very effort to contemplate or conceive it as a universal law would implicate one in some sort of contradiction or self-defeating incoherence. If a maxim is such that one cannot even imagine it as a universal law without implying some sort of contradiction or self-defeating incoherence, then obviously one couldn't turn around and will it to become universal law. So in such a case, one has a *perfect* duty to refrain from acting according to the maxim in question. The duty is perfect in the sense that the duty is fully and precisely specified and hence there is absolutely no variation or exception in how one must go about fulfilling it. For example, Kant thinks we have a perfect duty to refrain from false promising (for reasons we will return to below). And so, in his view, there simply is no variation on how one could fulfill this obligation other than to *not* engage in false promising—the duty is fully specific in this case.

Second, a maxim might be such that it could be contemplated as a universal law without implying a contradiction or self-defeating incoherence, but nonetheless one could not *will* it to become a universal law without thereby causing one to will two conflicting things at once. Accordingly, attempting to will such a maxim to become universal law would cause one to have a *contradiction of the will*. In such a case, one has an *imperfect* duty to abstain from acting according to that maxim. A duty is imperfect in the sense that the duty in question is not fully specified in how we are to go about fulfilling it. For example, Kant thinks we have an imperfect duty to help others in need (for reasons we will return to below), but this duty is imperfect in the sense that there is some latitude in precisely how and on which occasions we might extend that help. Keep in mind that, for Kant, imperfect duties are still full-blown moral duties—binding and absolute. The real difference between a perfect and imperfect duty is simply in terms of the specificity of the duty in question. In the case of perfect duties, one has a full and precise specification of what one is required to do or not do. In the case of imperfect duties, there is some underspecification of how one must discharge the duty, and hence one has some leeway in how to meet it.

As Kant sees it, practical reason commands rational creatures always and everywhere to act only on those maxims that one can at the same time will to become a universal law. We can see how all the various twists and turns of this categorical imperative hang together by considering the following flowchart (fig. 5.1), which captures each step of Kant's moral decision procedure. Take a moment and consider Figure 5.1 on the next page before moving on.

In Kant's view, there are moral duties that one owes to oneself and there are moral duties that one owes to others. What this means, then, is that given the distinction between perfect and imperfect duties, there are really four different categories of moral duties: (a) perfect duties owed to oneself; (b) perfect duties owed to others; (c) imperfect duties owed to oneself; and (d) imperfect duties owed to others (see fig. 5.2). Kant offers paradigmatic examples of each of these four types of duties. Reflecting on each of these examples will help to elucidate his decision procedure as well as the underlying distinctions he has in mind.

Figure 5.1. Kant's Moral Decision Procedure

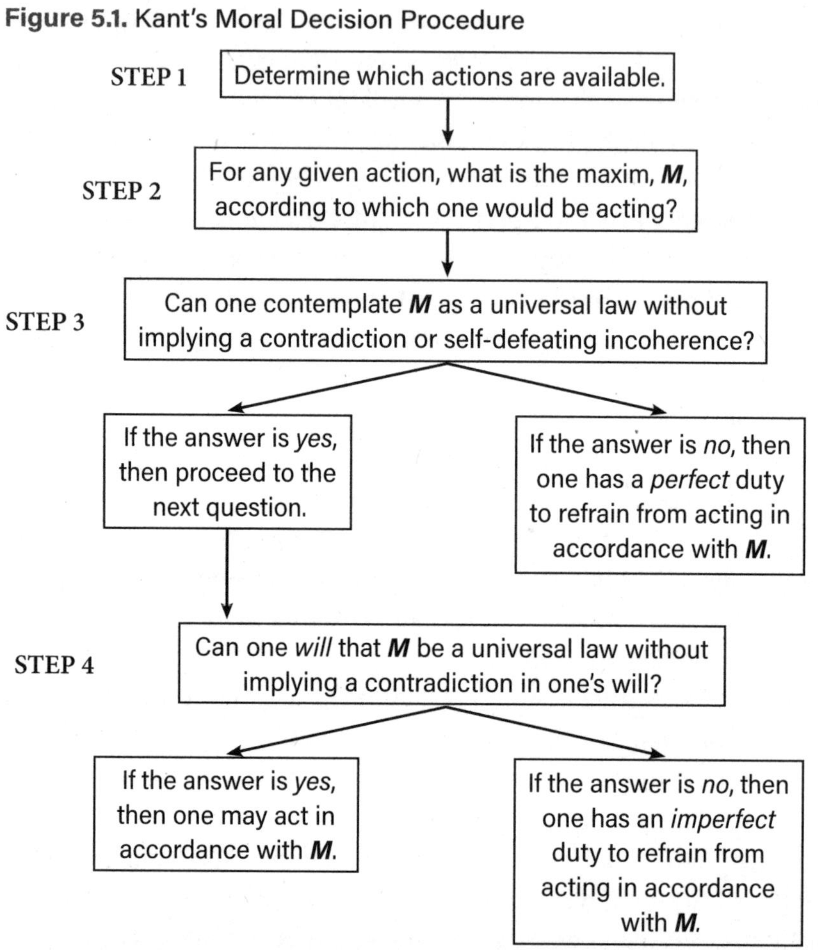

Figure 5.2. Kant's Basic Typology of Duties

WITH RESPECT TO . . .	PERFECT DUTY (i.e., the duty is fully specified)	IMPERFECT DUTY (i.e., the duty is not fully specified)
. . . oneself	To *not* commit suicide	To develop one's own talents
. . . others	To *not* make false promises	To help others

Take, first, Kant's paradigmatic example of the perfect duty that one owes to oneself: the duty to refrain from suicide. Why is this supposed to be a *perfect* duty in his view? Consider the maxim according to which one would be acting in taking one's own life, according to Kant: "From self-love

I make [it] my principle to shorten my life when its continued duration threatens more evil than it promises satisfaction."[7] To make things a bit more lucid, suppose we just reword this so that it fits more obviously into the formula of a maxim mentioned above: "I will end my life when circumstances have become unbearable in order to make my life better." Move now to STEP 3 of Kant's decision procedure. Can this maxim be contemplated as universal law without implying a contradiction or self-defeating incoherence? Not according to Kant. The thought here seems to be that if one no longer exists, one cannot be improved—and that's the contradiction: You cannot make your life better if you are dead.

Next, turn to what Kant regards as the paradigmatic example of a perfect duty owed to others: to refrain from making false promises. Imagine someone secures a loan by making a false promise to repay it. The maxim in this case is, "I will make a false promise when I'm in a pinch in order to promote my own advantage." Can this maxim be contemplated as universal law in a way that doesn't involve a contradiction or self-defeating incoherence? Not according to Kant. Imagine that everyone were to act on the basis of this maxim. If so, no one would then be able to pursue one's own advantage by means of making a false promise. Why is that? If *everyone* made false promises for the sake of pursuing one's own advantage, then no one would believe anyone's promises any longer, whereupon no one could actually use false promising as a means to pursue one's own advantage. Notice how the effort to contemplate the maxim as a universal law resulted in a self-defeating incoherence. Thus, in Kant's view, we have a perfect duty to refrain from false promising according to the categorical imperative.

Kant's paradigmatic example of an imperfect duty owed to oneself is to develop one's own talents. Why is this a *moral* duty? Suppose one chose to let one's talents go to waste. The lazy person's maxim would run something like this: "I will neglect the development of my talents in order to pursue my own pleasure." Can we contemplate this maxim as a universal law without implying some sort of contradiction or self-defeating incoherence? It seems so. It won't be a pretty picture perhaps, but there is no obvious contradiction involved here. So move to STEP 4 of Kant's decision procedure. The problem is that one cannot *will* the lazy person's maxim to become universal law precisely because in so willing, one would be willing something that conflicts with something else that is already willed by all rational beings—namely, that one's rationality be developed and attended to. Julia Driver explains this last point by saying that there is something that is essential to one's will: "What is essential to the will? This could be answered in a variety of ways—exercise of the will requires the capacity for autonomous decision making; and it also requires having our basic needs met in order to be autonomous agents."[8] Accordingly, one couldn't will the lazy person's maxim to become universal law without a contradiction of the will. So, in Kant's view, one has an imperfect duty to *not* let one's own talents go to waste. The duty here is still absolute, but notice how there remains some latitude—*under*specification, that is—in how one might go about developing one's own talents. That's why the duty here is *imperfect* in nature.

Lastly, Kant thinks we have an imperfect duty to help others in need. Suppose, for example, one were to neglect helping others even when one is in a position to help. One's maxim would be: "I will abstain from helping others who need my help (even when I'm in a position to do so) in order to focus on my own self-interests." Plausibly, this maxim can be contemplated as a universal law without implying any contradiction or self-defeating incoherence. That is, we seem to be able to imagine a world where everyone acts according to this maxim—we can imagine a world wherein everyone acts like an ethical egoist, for example. Yet Kant thinks one cannot *will* this maxim to become universal law because doing so would invariably conflict with something else that rational creatures necessarily always will: that one's own rational nature be developed and attended to. Imagine everyone acted according to the neglectful-of-others maxim in question. No one would ever help out anyone else in their times of need. Yet as a rational agent, one necessarily wills that one be helped by others when one needs help. So the effort to will this maxim as universal law results in a contradiction of the will, thereby generating an imperfect duty to refrain from so acting.

Kant further elaborates his system of moral duties in his *Metaphysics of Morals*.[9] In it, he enumerates a variety of specific examples of moral duties that one has—both with respect to oneself and with respect to others. Kant thinks, for example, that with respect to oneself, one has a duty to pursue the ultimate end of self-perfection, which he takes to mean the cultivation of one's natural endowments and capacities. This duty unfolds into the perfect duty to refrain from anything that would destroy, degrade, or otherwise diminish one's endowments and capacities—or anything that would impede progress in becoming an excellent moral being. Likewise, the underlying duty to pursue one's own self-perfection also results in the imperfect duty to develop one's natural endowments and capacities—both as a physical being and as a moral being—in pursuit of moral perfection and virtue. In turn, these duties entail even more specific duties owed to oneself (see fig. 5.3).

Figure 5.3. Examples of Specific Moral Duties Owed to Oneself, according to Kant

WITH RESPECT TO . . .	PERFECT DUTY TO REFRAIN FROM . . .	IMPERFECT DUTY TO DO OR PRACTICE . . .
. . . oneself as a physical being	Suicide	Self-preservation
	Self-dismembering or mutilation	Development of one's natural physical endowments and capacities
	Sexual self-abuse	Chastity
	Self-stupefaction through excessive enjoyment of food (gluttony)	Temperance
	Self-stupefaction through use of alcohol or other substances (drunkenness or intoxication)	
. . . oneself as a moral being		Search, test, and know oneself for the sake of pursuing moral perfection
		Removal of internal hindrances to moral perfection
		Development of predisposition to good will
	Lying	Veracity/honesty/sincerity/uprightness
	Miserly avarice (stinginess to the point of depriving oneself of needs)	Meeting one's own needs properly
	Servility (false humility)	Self-esteem and self-respect

In addition to pursuing one's own self-perfection, Kant also thinks one has an overarching moral duty to pursue the ultimate end of other people's happiness, which is to say that one should aim to improve others' satisfaction with their own conditions. This duty unfolds into perfect and imperfect duties related to love of humankind and duties related to respect of humankind (see fig. 5.4).

Figure 5.4. Examples of Specific Moral Duties Owed to Others, according to Kant

WITH RESPECT TO . . .	PERFECT DUTY TO REFRAIN FROM . . .	IMPERFECT DUTY TO DO OR PRACTICE . . .
. . . loving others	Hatred of humankind	Love of humankind
	Envy	Beneficence (make happiness of others an end for oneself)
	Ingratitude	Gratitude
	Malice	Sympathy
. . . respecting others	Contempt	Respecting others as ends and never degrading others to means only
	Pride (arrogance)	
	Slander	
	Mockery	

Kant's account of the right: the second formulation of the categorical imperative

Although Kant contends that there is only *one* categorical imperative issued by practical reason, he explains that this imperative can take several different expressions. And the second expression of it that he discusses is especially noteworthy. The second formulation of the categorical imperative goes like this: *Always act in such a way that treats human persons—whether oneself or others—as ends and never as means only.*

To appreciate what Kant has in mind here, we need to get a sense of what it is to treat a person as a *means* and what it is to treat a person as an *end*. Fortunately, the idea here is intuitive enough. One treats X as a means when one uses X for the sake of getting something else that one wants. Suppose, for example, you go to an ATM machine to withdraw some cash because you intend to buy some produce at a farmer's market that accepts only cash. You use the ATM machine as a means for getting cash. You use the cash as a means to buy the produce. And you use the produce to feed your family. Notice that you had an ultimate goal or end in mind: feed your family. And you used the ATM machine, the cash, and the produce as a means to that end. Of course, the ATM machine, cash, and the produce don't have any of their own goals or ends in mind; they are merely *things*, not persons. And things are unlike rational creatures who have ends in mind, or goals of their own.

The second formulation of the categorical imperative simply says one should never treat human persons (including oneself) like mere things to be used as a means in the pursuit of some end beyond them. Instead, one should always treat persons as rational creatures with goals and ends of their own. In other words: Don't treat persons like mere objects or things but as rational creatures who have ends of their own.

A point of clarification before moving on: Notice that the second formulation of the categorical imperative does not altogether forbid treating persons as a means; rather, it strictly forbids treating persons *merely* as a means or as a means *only*. It is sometimes permissible to treat a person as a means, but it is never permissible to treat that person as a means *only*. The key word here is the word "only." Think of it this way. Suppose you hire a landscaper to mow the unruly lawn you have been neglecting lately. You are indeed using this person as a means to your own end goal (i.e., getting the lawn mown). But if the landscaper has freely consented to mowing the lawn—presumably because you have contracted him to do the work for proper compensation—then you aren't using him as a means *only*. You are using him as a means, yes; but you are also regarding him as an end in himself, too. And you did this by recognizing him as a rational creature who has ends of his own in mind who can rationally and freely consent to the job for pay.

While most people find the second formulation of the categorical imperative intuitive enough, we might still wonder *how* it is supposed to be connected with the first formulation of the categorical imperative. Remember, Kant thinks these two different formulations are simply two different expressions of the very same underlying command of practical reason. But what does an injunction against treating person as a means only have to do with the injunction against acting on the basis of nonuniversalizable maxims? Aren't these two things very different?

There are at least two reasons for thinking these two things express the same underlying command of practical reason. The first is that both formulations of the categorical imperative, when consulted as guidance for how to make moral decisions, yield the same verdicts in a wide range of cases. To see the point here, return to Kant's four paradigmatic cases mentioned above (viz., suicide, false promising, neglecting one's own talents, and failing to help others). In each case, the two different formulations of the categorical imperative yield the very same verdict according to Kant. Given the second formulation of the categorical imperative, it is wrong for one to commit suicide because one is using one's own person, as it were, as a means for eliminating suffering.[10] Similarly, it is wrong for one to make false promises precisely because doing so uses other persons as instruments to one's own advantage—and without their informed consent. When one lets one's own talents go to waste, one fails to fully advance the end of humanity in one's own person. And when one fails to show benevolence toward others who need help, one's behavior fails to harmonize positively with humanity as an end in itself. Thus, given that the first and second formulations of the categorical imperatives converge on the same moral verdicts, we have incremental evidence that they are merely different ways of expressing the same underlying moral duty issued by practical reason.

A second reason for thinking they express the same duty is that both formulations of the categorical imperative point to the underlying importance of respecting rationality. When one acts in ways that one could wish to become universal law, one acts in ways that effectively take account of all other rational beings and the ends that they might have in mind to achieve. When one acts in a way that treats persons never as means only, one acts in ways that respect rational beings. And for Kant, the fundamental ground of morality must be something that is valuable as an end in itself and not merely because it is a means to some other end. What sort of thing has absolute worth as an end in itself? Kant's writes, "I say that man [i.e., humanity], and in general every rational being, exists as an end in himself and not merely as a means to be arbitrarily used by this or that will."[11] So human persons, and indeed all rational creatures, have a nature that deserves to be respected not merely as a valuable instrument to some other end but as something that must be respected as an end in itself.

A final note before moving on: The fact that both formulations of the categorical imperative point to rational beings as ends in themselves also underlines the importance of *autonomy* for Kant. One has autonomy when one is rationally self-governing and, hence, can live one's life from the inside out, as it were. When we act merely on the basis of our natural and unchosen impulses or appetites, we are not thereby directing our own behavior from the inside out. Rather, we are being driven by our contingent circumstances, circumstances that determined our impulses and appetites. In those cases, our lives are lived from the outside in, as it were. However, for Kant, since we are rational creatures, we can direct ourselves and choose our own laws, so to speak. That is, unlike mere things, rational creatures do not *have* to act in ways that are determined by external forces. When we exercise our autonomy to act in accordance with laws that we bestow upon ourselves (rather than acting as slaves to our appetites or to laws that come from outside of ourselves) we are fully free. This sort of freedom is exercisable only by rational creatures. And rationality requires us to respect that other rational beings have ends of their own choosing, too. That's precisely why we must treat rational creatures in ways that are governed by policies that we could will to become universal laws. If our treatment of persons is governed by policies that we couldn't will to become universal laws, then we treat other persons not as rational creatures but merely as means to our own ends. Thus, we can see that the first and second formulation of the categorical imperative are conceptually linked.

We are finally in a position to encapsulate Kant's account of the right. When contemplated according to the first formulation of the categorical imperative, we can summarize Kant's account of the right as follows: An action is morally obligatory if and only if the negation of its maxim cannot be universalized. An action is morally wrong if and only if its maxim cannot be universalized. And an action is optional if and only if its maxim (and the negation of that maxim) can be universalized.

Alternatively, when contemplated according to the second formulation of the categorical imperative, Kant's account of the right can be summarized as follows: An action is obligatory if and only if and because not doing it fails to respect persons as ends in themselves. An action is wrong if and only if and because it fails to respect persons as ends in themselves. And an action is optional if and only if and because it respects persons as ends in themselves. Notice that the first and second formulations of the categorical imperative are equivalent in the sense that they lead one to the same moral verdict. However, they are slightly different in the sense that the second formulation offers an accompanying explanation of *what makes* the action obligatory, forbidden, or optional.

5.2. The Case for Kantian Deontology

Because Kantian deontology is so multifaceted, commentators sometimes focus on explaining the various intricacies of Kant's view at the expense of making explicit what the argument for this particular theory of morality is supposed to be. So we should be careful to step back from the fray and ask: What is the basic case for Kantian deontology, and why might we be tempted to think that it is the correct view of morality? There are two main sorts of arguments we might point to. We will consider each in turn.

The unconditional value of persons argument

The first argument is perhaps easiest to see in connection to the second formulation of the categorical imperative: It is a case for thinking that human persons are priceless and, thus, should on every occasion be respected as ends in themselves.[12] Start by reflecting on the fact that human persons are rational and autonomous beings. So what? Well, rationality allows a person to reason about the various ends one might pursue, as well as about the means by which those ends might be pursued. This, in turn, allows a person to assign various objects value. Accordingly, things become valuable to a person simply by virtue of how they factor into the ends that the rational being has for them. In other words, rational beings are *valuers* in the sense that they bestow value on things.

That said, rational beings aren't *merely* valuers. They are *bearers* of value, too. But from whence does this value come?

Suppose at this juncture we were to say that rational beings—like mere objects—come to have their value simply in virtue of the fact that they are valued by, well, some *other* rational being. Suppose, in other words, that we were to posit that some particular rational being, A, is valuable simply because another rational being, B, bestows value upon A. What makes B valuable? If the answer were simply "another rational being, C," then notice how the threat of a regress would loom large. Why should one rational being have value that another rational being does *not* have such that one rational being needs another rational being to value it in the first place? One way around the regress problem here is to say that a person qua valuer is valuable in and of oneself, which is part of why one can *bestow* value in the first place. Yet not only does rationality give a person the capacity to bestow value on things, it also factors into the fact that a person is an autonomous being who can act in self-legislating ways—that is, in accordance with the various ends that a person selects for oneself, even ends that run contrary to a person's own subjective desires or natural appetites and impulses. Accordingly, or so the argument goes, we simply need to posit that rational and autonomous beings are valuable in themselves—and in a way that is beyond all price. They are unconditionally valuable and of absolute worth!

Now notice, if it is true that a rational and autonomous creature—that is, a *person*—is indeed valuable in this way, then it follows that this person should be respected as an end in itself and never treated as a means only. And that's exactly what the second formulation of the categorical imperative of practical reason says. Notice also that one way of respecting a person as an end in itself is to always act in accordance with maxims that one could wish to become universal law. When one does that, one is effectively attending to the fact that *all* persons are special enough to command respect.

How strong is this sort of case for Kantian deontology? We shouldn't ignore the fact that this argument seems to assume all along that rationality is something that makes a person unconditionally valuable. But, of course, we might wonder *how* and *why* rationality has the unique power to make a person valuable beyond all price. Notice how the Christian faith could explain this particular point by providing a deeper metaphysical backstory: Human persons are created in the image of a supremely perfect being—God—and being divine image-bearers thereby makes human persons uniquely valuable beyond all price. Without such a theistic backstory in place, it can seem less apparent why rationality *all by itself* is supposed to be so important. So while the proposition that rational creatures are unconditionally valuable might seem intuitive on many levels, it can be difficult to say *why* exactly this proposition might actually be true, especially without appeal to a theistic backstory.

Inference to best explanation

A second and different case for Kantian deontology comes in the form of an argument for best explanation. The underlying idea is this: The categorical imperative helps explain the data of our moral experience and intuition.[13] Consider the following data. We wince at the Hamas terrorist who treats Israel as something to be wiped off the face of the planet. We decry slavery and rape as profound violations of humanity. We are ashamed that six hundred African American men could ever be subjected to something as awful as the Tuskegee syphilis study. We abhor the atrocities committed by the Nazis during the holocaust. We recoil at paternalistic and autocratic behavior. Kant's moral theory helps explain why we have those reactions in each case: The actions in question cast persons as mere things that can be used or abused and thrown away like trash. The categorical imperative also helps explain why we feel justified in holding out hope for people—and for extending them second chances after second chances. And it helps explain why there might be such things as universal human rights.

To add to that, Kantian deontology can also seem to mesh nicely with views that are salient to the Christian faith—for example, the belief that morality is an objective matter and that humans are to be loved in ways that nonhuman animals or mere objects are not. Kantian deontology also meshes with the second table of the Decalogue (that is, the prohibitions against murder, adultery, theft, lying, covetousness), and it squares with the fact that Scripture can seem to presume in many ways the universality and absoluteness of moral duties.[14] Furthermore, it can be tempting at first glance to think that the first formulation of the categorical imperative—act only on those maxims that you could will to become universal law—sounds a lot like the Golden Rule: "Do to others what you would have them do to you" (Matt. 7:12 NIV). Finally, the intuition that morality is ultimately about obedience to the moral law and not about how one benefits from following that moral law fits nicely with Kantian deontology. So, ultimately, one might think Kantian deontology best explains the data of our moral experience and intuitions, including the witness of the Christian tradition.

Of course, we might wonder how strong this sort of argument really is—especially if those same data could be explained, and perhaps even better, by things other than Kantian deontology. What if those same data could also be explained—or explained better—by, say, divine commands or facts about human flourishing or some other set of considerations? And how tight, really, is the fit between Kantian deontology and the presuppositions of the Christian faith? Does Christianity really assume, for example, that *all* moral duties are absolute in nature?

Along similar lines, we should be careful in comparing the Golden Rule with Kant's first formulation of the categorical imperative. While they might entail many of the same moral verdicts, the categorical imperative and the Golden Rule aren't identical, and they even part company at various junctures. Notice, for example, that the Golden Rule would direct a person to focus on very particular and contingent facts about oneself—namely, facts about how *you* would want to be treated in this or that situation. By contrast, the categorical imperative says you should bracket out *all* those particularized, contingent facts about yourself and instead focus on whether your maxim is universalizable. Yet it is certainly plausible that one might want to be treated in ways that one couldn't turn around and will to become universal law—and that's where some sunlight between Kant and Jesus starts to emerge. For example, imagine a person who sincerely wouldn't want to learn the truth about certain topics that would be utterly heartbreaking and devastating to discover. What should this particular individual do, then, when she is asked by her frail and dying mother to tell her about her son who, unbeknownst to the mother, was recently murdered in a particularly gruesome fashion? In this sort of case, as well as in others, the Golden Rule might seem to cut against the verdicts of the categorical imperative.[15] Similarly, notice how the first formulation of the categorical imperative would entail that one has duties to oneself, whereas the Golden Rule simply offers no instruction about how one should treat oneself. So, clearly, the two cannot be identical, even if they converge at key points.

5.3. The Case against Kantian Deontology

Kantian deontology is not without its critics, and we need to ask whether Kant's moral theory can be defended against the concerns that arise. The first three objections we consider in this section are relatively standard problems found in the literature. The final two are of special significance for Christians. We will consider each in turn.

Kantian deontology has problems related to how one depicts one's maxim

One of the standard objections to Kantian deontology centers on how the first formulation of the categorical imperative requires one to determine whether one could will one's maxim to become universal law. However, whether one could indeed will one's maxim to become universal law appears to hinge, at least in part, on how one construes the maxim in the first place.

To see the point here, return to Kant's paradigmatic example of a perfect duty owed to others concerning false promises. In Kant's view, one always and on every occasion has a fully specified, absolute duty to *not* violate one's promises—period. Now suppose you have solemnly promised your boss to be present at a very important business meeting. (Imagine, for example, this meeting will determine whether the company survives into the future, and you are the clutch player.) But suppose that en route to that meeting, you get a phone call from your spouse who tells you that your daughter needs your help immediately, and that she could even die if you don't help right now. The emergency will, however, require you to skip the meeting. To keep things interesting, suppose that the meeting cannot be rescheduled and that your boss is a stubborn person who will not release you from your prior commitment to be at said meeting. Should you break the promise you made to your boss? Take a moment and think it over.

Now look back at Kant's decision procedure in section 5.1 above. The problem at hand centers on STEP 1 of the decision procedure: The way one chooses to construe the maxim in this particular case appears to determine whether the maxim in question is universalizable and hence whether it is permissible according to Kant's first formulation of the categorical imperative. Consider two possible articulations of the maxim you would be acting on in this case:

> MAXIM 1: "I will break a promise when I am in a difficult situation in order to pursue my own advantage."
> MAXIM 2: "I will break a promise in circumstances wherein a child might die in order to save her life."

If MAXIM 1 is correct in this case, then (assuming you follow the rest of Kant's moral decision procedure) you cannot even contemplate your maxim as a universal law without some sort of contradiction or self-defeating incoherence. Why? If everyone broke one's promises when in a difficult situation in order to pursue one's own advantage, then no one would be able to pursue one's own advantage by means of a broken promise. Thus, you have a *perfect* duty to abstain from acting in accordance with MAXIM 1.

But notice how if MAXIM 2 is accurate in this case, then you could quite plausibly contemplate your maxim as a universal law without implying a contradiction, and you could quite plausibly *will* that such a maxim become universal law, too. (At the very least, it is unclear why you *couldn't* will MAXIM 2 to become universal law.) Thus, plausibly, it would be permissible for you to act according to MAXIM 2.

Obviously enough, there is a serious problem here. After all, the action in question remains precisely the same, no matter how you or anyone else might describe it. And to make matters worse, this very sort of problem replicates itself in a wide range of cases that might admit of multiple descriptions. So unless there is a principled, objective way of stabilizing the articulation of one's maxim in *all* such cases, then there is no clear way of getting stable (or noncontradictory) results from Kant's moral decision procedure. And that *is* a problem.

Perhaps, though, this need not be seen as a fatal objection to Kantian deontology. After all, a Kantian might try to argue that there is indeed an objectively correct, stable articulation of one's maxim in each case. Accordingly, one might try to claim, despite how things might seem on first pass, that there is really *one* and *only one* correct articulation of the maxim in this sort of case. For example, one might try to claim that MAXIM 1 is the correct articulation of the maxim in question because it captures the description of the action, the circumstances, and the end at the appropriate level of generality. Of course, this move will almost inevitably invite the worry that this generalized articulation of the maxim fails to capture everything that is morally relevant in this situation. So, alternatively, a Kantian might try to argue that MAXIM 2—and *not* MAXIM 1—is actually the proper articulation in this case precisely because it captures all the specific, morally salient information relevant to this situation to the extent that it captures the pertinent information pertaining to human persons—including information about the life of the child—which is information omitted in MAXIM 1. A remaining, complicating factor for proponents of the second strategy is this: Kant himself seemed pretty committed to saying that one must always and in every case keep one's promises—period. But perhaps Kant is not the best interpreter of his own view.

Kantian deontology cannot adjudicate conflicts of absolute duties

One of the most notable features of Kantian deontology is that it regards our moral duties to be absolute in nature. Take, for example, the duty to be truthful. Kant regards this particular moral duty be "a sacred and unconditionally commanding law of reason that *admits of no expediency whatsoever*."[16] In other words, Kant contends that the duty to be truthful (or the duty to abstain from lying) is absolute and exceptionless—even in those cases where telling the truth would result in terrible consequences for oneself or others. The same goes for our other moral duties as well—they, too, are absolute. Take, for example, the duty to help others in need. While this is an imperfect duty in the sense that there is underspecification in how to discharge it, the duty remains absolute in nature.

Now for the worry facing Kantian deontology's absolutism: What should happen if one's absolute duties were ever to come into conflict? How does Kantian deontology provide guidance in situations wherein one is confronted with multiple absolute duties that, due to the force of the circumstances at hand, cannot all be discharged simultaneously? Could there be situations like that in the first place?

Consider the predicament faced by Corrie ten Boom (1892–1983) and her family during World War II.[17] The ten Boom family lived in an apartment just above her father's watchmaker shop in the town of Haarlem, Netherlands. From May 1940 to February 1944, Corrie and her older sister, Betsie, along with their father, Casper, were motivated by their Christian convictions to use a secret room in their home to hide Jews escaping from the Nazis until the family was betrayed by an informant. Despite the ten Booms being interrogated by the Gestapo, none of the Jews who had been sheltered by the Dutch family were ever found. For their part, the ten Booms were sent to prison, where the eighty-four-year-old Casper died just a few days later. Corrie and Betsie were then transferred to Kamp Vught and then eventually to the infamous Ravensbrück concentration camp, where they were exposed to extreme cruelties. Betsie died there at the age of fifty-six. Then, just before being sent to the gas chamber with the other women in her age bracket, Corrie was released from the camp due to a clerical mistake. She went on to chronicle her family's harrowing experience in her famous book, *The Hiding Place* (1971). Corrie died in 1984 at the age of ninety-one. Because the ten Booms helped to save as many as eight hundred Jewish lives during the holocaust, they were formally declared Righteous Among the Nations by the State of Israel.

Now imagine a Gestapo officer had knocked on the door and asked whether the family was sheltering any Jews. Would it have been morally permissible for Corrie ten Boom to lie in this case? Take a moment and consider your answer.

On the one hand, if Kant is right, ten Boom would have had an absolute duty to tell the truth. On the other hand, so it seems, ten Boom would also have had an absolute duty to protect the lives of those she was sheltering—to prevent their unjust persecution and extermination by the Nazis. After all, if ten Boom had told the truth, the Jews (along with her own family) would have surely been ruthlessly killed by the Nazis. So notice the conflict of absolute duties here: Corrie ten Boom either (a) tells the truth or (b) helps the Jews who are fleeing the Nazis. The problem for Kantian deontology is that, insofar as it contemplates moral duties to be absolute and exceptionless, there is no clear-cut way to adjudicate conflicts of this sort. If a moral theory is going to assert that there are absolute moral duties, then it needs to provide a mechanism by which to adjudicate in situations wherein these duties come into conflict.

Does Kantian deontology have the resources to respond to this problem? Perhaps the distinction between perfect and imperfect duties can do some of the heavy lifting here. One might suggest that *perfect* duties (precisely insofar as they are fully specified and, hence, admit no latitude in how they can be discharged) should be prioritized over *imperfect* duties (which *do* have some latitude in how they can be discharged) in cases where they might come into conflict. Admittedly, this prioritization strategy might adjudicate the conflict of duties in the Corrie ten Boom case, but it would provide no guidance whatsoever in cases where two perfect (or two imperfect) duties might conflict. At any rate, and unfortunately for Kant, this strategy of adjudicating the conflict seems to many critics to produce the exact wrong answer. After all, Kant is adamant in construing the duty to tell the truth as a *perfect* duty, whereas the duty to help is only *imperfect*. Accordingly, if we were to prioritize perfect over imperfect duties in this case, Kantian deontology would advise Corrie ten Boom to tell the truth to the Gestapo over protecting the lives of innocent humans. Many see this particular implication of Kantian deontology as a bullet they are perfectly unwilling to bite.

For that reason, some philosophers recommend a different tack altogether: Hang on to certain key elements of Kantian deontology without hanging on to *all* of them. In particular, some philosophers recommend that we forfeit the Kantian assumption that moral duties are absolute in nature. One such strategy, for example, is offered by the early twentieth-century British philosopher Sir W. D. Ross (1877–1971). To see how this particular strategy could be deployed, we need to pause and consider Ross's unique approach to deontology more generally.

In Ross's view, we apprehend simply by means of moral intuition that we have a *plurality* of moral duties. Importantly, these multiple duties are not reducible to some singular, underlying imperative of practical reason such as Kant's categorical imperative. Rather, Ross holds that we intuitively discern that we have seven basic categories of duties, including duties of fidelity, reparation, gratitude, justice, beneficence, self-improvement, and nonmaleficence (see fig. 5.5).[18] More specifically, Ross contends that we apprehend these various categories of duty (and, hence, the moral rules they would entail) in the same sort of way one might come to see that a mathematical axiom is self-evidently true: "Not in the sense that it is evident from the beginning of our lives, or as soon as we attend to the proposition in the first time, but in the sense that when we have reached sufficient mental maturity and have given sufficient attention to the proposition it is evident without the need of proof, or of evidence beyond itself."[19] In short, we encounter the existence of these seven categories of duties as self-evident.

Figure 5.5. W. D. Ross's Categories of Duties

FIDELITY	Duties to keep one's promises and to tell the truth
REPARATION	Duties to make amends for previous wrong acts
GRATITUDE	Duties to be grateful to others for their services to oneself
JUSTICE	Duties to align the distribution of happiness to merit
BENEFICENCE	Duties to improve the virtue, intelligence, and pleasure of others
SELF-IMPROVEMENT	Duties to improve one's own virtue, intelligence, and pleasure
NONMALEFICENCE	Duties to not harm others

However, in Ross's view, these self-evident duties are simply *prima facie* duties. In other words, they are duties *on the first face of it*, so to speak—that is, they are duties that bind us unless and until they are overridden by some more pressing duty that conflicts in a specific, concrete situation. Accordingly, contra Kant, these duties are not absolute in nature. In fact, these prima facie duties aren't actually full-throated duties in the first place. Rather, they are more like pressing reasons in favor of doing something, reasons that can be trumped by other considerations. Still, reasons are reasons, and we always have a pressing reason to follow the rules entailed by the seven categories of duties listed above (e.g., exercise fidelity, make amends, show gratitude, etc.), which is precisely why we tend to regret not having followed one of these rules even when it gets overridden by one of the other rules in question.

How does Ross's moral theory provide a strategy of adjudicating between conflicting duties? According to Ross, the prima facie duty that should ultimately reign supreme will be illuminated by the details of the situation that brought about a conflict of prima facie duties in the first place. How so? Not through a clean moral decision procedure of the sort Kant imagines but through the exercise of a kind of moral judgment whereby one takes into account all the morally relevant factors involved in the situation and then spots which prima facie duty is the *most* pressing. Ross explains: "There is no principle by which we can draw the conclusion that is on the whole right or on the whole wrong. In this respect the judgment as to the rightness of a particular act is just like the judgement as to the beauty of a particular natural object or work of art."[20] Moral judgment, when properly honed, allows one to adjudicate among the conflicting prima facie duties to determine which one is actually the most important duty—and hence the ultimate, overriding duty—in a situation.

Now notice how, if we interpret Kantian deontology along the lines of Ross's intuitionism, the difficulties of adjudicating between conflicting moral duties start to dissipate, along with the objection on offer. Of course, this strategy comes at a cost, in no small part because Ross's intuitionism invites problems of its own. Is Ross's list of moral duties really self-evident to everyone? Why aren't these duties reducible to some more fundamental, underlying imperative of practical reason? And is the appeal to moral judgment—and a lack of a fixed strategy for ranking these prima facie duties—something like an appeal to a moral Spidey-sense? Is this an adequate account of the moral life?

Even if the answers to those questions are ready at hand, another question remains in the wings: How should the rejection of absolutism be viewed from the perspective of the Christian faith? On the one hand, the duties outlined in the Decalogue might seem to be absolute in nature—no exceptions. They are, after all, *commandments*, not suggestions. On the other hand, there are places in Hebrew and Christian Scriptures where exceptions to some of those very same commandments might seem to be implied.

Consider, for example, the situation facing two Hebrew midwives, Shiphrah and Puah, as described in the first chapter of Exodus. The midwives had been ordered by the Egyptian pharaoh to kill any baby boy born to a Hebrew woman. Shiphrah and Puah rightly refused. When they were summoned by the pharaoh to explain why they were allowing the babies to live, they responded by saying, "Hebrew women are not like Egyptian women; they are vigorous and give birth before the midwives arrive" (Exod. 1:19 NIV). According to the text, God was kind to the midwives and rewarded them with families of their own.

Or consider the case of the prostitute Rahab of Jericho as recounted in the book of Joshua. Rahab hid two Israelite spies who had been staying at her house. When she was ordered by the king of Jericho to turn over the two spies, she replied: "Yes, the men came to me, but I did not know where they had come from. At dusk, when it was time to close the city gate, they left. I don't know which way they went. Go after them quickly. You may catch up with them" (Josh. 2:4–5 NIV). Ultimately, precisely because she helped the spies, Rahab's life was spared. What is more, the author of the book of Hebrews even identifies Rahab as an exemplar of faith.

Lastly, in this connection, consider the case in which Jesus appears to allow for exceptions to laws that ordinarily forbade Jews from picking grain on the Sabbath. Jesus cites David's justification for eating the consecrated bread that was ordinarily lawful only for priests. According to Jesus, David was justified in his situation because "he and his companions were hungry and in need" (Mark 2:25 NIV).

Did Shiphrah and Puah actually *lie* in the case mentioned above? Or was their response to the pharaoh technically correct—namely, that the Hebrew women were having their babies *before* the midwives arrived? In a similar vein, was Rahab's answer to the king of Jericho technically true? Or was she intentionally deceiving the king in order to protect the lives of the Israelite spies? (After all, she eventually went to the spies in the very location they had been hiding: her roof.) If the midwives or Rahab weren't telling the truth, do either or both of these cases present us with an exception to the prohibition against bearing false witness (in order, say, to protect innocent lives), and hence a scriptural reason to question moral absolutism? Does Jesus's case present us with an exception to the commandment to remember the Sabbath and keep it holy (in order, say, to prevent starvation), and hence a reason to question moral absolutism? We leave the matter for readers to decide.

Kantian deontology has it wrong on moral motivation

Suppose the previous concerns can be adequately addressed. A very different objection to Kantian deontology pertains to Kant's account of the good. Recall that, in Kant's view, a good will is defined as a will that moves one to do one's duty *for the sake of doing one's duty*. Accordingly, one's dutiful actions are morally praiseworthy only if they are done for the sake of doing one's moral duty—and not for some other reason like pursuing one's self-interests or acting out of habit or inclination. Notice that the underlying motivation of a good will is simply to do one's duty.

Some critics worry that, in at least some cases, Kant simply fails to capture the correct view about *why* one should be motivated to be moral. To see the worry here, consider an intriguing example offered by Michael Stocker:

> Suppose you are in a hospital, recovering from a long illness. You are very bored and restless and at loose ends when [your friend] Smith comes in. . . . You are now convinced more than ever that he is a fine fellow and a real friend—taking so much time to cheer you up, travelling all the way across town, and so on. You are so effusive with your praise and thanks that he protests that he always tries to do what he thinks is his duty, what he thinks will be best. You at first think he is engaging in a polite form of self-deprecation, relieving the moral burden. But the more you two speak, the more clear it becomes that he came to see you, not because you are friends, but because he thought it his duty, perhaps as a fellow Christian . . . or simply because he knows of no one more in need of cheering up and no one easier to cheer up.[21]

Now for the million-dollar question. Suppose *you* were the one in the hospital. Would *you* be disappointed in Smith? Do *you* think Smith had the wrong motivation for coming to see you? Does Smith's behavior strike you as morally *praiseworthy*?

If Kant is right, Smith has exhibited a good will in this case: He has done his duty (visiting you in the hospital) not for *your* sake or even for *Smith's* own sake but simply *for the sake of doing his duty*. Yet some of us will no doubt disagree with Kant and agree with Stocker's assessment that something seems to be lacking here—something "lacking in moral merit or value."[22] In Stocker's view, "the wrong sort of thing is said to be the proper motive."[23] Notice how Kantian deontology excludes as a proper motive for moral behavior the following things: acting for the sake of one's friend; acting out of care or compassion for someone who is suffering; acting out of love for one's neighbor; acting for the sake of pursuing the good life or fulfilling one's nature; acting out of an intentionally cultivated habit of visiting the sick and shut-in; acting for the sake of manifesting the fruits of the Holy Spirit (e.g., love, kindness, gentleness, faithfulness, etc.); acting for the sake of glorifying God; acting for the sake of pleasing God or doing God's will, and so on. Accordingly, or so one might conclude, Kantian deontology has either a flawed answer or an incomplete answer to the question of "Why should one be moral?"

Kantian deontology trusts practical reason over divine revelation

While Kant's moral theory might seem to fit with certain Christian presuppositions and affirmations about the nature of morality, in other ways it can seem to clash. One general sort of concern a Christian might have with Kantian deontology is that it upholds *reason*—and specifically the categorical imperative of practical reason—as that which is to be trusted over all things—even over divine revelation (as conveyed in Scripture, for example).[24] In Kant's view, for example, if some part of Scripture (or any other putative source of divine commands) were ever to conflict with the requirements of the categorical imperative, then we should simply reject it as being not *from God* in the first place. That's because, for Kant, God could never and would never command something contrary to the categorical imperative of practical reason. Effectively, then, God is subject to something independent of God's will, namely something like an objective moral law. In fact, Kant comments that "God is Himself good and Holy because His will conforms to this objective law."[25]

Pay attention to the implications of Kant's view when we reflect on what appears to be God's command to Abraham to sacrifice his son Isaac (Gen. 22) or for the Israelites to plunder Egypt (Exod. 11). Notice how Abraham's maxim in particular ("I will kill my son when . . .") would seem to be perfectly nonuniversalizable. So, in Kant's view, reason tells us in no uncertain terms that we have a perfect duty to refrain from child sacrifice. Accordingly, it would seem that Kant's recommendation, then, is essentially to remove (or substantially reinterpret) a page from the biblical canon. In fact, Kant explicitly says, "Abraham should have replied to this supposedly divine voice: 'That I ought not kill my good son is quite certain. But that you, this apparition, are God—of that I am *not* certain, and *never can be*, not even if this voice rings down to me from (visible) heaven.'"[26] The bottom line for Kant is that we should trust reason over Scripture or, for that matter, direct divine commands.

Does this constitute a fatal objection to Kantian deontology from a Christian perspective? Perhaps one might suppose that reason should simply be used in precisely the manner suggested by Kant to properly discern (or interpret) what are—and what are *not* and *could not be*—God's commands. But at least some tension remains, to be sure, as do some hard questions. Should we trust practical reason *over* divine revelation? Does reason simply chasten our view of what counts as divine revelation in the first place—and hence dictate how to interpret Scripture? Or should reason be chastened by divine revelation?

The right cannot be prior to the good

Even if the previous objections and worries can be mitigated on Kant's behalf, there is at least one final concern facing Kantian deontology from the perspective of the Christian tradition. Recall that Kantian deontology is committed to thinking that the *right* is prior to the *good*. After all, Kant defines that which is intrinsically and unqualifiedly good (the good will) in terms of what is right—doing one's duty for the sake of doing one's duty. Precisely because the good (namely, good will) is defined in terms of the right (namely, duty), the right explanatorily *precedes* the good in his view. In other words, the right is more *fundamental* than the good. That's why, in Kant's view, God is good—that is, God has a good will—*because* God somehow conforms to what is right as defined by an objective moral law (which is presumably independent of God).

But all of that seems to conflict with a key assumption of Christian theism, and here's why. The Christian tradition contemplates God as that than which nothing greater can be conceived—that is, God is understood to be a perfect being. At least part of what it means to be the perfect being is to be what explains everything else. (If something else did part of the explaining in question, then we could think of something greater, namely that which did *all* the explaining.) And to be the explainer of all else is to be explanatorily prior to all else. Assuming a perfect God exists, then God is explanatorily prior to all else. Now if something is a perfect being, then it is necessarily good. (If something is only contingently good, then we could think of something greater, namely something that is necessarily good.) So if God is explanatorily prior to all else *and* necessarily good, then that which is necessarily good (God) would have to be explanatorily prior to any and all moral duties that God might ever incur (if, indeed, God has any moral duties). In other words, if a perfect being such as God exists, then it would be fair to say—contra Kant—that the good is prior to the right.

chapter six

SOCIAL CONTRACT THEORY

Just two years after the end of the US Civil War, Congress formed a commission to negotiate a peace agreement between the federal government and several American Indian nations of the southern Great Plains. Distrust, antagonism, and bloodshed had long marked the relationship between Native American tribes and the White Americans who increasingly expanded their new country's western frontier. The construction of North America's first transcontinental railroad during the 1860s served only to exacerbate the friction and violence in the flatlands. All sides were motivated to seek a truce. Among other things, the American Indian tribes wanted some assurance that continued encroachments into their territories would cease and desist. The US government, for its part, calculated that the inevitable concessions of a peace settlement would ultimately prove less deadly—and less costly—than continued and prolonged military engagements. So in October 1867, the government's peace commission, led by Senator John Henderson of Missouri, met with representatives of the Kiowa, Comanche, Arapaho, and Kiowa Apache nations—and eventually with the Southern Cheyenne nation—to hash out the terms of three separate but largely identical treaties at Medicine Lodge Creek, a sacred site located in what is today Kansas. In exchange for amity and relocation away from traditional tribal lands—and, hence, away from the path of westward US expansion—the tribes were granted millions of acres of land in western Indian Territory (in what is now Oklahoma) along with provisions of food and equipment, as well as buffalo hunting rights. Importantly, under Article 12 of those treaties, the tribes were guaranteed that no cession of their new reservation lands could take place in the future unless three-fourths of the Native American adult male population approved. The treaties were signed by several Indian chiefs and ultimately ratified by the US Senate in July 1868.

Within a year, however, allotments to the American Indian tribes came to a halt. And the infamous Union general William Tecumseh Sherman—who had also served on the federal government's peace commission—acted to prevent the hunting rights defined under the treaties. In due course, the federal government started chipping away at the size of the Indian reservations—and without the required approval of the affected tribes. In turn, the American Indian tribes retaliated, and the old hostilities resumed. By the dawn of the twentieth century, the controversy came to a boiling point. Kiowa Chief Lone Wolf the Younger filed a lawsuit against the Secretary of the Interior, claiming that Article 12 of the Medicine Lodge Creek treaties had been violated. That landmark case, *Lone Wolf v. Hitchcock* (1903), eventually worked its way to the Supreme Court. The justices of the high court ultimately ruled that Congress held "plenary power" on the matter—that is, absolute and unlimited power—and could thereby simply nullify any and all prior treaties with the American Indians, whom the court dubbed an "ignorant and dependent race" who are effectively "wards" of the federal government.[1]

At least part of the indignation one can feel when reflecting on this episode in American history is connected to an intuition that many regard as central to the nature of what we owe each other as people—namely, the intuition that *agreement* matters in a special, unique, and even fundamental way. A theoretical framework that builds on this intuition in particular is often known as social contract theory (or contractualism, contractarianism, or constructivism). This general framework is perhaps most often discussed within the context of political philosophy, in part because it also provides a helpful explanation for what might justify the use of the coercive power of government. But this framework can also be contemplated as a theory of morality, which is the focus of the present chapter.

Both as a theory of politics and as a theory of morality, social contract theory (hereafter, "SCT") has a long and prominent role within Western civilization, spanning from Greek antiquity up through the American civil rights movement of the 1960s. Key elements of the SCT tradition can be seen in the works of Plato (ca. 429–347 BC), particularly in his *Crito* and also his *Republic*. But the SCT tradition has been especially prominent in the modern era since the sixteenth century. Perhaps the most famous presentation of SCT is found in the work of the English philosopher Thomas Hobbes (1588–1679), though it was further developed in the work of key Enlightenment thinkers such as John Locke (1632–1704), Samuel Pufendorf (1632–1694), and Jean-Jacques Rousseau (1712–1778), among others. In many respects, the SCT tradition has played an especially salient role within American history, in no small part because of its influence on several of the key figures involved in the initial framing of the US government and its surrounding legal and political culture. And the influence of SCT can be seen in the language of several key founding documents of the United States, including the Declaration of Independence and the Constitution.

6.1. What Social Contract Theory Says

SCT depicts the moral life as being governed by the set of rules by which free, equal, rational, and self-interested individuals would agree to be bound, provided others agree to be bound by them as well. In other words, according to SCT, our moral obligations and duties are defined by a set of rules to which free, equal, rational, and self-interested individuals would agree in a fair initial negotiation. Accordingly, we would have moral obligations to refrain from, say, murder or theft precisely because such actions would run afoul of a general rule (e.g., "Don't do unto others what you don't want done unto yourself") that free, equal, rational, and self-interested individuals would agree to follow if they were to establish the basic contours of society from scratch. Accordingly, moral behavior can be thought of as the terms of a freely entered agreement—a contract—hashed out by the individuals who make up society.

There are five key features—three central affirmations and two noteworthy characteristics—of SCT that we will highlight moving forward:

i. The moral status of one's action depends on whether it conforms to certain rules, and the status of those rules ultimately depends on agreement.
ii. The relevant parties to this agreement are free, equal, rational, self-interested individuals.
iii. The rules to which these individuals would agree in a fair initial negotiation are of special importance.
iv. SCT represents a minimalist approach to moral theory.
v. SCT presupposes a thin account of the good.

The first central affirmation of SCT is what we might think of as an *agreement-dependency thesis* according to which the rules of morality are most fundamentally a product of a special sort of agreement. Importantly, this special agreement is the most fundamental right-making (or wrong-making) mechanism. Notice how such an agreement-dependency thesis distinguishes SCT from other theories that hold that morality most fundamentally depends on, say, culture, the maximization of best consequences, concerns about universalizability of maxims, facts about human nature, or God's commands. For SCT, agreement among free, equal, rational, and self-interested individuals does all the heavy lifting.

Second, SCT affirms the *centrality of individuals*. In other words, individual persons—as opposed to families or tribes or communities or society as a whole—take center stage in the imagination of SCT. Importantly, the individual parties to the contract—the contractors, so to speak—are contemplated as being, by nature, fully autonomous and wholly discrete from one another and of a certain quality. Namely, in their most natural state, individuals are imagined to be free (versus coerced or compelled from outside), roughly equal to one another in their capacities, rational (versus nonrational), and concerned with furthering their own self-interests (even if they are not exclusively concerned with their own interests). These points are commonly thought to be relatively uncontroversial assumptions about what humans are like in their most natural, presocietal state.

Third, SCT places special emphasis on what individual contractors would agree to in a fair initial negotiation. Notice, for starters, how we would need to imagine an initial negotiation that is *fair*. Why? Terms derived though unfair, prejudiced, or biased means don't really reflect the will of (all) the parties involved in a negotiation. Accordingly, terms obtained in an unfair negotiation wouldn't be binding upon the contractors, and hence those terms *couldn't* produce the rules of morality. So the negotiation must be fair. Furthermore, notice also how we need to imagine what contractors would agree to in an *initial* negotiation. The thought here is that we need to imagine what contractors would agree to if they had a chance to select the rules that would form and regulate their society from the ground up. Now, it can be easy to get the wrong impression here. The point here is *not* that this initial negotiation is, say, a description of some actual historical event that took place long ago. Nor should we contemplate the initial negotiation as a model for deliberations that we could actually set up in the future. Rather, for SCT, describing an initial negotiation among free, equal, rational, and self-interested contractors is basically a thought experiment—an intellectual device—that helps us imagine what such contractors *would agree to* if such a negotiation were ever to occur. Such a thought experiment, in turn, helps us identify the basic rules of morality precisely because it helps isolate rules that would be *freely* accepted by *rational* individuals who are concerned with their own interests under *fair* conditions of *equality*.

A fourth key feature of SCT is that it does not require especially deep assertions (or denials) about the fundamental nature of reality. For example, a noteworthy characteristic of SCT is that it can seem to remain neutral about such matters as God's existence, remote consequences until the end of history, controversial claims about human nature or psychology, robust accounts about what humans desire, need, or require for happiness or flourishing, and so on. Accordingly, SCT appears to represent a relatively modest and even minimalist approach to theorizing about the nature of morality. SCT travels light, as it were. It remains metaphysically neutral and stays on the surface, philosophically speaking—or so it seems.

Lastly, and along similar lines, SCT presupposes what we might think of as a *thin account of the good*. In other words, SCT has very few (if any) commitments about what is intrinsically good or intrinsically evil and maintains instead something of a neutral position toward the competing accounts of the good that might be endorsed or presupposed by the free, equal, rational, and self-interested contractors involved in the initial negotiation. Practically speaking, SCT simply has very little to say about good and evil and, instead, focuses on providing a process for determining the rules that, in turn, determine what is obligatory, optional, or wrong. In effect, the only account of the good that factors prominently in SCT pertains to the interests, goals, and preferences the individual contractors might have in mind. Accordingly, social contract theory does not offer or presuppose a singular account of the good in any straightforward sense, and this fact helps distinguish SCT from nearly all other theories of morality.

We are now in a position to summarize an SCT account of the right in the following way. An action is morally obligatory if and only if and just because it is required by the rules that free, equal, rational, and self-interested individuals would in a fair initial negotiation agree to follow, provided that others do so as well. An action is morally wrong if and only if and just because it violates one of those rules. And an action is optional if and only if and just because it does not violate one of those rules. Accordingly, SCT's moral decision procedure can be stated as follows:

> STEP 1: Determine the set of rules that would be agreed to by free, equal, rational, and self-interested individuals in a fair initial negotiation.
>
> STEP 2: Determine whether a given action is required by or violates one of those rules.
>
> STEP 3: Act accordingly.

6.2. The Case for Social Contract Theory

Various arguments for SCT have been formulated throughout the centuries. We will here attempt to reconstruct two of the most formidable sets of considerations in favor of SCT. Although we will present these as though they are separate arguments, they can be regarded as working in tandem to offer a cumulative case for SCT. We close this section with a brief critical reflection on some of the worries facing the overall case for SCT.

The Hobbesian state of nature argument

Perhaps the most famous case for SCT hails from the dramatic thought experiment in Thomas Hobbes's *Leviathan* (1651), which runs roughly as follows. Imagine what we humans would be like in our most natural, primitive, undeveloped, unmodified, unadulterated, prepolitical state. Imagine, in other words, what we would be like in what Hobbes calls the *state of nature*. There would of course be no government, no laws, no rulers, no police, no courts, no schools, no libraries, no institutions, and no other artifices of society in the state of nature. We would be left to our own devices, as it were—stripped of everything we didn't come into existence with as individuals.

What exactly does that include? It is safe to assume that in the state of nature individuals would be capable of reasoning about their interests and about how to pursue them. Humans are rational creatures, after all. And it seems safe enough to assume that individuals in a state of nature would indeed be concerned with their own self-interests—about how to secure sufficient food, shelter, clothing, and so on. And individuals would be free in a state of nature—maximally free, in fact—to pursue those interests *by any means necessary*. Why is that? Remember, in a state of nature, there would be no social artifices in place to limit what individuals may do. So, in a state of nature, individuals would be rational, self-interested, and maximally free. What is more, though, individuals in a state of nature would be roughly equal to one another. Sure, some individuals might be bigger or taller or stronger in one sense. But in another sense, individuals would be more or less equal in their ability to pursue their interests; there would be neither king nor peasant in the state of nature.

Now, although individuals would be more or less equal in their ability to pursue their own interests, there would still be a limited, finite supply of resources in a state of nature. What that means is that, because individuals would be free to pursue their own interests by any means necessary, the state of nature would inevitably become a struggle of competing interests:

Everyone would want the very same supply of resources, but not everyone could have it all at the same time. One individual would need what another individual would have, and there would be no rules or government or other artifices of society to prevent the one from taking it by force. Hobbes depicts the situation as akin to a state of war:

> Whatsoever therefore is consequent to a time of Warre, where every man is Enemy to every man; the same is consequent to the time, wherein men live without other security, than what their own strength, and their own invention shall furnish them withall. In such condition, there is no place for Industry; because the fruit thereof is uncertain: and consequently no Culture of the Earth; no Navigation, nor use of the commodities that may be imported by Sea; no commodious Building; no Instruments of moving, and removing such things as require much force; no Knowledge of the face of the earth; no account of Time; no Arts; no Letters; no Society; and which is worst of all, continuall feare, and danger of violent death; and the life of man, solitary, poore, nasty, brutish, and short.[2]

To put it mildly, the state of nature is no walk in the park. Notice that, as Hobbes describes the situation, individuals in the state of nature would inevitably find themselves fearing the rather imminent possibility of violent death. Why is that? In a state of nature, everyone would be free to pursue one's own interests *by any means necessary*. When conflict inevitably arises due to the limited, finite supply of the resources, violence would erupt, and each would be left to fend for oneself. So individuals in a state of nature would need to sleep with one eye open, so to speak.

The fear of imminent death is of course a powerful thing. And it would provide individuals in a state of nature with some rather serious motivation to get out of their predicament. Accordingly, individuals in a state of nature would have ample reason to seek a truce—some way of getting along with others so they wouldn't be at each other's throats continually. Since they would be rational, they would understand this. And since they would be self-interested, they would certainly want this, too.

How far would individuals be willing to go to exit the state of nature? In Hobbes's depiction, they would be willing to agree with one another to forfeit at least a portion of the otherwise unlimited freedom they would possess in the state of nature—to be bound in certain ways, that is—on the condition that others do so as well. In so doing, individuals would effectively band together and negotiate a contract of sorts, as if to say, "To endeavor peace, I will forfeit my natural liberty of pursuing my own self-interests *by any means necessary* as long as you do the same!" In so agreeing with one another, individuals exiting the state of nature would freely agree to certain contractual terms—that is, general rules that govern human behavior—which thereby become binding moving forward. John Locke explains why they would be willing to do this:

> If man in the state of nature be so free, as has been said; if he be absolute lord of his own person and possessions, equal to the greatest, and subject to no body, why will he part with his freedom? Why will he give up this empire, and subject himself to the dominion and controul of any other power? To which it is obvious to answer, that though in the state of nature he hath such a right, yet the enjoyment of it is very uncertain, and constantly exposed to the invasion of others: for all being kings as much as he, every man his equal, and the greater part no strict observers of equity and justice, the enjoyment of the property he has in this state is very unsafe, very unsecure. This makes him willing to quit a condition, which, however free, is full of fears and continual dangers: and it is not without reason, that he seeks out, and is willing to join in society with others, who are already united, or have a mind to unite, for the mutual *preservation* of their lives, liberties and estates, which I call by the general name, *property*.[3]

Notice how the terms agreed upon by the contractors in the initial negotiation give birth to what is obligatory, forbidden, and optional moving forward. Since the individual contractors would be concerned with their own self-interests—even if they wouldn't be concerned with them exclusively—they would of course agree only to those rules that they would perceive as amenable to their understanding of their own interests. Since individuals would be equal in the initial negotiation, there would be no unfairness to mislead them in the process of deciding which rules to agree to. Since they would be freely entering the contract, they would be uncoerced. And since they would freely agree to follow certain rules (provided others do so as well), those rules would be effectively self-selected, which is why they would be morally binding. Who or what makes those rules morally binding? The contractors. By what means? Agreement! Or so goes the Hobbesian state of nature argument for SCT.

We can outline the basic argument implied by this thought experiment in the following manner:

(1) In a state of nature, individuals would be free, equal, rational, and self-interested.

(2) Due to limited resources, the state of nature would inevitably result in violent conflict.

(3) Because they would fear death in the state of nature, it would be rational for equal and self-interested individuals to seek a truce.

(4) To achieve this, equal, rational, self-interested individuals would *freely* agree to be bound by certain rules, provided others do so as well.

(5) If equal, rational, and self-interested individuals would freely agree to rules R_1–R_n, then R_1–R_n would be morally binding on them (because R_1–R_n would be rationally judged to be advantageous, and they would be fairly and freely selected by those to whom they would apply).

(6) Thus, SCT is the correct theory of morality.

The explanatory and practical benefits argument

We can also supplement the case for SCT in far less dramatic ways by simply highlighting the explanatory and practical benefits of the theory itself. Suppose we found ourselves thinking in the ruins, so to speak. In other words, suppose all the other rival stories about the foundations of morality have failed and, hence, that they cannot explain key features of our experience as moral creatures. Yet surely those salient features of our experience stand in need of some sort of explanation, not least that we have moral obligations in the first place. And it is here where one might argue that SCT provides a helpful framework for explaining what stands in need of explanation.

Consider a few of the things that SCT brings to the table, explanatorily speaking.[4] First, SCT can help explain why we ought to follow certain common-sense rules—that is, rules that seem intuitively correct, like "don't kill wantonly," "don't cheat," "don't steal," and so on. According to SCT, we should abide by those rules precisely because they are what free, equal, and rational individuals would agree to in a fair initial negotiation. Why would they do so, exactly? Well, such rules, when followed, will allow everyone to get along; they provide for peaceful coexistence in society. Notice, then, how SCT seems to provide an objective basis for morality in a way that can seem to circumvent the need to weigh in on controversial questions about, say, theories of psychology (such as psychological egoism), or robust accounts of human happiness, or universalizability, or even whether God exists.

Second, SCT can seem to provide a satisfying answer to the question, Why should one be moral? The answer offered by SCT goes thusly: In the long run, it is in one's own best interest to be moral—that is, to follow the rules that free, equal, rational, self-interested parties would agree to—even if following those rules can sometimes play to one's own personal disadvantage. That's because one faces social sanctions and punishment if one does not follow those rules. And *in general*, being a part of a society that enforces such rules is far superior to the nastier, more brutish, and shorter alternative (i.e., the state of nature), hands down.

Third, SCT can help explain why and under which circumstances it might be justifiable to *not* follow the rules—namely, when the terms of the contract have been violated, or when the parties who should have been included in the initial negotiation weren't actually included or represented in the first place. Consider the first kind of case, where the terms of the contract have been broken. Suppose a rule that contractors would agree to is "don't do to others what you don't want them to do to you." Now imagine someone acts in ways that violate this rule, either by defrauding someone else, or stealing another's property, or by killing them. That individual would thereby forfeit his claim to having others refrain from treating him in undesirable ways: There would now be justification for, say, locking up the perpetrator or for punishing him by some other means. SCT provides a framework for explaining this.

Or imagine cases where parties who *should* have been included in an initial negotiation were neither included nor represented. This is the sort of complaint made by key figures in the American civil rights movement. For example, in 1955, Rosa Parks (1913–2005) refused to obey the city ordinance of Montgomery, Alabama, that would have required her to give up her bus seat to a White man. Part of the point of doing this was to bring public awareness to the fact that the civil rights of African Americans—their rational self-interests—had been historically and systematically excluded from consideration throughout the segregated Jim Crow South. In other words, Parks helped illuminate the fact that African Americans had been excluded from the negotiation of the rules that governed the social contexts in which they lived. The actions taken by Rev. Martin Luther King Jr. (1929–1968) can be interpreted along similar lines. After being locked up in April 1963 for violating a court injunction and leading a protest, King explained his civil disobedience in his famous "Letter from a Birmingham Jail":

> You may well ask: "Why direct action? Why sit ins, marches and so forth? Isn't negotiation a better path?" You are quite right in calling for negotiation. Indeed, *this is the very purpose of direct action.* Nonviolent direct action seeks to create such a crisis and foster such a tension that a community which has constantly refused to negotiate is forced to confront the issue. It seeks so to dramatize the issue that it can no longer be ignored. My citing the creation of tension as part of the work of the nonviolent resister may sound rather shocking. But I must confess that I am not afraid of the word "tension." I have earnestly opposed violent tension, but there is a type of constructive, nonviolent tension which is necessary for growth. Just as Socrates felt that it was necessary to create a tension in the mind so that individuals

> could rise from the bondage of myths and half truths to the unfettered realm of creative analysis and objective appraisal, so must we see the need for nonviolent gadflies to create the kind of tension in society that will help men rise from the dark depths of prejudice and racism to the majestic heights of understanding and brotherhood. *The purpose of our direct action program is to create a situation so crisis packed that it will inevitably open the door to negotiation.*[5]

Notice how King endeavored to draw widespread attention to the fact that the rules he and others disobeyed were not those that *all* free, equal, rational, and self-interested parties would agree to in a fair initial negotiation—precisely because African Americans were never included in the initial negotiation of those rules to begin with, which is why King sought to "open the door to negotiation," as he put it. This highlights a point relevant to the overall case for SCT. SCT provides an explanation for why, and under which conditions, we might be justified in *not* following certain rules: when the negotiation that inaugurated those rules wasn't fair precisely because it excluded those who should have been included in the negotiation.

Lastly, in addition to the explanatory work provided by the theory, proponents of SCT can also point to very practical things for which social contracts can provide. For example, they can provide for social coexistence, peace over war, a reduction of human suffering, improved odds for individuals to pursue their own interests as they understand them, and a way of resolving real-life conflicts.[6] These benefits provide incremental evidence in favor of thinking SCT is the correct account of morality—or so the thought goes.

How strong is the overall case for SCT? When evaluating it critically, we should pay attention to the fact that it assumes, on some level, that rival accounts of morality are insufficient to the task at hand. Of course, the better those rival accounts actually are, the less motivated SCT will seem. This particular point is perhaps especially salient for *theists*. After all, whether it is actually an advantage of SCT that it does not require buy-in on what some might regard as controversial metaphysical assumptions (e.g., God's existence) hangs on whether one finds those assumptions controversial in the first place. If one accepts the metaphysical claims of alternative accounts of morality (after all, theists believe that God exists), one will be less motivated to accept SCT as the way to think our way out of the ruins, as it were. Admittedly, theists might still welcome the thought that we indeed ought to abide by the rules that free, equal, rational, and self-interested people would accept in a fair initial negotiation—even while denying that the rules are morally binding on us *just because* free, equal, rational, and self-interested contractors would accept them. In other words, so the theist might say, perhaps there is an even better explanation for what makes those rules morally binding in the first place.

There is another worry in the vicinity. While SCT is often taken to be metaphysically minimalist in nature, it is not without metaphysical controversies of its own. After all, SCT appears to smuggle in certain assumptions about the fundamental nature of reality that are at least debatable. Focus on premise 1 of the Hobbesian state of nature argument above, for example. Notice how SCT presupposes that individuals in the state of nature would be—in their most natural state—free, equal, rational, and self-interested. What also seems to be assumed in the background here is that these individuals would be fully autonomous and independent of one another. That is to say, SCT seems to presume that human beings are, in their most natural state, atomistic, unencumbered selves who are wholly discrete and fully detached from one another, which is precisely why the uncoordinated pursuit of their individual self-interests would inevitably result in violent conflict and insecurity, which in turn would motivate them to seek a truce. In fact, the Hobbesian argument for SCT banks on this being an accurate representation of what humans are like in our most natural state.

But this picture is at least debatable, if not just plainly false. And the reason is that, in many ways, we humans are actually situated, *encumbered* selves.[7] That is, in reality, we come into the world not as discrete, autonomous, atomistic individuals but always already as sons and daughters, brothers and sisters, members of this or that community, here and now, with this or that history and tradition—for better or worse. Those facts about us at least partially stake out the parameters within which our lives in turn are animated, and they lay the groundwork for certain obligations for us, too—obligations that we did nothing to select or agree to. Accordingly, when we imagine ourselves in a state of nature in the way that the SCT seems to envision, we are contemplating abstracted and idealized versions of ourselves, bracketing off those encumbrances that at least partially define us as real, living human selves. What that means, then, is that the thought experiment Hobbes invites us into runs the risk of having us imagine ourselves in ways that don't actually reflect what we are, by nature, actually like. At the very least, SCT banks on a controversial account about human nature.

Along similar lines, we might worry that SCT also smuggles a controversial account of the good through the back door, so to speak—all under the guise of seeming *neutral* with respect to competing accounts of good and evil. SCT seems to assume that something is good solely in virtue of the fact that individuals value it—and for no other reason. But such a presupposition about the nature of the good would certainly conflict with an alternative account of the good according to which certain things are *intrinsically* good, regardless of whether they are valued by any human valuer. So even if SCT intends to remain neutral with respect to competing comprehensive accounts of the good, it is not clear how SCT can follow through on that intention.

6.3. The Case against Social Contract Theory

Even if the positive case for SCT can withstand scrutiny, SCT still invites a host of objections. We will briefly mention four such objections, with some attention to what can be said in defense of SCT. The final objection is of special concern to Christians.

SCT cannot explain why the contract is morally binding

SCT envisions free, equal, rational, self-interested individuals entering into a solemn agreement to be bound in certain ways, provided others do so as well. One concern with SCT stems from the simple fact that this initial negotiation never actually took place—that is, it was never a real, historical event in the past. The worry, of course, is that a negotiation that never occurred—like a contract that was never signed—doesn't do anything for anybody. But suppose such an agreement *did* take place in the past. In other words, suppose our ancestors actually sat down at the table of a fair initial negotiation. The problem now becomes this: Why should the terms agreed upon by our ancestors in the *past* be morally binding on us *now*? After all, their contract surely wasn't *our* contract, was it? Or so the critic might ask.[8]

Perhaps the correct response to this last question is something akin to what Socrates offers to his interlocutors in Plato's *Crito*—namely, that we somehow tacitly consent to the terms of our ancestors' social contract by remaining in the society they formed, by receiving its benefits, and by *not leaving*. The underlying thought here is that, in principle, we could always exit the contract hashed out by our ancestors by simply leaving the society into which we were born. Of course, one of the problems with this line of defense is that we cannot actually exit stage left to the Hobbesian state of nature, as it were—*that* option isn't really open to us. Sure, we might migrate to, say, another country or continent. But there is really nowhere we can go where someone else couldn't turn around and claim that we now have stepped into an implied social contract by being in that new place.

To circumvent this sort of concern, we might just restrict ourselves to contemplating the social contract as being strictly *hypothetical* in nature. In other words, the social contract is merely what free, equal, rational, self-interested individuals *would* agree to if they ever *were* to negotiate things out. Notice the use of counterfactual, subjunctive language here. The claim here is decidedly not that contractors actually sat down at the initial negotiation at some point in the past and agreed on rules that are somehow still binding on us. Rather, the claim is that, hypothetically speaking, idealized free, equal, rational, self-interested individuals *would* agree to this or that rule if they ever *were* to come to the table of an initial, fair negotiation.

Three problems remain for SCT though.[9] First, why should we suppose there is any fact of the matter about what such hypothetical contractors would agree to? Second, even if there are such subjunctive facts, why should we suppose we could ever figure out what they are? And, third, even if there are such facts, and even if we could correctly discern what they are, we might wonder how exactly such a hypothetical agreement by hypothetical people has binding power on *us*—that is, *actual people*. After all, if our ancestors' agreements aren't morally binding on us, then why would the agreement of nonexistent hypothetical persons be any different?

Perhaps those question can be satisfactorily addressed. But if they cannot be addressed, then SCT has not and cannot explain *why* the terms of the social contract are supposed to be binding on us, in which case it has failed to offer an explanation of the rules of morality.

SCT cannot explain why rational free riders are immoral

Even if hypothetical agreements made by hypothetical persons are morally binding on actual people (namely, us), SCT faces another problem: explaining why those who would appear to be acting rationally in pursuit of their own self-interests are nonetheless acting immorally. To see the problem at hand, consider what we might think of as the case of *rational free riders*. In general, we can think of a free rider as someone who benefits from the collective sacrifice of most folks in the community in pursuit of some common good but who makes no accompanying sacrifice oneself. A problem for SCT arises in cases wherein a free rider might seem fully rational in taking the free ride.

An illustration will help. Just two years after the initial outbreak of the COVID-19 pandemic, more than 6.3 million people worldwide had died of the virus, with more than a million of those deaths occurring in the United States. Those are terrible data, to be sure. However, before global vaccination efforts took full effect, as many as three hundred million people worldwide died of smallpox during the twentieth century—more than were killed in all the world's wars during the same period.[10] Now imagine a moment prior to the eradication of smallpox. Suppose a healthy young man refuses to be vaccinated, while nearly everyone else gets vaccinated. In this case, the anti-vaxxer would be a classic free rider: He benefits from the fact that virtually everyone else shoulders the inconvenience and (minor) medical risks associated with getting immunized, and because the threat of transmission is flattened by the mass vaccinations, he gets all the benefit without making any sacrifices himself.

Now suppose this individual reasoned through his decision to refuse the vaccine in the following way: "Why should *I* get vaccinated? Everyone else is doing it—in fact, far more than is necessary to ensure eradication.

So it would be superfluous for *me* to get vaccinated too. If I were to do so, no one would be made better off. My own personal costs (inconvenience or potential risks) would only go up. But why should I accept even a small cost for no resulting benefit? That would be irrational. So I'll just refuse the vaccination and enjoy the benefit of what everyone else has done while incurring none of the costs myself." In this sort of case, then, the anti-vaxxer might seem to be a *rational free rider*.

It can be tempting to think that the free rider in this case is behaving immorally. For one thing, the free rider can seem selfish: He gets all the gain with none of the pain, so to speak. Plus, he isn't following the rules that, presumably, would be agreed to by hypothetical contractors in the hypothetical initial fair negotiation. But why should that matter? After all, the anti-vaxxer in this case still seems to be behaving in a rational, self-interested way. Why should he embrace the slogan "no pain, no gain" if he can get all the gain without any of the pain? So here's the rub: Given that SCT depicts morality as consisting in the set of rules that would be agreed to by free, equal, rational, self-interested individuals, it seems like a problem that our free riding anti-vaxxer is behaving in a way that can appear *both* rationally self-interested *and* immoral. How can SCT explain this? Can there actually be cases wherein rationally self-interested behavior is indeed *immoral*? Or is the free rider here actually not acting *rationally*? To add to the problem, one of the putative advantages of SCT is that it supposedly explains why one should engage in moral behavior, and it does so in a way that doesn't require someone to accept (allegedly) controversial metaphysical claims. And yet it seems hard to find a motivation from within SCT to convince the free riding anti-vaxxer to get the vaccine anyway!

It is not entirely clear how the proponent of SCT should respond to the problem of the rational free rider. One possibility is to emphasize that the rules of the social contract are those that free, equal, rational, self-interested individuals would adopt *on the condition that others adopt them as well*. Accordingly, in a world wherein we could achieve *perfect* enforcement of the agreed-upon rules, we could simply circumvent the problem that the rational free rider presents. And perhaps it is enough that SCT shows that rational self-interested behavior *almost always* or at least *usually* entails acting morally. Lastly, even if there are indeed some occasions wherein rational self-interested behavior is *consistent* with acting immorally, that doesn't entail that the individual in question would *necessarily* act immorally. Acting in one's rational self-interests doesn't somehow entail, for example, that one must refuse the vaccine in the conditions of widespread vaccination. After all, someone might be interested in being part of a larger cooperative effort. Such a person could happily be part of the cooperative effort without inviting any charge of irrationality.

Either the agreement-dependency thesis is false, or SCT is arbitrary

According to SCT, morality consists in the set of rules that would be freely adopted by rationally self-interested individuals in a fair initial negotiation.[11] Now suppose the contractors would agree to some given rule, R. Accordingly, given social contract theory, R is a rule that we morally ought to follow. *How* did R become a morally binding rule in the first place? Given the agreement-dependency thesis, R became morally binding just because the free, equal, rational, self-interested contractors would agree to it.

But suppose we ask a slightly different question at this juncture: *Why* did (or would) the contractors agree to it? To keep things interesting here, imagine we could somehow consult one of the contractors and ask, "Why did (would) you agree to R?" Presumably, her answer would at least in part center on how R would advance her self-interests. After all, she is a *rational* and *self-interested* contractor. So, surely, the contractor has some such *reason* for adopting the rules she adopts in the initial negotiation.

But this presents a problem for SCT, and here's why. If the contractors indeed have *reasons* for adopting R, then those reasons for adopting R would seem to be sufficient all by themselves to explain why we morally ought to follow R—not the mere fact that the contractors *agreed* to R. So the salient thing here wouldn't be the act of agreement but the reasons upon which rationally self-interested contractors would have made their selections. Indeed, the fact that the contractors *agreed* to R seems to be an explanatorily unnecessary fifth wheel, so to speak. But if that's the case, then one of the key features of SCT, namely the agreement-dependency thesis, is simply false.

To avoid this embarrassing conclusion, proponents of SCT might be tempted to argue that the hypothetical contractors in question don't actually need to have reasons for the rules they agree to. Presumably, taking this line of defense might save the agreement-dependency thesis from the ash heap. Unfortunately, it does so at too high a cost: It would entail that morality is based on the arbitrary will of hypothetical people. But the arbitrary will of *actual* people is bad enough. Surely, the arbitrary will of *hypothetical* people is no better. So SCT faces a difficult dilemma: Either the agreement-dependency thesis is just false, or SCT is unacceptably arbitrary. Neither horn of this dilemma leaves SCT in very good shape.

SCT leaves too many and too much out of the moral community

Suppose all the prior objections to SCT can be adequately handled. A separate problem remains. If morality is indeed dependent upon agreement among rational contractors—hypothetical or otherwise—then what is the status of those who are simply incapable of *rational* agreement in the first place? Presumably, anyone or anything incapable of rational agreement could not play a role in the moral community—at least not in any *direct* sense. In the words of one of the leading contemporary proponents of SCT, David Gauthier, "animals, the unborn, the congenitally handicapped and defective, fall beyond the pale of a morality tied to mutuality."[12] To this unfortunate list of excluded parties we could also include those who are insane or senile, the environment, future generations, or past generations.

Why exactly are those folks or things "beyond the pale" of a conception of morality tied to mutual agreement such as SCT? To quote Gauthier again, "The disposition to comply with moral constraints . . . may be rationally defended *only within the scope of expected benefit*."[13] In other words, it can be rational to be bound by considerations about someone or something else's interests only if there is some expected benefit in return for doing so. And sadly, those folks and things named above can provide only limited benefit, or even *no* such expected benefit, to rationally self-interested contractors. The result is difficult to shake: SCT effectively leaves many of the *most* vulnerable out of the moral community.

Such a result—so it seems—should be especially problematic for Christians, especially those who take Jesus's words in Matthew 25 seriously. Consider Jesus's parable of the sheep and the goats:

> When the Son of Man comes in his glory, and all the angels with him, he will sit on his glorious throne. All the nations will be gathered before him, and he will separate the people one from another as a shepherd separates the sheep from the goats. He will put the sheep on his right and the goats on his left. . . .
>
> Then he will say to those on his left, "Depart from me, you who are cursed, into the eternal fire prepared for the devil and his angels. For I was hungry and you gave me nothing to eat, I was thirsty and you gave me nothing to drink, I was a stranger and you did not invite me in, I needed clothes and you did not clothe me, I was sick and in prison and you did not look after me."
>
> They also will answer, "Lord, when did we see you hungry or thirsty or a stranger or needing clothes or sick or in prison, and did not help you?"
>
> He will reply, "Truly I tell you, whatever you did not do for one of the least of these, you did not do for me." (Matt. 25:31–33, 41–45 NIV)

Two points are worth noticing here. Notice how Jesus places special emphasis on the treatment of those whom he identifies as "the least of these"—the poor, the stranger, the sick, and the imprisoned. In other words, Jesus seems to be saying that we should have special regard for those who are the *most vulnerable* in our midst. What is more, notice how in this parable the Son of Man ultimately identifies *himself* with the "least of these," such that those who neglected the most vulnerable thereby neglected the Son of Man himself. One very plausible interpretation of this is that when we neglect the least of these in society, we thereby neglect Jesus. By extension, a theory of morality that excludes the most vulnerable from the moral community thereby simply excludes *Jesus*.

That exclusion connects up with a broader point worth observing: SCT seems to leave *God* out of the picture from the very start. Remember,

SCT holds that our moral obligations and duties are defined by the set of rules that free, equal, rational, self-interested individuals would agree to follow, provided others would do so as well. But notice how this occludes God almost by definition. Sure, God is plausibly conceivable as free, as rational, and perhaps even as self-interested on some level. But there is surely no meaningful sense in which God is equal to the rest of us. So, as it is standardly conceived, SCT would have to exclude God as a hypothetical contractor, which would imply that humans neither have moral obligations *to* God nor any obligations *because* of God. And those entailments would appear to conflict pretty squarely with the presuppositions and affirmations of the Christian faith.

chapter seven

VIRTUE THEORY

On January 21, 1998, the *Washington Post* reported that President Bill Clinton had been accused of urging a former White House intern named Monica Lewinsky to give false testimony in connection to an ongoing sexual harassment case brought against the president by Paula C. Jones.[1] Although Jones eventually dropped her lawsuit in exchange for $850,000, in the months leading up to that settlement, Jones's lawyers had questioned Lewinsky about her relationship with Clinton during her time at the White House. In a sworn affidavit, Lewinsky denied having had a sexual relationship with Clinton. And just a few days after the allegations made the headlines, during a televised press conference, President Clinton stood next to his wife, the future US Senator and Secretary of State Hillary Rodham Clinton, and said this:

> I want to say one thing to the American people. I want you to listen to me. I'm going to say this again: *I did not have sexual relations with that woman*, Miss Lewinsky. I never told anybody to lie, not a single time; never. These allegations are false. And I need to go back to work for the American people. Thank you.[2]

It soon came to light that Clinton had indeed lied: Lewinsky had confided in a coworker, Linda R. Tripp, that she had engaged in sexual activity with the president on multiple occasions over the span of several months. In fact, Tripp had recorded her conversations with Lewinski and had also convinced her to keep her blue, semen-stained dress—a dress that provided definitive DNA evidence eventually turned over to the independent counsel, Kenneth W. Starr. President Clinton was ultimately impeached by the House of Representatives for lying under oath and for obstruction of justice.

Political foes complained that Clinton's adulterous escapades with a twenty-one-year-old intern, together with his subsequent dishonesty, portrayed a character unfit for public office. One such critic was Bill Bennett, who had served as the Secretary of Education during the Reagan administration and whose older brother Robert Bennett (ironically) served as Clinton's personal attorney in the Paula Jones case. Incensed that the Senate did not convict Clinton on the impeachment charges, former Secretary Bennett argued that letting Clinton off the hook ushered in "a lower common denominator of behavior and leadership than we Americans ought to accept."[3] Along similar lines, the pro-family activist and conservative icon Phyllis Schlafly conveyed her outrage in her widely circulated *Eagle Forum* newsletter. Her articled was entitled "Schlafly Appalled at the New Teen Fad: Is This the Bill Clinton Legacy?" The fad in question was the uptick in oral sex among middle schoolers.[4] Like Bennett, Schlafly believed Clinton's lack of moral fiber disqualified him for public office.

Judgments of this sort have hardly been reserved for Clinton—or for Democrats or liberals. During the run-up to the 2016 presidential election (and long thereafter), critics from across the political spectrum denounced Republican presidential hopeful Donald J. Trump. From the left, critics voiced their umbrage over Trump's questionable relationship to wealth, women, norms of civility, and truth-telling. Critics on the right spoke up as well. For example, the conservative megachurch pastor and best-selling author Max Lucado broke with his usual silence on political matters and argued that Trump couldn't clear even a basic decency test that he would expect someone wanting to date his daughter to pass. Lucado wrote:

> I don't know Mr. Trump. But I've been chagrined at his antics. He ridiculed a war hero. He made a mockery of a reporter's

> menstrual cycle. He made fun of a disabled reporter. He referred to the former first lady, Barbara Bush as "mommy," and belittled Jeb Bush for bringing her on the campaign trail. He routinely calls people "stupid," and "dummy." One writer catalogued sixty-four occasions that he called someone "loser." These were not off-line, backstage, overheard, not-to-be-repeated comments. They were publicly and intentionally tweeted, recorded, and presented. Such insensitivities wouldn't be acceptable even for a middle school student body election. But for the Oval Office? And to do so while brandishing a Bible and boasting of his Christian faith?[5]

Of course, it can sometimes be tempting to assume that the indignation directed at public figures is motivated more by partisanship than an actual concern for ethics. Take the simple fact that many of the very same right-wing pundits who condemned Clinton as unfit for office—including Bill Bennett and Phyllis Schlafly in particular—went on to publicly endorse Trump for president in 2016, even after allegations of Trump's own sexual indiscretions and coverups made the headlines. Similarly, many of those on the left who expressed the most outrage over the accusations of sexual assault brought against Supreme Court Justice Brett Kavanaugh during his 2018 Senate confirmation hearings fell silent or even went on the defense when similar claims were made against the then 2020 presidential candidate Joseph R. Biden.[6]

Still, while it might be tempting to think the ire over a politician's moral character amounts to nothing more than political posturing, such cynicism betrays a crucial truth nonetheless: If the public never felt any sense of outrage about a politician's character, the attempts to use it to exert political influence would prove feckless. Yet we *do* think the character of our public figures matters—and matters quite a bit. And the fact that we are often quite attuned to their flaws helps to underscore that morality can seem to involve more than just evaluation of this or that *action* but also an evaluation of a person's underlying *character*. This chapter is dedicated to an ancient theory of morality that places the evaluation of character traits front and center: virtue theory.

7.1. What Virtue Theory Says

Virtue theory depicts the moral life as being more about character traits than about, say, actions, rules, and policies. In other words, virtue theory holds that we should concern ourselves first and foremost with the various excellences a person should acquire. Roughly put, virtues are the praiseworthy character traits that direct us toward our appropriate end or ends—whatever those may be—whereas vices steer us away from the bullseye, so to speak. But if we think about virtues as those character traits that enable us to be and do what we ought to be and do, notice how the pressing question of whether this or that character trait should count as a virtue or vice is ultimately going to pivot on the prior question of which end or ends we should be aimed at. So what are the ultimate ends toward which we should be directed in the first place?

One of the most influential approaches to answering this question comes from the ancient Greek philosopher Aristotle (384–322 BC), particularly in his *Nicomachean Ethics*. For Aristotle, everything in the world has a *telos*—that is, some ultimate end or goal toward which it is aimed, given the kind of thing it is. And the telos of a thing is connected in important ways with its unique function—what it does that nothing else does. The telos of a knife is to *cut*, for example. The telos of an eye is to *see*. Accordingly, when the eye sees well, it is performing its unique function well and, thus, it is a good eye. By functioning in this way, the eye is in a state of excellence or perfection for the kind of thing it is. When the eye sees poorly, it is deficient and, thus, stands in need of correction. Of course, we aren't concerned with excellences of knives or eyes here but with those of humankind more generally. Nor are we concerned with the traits that would best equip someone to succeed in this or that specific role or occupation, say, as a professor or student or banker or farmer or mother. Instead, we are wondering about the character traits that would be excellent for us to have *simply insofar as we are human*. What are those?

To answer that question, we would first need to know what the ultimate human telos is. Aristotle argues that the human telos is *eudaimonia*, which often gets translated as "happiness" but which is probably better understood as something along the lines of *the objectively well-lived life*—that is, a flourishing life. But why should we think that eudaimonia is the ultimate telos of human endeavor?

Aristotle contends that for something to qualify as the ultimate telos in the first place, it would have to meet four key criteria: It would have to be (a) that for the sake of which all other ends are ultimately pursued; (b) that which is valuable in and of itself; (c) that which isn't pursued for the sake of something else beyond it; and (d) that which is self-sufficient in the sense that it makes life choiceworthy and, hence, lacking in no way.[7] Accordingly, if something fails to meet one or more of these key criteria, then it really wouldn't qualify as the ultimate telos of human endeavor.

But notice how these four criteria effectively rule out a variety of things that we commonly pursue in our lives—even things we sometimes value for their own sakes. Take, for example, pleasure or desire-satisfaction. The satisfaction of desires and the enjoyment of pleasures couldn't qualify as the final highest end according to Aristotle precisely because we pursue pleasure (or the satisfaction of our desires) as a means to some other end (viz., so that we can live well). Pleasure or desire-satisfaction are also not enough to make life lacking in nothing. After all, one could indulge in lots of pleasures and satisfy all of one's desires but still lead an empty and hollow life. The same general point holds for other things such as money, honor, status, and even virtue: We pursue those things as a *means* to something else (viz., to live well). So they cannot qualify as the ultimate human telos. What, then, is the final highest end according to Aristotle? *Eudaimonia*—the flourishing life. After all, eudaimonia is valuable in and of itself and is never sought because of something else beyond it, and all other ends are pursued for the sake of achieving it. Furthermore, eudaimonia is self-sufficient in the sense that achieving the objectively well-lived life makes life choiceworthy and, hence, lacking in no way.

But what, exactly, does eudaimonia consist of? Since we are seeking to understand *human* eudaimonia in particular, we will need to start by reflecting on the basic nature of humankind. So what is our essential nature as humans? Aristotle's answer starts by trying to identify our *unique* function relative to everything else. What do humans possess or do that nothing else possesses or does? It cannot be the fact that we take nutrition and reproduce, since we share that capacity with lots of things, even plants.

Nor is our capacity for sense perception unique to us, since we share that with nonhuman animals such as horses and oxen. However, there is one capacity that is ours and ours alone: *rationality*. Naturally enough, then, rationality is central to our unique function, and hence it is connected in a central way to Aristotle's conception of eudaimonia. In his view, the final end and highest good for humans consists in a life that expresses reason and expresses it with excellence. In other words, a flourishing life is one lived in accordance with right reason. And we live in accordance with right reason *excellently* by cultivating and practicing certain character traits within the different domains of human life. The virtues, then, are the character traits that direct us toward our human telos of eudaimonia; the vices, by contrast, direct us away from this end.

It is important to keep in mind that while the virtues clearly pertain to a person's outward-facing behavior, they are also connected in important ways to a person's *internal life*, so to speak. This includes (a) how one perceives, (b) what one believes and knows, (c) how one is motivated, and (d) how one feels emotionally. Notice, for example, how a person's character traits can influence what one perceives in a situation. Someone who is generous and caring will inevitably be more attuned to needy people in one's midst, while a stingy person might not even notice that they exist. A gluttonous man may be more aware of how much cake is left on the serving plate in the distance than the temperate woman. And so on. So virtues can affect what we perceive in the first place. Character traits also affect our cognitive states. Aristotle rightly holds that the truly virtuous person does not just get lucky and do the virtuous act by accident. Rather, the virtuous person *knows* that what one is doing is virtuous. (In fact, in Aristotle's account, knowing that one's action is virtuous is a necessary condition for having the virtue in question.)

Other internal conditions are required for virtue, too—what we might think of as motivational and affective conditions. Virtuous people are moved to act in certain kinds of ways—that is, they are *motivated* by certain reasons—and they have positive (or at least not negative) emotional responses to those ways of acting. For example, a truly courageous person is moved to act through the desire to preserve or pursue some good thing, despite the obstacles and dangers of doing so, and the virtuous person is not overly pained internally in the process. A truly temperate person is moved to eat or drink an appropriate amount precisely because the temperate person has disciplined one's appetites to desire (and not be pained by) the proper amount of food and drink for one's body, and to *not* want some improper measure of food and drink. Notice how virtuous people are motivated to act for these good reasons, and not for other sorts of reasons. And the affective states of virtuous people are, as it were, in alignment with the behavior they are motivated to engage in. That is, they feel pleased (or at least not pained) by the virtuous act.

Virtues are more than just a string of discrete behaviors and internal states—they are *dispositions* to perceive, to believe, to feel, to be motivated, and to behave in certain ways in certain circumstances. Aristotle contemplates these dispositions as *states of the soul.* Think of these as, roughly, what make up the internal architecture of a person. In turn, the internal architecture of a person affects what happens under this or that condition. Just as glass generally breaks when it is hit by a hammer (although brass does not), the virtuous person typically acts in certain ways when certain conditions arise. The glass breaks (whereas brass does not) precisely because of glass's composition on the inside, so to speak. That is, the glass is disposed to break under those conditions, and it is so disposed because of its internal architecture. Similarly, a virtue is the internal state of a person that leads one to hold up in certain ways under certain circumstances, and in ways that ultimately contribute to that person's overall well-being.

Lastly, in Aristotle's depiction, virtues are character traits that are *stable* over time—they aren't wishy-washy or fly-by-night, which is why Aristotle says a virtuous person acts from an unchanging, resolute state. After all, a knife that stays sharp for only a few strokes before going dull is hardly a prized tool in the hands of a craftsman. Similarly, one who acts courageously or temperately or generously only on this or that occasion isn't *truly* courageous nor truly temperate nor truly generous. *Real* virtues are durable and lasting across a range of relevant circumstances over time. But, of course, just as we might have diachronically stable traits that contribute to our well-being, so too we might have stable traits that ultimately damage us. Those traits are the vices.

With this brief historical backdrop in tow, we want to highlight five common affirmations of a virtue theory approach to moral philosophy:

i. Moral theory is agent-focused as opposed to action- or rule-focused.
ii. Certain character traits are virtuous and others traits are vicious.
iii. Why certain character traits are either virtuous or vicious can be explained in reference to the theory's underlying account of the good.
iv. The moral status of an action is indicated by what a virtuous person would do.
v. The good is prior to the right.

First off, notice that virtue theory is agent-focused, as opposed to action- or rule-focused. What this means is that, for virtue theory, the heart of moral philosophy is less about evaluating particular actions or even rules or maxims or principles and more about evaluating character traits. Some philosophers contemplate this orientation as something of a first-things-first approach to doing ethics. The basic idea is that if we concern ourselves first with what is required to become a virtuous person, then the rest will follow naturally enough. In other words, all the right actions and rules and maxims and principles can be discovered downstream from the virtuous character, as it were.

The second and third affirmation of virtue theory get reflected in a theorist's list of the virtues and vices, together with the explanation of why those particular traits should count as virtues or vices. Even among competing versions of virtue theory, there is almost always some overlap to such lists of the virtues and vices; but these lists and explanations nonetheless do vary from theorist to theorist. In all cases, though, these lists express the central convictions of the theorist in question, thereby reflecting the theorist's views on the underlying account of the ultimate good or goods toward which human life ought to be directed.

Fourth, virtue theory affirms what we might think of as a *virtue-indicative thesis*, according to which the virtuous person's behavior indicates an action's moral status. More specifically, facts about how the virtuous person would behave in this or that circumstance signal whether an action is morally obligatory, optional, or forbidden. Still in other words, the moral status of an action is effectively illuminated by paying attention to how the virtuous person would behave. Some virtue theorists want to go even further and claim that facts about how a virtuous person would behave not only *indicate* what is right but also show what *make* the action in question right. Accordingly, the moral status of an action isn't just illuminated by how the virtuous person would behave. Rather, the moral status of an action is causally dependent on how the virtuous person would behave. Call this more stringent claim the *virtue-dependency thesis*. In our view, virtue theory need not be committed to the virtue-dependency thesis, though it is committed to the weaker virtue-indicative thesis.[8] That is to say, virtue is the right-indicating mechanism, so to speak, even if virtue is not the right-making mechanism. Similarly, vice is the wrong-indicating mechanism, even if it is not the wrong-making mechanism. This is a point to which we will return below.

Lastly, virtue theory most typically contemplates the good as being explanatorily prior to the right. Put differently, what is right or wrong can be explained by reference to morally praiseworthy (virtuous) or reprehensible (vicious) character traits—that is, the goodness or badness of persons. Most virtue theorists, like Aristotle, contend that the various virtues are good precisely because they aim us toward, or equip us to achieve, some higher good—like eudaimonia, for example. Other virtue theorists hold that the virtues themselves are the most fundamental or intrinsically valuable goods at play. Notice, though, that most versions of virtue theory hold that what is good (and bad) is explanatorily prior to what is right (and wrong). The good explains what is right, in other words—not the other way around.[9]

Now, unfortunately, there is no easy way to encapsulate virtue theory's underlying account of the good. The difficulty here results from the simple fact that there are competing accounts of the ultimate human telos—and hence accompanying accounts of the good—at play among differing proponents of virtue theory, which also helps explain why there are differences in their various lists of virtues and vices. (Keep in mind that one's underlying account of the ultimate human telos will, in turn, affect one's vision of what counts as virtues or vices.) One exceedingly influential account of the good in the virtue tradition is, unsurprisingly, Aristotle's *perfectionist* account, which runs roughly as follows. Something is good for us if and only if and just because it contributes to what perfects or completes us given the kind of creatures we are. Something is bad if and only if and just because it somehow inhibits our perfection or completion. And something is value-neutral if and only if and just because it neither aids nor inhibits our perfection or completion. Of course, for Aristotle, perfection or completion is contemplated specifically in terms of his understanding of eudaimonia.

Other virtue theorists, such as the medieval philosopher Thomas Aquinas (1225–1274), accept the basic structure of Aristotle's perfectionist account of the good, though with an important and decidedly Christian twist. Aristotle's conception of eudaimonia—and hence his account of the good—is about rational functioning in *this earthly* life. In other words, his notion of eudaimonia is very much a this-worldly sense of flourishing. By contrast, in Aquinas's view, the ultimate telos of humanity, and hence true flourishing, is not exclusively about this earthly life but rather about union with God in the resurrected life to come. Aquinas contemplates the ultimate telos and highest good for humans as a union with God that occurs in an intellectual beholding of God that is sometimes called the *beatific vision*. Other virtue theorists in the Christian tradition modify Aquinas's specific account of the highest human good. For example, some thinkers hold that the ultimate telos isn't a static state of the intellect in the beatific vision but rather a dynamic participation in the kingdom of heaven.[10]

Other virtue theorists eschew the general structure of Aristotle's perfectionist account of the good altogether. Some do so precisely because they think we cannot legitimately infer an account of the good from descriptive facts about human nature—such an inference, in their view, represents an illicit move from is-claims to ought-claims.[11] Accordingly, these thinkers offer an account of human goods that avoids a reliance on Aristotelian teleology or perfectionism altogether. Still other virtue theorists part ways with the Aristotelian perfectionist account of the good because they see it as problematically self-regarding. The basic thought here is that morality is not fundamentally about what is good *for us*—either our ultimate flourishing or the proper pursuit of human goods—but about obedience to God and faithfulness to what God wants us to be. For such thinkers, the account of the good starts not with a vision of what is good for humans or what leads to our flourishing or perfection but simply with God himself: God is the ultimate good. Accordingly, in this view, ethics is not primarily about becoming the kind of person who can flourish or be perfected but about conforming to the will of God.

While different versions of virtue theory are underwritten by differing accounts of the good—and this is a point to which we will return below—virtue theory can still provide a relatively straightforward account of the *right*—in one sense, at least. Predictably, such an account centers on the virtues: An action is morally obligatory if and only if the virtuous person would always do it in the relevant circumstances. An action is morally wrong if and only if the virtuous person would never do it in the relevant circumstances. And an action is morally optional if and only if the virtuous person might (though might not) do it in the relevant circumstances. Notice how this account of the right, as stated here, does not assert that facts about how the virtuous person would behave are what *make* an action obligatory, wrong, or optional. Rather, it simply highlights the necessary and sufficient conditions for indicating when an action can properly be said to be obligatory, wrong, or optional. Remember that, in our view, virtue theory is committed to the virtue-indicative thesis and not necessarily the virtue-dependency thesis.

At any rate, such an account of the right naturally suggests the following moral decision procedure: *Follow the example of the virtuous person!* Obviously enough, this doesn't mimic any of the other decision procedures we have examined thus far in this book. That's because, for virtue theory, if one wants to know how one should behave, one should look to what the virtuous person would do in a relevantly similar circumstance—and to why the virtuous person would do so—and then try to comport oneself similarly. For the virtue theorist, there is no more straightforward a principle to which one might helpfully appeal, in part because (so one might say) the moral life is not further codifiable. That is to say, the moral law cannot be reduced into precise codes, laws, rule, or principles that other theories deal in. Notice, then, the vital role for moral exemplars. Instead of recommending a consequential analysis or following some Kantian flowchart, and instead of appealing to decontextualized moral principles, virtue theory recommends a careful study of the life of heroes, saints, leaders, community elders, and others who embody the virtues. And notice also that virtue theory stresses not only that we *do* what the virtuous exemplar would do; we should become *like* the virtuous person (which includes doing what the virtuous person would do for the reasons the virtuous person would do it). Becoming virtuous involves intentionally cultivating the internal architecture of the virtuous person. To be courageous, for example, we of course first need to do what the courageous person would do. But when we *force* ourselves to do what the courageous person would do, we aren't exactly courageous yet—because we are not doing the courageous act with the same internal state as the fully courageous person. However, over time, and with practice, our internal architecture molds and hardens in ways that match the internal architecture of the courageous. We *become* like the courageous person. That is, we *cultivate* and eventually *practice* the virtues in our lives. This is moral character development.

7.2. Identifying the Virtues and Their Vices

Perhaps the most crucial element of any virtue theory is the task of identifying the various virtues and vices—along with the task of explicating them, charting the various relationships between them, and explaining how we order and prioritize them. In this section, we briefly reconstruct some of the more influential of these accounts. We start with Aristotle, then turn to a representative sample of thinkers in the Christian intellectual tradition, and then move to the various lists of virtues and vices in the New Testament.

Aristotle on the virtues and vices

Aristotle offers one of the earliest and most prominent lists of virtues and vices. To get a feel for his list, it is helpful to start by focusing on two specific virtues that he discusses at some length (namely, courage and temperance), before turning to twelve other important virtues (and their vices) that he highlights. In Aristotle's account, courage is having the proper amount of confidence and fear in the face of danger or difficulty, especially in circumstances in which something of value is threatened. And it should be easy enough to see why such a character trait would be a virtue: One who has absolutely no confidence in fearful or trying circumstances is unlikely to flourish in life because one would be unlikely to bridle one's fear at times when one needs to. For example, such a person would lack the internal fortitude to proceed in battle or handle a cancer diagnosis—and one would never take on the risks of trying out for the team, or taking on a new job, or asking for the date, or blowing the whistle on a shady boss. When one lacks the proper confidence in these scenarios, one lacks something that is needed to live well; one is cowardly. Of course, it is possible to have *too much* confidence in the face of danger or an obstacle, even if most of us are inclined to have too little confidence. Yet there are times when one should be reasonable and recognize that one is just not cut out to undertake the difficulty or surmount the hurdle at hand. Those who have too much confidence in fearful circumstances are rash, and they are not likely to flourish either.

Notice how, with respect to feelings of fear and confidence, the virtue in question falls between two extremes. At one end of the spectrum is the vice of deficiency (cowardice), and at the other end is a vice of excess (rashness). For Aristotle, many (though not all) of the most significant virtues conform to this pattern. Consider temperance, for example, which pertains to one's appetite for food, drink, and sex. The temperate person's appetite is moderated or attuned—*tempered*, in other words—in such a way that one experiences pleasure and pain with respect to food, drink, and sex in the most reasonable way. Lots of people love ice cream, and so the thought of eating, say, *five* heaping bowls might sound enticing on first pass. But reasonable people won't actually go that far in a single sitting; they typically stop at some point, precisely because reason kicks in and reminds them that eating five bowls would be a pretty bad idea. Notice how there can be something of a tug-of-war between one's rational self and one's appetite for the pleasures of the table (or with what Aristotle calls the "pleasures of Aphrodite"). But suppose one's appetites were trained in such a way that one felt pleasure only in eating in the most reasonable way—the right food, in the right amount, in the right manner, at the right time, and so on. And suppose the same were true also with respect to indulging in the pleasures of drink and sex. If one is tempered in these ways, one has greater odds of leading a healthy and flourishing life; one is temperate. Admittedly, just as one might take excess pleasure in food, drink, and sex, it is possible for someone to fail to take *enough* pleasure in them, too. Aristotle contemplates such a vice of deficiency as insensibility, though he points out that it is all-too-human to be inclined toward the vices of excess when it comes to food, drink, and sex, and there is something not very human at all about insensibility.

At any rate, for Aristotle, the virtues of character often follow the same pattern on display with respect to courage and temperance, where the virtue in question falls between a vice of excess and a vice of deficiency along some particular axis of human experience. The following chart (fig. 7.1) is meant to capture the basic gist here, as well as most of Aristotle's list of virtues and vices.

Figure 7.1. Aristotle's (Partial) List of Virtues and Vices

WITH RESPECT TO . . .	VICE (DEFICIENCY)	VIRTUE (MEAN)	VICE (EXCESS)
. . . feelings of fear and confidence	Cowardice	Courage	Rashness
. . . pleasures and pains related to food, drink, and sex	Insensibility	Temperance	Gluttony or piggishness
. . . giving and getting wealth (in small matters)	Stinginess (takes in money to excess but is deficient in spending/giving)	Generosity	Wastefulness (too much spending but deficient in taking in money)
. . . giving wealth (in large matters)	Miserliness	Magnificence	Ostentatiousness or vulgarity
. . . honor and dishonor (in large matters)	Pusillanimity or smallness of the soul	Magnanimity, or greatness of the soul	Conceitedness
. . . honor and dishonor (in small matters)	Indifferent to honor	Appropriate regard for honor	Honor-lover
. . . anger	Too easygoing	Mild-mannered or good-tempered	Irascibility or bad-tempered
. . . relaying facts about oneself to others	Self-deprecating	Truthfulness	Boastfulness

WITH RESPECT TO . . .	VICE (DEFICIENCY)	VIRTUE (MEAN)	VICE (EXCESS)
. . . providing amusements in conversation	Boorishness	Wittiness	Buffoonery
. . . being a source of pleasure in life generally	Quarrelsomeness or disagreeableness	Friendliness	Ingratiating or flattering
. . . one's feelings about oneself	Shamelessness	Proper sense of shame	Overly shameful
. . . feeling pleasure and pain about others	Spitefulness (enjoys other people's misfortunes)	Proper sense of indignation (pain when the undeserving does well)	Envy (pain at other people's good fortune)

It is important to note that not all the virtues Aristotle discusses conform to the pattern on display in Figure 7.1. In fact, two of the most important virtues in his account do not: *justice* and *prudence* (or practical wisdom). Nonetheless, justice and prudence are of special importance precisely because justice and prudence, along with courage and temperance, comprise the *cardinal virtues* (see fig 7.2). Cardinal virtues are thought to be of paramount significance because they are needed to make any progress in cultivating the other virtues. Accordingly, the cardinal virtues act as a sort of hinge upon which the development of the other virtues turns. In fact, the word "cardinal" comes from the Latin word "*cardo*," meaning "hinge."

Figure 7.2. The Cardinal Virtues

COURAGE	The appropriate level of confidence in fearful circumstances
TEMPERANCE	Proper state of the appetite for food, drink, and sex
JUSTICE	Disposition to give people what is fair and act according to proper laws
PRUDENCE	Proper use of reason to choose ends and the means to those ends

Suppose, for example, that a stingy person—that is, one who feels pain in giving to others—wants to become generous and, hence, capable of feeling pleasure in giving to others. One will of course need to cultivate the habit of doing what the generous person would do with respect to wealth (even if it pains one to do so at first). But notice how one would also first need to already have other traits in place in order to make progress toward becoming generous: One would need to be temperate enough to obey one's intellect over one's appetite for additional wealth; one would need to be courageous enough to face the pain required to give generously; and one would need to be prudent and just in order to discern the proper amount to be given in the first place.

That brings us back to justice and prudence. Unlike the virtues cataloged in Figure 7.1, justice does not simply lie at the mean between two extremes (of, say, too little justice and too much justice). Instead, according to Aristotle, we can approach the task of contemplating the nature of justice by first paying attention to what is unjust. And an unjust person is one who either doesn't follow the proper laws or is unfair to others. So by contrast then, justice is about fairness or following the proper laws (for the right reasons). Accordingly, justice is relational in nature in the sense that it arises within a social context. Part of what this means is that justice can be expressed both within societies at large and within the individual persons who make up societies. A just society gives people what they are due from society. Similarly, a just person gives to others what they are owed from oneself, too. So a just person is disposed to see and understand what is required of oneself according to the laws and norms of one's society and is appropriately motivated to act in accordance with those reasonable laws—and the just person is disposed to give to people what they are due, and for the right reasons. Notice that while injustice is opposed to justice, the two dispositions do not neatly conform to the pattern on display in Figure 7.1, where the virtue falls between a vice of excess and a vice of deficiency.

Nor does prudence (or practical wisdom) fit such a pattern. For Aristotle, prudence is special because it operates as a sort of bridge between the life of the mind and one's character more generally. That's because prudence is an *intellectual* virtue that undergirds, and is necessary for, the cultivation and practice of the *character* virtues. After all, one needs to be prudent in order to know how to be temperate with respect to food. And one needs to be prudent in order to know how confident or fearful one should be in this or that circumstance. And so on. Prudence, in short, is the disposition to reason rightly in selecting both the ends one should pursue in life *and* the means to those ends. The prudent person is one who habitually deliberates, judges, and makes decisions properly about what is truly good and advantageous for human life in general. In so doing, the prudent person uses right reason to navigate various complexities and intricacies one encounters in the pursuit of a flourishing life.

Unfortunately, there are lots of vices that can oppose the virtue of prudence (e.g., thoughtlessness, indecisiveness, negligence, ignorance), in part because there are simply so many ways to go wrong in reasoning about worthy ends and how to achieve them. Aquinas, who was profoundly influenced by Aristotle's virtue theory, highlights one such vice that opposes prudence—what Aquinas refers to as "prudence-of-the-flesh."[12] He depicts prudence-of-the-flesh as the vice that causes one to seek merely carnal ends—ends solely about this earthly or fleshly life—as though they were of ultimate, highest value. In so doing, prudence-of-the-flesh causes a person to neglect higher, spiritual ends related to beatitude in the resurrected life. To be clear, Aristotle does not discuss prudence-of-the-flesh (and probably would have rejected the thought that such a disposition is a vice in the first place). But we mention Aquinas's input here as a reminder of how different virtue theorists offer different lists of the virtues and vices in light of their different conceptualizations of the ultimate human telos and the underlying account of the good that it represents.

In the same way that Aquinas's treatment of the virtues and vices was influenced by Aristotle, it is worth noting that Aristotle was himself an inheritor of a nascent intellectual tradition and background culture that presupposed the importance of the virtues and the vices as a way of contemplating the moral life. That is to say, it is not as though virtue theory or philosophical reflection on virtues and vices somehow originated with Aristotle. Rather, it was an assumed feature of much of the ancient world. For one thing, Aristotle's virtue theory was clearly informed on some level by his teacher, Plato (ca. 429–347 BC), who discusses the cardinal virtues throughout his work and simply presumes their importance. And Plato was no doubt influenced by Socrates (469–399 BC), who dedicated his life to getting clear on the virtues in his dialogues with others. And so on.

Likewise, virtue theory is not exclusive to the ancient Greeks (or the Western tradition, more generally), as expressions of it can be seen in the work of East Asian thinkers such as Confucius (551–479 BC) and Lao-Tze (ca. sixth century BC). Importantly, some elements of virtue theory are clearly on display in ancient Hebraic culture too. For one thing, a variety of passages in the Hebrew Bible—some dating back as far as 700 BC—clearly presume a concern for virtues and vices.[13] And consider the book of Wisdom, which is thought to have been written around 300 BC for Jews living outside of Israel. The author praises courage, temperance (self-control), justice, and prudence in particular as needed for living a profitable life.[14] It is significant that an explicit mention of the cardinal virtues appears in a Jewish book written three centuries before Christ because it provides at least some reason to imagine that Jesus himself taught in a cultural context in which a discussion of the cardinal virtues may have been in the air, so to speak.

We turn now to a brief survey of the intellectual tradition following Jesus Christ—from the early church fathers through Aquinas—before returning to a discussion of how virtues and vices appear to be portrayed in the New Testament.

Virtue and vice in the Christian tradition

Reflection on virtues and vices can be found within the broader Christian intellectual tradition dating back to the time of Christ—including among a diverse array of important non-canonical Christian documents written during the same time period as, or in the generations immediately after, many of the texts canonized in the New Testament. Take, for example, the *Didache*, which dates to AD 50–120 and is thought to be one of the earliest Christian catechisms and reflections on Christian ethics. In it, the author instructs readers to love, bless, and forgive others and to be generous (chapter 1), and to avoid anger, jealousy, lust, dishonesty, greed, and vainglory (chapter 3).[15] Or consider 2 Clement, dated to AD 130–160, in which the author exhorts: "Let us earnestly follow after virtue, but forsake every wicked tendency [vice] which would lead us into transgression" (2 Clement 10).[16] Among other things, the author instructs readers to be loving, continent, compassionate, good, and sympathetic and to abstain from adultery, ill-speaking, and avarice (2 Clement 4). Of course, there are several other prominent pre-Nicene Christian thinkers who seem to appropriate elements of the virtue theory tradition, including such prominent figures as Justin Martyr (ca. AD 100–165),[17] Tertullian (ca. AD 155–220),[18] and Clement of Alexandria (AD 150–ca. 215),[19] among many others.

By the fourth century, reflection on the virtues and vices had permeated the work of several important Christian writers, including the Roman poet Aurelius Prudentius Clemens (348–405), commonly known as Prudentius.[20] In his influential allegorical poem *Psychomachia*, for example, Prudentius depicts the personification of seven virtues (Faith, Chastity, Patience, Lowliness, Sobriety, Concord, and Good Works) as engaging in an epic battle with the personification of seven vices (Paganism, Lust, Wrath, Pride, Indulgence, Discord, and Avarice).[21] During the same time period, the cardinal virtues were discussed explicitly in the works of Augustine of Hippo (354–430).[22] For example, Augustine contemplates each of the cardinal virtues as a different "movement of love," thereby framing the cardinal virtues in a decidedly Christian light:

> I hold that virtue is nothing other than the perfect love of God. . . . Temperance is love preserving itself entire and incorrupt for God; courage is love readily bearing all things for the sake of God; justice is love serving only God, and therefore ruling well everything else that is subject to the human person; prudence is love discerning well between what helps it toward God and what hinders it.[23]

Later Christian thinkers—perhaps most notably Aquinas—came to emphasize not only the cardinal virtues (which are needed to lead a flourishing earthly life) but also decidedly *theological* virtues, namely, faith, hope, and charity (or love). Remember that Aquinas, unlike Aristotle, contemplates the ultimate human telos as being about more than this-worldly flourishing. Instead, in Aquinas's view, the final, ultimate end of human existence is a sort of supernatural flourishing—*beatitude*—that comes with union with God in the resurrected life. What this means, then, is that while the traditional cardinal virtues are needed to direct us toward our natural, worldly end, they aren't enough to direct us toward our ultimate and final *super*natural end. For that, we need something additional, namely, the *theological virtues* (see fig. 7.3). The theological virtues are unlike natural virtues in at least three respects: The theological virtues have God as their object—they are about God, in other words; they are habits that are infused in us by God's grace rather than through our natural efforts; and they are discoverable by us only by means of divine revelation.

Figure 7.3. The Theological Virtues

FAITH	Disposition to believe what God says
HOPE	Disposition to expect future goods that are difficult to obtain and trust that God will deliver
CHARITY	Disposition to love God for his own sake

First, take the virtue of faith. Aquinas depicts faith as the disposition to believe divinely revealed propositions (in, say, Scripture) simply on the credibility of the one proposing them (namely, God). This is not merely an act of the intellect for Aquinas but also an act of the will. The will is drawn to God, and consequently the will directs the intellect to accept what God says. Second, the virtue of hope is the disposition to anticipate and strive for some future good that is difficult (though not impossible) to obtain—namely, it is the movement of expectation toward our future union with God. This is not a blind wish for something far-fetched; instead, it is a disposition to trust that, by God's grace, our ultimate good will indeed be realized. And third, Aquinas contemplates charity as the disposition to love God for his own sake—and not simply because of what God can do for us, as though God were an instrument. To be drawn to God for his own sake is to be drawn, by God's grace, to our highest end, by which our fallen wills are perfected. The spillover effect of this divinely infused virtue is that we are also enabled to love our neighbors as ourselves. Notice the connection among the theological virtues: Faith is needed to develop hope; hope is needed to develop charity; and charity is needed to achieve beatitude.

The manifestation of virtue theory within the Christian tradition is by no means restricted to a reflection on the virtues. In fact, reflection on the *vices* has been equally important and enduring within the Christian tradition.[24] One of the earliest and most important reflections on the vices comes to us from the so-called Egyptian Desert Fathers, in particular from the Christian monk and ascetic Evagrius of Pontus (345–399). During the fourth century, Evagrius joined a monastic community in the desert near Alexandria, Egypt. Members of this order had journeyed into the desert to engage in prayer, vigorous self-examination, diagnosis, confession, and penance. The basic goal was to do battle with one's temptations as a way of following the example of Christ's temptation in the wilderness after his baptism (Matt. 4:1–11). In due course, Evagrius penned a list of very practical recommendations and remedies for other monks with respect to the various sorts of temptations they would almost inevitably have to confront. He enumerated eight such *logismoi* (literally, "bad thoughts"): gluttony, lust, avarice, sadness (at another's good fortune, for example), anger, acedia (sloth), vainglory, and pride.[25] While a modified version of this list would eventually come to be known as the "seven deadly sins," it is more fitting to describe Evagrius's list as a list of *capital* vices, where the word "capital" comes from the Latin word "caput," which simply means head. After all, in Evagrius's depiction, the vices operate as internal dispositions to act in characteristic ways for characteristic reasons, all of which direct one *away* from one's proper end. Accordingly, this is not a list of "sins," per se, in the sense of being a list of discrete, blameworthy, individual actions. Instead, when one is beset with one of these *logismoi*, one has a certain disposition or likelihood to sin in specific sorts of ways; the *logismoi* are perversely fecund proclivities. For example, a person who suffers from the vice of avarice (or greed) will be more likely to lie or cheat to get money when in a pinch. The vicious internal state leads to particular sinful behaviors; but the internal state is not reducible to those individual actions.

Each of these vicious character traits has been the subject of elucidation and application by other writers throughout the Christian tradition—from Evagrius's time through such late medieval authors as Dante Alighieri (1265–1321) and Geoffrey Chaucer (1340–1400), and beyond. Evagrius's own disciple, John Cassian (ca. 360–435), made significant contributions to the capital vices tradition, in part by dividing Evagrius's list into the two subcategories of carnal vices and spiritual vices. Whereas carnal vices are those whose object is bodily in nature, spiritual vices are those whose object is not. For example, the carnal vices include gluttony (disordered love of *food*), lust (disordered love of *sex*), and avarice (disordered love of *money*). Meanwhile, wrath, sadness, and acedia aren't centered on something physical in nature; instead, they ultimately thwart spiritual maturation in different ways. Vainglory and pride are special in Cassian's view because, unlike the other six vices, they have the unique ability to contaminate the progress one may have made in battling the other six vices. (For example, as a result of one's conquest over, say, gluttony or avarice, one might come to love one's own excellence in this regard too much, which is prideful.)

Pope Gregory I (540–604) further refined and modified Cassian's list by contemplating pride as the root source of the other capital vices—rather than being merely one among the others—thereby trimming his list of capital vices from eight to seven. Gregory's list of seven vices—as well as his affinity for the number seven in general—became the definitive list among Christian theologians for the next seven hundred years leading up to the time of Aquinas in the thirteenth century. Because Aquinas routinely engaged with the work of early church fathers, it is hardly surprising that he adopted the list of vices he inherited within church tradition. In fact, he more or less adopted the list first developed by Evagrius and honed through Cassian and Gregory—although he did emend Gregory's emphasis on sadness with an emphasis on sloth (see fig. 7.4).[26]

Figure 7.4. Capital Vices from Evagrius to Aquinas

EVAGRIUS (4th cent.)	CASSIAN (4th/5th cent.)	GREGORY I (6th cent.)	AQUINAS (13th cent.)
1. Gluttony	1. Gluttony	1. Vainglory	1. Vainglory
2. Lust	2. Lust	2. Envy	2. Envy
3. Avarice	3. Avarice	3. Sadness	3. Sloth
4. Sadness	4. Wrath	4. Avarice	4. Avarice
5. Anger	5. Sadness	5. Wrath	5. Wrath
6. Acedia (Sloth)	6. Acedia (Sloth)	6. Lust	6. Lust
7. Vainglory	7. Vainglory	7. Gluttony	7. Gluttony
8. Pride	8. Pride	Root = Pride	Root = Pride

It is worth noting here that, in addition to his influential list of seven capital vices, Gregory also elucidated a list of seven key virtues aimed at combating the capital vices. In some ways, his list of corrective or remedial virtues is reminiscent of the characters portrayed in Prudentius's allegory (viz., Faith, Chastity, Patience, Lowliness, Sobriety, Concordia, and Good Works), which together do battle with the seven vices. Prudentius's personified virtues eventually came to be seen by some in the Christian tradition as the fitting antidotes for the capital vices. And nearly two centuries after Prudentius, Gregory offered his own list of the corrective virtues (see fig. 7.5).

Figure 7.5. Corrective or Remedial Virtues in Prudentius and Gregory I[27]

PRUDENTIUS (4th/5th cent.)		GREGORY I (6th cent.)	
CORRECTIVE VIRTUES	**VICES**	**CORRECTIVE VIRTUES**	**VICES**
Faith	Paganism	**Chastity**	Lust
Chastity	Lust	**Temperance**	Gluttony
Patience	Wrath	**Charity**	Greed
Lowliness	Pride	**Diligence**	Sloth (Acedia)
Sobriety	Indulgence	**Kindness**	Envy
Good Works	Avarice	**Patience**	Wrath
Concord	Discord	**Humility**	Pride

Virtue and vice in the New Testament

When we recognize the prevalence of virtue theory in pre-Christian Greek and Hebrew influences on the early church, as well as in the Christian intellectual tradition following Christ, it becomes far less surprising to see key features of virtue theory operating in the background of the New Testament. Take, for example, the Sermon on the Mount, where there are at least three key passages that seem to presume virtue theory on some level. The sermon begins with Jesus identifying several different groups of people whom he pronounces as "blessed" (e.g., "Blessed are the poor in spirit," "Blessed are the meek"). One leading New Testament scholar, Jonathan T. Pennington, argues that the Greek word typically translated as "blessed" (namely, *makarios*) should be understood as including the concept of eudaimonia, or flourishing.[28] Taking this interpretation, we can plausibly render the so-called beatitudes roughly as "Flourishing are the poor in spirit," "Flourishing are the meek," and so on. With this translation, notice how a key element of virtue theory seems to be operating in the background of the Sermon on the Mount—namely, a contemplation of the ultimate human telos as flourishing. Of course, Jesus's conception of makarios is not identical to the Aristotelian conception of eudaimonia. For one thing, Jesus seems to be claiming that the *meek* can flourish. Aristotle seems to regard the meek as viciously small-minded.

A second relevant passage comes later in the Sermon on the Mount in which Jesus explains that we can identify a false prophet by looking at the fruit his life yields: "Every good tree bears good fruit, but a bad tree bears bad fruit. A good tree *cannot* bear bad fruit, and a bad tree *cannot* bear good fruit" (Matt. 7:17–18 NIV—emphasis added). Obviously enough, Jesus is concerned here with people, not fruit trees. Notice how this claim is consistent with elements in the virtue theory tradition: One whose internal architecture is as it should be—one whose perceptions, beliefs, motives, and affections are geared toward one's proper end—*naturally* produces good fruit, so to speak. In fact, Jesus adds that what sullies a person is not something outside of him (such as eating food with unwashed hands) but something on the inside: "For it is from within, out of a person's heart, that evil thoughts come—sexual immorality, theft, murder, adultery, greed, malice, deceit, lewdness, envy, slander, arrogance and folly. All these evils come from inside and defile a person" (Mark 7:21–23 NIV). And consider how Jesus concludes the Sermon on the Mount with an illustration about one man who built his house on a good foundation (rock) and another man who built his house on a poor foundation (sand)—things go well for the former and poorly for the latter. Notice the parallel. The virtuous person—one whose internal life is constructed on good foundations—has the capacity to overcome difficulty and flourish.

To be clear, we are not insinuating that Jesus Christ was (or is) *merely* a virtue theorist. But we do mean to suggest that his teachings plausibly presume at least some elements of virtue theory on some level. After all, consider what Jesus says about himself in John 10:10: "I have come that they may have life, and that they may have it more abundantly" (NKJV). Here, Jesus appears to be saying that the reason he came into the world was so humans could live more abundantly. In other words, he seems to be saying that the purpose of his own life—and hence the *incarnation*—is so that humans may truly flourish. Second, if indeed the goal of Jesus's coming into the world was to enable humans to truly flourish, then that would seem to imply that the ultimate telos of humanity is flourishing. Why? The one who creates an artifact is the very one who decides the purpose of the artifact. A knife has the telos of cutting precisely because that is precisely what its maker designed it to do. If indeed the creator of humanity designed us to live an abundant life, then that is the ultimate telos of humanity.

Beyond Jesus's own teaching, elements of virtue theory are scattered throughout the New Testament. Consider, for example, the apostle Paul's epistle to the Galatians, in which he draws a distinction between a life lived in accord with the Holy Spirit and a life lived according to the flesh, which is connected to the desires of our sinful nature. Paul writes, "Those who belong to Christ Jesus have crucified the flesh with its passions and desires" (Gal. 5:24 NIV). Accordingly, those who belong to Christ should no longer manifest the works of the flesh, which include "sexual immorality, impurity and debauchery; idolatry and witchcraft; hatred, discord, jealousy, fits of rage, selfish ambition, dissensions, factions and envy; drunkenness, orgies, and the like" (Gal. 5:19–21 NIV). A fairly natural way of reading this point would be that those who live according to the flesh are practicing the vices that misguide them in Christian living, and thus they will miss out on the truly flourishing life. Hence, Paul explicitly warns that they "will not inherit the kingdom of God." Instead, Paul exhorts his readers to "walk by the Spirit," and he outlines how the fruits of doing this will become manifest in their lives as "love, joy, peace, forbearance, kindness, goodness, faithfulness, gentleness and self-control" (Gal. 5:22–23 NIV). Notice how this list is in some ways reminiscent of some of the cardinal virtues, and it prefigures at least some of Aquinas's theological virtues as well.

The lists of virtues and vices are not restricted to the Pauline epistles within the New Testament. Consider the apostle Peter's instruction:

> Make every effort to add to your faith goodness; and to goodness, knowledge; and to knowledge, self-control; and to self-control, perseverance; and to perseverance, godliness; and to godliness, mutual affection; and to mutual affection, love. For if you possess these qualities in increasing measure, they will keep you from being ineffective and unproductive in your knowledge of our Lord Jesus Christ. But whoever does not have them is nearsighted and blind. (2 Pet. 1:5–9 NIV)

Notice not only the clear hint of some of the cardinal and theological virtues at play here but also the fact that these qualities are presented as internal traits the cultivation of which equips one to become more effective and productive in one's life as a Christian.

In fact, there are quite a few lists in the New Testament that can be reasonably understood as lists of *virtues* and *vices*. Admittedly, there is no effort in the New Testament to articulate, explain, or defend some sort of theoretical framework that gives pride of place to internal dispositions to perceive, feel, be motivated, and act in certain ways. However, our point is that such a framework appears to be presumed on some level (see fig. 7.6).

Figure 7.6. Some Lists of Virtues and Vices in the New Testament[29]

PASSAGE	VIRTUES (OR, GOOD WORKS)	VICES (OR, SINS)
Matt. 5:3–11	Poor in spirit, mourn, meek, hunger and thirst for righteousness, merciful, pure in heart, peacemakers, persecuted because of righteousness	
Matt. 15:19 Mark 7:21–23		Evil thoughts, murder, sexual immorality, theft, false testimony (deceit), slander, greed, malice, lewdness, envy, arrogance, folly
Rom. 1:29–31		Wickedness, evil, greed and depravity, envy, murder, strife, deceit and malice, gossips, slanderers, god-haters, insolent, arrogant and boastful, invent ways of doing evil, disobey parents, no understanding, no fidelity, no love, no mercy
Rom. 13:13		Sexual immorality, drunkenness, debauchery, dissension, jealousy

PASSAGE	VIRTUES (OR, GOOD WORKS)	VICES (OR, SINS)
1 Cor. 5:10–11		Sexually immoral, greedy, swindlers, idolators, slanderer, drunkard
2 Cor. 6:4–7	Endurance, hard work, purity, understanding, patience, kindness, sincere love, truthfulness, righteousness	
Gal. 5:19–23	Love, joy, peace, forbearance, kindness, goodness, faithfulness, gentleness, self-control	Sexual immorality, impurity and debauchery, idolatry and witchcraft, hatred, discord, jealousy, fits of rage, selfish ambition, dissensions, factions and envy, drunkenness, orgies
Eph. 4:2–3	Humility, gentleness, patience, bearing with one another in love, unity, peace	
Eph. 4:25–32	Truthfulness, diligence, kind, compassionate, forgiving	Falsehood, anger, theft, unwholesome talk, bitterness, rage, brawling, slander, malice
Eph. 5:3–6		Sexual immorality, impurity, greed, obscenity, foolish talk, coarse joking, idolatry, empty words, disobedience
Col. 3:1–16	Compassion, kindness, humility, gentleness, patience, forbearance, forgiveness, ("and over all these virtues put on love, which binds them all together in perfect unity"), peace, thankfulness, wisdom	Sexual immorality, impurity, lust, evil desires, greed, idolatry, anger, rage, malice, slander, filthy language, lying
1 Thess. 5:12–22	Hard work, caring, peace, helping the weak, patience, doing good, rejoicing, praying	Idleness, disruptiveness, repaying wrong with wrong
1 Tim. 1:9–10		Lawbreakers and rebels, ungodly and sinful, unholy and irreligious, those who kill their fathers or mothers, murderers, sexually immoral, those practicing homosexuality, slave traders, liars, perjurers
1 Tim. 3:2–11	Above reproach, faithful to spouse, temperate, self-controlled, respectable, hospitable, able to teach, gentle, trustworthy	Drunkenness, violent, quarrelsome, love of money, conceited, malicious talkers
1 Tim. 6:4–5		Envy, strife, malicious talk, evil suspicions, constant friction, corrupt mind

PASSAGE	VIRTUES (OR, GOOD WORKS)	VICES (OR, SINS)
Titus 1:7–10	Blameless, hospitable, loves what is good, self-controlled, upright, holy, disciplined, holds firm to what is trustworthy	Overbearing, quick-tempered, drunkenness, violent, dishonest
James 3:13–18	Humility, wisdom, pure, peace-loving, considerate, submissive, full of mercy and good fruit, impartial, sincere	Envy, selfish ambition, boasting, dishonesty, disorder, evil practices
1 Pet. 4:3–5		Debauchery, lust, drunkenness, orgies, carousing, idolatry, reckless, wild living
2 Pet. 1:5–9	Faith, goodness, knowledge, self-control, perseverance, godliness, mutual affection, love	Ineffective, unproductive, nearsighted, blind, forgetful of gifts
Rev. 21:6–8		Cowardly, unbelieving, vile, murderers, sexually immoral, those who practice magic, idolators, liars

7.3. The Case for Virtue Theory

There are any number of arguments in support of virtue theory; we will consider three in this section. The first argument highlights the advantages of virtue theory relative to modern rivals. A second emphasizes the fact that virtue theory is compatible with a variety of plausible accounts of the good. And the third argument is premised on an acceptance of the Christian tradition. While we will consider each of these independently, they are perhaps best regarded as working in concert with one another to provide a cumulative case for virtue theory.

Comparative advantages argument

One way of arguing for virtue theory is to highlight its advantages relative to other moral theories. To get a sense of how this sort of argument might get off the ground, compare virtue theory to utilitarianism and Kantian deontology, which are perhaps the two most prominent moral theories of the modern era. The virtue theorist might complain that utilitarianism and Kantian deontology both seek to do the impossible, namely to *codify* the moral life. That is, they seek to articulate a precise principle that can be applied to any highly contextualized situation and yield the proper moral verdict every single time. To see the point, start with a simple question: Is it morally permissible to drive one hundred miles per hour through a school zone while kids are present? "No," says the utilitarian: "Doing so wouldn't maximize utility." And, "No," says the Kantian deontologist: "Doing so would fail to respect persons as ends in themselves." Notice how both accounts might seem to offer plausible enough explanations at first glance. The problem, however, is that both utilitarianism and Kantian deontology appear to render perfectly *incorrect* judgments in other important cases of applied ethics. Utilitarianism, for example, would permit scapegoating innocent persons in at least certain situations. And Kantianism says we should tell an inquiring murderer the truth about where his innocent victim is. By underscoring how utilitarianism and Kantianism *fail* to render proper judgements in a variety of cases, one can then point to a comparative advantage of virtue theory: Virtue theory does not even attempt to codify the moral life in the same way that modern moral theories like utilitarianism and Kantianism do. Hence, virtue theory is better positioned to render proper judgments in specific, highly contextualized situations.

To further illustrate the point here, consider the so-called "trolley problem" made famous in recent decades by Phillipa Foot (1920–2010).[30] Suppose a trolley is barreling in the direction of five innocent people who are, for whatever reason, tied to the train tracks. If the trolley stays on its course, they will surely die. Suppose you happen to be standing next to a lever that could shift the trolley to an alternate set of train tracks, thereby saving these five unfortunate people. Sadly, there is one poor fellow who is tied to the alternate set of train tracks, and he will surely die if you pull the lever. What would *you* do?

Among those surveyed, the vast majority of respondents said *they would* pull the lever.[31] Those moral data, so to speak, seem to be in alignment with, or best explained by, the utilitarian principle: We should pursue the course of action that maximizes happiness (or minimizes harm). But suppose the situation were modified just a bit.[32] Imagine that the trolley is still on target to kill five people, but this time around, there are no alternate tracks onto which you can shift the trolley. Suppose, though, that you are watching the impending collision from a bridge overlooking the train tracks. And suppose also that, although you happen to be a rather skinny chap yourself, you are standing next to a very large, portly man. It occurs to you that if this fat man were somehow to fall onto the tracks, his body mass would surely be enough to throw the trolley off its deadly course. What would you do *now*? If you were to push the fat man off the bridge, he would surely die, but five others would live. Should you maximize happiness with a quick shove?

As it turns out, the vast majority of those surveyed said they would *not* push the fat man, even if doing so were indeed the only way to save the five people on the tracks.[33] Notice how the moral data in the second case would seem to align with, or be suggestive of, Kantian deontology: We shouldn't treat any human as a means only. So what are we to make of the inconsistency in the data? If one is permitted or even obligated to pull the lever in the first case precisely because saving five lives is better than saving one life, then why wouldn't one also be permitted or even obligated to push the hefty man off the bridge for the very same reason? Shouldn't a moral theory be able to articulate the underlying standard or principle that would explain specific evaluative judgments across a variety of cases? In other words, shouldn't our moral theory predict and explain—again, with consistency—the correct moral verdicts in applied ethics?

Some philosophers contend that the task of trying to explain *all* the correct moral verdicts of applied ethics by appeal to a singular moral principle (or even a set of principles) is an utterly futile endeavor precisely because the moral life is too irreducibly complex to be captured so neatly. Some philosophers go even further to contend that *no* correct moral verdict can be explained by any moral principle in the first place.[34] We need not go as far as that to see the basic point at hand. One need only to think that in order for a moral principle to yield correct moral verdicts across a variety of applied cases, that principle must lack rigid precision. This can seem to be Aristotle's point when he says we shouldn't expect "the same exactness in everything but, in each case, the one that is in accord with the subject matter and the degree sought by the method of inquiry that properly belongs to it."[35] In other words, Aristotle seems to suggest that we shouldn't expect a high degree of precision with respect to ethics.

This general point on offer here is sometimes made by claiming that the moral life is *noncodifiable*. That is to say, correct moral judgments cannot be expressed or explained by appeal to some singular principle or even by some tidy set of precise laws. If it is true that morality is noncodifiable, then we will eventually err in trying to reduce all correct moral judgments to precise moral principles, which is why modern moral theories such as utilitarianism and Kantianism fail to explain *all* the relevant moral data of our considered moral judgments. Thus, we should seek an alternative such as virtue theory—or so the argument might go. We can outline this line of reasoning as follows:

(1) Modern moral theories attempt to codify the moral life via precise moral principles.
(2) But the moral life is noncodifiable.
(3) Virtue theory does not attempt to codify the moral life in the same way that modern moral theories do.
(4) So, virtue theory offers a more plausible outlook.

There are of course limitations to this sort of argument, even if its premises are all true. (And it is debatable whether premise 2 is true!) Notice that the premises above, even if true, do not entail that virtue theory is per se the *correct* theory of ethics. Rather, if true, the premises entail only that virtue theory would have a comparative advantage to moral theories that endeavor to codify the moral life. So to bolster this kind of argument for virtue theory, one might look for other ways that virtue theory can outperform its rivals.

Consider three such advantages, according to advocates of virtue theory. First, one might contend that virtue theory offers better instruction than its competitors on how to lead a good, ethical life. The virtue theorist might contend that a moral theory really needs to do more than merely give us rules or explain when an action is right or wrong. It also needs to guide us on *who* we ought to become, *which* internal traits we ought to cultivate, *how* we should live, *why* we should act in this or that way, and *what* kind of things we should care about and desire and feel good about. And virtue theory can offer what is needed here, or so say its proponents. After all, virtue theory does not merely judge that one should or should not torture a terrorist or pull a trolley lever or pursue one's self-interests or honor a contract or whatever. Rather, virtue theory speaks to the characteristic ways in which human behavior tends to go wrong or right, and it offers a model to follow. For example, Aristotelian virtue theory says people tend to go wrong by not having enough confidence in fearful circumstances, and we are more likely to be cowardly than rash. Notice the practical guidance on offer: In general, if we want to become courageous, we should lean in the direction of rashness (though not too far!) to cultivate the virtue of courage. In this way, virtue theory has the advantage of better equipping us to grow morally.

A second advantage virtue theorists might point to relates to the underlying question of why someone should be moral in the first place. A common complaint is that Kantian deontology and utilitarianism do not or cannot provide a very satisfying answer. The utilitarian answer goes roughly as follows: If you admit that your own happiness is desirable as an end (and thus potentially motivating to you), then, *on pain of irrationality*, you should also recognize that the happiness of society as a whole is desirable as an end for the aggregate, and thus it is an end that you, too, should seek. In other words, you should care about other people's happiness because failing to do so would mean you accept the motivating power of your own happiness while irrationally refusing to accept the motivating power of general happiness. Why is this answer unsatisfying? Part of the problem is that the utilitarian answer vacillates between what is desirable to an individual and what is desirable to the *aggregate* of persons. We know what it means to say that such-and-such is desirable to an individual, but it is less obvious what it means to say that such-and-such is desirable to an aggregate. But even if we just ignore that worry and concede that acting immorally (by *not* maximizing general happiness) implies a failure to act rationally, the utilitarian answer can still seem unsatisfying. "So what?!" the critic will ask. "Why should I care if *my* action is irrational if it still benefits *me* in some way?" As it turns out, Kantian deontology's answer to the question faces the same worry. Kant held that acting on a maxim that isn't universalizable is tantamount to violating the categorical imperative of practical reason. Notice how the critic will just raise same question as above: "Why should I care if *my* maxim is irrational if acting on it benefits *me* in some way?" So, as far as the critic is concerned, the question of why someone should be moral remains largely unanswered. Virtue theory can circumvent this worry altogether by offering a more compelling answer to the question at hand: Failing to act morally—that is, failing to live a life of virtue—decreases your chances of flourishing, given the kind of creature you are. And *that's* precisely why you should care.

A third advantage of virtue theory is that compared to its modern rivals, virtue theory seems far better equipped to allow close personal relationships to generate meaningful moral reasons. For example, virtue theory can recognize how morally relevant reasons arise from considerations about, say, compassion for others or loyalty to one's friends. Not so with utilitarianism and Kantianism. For utilitarianism, the only morally relevant considerations are those related to an impartial and egalitarian assessment of how to maximize utility in the world. And for Kantian deontology, all that matters is acting from a motivation to obey the moral law and thereby do one's duty, with no regard to the various partialities that might define us as selves. Notice the strange light this casts when we reflect on something as simple (and as important) as a mother's relationship to her newborn baby. As far as utilitarianism is concerned, a mother's reason to provide for her child (or not) depends solely on whether doing so maximizes utility. So for utilitarianism, whether the mother actually *loves* or *cares about* her child makes no real moral difference. But surely that's false. Along similar lines, for Kantian deontology, a mother's reason to provide for her child reduces to nothing more than considerations about doing her duty for the sake of doing her duty. Accordingly, from a Kantian perspective, the mother who *truly wants* to provide for her child *and* does so in obedience to the moral law wouldn't be morally superior to the mother who *doesn't want* to provide for her child but does so anyway strictly out of obedience to the moral law. But that seems wrong. So both the utilitarian and the Kantian perspective seem deficient in this case. It is at least plausible that a person's closeness to us matters in a moral sense, and so, plausibly, we have obligations to family members that cannot be explained by considerations about general utility (contrary to utilitarianism). Similarly, it is at least plausible that we are morally better off if we come to act from certain desires and motivations that go beyond mere obedience to the moral law (contrary to Kantian deontology).

We are now in a position to extend and enhance the comparative advantages argument for virtue theory in the following way:

(1) Modern moral theories attempt to codify the moral life via precise moral principles.
(2) But the moral life is noncodifiable.
(3) Virtue theory does not attempt to codify the moral life in the same way that modern moral theories do.
(4) Additionally, virtue theory outperforms modern moral theories in providing moral guidance for why someone should be moral and in allowing for moral reasons to arise in connection to close personal relationships.
(5) Thus, we have good reasons to accept virtue theory as the correct moral theory.

Whether this proves to be a compelling argument for virtue theory will of course depend in part upon whether premises 2 and 4 are true. But, importantly, even if premises 1–4 are true, we would still need to ask whether they provide us with *definitive* reasons for thinking that virtue theory is correct or just reasons *in favor* of accepting it over, say, utilitarianism and Kantianism.

Virtue theory is compatible with the proper account of the good

As we mentioned above, there is no easy way of encapsulating virtue theory's account of the good precisely because different virtue theorists presume different accounts of the good (and hence articulate differing lists of the virtues and vices). For example, a diverse array of thinkers with very different accounts of the good (from Aristotle to Aquinas to Nietzsche to Ayn Rand) have been interpreted on some level as virtue ethicists. On the one hand, this particular feature of virtue theory underscores why virtue theory, taken by itself, is incomplete and stands in need of supplementation—any virtue theory relies on some underlying account of the good. On the other hand, this very same fact about virtue theory ironically counts as a point in its favor. Since virtue theory can be rendered compatible with competing accounts of the good, virtue theory is malleable—in fact, malleable enough to be compatible with whatever turns out to be the correct account of the good. Notice how this malleability differentiates virtue theory from utilitarianism, Kantianism, and ethical egoism; each of those theories of morality bank on a specific account of the good and, hence, rise or fall with that account. For example, if happiness is not the only good, Mill's utilitarianism is in big trouble. If doing one's duty for the sake of doing one's duty is not the only intrinsically and unqualifiedly good thing, then Kantianism is up a creek. And if one's own rational self-interest is not the only good, ethical egoism is doomed. This is not the case for virtue theory. And that's because, in contrast to its modern rivals, virtue theory can accommodate whatever is, in fact, the correct account of the good.

There is an added bonus in the mix: Virtue theory can also provide something of a bridge between whatever turns out to be the correct account of the good on the one hand and the proper discernment of right action on the other hand. To explain, once we have identified the correct account of the good, we can then start to elucidate which traits would facilitate the achievement of that good (the virtues) and which traits would thwart it (the vices). And once we know which traits are virtues, we can then use that list to imaginatively discern what someone with those very same traits *would* do in this or that specific situation. The virtuous person, as it were, illuminates what is right. This is *not* to say that the action is right *just because* the imaginary virtuous person would do it. Rather, our point is simply that the intellectual work that led us to believe that the virtuous person would do this or that serves as a helpful epistemic aid for determining right and wrong action. So, in sum, careful reflection on the virtues provides a bridge between the correct contemplation of the good and an appropriate discernment of the right.

Of course, these considerations do not, on their own, entail that virtue theory is the correct theory of morality. But, or so one might argue, they do offer reasons in the favor of virtue theory, which can play a role in a larger cumulative case for it.

An argument from Christianity

Virtue theory's prominence within the Christian tradition could easily be reformulated as an argument *from Christianity* for virtue theory. We will not here repeat what we said above in section 7.2. However, it is worth stating explicitly these points from the Christian point of view:

(1) If it's true that Jesus taught from a backdrop of virtue theory, and if it's true that Paul and other biblical writers presumed some components of virtue theory, and if it's true that the early church fathers accepted key elements of virtue theory, and if it's true that virtue theory remained a dominant and increasingly developed moral theory within the Christian tradition for thirteen hundred years, then Christians have good reason to take virtue theory seriously as an approach for understanding the moral life.

(2) Those things are true.

(3) So, Christians have good reason to take virtue theory seriously as an approach for understanding the moral life.

Whether this sort of argument has any purchase will perhaps inevitably pivot on two questions. First, is the Christian religion true in the first place? If not, then this argument is of course worthless. But if the Christian religion *is* true, then the considerations in premise 1 are powerful indeed. And second, is it true that Jesus, Paul, early Church fathers, and others in the Christian tradition are indebted to the virtue theory approach as we have interpreted them?

7.4. The Case against Virtue Theory

Virtue theory, of course, has its critics. In this section, we will discuss several common objections to virtue theory—and one concern that should be of special interest to Christians in particular. We will consider each objection in turn.

Virtue theory has an epistemic problem

Virtue theory holds that we can discern what is right or wrong in this or that situation by looking to the example of how the virtuous person would or would not behave. But how are we supposed to know what the virtuous person would do in *unprecedented* circumstances? Suppose that a completely novel dilemma arises because of technological advances heretofore unknown to anybody, virtuous or not. When we ask what the virtuous person *would* do in such a case, it seems like there is no actual answer to which we might turn for guidance. If it is true that no real person has ever been in the situation before, then when we speculate about what the virtuous person *would* do, it seems like we are speculating about a strictly *hypothetical* person. But on what basis are we supposed to determine what this entirely hypothetical virtuous person would do?

In one way, this worry runs parallel to epistemic problems facing social contract theory, as well as those facing utilitarianism. For now, focus on the epistemic problem facing utilitarianism, namely, that it is impossible to know (prior to acting) which action will maximize utility in the long run. One line of defense offered by utilitarians is to draw a distinction between *expected* and *actual* utility and simply to require that we do the best we can by maximizing expected utility. Of course, utilitarians will then have to concede that, on final analysis, the action that actually maximizes utility might not be the same as the one we reasonably expected to do so. Accordingly, *expected* utility might be our *guide* before we act, but *actual* utility is the *judge* in the end.

Perhaps the virtue theorist can mimic the utilitarian's strategy by drawing a distinction between (a) what we can reasonably *expect* that the virtuous person would do in the situation and (b) what the virtuous person would *actually* do in a situation. From there, the virtue theorist might recommend that we do what, *to the best of our knowledge*, the virtuous person would do—even if that action proves to be something that, on final analysis, the virtuous person wouldn't actually do. Accordingly, the virtue theorist might say that (a) is our guide even if (b) is our final judge, so to speak. This can seem like a strange predicament, to be sure; but the virtue theorist actually fares better than the utilitarian in making this move for two reasons. For starters, utilitarians are committed to saying that, in the end, we are morally culpable whenever we fail to maximize *actual* utility (even if we should guide our action based on expected utility). But virtue theory need not be committed to the claim that *all* cases of failing to do what the virtuous person would do result in moral culpability. If, through no fault of our own, we are in a situation where we could not possibly know what the virtuous person would do, perhaps moral culpability simply does not apply. In other words, perhaps it is true that we ought to do what the virtuous person would do, but not all failures to do this cause us to be morally guilty.

There is a second way in which virtue theory might fare better than utilitarianism. Recall that a critic might worry that there is simply *no fact of the matter* about which action will ultimately maximize utility. One might similarly worry that, at least in certain unprecedented situations, there is likewise just *no fact of the matter* about what a virtuous person would do because the virtuous person hasn't been there before. But notice, if there is no fact of the matter about which action maximizes utility, then utilitarianism faces a fatal problem. That's because, for utilitarianism, the fact that an action maximizes utility is what fundamentally explains why the action is obligatory. Not so for virtue theory. A virtue theorist can consistently hold that facts about what the virtuous person would always do illuminate or indicate the moral status of an action without saying those same facts *make* the action in question right or wrong. We will return to this point below.

The virtues sometimes can (and do) come into conflict

For now, though, turn to a separate worry in the vicinity of the epistemic problem. One might object to virtue theory on the grounds that there are at least some cases where the virtues clash, as it were. And in those cases, virtue theory becomes a perfectly useless guide. To illustrate the worry, start with the fact that in nearly any serious version of virtue theory, honesty, loyalty, and justice are all going to be praised as key virtues. But which virtue takes priority in cases where they come into conflict with one another? Should you testify against a spouse or family member whom you *know* to be guilty of a crime? If you don't testify, are you fully honest? If you do testify, are you loyal? Or consider the infamous case of the inquiring murderer. Honesty would seem to lead you to tell the truth; justice would seem to lead you away from aiding and abetting a murderer. What is the virtuous person to do in these sorts of cases? What we appear to need in these cases is some sort of rule or principle that tells us *which* virtue should take priority. Unfortunately, it is at least not obvious that a precise rule or principle can always be given, and—what seems worse—virtue theory by itself doesn't even endeavor to articulate one.

The virtue theorist can respond to this objection by arguing that the adjudication of these sorts of conflicts requires not so much the application of a rule as it requires the exercise of the cardinal virtue of *prudence* (or practical wisdom) in the moment. Recall that prudence is the disposition to use reason properly to choose both the ends one should pursue and the means to pursue those ends. Accordingly, prudence might express itself as a sort of capacity for insight or judgment about how one should behave in the heat of tough and highly textured situations—an insight that simply isn't reducible to the application of precise rules or principles.[36] And if there is indeed a clash of virtues where no prioritizing rule is available, then this situation would be the very sort of occasion in which we would need something like prudence. And perhaps that is just what we should expect to rely on—as opposed to expecting to rely on a rule or principle. After all, there are a million little factors that could plausibly influence whether justice or honesty should be prioritized.

For example, in the case of the inquiring murderer, just who is this man knocking at the door? What is your history with him? And what about the victim? What kind of door is it? Is that door sturdy enough that you could just close it quickly and lock it? What *other* means are at your disposal such that you might pursue both honesty *and* justice at the same time? And assuming there is simply no way to pursue both, what other salient factors in *this* nuanced circumstance might affect your decision? And so on. The point here is that there are lots of details—perhaps too many to name or even fully acknowledge in the moment of the actual decision-making—that the truly prudent person would rightly weigh in deciding how to handle the situation, and not all of those relevant factors can be articulated so neatly in a precise rule.

Virtue theory invites relativism

Return to the differing lists of virtues and vices offered by different virtue theorists. We discussed the ancient Greek virtues and the early Christian theological virtues above. But there are, of course, *other* important lists.[37] For Hinduism, nonviolence, truth, purity, and self-control are key virtues. Confucius listed courtesy, generosity, honesty, persistence, and kindness as virtues. Turning to the modern era, Thomas Hobbes held that keeping contracts, gratitude, sociability, and avoiding hatred were among the key virtues, in part because they are needed to exit the nasty, brutish, and short life in the state of nature. For Immanuel Kant, sobriety, self-control, veracity, beneficence, and respect for humans (both in oneself and in others) are among the chief virtues. Even Friedrich Nietzsche is sometimes regarded as something of a virtue ethicist. He despised the thought that meekness or gentleness or forgiveness would be considered virtues. As he saw it, power and self-realization are the only real goods, and so a trait would be virtuous if it facilitated an honest will-to-power—so things like overcoming resistance, authenticity, assertiveness, creativity, risk-taking, self-confidence, and mercilessness would effectively emerge as virtues.[38] Along similar lines, Ayn Rand argued that productivity, pride, independence, rationality, and *selfishness* are among the chief virtues in a capitalist society precisely because they help one secure one's own self-interest, which is the ethical egoist's conception of the ultimate good. And so on. The key point here is that what one depicts as a virtue will ultimately depend on the end or ends that those virtues are supposed to serve. Some say the proper end is this-worldly human flourishing; others say it is found in other-worldly union with God. Some say the ultimate end is power; others say it is obedience to the moral law. In any case, notice that what one affirms as the ultimate human telos will, in turn, drive what one thinks is conducive to that end. Put differently, what one takes as the proper account of the virtues will inevitably depend on one's underlying account of the good. And the level of disagreement among virtue theorists about the underlying account of good is not insignificant. Hence the objection on offer: Virtue theory invites a relativism problem. The basic worry is that *any* list of virtues invariably will be indexed to one's culture or background assumptions about human ends or goods.

One way of defending virtue theory against this worry is to point out that human fallibility and disagreement about the nature of morality is perhaps inevitable and to emphasize that this fact holds true for *any* moral theory. Accordingly, if disagreement about which traits count as virtues creates a relativism problem for virtue theory, then other forms of disagreement would present the same problem for every other moral theory too. After all, utilitarians disagree about what maximizes utility; Kantians disagree about which actions accord with universalizable maxims; and so on. So what remains a problem for *all* moral theories surely doesn't qualify as a problem for just one *particular* moral theory. What is more, the simple fact that there is disagreement among the various lists of virtues does not somehow entail that there is no correct list. So human fallibilism and disagreement, in themselves, don't actually entail relativism, even if they recommend that we should practice humility in the effort to articulate the correct list of virtues. That said, reflecting on the fact that there are indeed competing lists of virtues should force us to recognize an incompleteness to virtue theory: It relies on some deeper account of the good to drive its vision of the ultimate telos of humanity. What that means is that virtue theory cannot be a stand-alone account of ethics; it requires supplementation.

Virtue theory gets the order of explanation wrong

Some critics complain that virtue theory fails to offer the appropriate kind of explanation for what actually makes an action obligatory, optional, or wrong. To illustrate the worry, start with the fact that a virtuous person would never abuse a child. According to some interpretations of virtue theory, the simple fact that a virtuous person would never do such a thing is what most fundamentally explains why child abuse is so horribly wrong. In other words, according to this interpretation of virtue theory, the fact that the virtuous person would never abuse children is what *makes it true* that child abuse is wrong. But notice the problem. What makes child abuse wrong isn't the fact that virtuous persons would never do such a thing. Rather, what makes child abuse wrong surely has more to do with, say, facts involving the unreasonable harm, damage, and humiliation inflicted upon innocent and vulnerable persons of immeasurable worth. Indeed, those very same facts are what explain why virtuous persons would never abuse a child in the first place—not the other way around. Thus, says the critic, virtue theory gets the order of explanation exactly backward.[39]

While this may seem like a trenchant objection on first pass, there is a plausible path forward for virtue theory. However, the virtue theorist will need to deny that what the virtuous person would do is the right-making mechanism within virtue theory and insist instead that what the virtuous person would do is merely right-indicating. (This is why we said at the outset of this chapter that virtue theory is committed to the virtue-indicative thesis but not to the virtue-dependency thesis.) Return to our presentation of virtue theory's account of the right: An action is morally obligatory if and only if the virtuous person would always do it in the relevant circumstances. An action is morally forbidden if and only if the virtuous person would never do it in the relevant circumstances. And an action is morally optional if and only if the virtuous person might (though might not) do it in the relevant circumstances.

Notice this account does *not* assert that an action is right or wrong *just because* of what the virtuous person would or wouldn't do. Instead, it says something much more modest: What the virtuous person would or wouldn't do effectively *illuminates* the deontic status of an action. And, in truth, virtue theory is not—and ought not be—committed to saying that what the virtuous person would do is what most fundamentally *explains* the deontic status of an action. After all, one of the most important and paradigmatic virtue theorists of all time—Thomas Aquinas—clearly did not think that what most fundamentally explains why the action in question is obligatory is the fact that the virtuous person would always do it. Rather, as both a proponent of virtue theory *and* natural law theory, Aquinas contends that what most fundamentally makes an action right or wrong centers on facts about the rational pursuit of human goods. So the critic's complaint against virtue theory really only defeats certain *versions* of virtue theory—and nonparadigmatic versions of virtue theory at that.

Still, there is an important lesson to learn here: If defensible versions of virtue theory must avoid saying that facts about how the virtuous person would behave are what make an action obligatory, optional, or wrong, then the virtue theorist has a responsibility to provide a supplementary account of what *does* cause an action to be obligatory, optional, or wrong. So we return again to a point made above: To provide a robust account of the moral life, virtue theory stands in need of supplementation by sources beyond itself. Previously, we saw that virtue theory is incomplete as a moral theory insofar as it does not, by itself, offer a singular account of the good. We now see another way that virtue theory is incomplete: It must bank on more than just facts about what the virtuous person would or wouldn't do to explain what *causes* or *makes* an action obligatory, optional, or wrong.

Robust virtues don't even exist

Virtue theory presupposes that people have (or at least can come to develop) diachronically stable character traits that are consistent across a wide range of situations—in other words, virtue theory presumes that there are such things as virtues and vices. However, according to the so-called *situationist objection* to virtue theory, no such robust character traits actually exist. Instead, according to situationists, a person's behavior is really just driven by the details of the situation in which one finds oneself—the details of which one is often unaware—rather than, say, differences in the internal architecture of a person's character.[40] To support this view, situationists point to experiments in social psychology such as the famous "dime study," in which adults were tested for how likely they would be to help a stranger.[41] The experiment goes roughly as follows. The subject of the study enters a phone booth in a shopping mall. Unbeknownst to this person, a dime had been placed in the return slot of the phone booth. A confederate of the study walks by and pretends to accidentally drop a stack of papers just as the subject of the study exits the phone booth. Of the sixteen people who found the dime in the return slot, fourteen stopped to help the stranger pick up the spilled papers. Of the twenty-five who didn't find the dime, only one stopped to help. Notice how it can seem as though perfectly mundane situational factors—like whether one finds a dime, for example—affect whether the subject helps the stranger, not some underlying, robust internal trait (such as a virtue).

To be sure, the dime study is hardly enough to *prove* the situationist objection to virtue theory, in part because of the tiny sample size of the study, and in part because several efforts to replicate it have not produced similar results.[42] But other experiments in social psychology can seem to lend support to the situationist objection. For example, a group of three related studies measured whether being in a group (versus being alone) would affect a person's tendency to help others.[43] Subjects of the study were presented with an apparent emergency situation (e.g., smoke coming from the office next door, or a woman crying in pain next door, or a student having a seizure on the other end of an intercom). Some of the subjects of the study were placed in these situations by themselves, and others were placed in these situations in groups or in pairs. As it turns out, in each case, being alone appears to have made people *more* likely to help.

Now notice how the situationist complaint against virtue theory would go. Virtue theory presumes that because of the internal architecture of one's character, a virtuous person acts virtuously across a wide range of relevantly similar situations and not merely in very narrowly defined situations prompted by seemingly mundane situational factors. Yet "found-a-dime kindness" and "only-when-alone compassion" surely don't count as, or reveal the workings of, robust virtues (i.e., kindness and compassion). The problem seems to be that virtue theory *mistakenly* assumes that robust character traits exist in the first place. But, says the critic, only situationally dependent traits exist. Thus, says the situationist, virtue theory is empirically inadequate and outdated.

One way of taking the sting out of this objection is by simply denying that virtue theory requires character traits to be as robust as the situationist objection seems to suggest. Robert C. Roberts emphasizes the scalar nature of character traits and contends that virtue and vice could come in differing depths of ingression.[44] In this view, a person might be *deeply* virtuous or *deeply* vicious such that situational factors (like finding a dime or being alone) wouldn't deter a person from the underlying virtue or vice. Meanwhile, most of us might tend to fall along a spectrum ranging from deep virtue to deep vice. Only the people in the very middle of this spectrum would be truly character-less (and hence driven entirely by situational factors). Given this scalar view of character, it seems silly to say that *only* folks at the extreme ends of the spectrum have distinctive character traits. Rather, we should say that people at the extreme ends have *more* distinctive or enduring character traits than those along the spectrum. Roberts illustrates this point by imagining a wax figurine. The figurine retains a distinctive character *even if* that character can be overcome in some situations (e.g., at a certain hot temperature).

Return to the bystander experiments mentioned above and notice how they involve situations that are admittedly *trying* to the subject of the study. Perhaps it is more psychologically difficult to step up to the plate and help out when one has the option of relying on others to do so. And it is perhaps easier to be compassionate when one recognizes that there is simply just no backup option, as it were. Even though these trying situations may have melted away the virtuous character of all but the most tempered of the subjects of the study, perhaps we shouldn't so easily conclude that everyone who failed to help is devoid of any virtue or character whatsoever. We should rather say that their characters, much like the wax figurine's, were not sufficiently tempered to handle these more trying situations. So there is more at play than mere situational factors: Character traits *do* exist, even if situational factors can try them—or even obliterate them—in much the same way that heat can test and eventually obliterate a wax figurine. None of this is to ignore the findings of social psychology. Admittedly, we all find ourselves in situations that are, at various times, conducive or detrimental to the exercise of virtue. Proponents of virtue theory can accept this point and simply advise us to be disciplined in how we place ourselves in situations—and to become increasingly aware of how those situations might affect us psychologically with respect to behaving as the virtuous person would behave. For example, we might tell our friends about our intention to lose weight, hoping that by doing so we are putting ourselves in a situation that makes it more likely that we will eat temperately. Over time, as the virtuous behavior becomes more habituated in us, we learn to eat well even without relying on the social pressures being in place.

Virtue theory conflicts with the priority of obedience in the Christian life

A final objection to virtue theory is of perhaps special concern to Christians. Recall virtue theory's answer to the question of why someone should be moral. According to virtue theory, you should be moral because doing so helps you flourish, given the kind of creature you are. Decidedly *Christian* versions of virtue theory can extend that answer a step further: You should be moral because doing so means cultivating the internal dispositions needed for the beatific vision, for union with God, or for enjoying everlasting life in God's kingdom. Notice how each of these explanations for why one should be moral appeals to one's own flourishing or happiness or well-being, albeit perhaps in a long-term sense. The view that our choices should be governed by considerations related to flourishing is sometimes called *eudaimonism*. One might be tempted to think that Christians should be uncomfortable with eudaimonism—and hence virtue theory—on the grounds that the ultimate point of morality is not most fundamentally about *our* flourishing but about obeying *God*. Admittedly, flourishing might be a byproduct of obeying God, but it is not actually the ultimate goal. Instead, the ultimate goal is to love God by respecting his authority and obeying his commands and law.

In one way, Kant holds something of an analogous position. In his view, our choices should be directed by the will to obey the moral law simply *because it is the moral law*—doing one's moral duty for the sake of something other than doing one's duty lacks praiseworthiness. If one's choices are motivated by, say, the pursuit of one's own flourishing, then one fails to express a good will. Imagine how a Christian spin on this Kantian line of reasoning could run. Consider, for example, a claim made by Robert Richardson (1806–1876), a nineteenth-century Protestant thinker: "The best and highest reason that can be given for any action is, that *God commands it*. Whatever it may have in itself of manifest suitableness or of probable utility, will, if it become a motive to its performance, but detract to that extent from the obedience of faith."[45]

There are reasons why a Christian might want to follow Richardson in rejecting eudaimonism in favor of prioritizing obedience to God in connection to the moral life. For example, Scripture seems to emphasize "dying to oneself" (Luke 9:23–24; Rom. 6:11–14; Eph. 4:22–24; Gal. 2:20), putting the needs of others before one's own (Rom. 12:10), and not operating from a self-regarding maxim (Phil. 2:3–4). Furthermore, reflect on what is involved in confessing that Jesus is Lord. Such a confession implies, foremost, that you are *not* the Lord. And accepting that Jesus is the Lord means, among other things, that you recognize his authority over you—and that you are *willing* to submit to it. All that can seem to mesh with Jesus's final charge to his disciples before his ascension: "*All authority in heaven and on earth has been given to me*. Therefore go and make disciples of all nations, baptizing them in the name of the Father and of the Son and of the Holy Spirit, and teaching them to *obey everything I have commanded you*" (Matt. 28:18–20 NIV—emphasis added). Notice the emphasis on obedience.

Of course, it is worth repeating that one of Jesus's stated reasons for coming to earth was so that people might have abundant life (John 10:10). He also says we should store up treasures for ourselves in heaven (Matt. 6:20). And he sometimes seems to motivate folks by letting them know that following *his* way is ultimately in *their* best interest (Matt. 11:28–30). In other words, when describing the moral life, Jesus at least sometimes seems to emphasize things *other* than obedience. In fact, he even goes as far as suggesting that rote rule-following and mere behavioral compliance aren't enough for true righteousness. For example, after explaining that one's righteousness must surpass that of the Pharisees and teachers of the law to enter the kingdom of heaven, Jesus contrasts the righteousness of the teachers of the law with the righteousness in God's kingdom. He does this by commenting on six well-known commands. Consider his reflection on the first of these:

> You have heard that it was said to the people long ago, "You shall not murder, and anyone who murders will be subject to judgment." But I tell you that anyone who is angry with a brother or sister will be subject to judgment. Again, anyone who says to a brother or sister, "Raca," is answerable to the court. And anyone who says, "You fool!" will be in danger of the fire of hell. (Matt. 5:21–22 NIV)

The implication here seems to be that merely acting in compliance with the divine prohibition on murder presented by Moses in the Decalogue isn't enough to rise to the level of righteousness of those who enter the kingdom of heaven. Why? Because merely acting in accordance with the law—even if one does so *for the sake* of obeying God—wouldn't necessarily be enough to form and shape the relevant feature of one's internal life, which Jesus is clearly concerned about here. Think about where murder comes from in the first place. Cain killed his brother Abel precisely because Cain was full of wrath (Gen. 4:5). If Jesus is correct, Cain was subject to judgment *prior to*—and even *independent of*—killing Abel. So righteousness that exceeds that of the Pharisees would come not just from one's outward behavior but also from *who one is* on the inside. If this sort of interpretation is correct, it would challenge the thought that acting strictly for the sake of conforming to a divine command is the only or even the primary motive undergirding moral goodness.[46] The emphasis falls on something other than obedience.

So what are we to make of all this? Perhaps the Christian faith doesn't assume we should act *solely* for the sake of obeying God or that we should *only* ever act for the sake of ultimate flourishing, although both do get emphasized. Perhaps Christian versions of virtue theory should hold that obedience and flourishing are, in the end, *jointly fundamental* with respect to the governance of our choices. After all, or so one might contend, flourishing and obedience merge in the age to come—obedience to Christ and flourishing in his presence both come naturally to the fully sanctified (i.e., *truly* virtuous) citizens of God's community. Happily, it is available for the Christian virtue theorist to say that we should cultivate the virtues *both* for the sake of obeying God *and* for the sake of flourishing.

chapter eight

NATURAL LAW THEORY

The journal *Psychopathology* published a case report in 2022 about a twenty-four-year-old European who was admitted to the hospital after following through on a carefully premeditated plan to cut off one's own hand using an electric saw.[1] Having long fantasized about life without a left hand, this individual exhibited telltale signs of *apotemnophilia*, or body integrity identity disorder (BIID). Such a condition is characterized by "a mismatch between the mental body image and the physical body" together with the desire to amputate a healthy limb or otherwise to become paralyzed.[2] While cases of BIID are thought to be uncommon, it remains unclear just how rare they may be because they are often shrouded in secrecy. At any rate, they do occur. But they can of course seem baffling, in no small part because they involve perceptions or desires that conflict with biological facts about the individuals involved.

A similar perplexity arises in connection to people who contemplate and represent themselves not as singular entities but rather as plural—that is, as having multiple alters or *headmates*.[3] One prominent child psychiatrist, Devid Rettew, recently noted in *Psychology Today* that there has been a recognizable increase of adolescents throughout the United States who claim that "within themselves there are a number of different personalities that emerge at different times." He speculated that "much of this seems to be driven by a small number of influential people" who discuss their plural self-identities on popular social media platforms such as TikTok.[4]

Other phenomena can leave us scratching our heads not only because they involve perceptions or desires at odds with empirically verifiable facts but because they also involve a denial that, as a biological creature, one belongs to the human category in the first place. For example, some people—sometimes known as *otherkin*—claim that they belong to one or more nonhuman species. These individuals identify either partially or wholly as nonhuman animals (such as foxes or cats), or even as members of fictional species (such unicorns or goblins). While there is no precise way of estimating how many folks identify in this way, there has been a notable uptick of otherkin personae in online forums in recent years.[5] Admittedly, it can be hard to know what to make of these. Just how serious are they? At least one of them, Tiamat Legion Medusa, was apparently serious enough to spend more than $75,000 (and counting) on cosmetic surgeries to bring Medusa's body into better alignment with a projected self-identity as a genderless dragon: Medusa's surgical procedures included tongue splitting, nose modification, ear removal, horn implantation, and castration.[6]

Other situations can seem difficult to process because they involve (among other things) appetites and behaviors that transgress the typical borders of human experience in particularly alarming ways. One such example is the tragic case of the notorious porn-star-turned-anti-porn-advocate Linda Susan Boreman, also known as Linda Lovelace.[7] In 1972, Boreman was allegedly forced at gunpoint to engage in sexual acts with a dog while being filmed for a pornographic movie. By Boreman's own account, the problem was not exclusively about her lack of consent. Although she had been raped and abused throughout her career, she explained that she was haunted by the event in question because it had, in her own words, crossed a "huge dividing line."[8] Yet as devastating as Boreman's personal story is, voluntary acts of bestiality and zoophilia are more commonplace than one might suspect. According to two frequently cited (albeit dated) studies on the matter, between 5 and 8 percent of the American males surveyed have had sex with a nonhuman animal.[9] Some of the same men surveyed admitted that they were deeply upset when the relationships with their animals were ended. Consistent with such emotional connections, there have been reports in recent years of people trying to enter into marriage-type arrangements with animals.[10] And, apparently, acts of bestiality are still being filmed and distributed. One such filming session near Seattle made national headlines in 2005 when a forty-five-year-old man died from complications related to a perforated colon after engaging in sexual acts with a horse, which promptly led the state of Washington to ban bestiality.[11]

Cases such as these can cause us to wonder whether there is something *morally* salient at stake. One might wonder, for example, whether severing a perfectly healthy hand is not only pathological but also immoral—in part because human beings *as a kind* have two hands, even if some individuals are born without two or lose one in an accident. Along similar lines, it can seem tempting to assume that people come packaged one per brain, and not in sets of two or more. And one might be tempted to think that otherkin folks like Tiamat Legion Medusa ought not modify their bodies to look more like dragons or cats because, after all, they are actually human beings, not dragons or cats. Similarly, one might suppose that acts of bestiality are morally illicit not because the animals involved don't or can't consent but because such cross-species sexual acts fly in the teeth of facts about human nature, including facts about anatomy and physiology. And so on.

The thought that a correct appraisal of human nature provides us with information pertinent to the moral life is one of the motivating ideas behind natural law theory (hereafter, "NLT"), which is the focus of the present chapter. NLT has a long and impressive pedigree, and elements of it can be traced back to such thinkers as Plato (ca. 429–347 BC), Aristotle (384–322 BC), and Cicero (106–43 BC), among many others. For that reason, if no other, there have been different formulations of NLT throughout the history of ethics. While NLT is sometimes depicted in purely secular terms, it is perhaps most commonly contemplated as a *religious* theory of ethics, in part because proponents of NLT often hold that human nature (along with everything else) was created by God. And although NLT predates Christianity, it has nonetheless featured prominently within important streams of the Christian tradition—most notably within the Roman Catholic tradition—thanks in no small part to the influence of Thomas Aquinas (1225–1274). In fact, NLT continues to provide much of the conceptual framework for Catholic moral theology, perhaps most visibly these days with respect to sexual ethics in particular. Consider, for example, the doctrine on birth control set forth by the famous 1968 papal encyclical *Humanae Vitae*:

> An act of mutual love which impairs the capacity to transmit life which God the Creator, through specific laws, has built into it, frustrates His design which constitutes the norm of marriage, and contradicts the will of the Author of life. Hence to use this divine gift while depriving it, even if only partially, of its meaning and purpose, is equally repugnant to the nature of man and of woman, and is consequently in opposition to the plan of God and His holy will.[12]

The underlying idea here is that sexual behavior that intentionally impedes or occludes reproduction is in opposition to human nature, which was designed by God with certain capacities geared toward certain teleological ends. Accordingly, sexual practices that intentionally thwart these ends are disordered and hence morally illicit. Such immoral practices include artificially contracepted sex between a husband and wife, oral sex, anal sex, onanism, masturbation, homosexual sex, and bestiality. To be sure, while many non-Catholic defenders of NLT reject that NLT entails these granular-level conclusions with respect to sex, our point here is simply that NLT has indeed been appropriated within important branches of the broader Christian tradition and has, in turn, helped inform Christian views for centuries. This chapter is dedicated particularly to the consideration of NLT as expressed in the work of Aquinas, who is widely recognized as having offered the paradigmatic articulation of NLT.

8.1. What Natural Law Theory Says

According to NLT, there is something like a divinely imprinted grain to the universe, and so the better part of wisdom is to discern the direction of that natural grain and act *with* it and not against it. More precisely, NLT holds that there is a set of objective moral principles, or laws, that arises in connection to facts about the sort of creatures we are by nature—facts that we can discover and reason about for ourselves, facts for which God is responsible. There are seven key affirmations at the heart of Thomistic NLT that we will highlight moving forward:

i. The moral law is grounded in human nature.
ii. We can discern that moral law through reason.
iii. The good is prior to the right.
iv. It is self-evident that what is good is to be pursued and what is evil is to be shunned.
v. The good is that which perfects or completes us.
vi. There are a variety of human goods.
vii. Practical reason provides guidelines on how we should pursue those human goods.

The first two theses above give expression to the two different ways morality might be thought to be natural. According to the first thesis—what we can label NLT's *grounding thesis*—the principles or laws of morality are natural in the sense that they are importantly connected to facts about the kind of creatures we are, and so those moral laws are binding on us just insofar as we have the nature that we have as human beings. Put differently, according to the grounding thesis, facts about human nature provide an essential objective basis for determining what is and is not morally appropriate for humans. And precisely because morality is grounded in human nature in this way, we can say that morality is natural to us.

There is a another sense in which morality is natural, which brings us to the second thesis above—what we can label NLT's *epistemic thesis*. According to this thesis, we can come to discern the laws of morality through the proper use of supernaturally unaided human reason. Put differently, we have all the relevant equipment we need as humans to learn about what we morally ought to do and who we should become—and we have that equipment naturally. So in this second sense, the moral law is natural to us.

The third key affirmation of NLT is that the account of the good is logically prior to the account of the right. That's because, according to NLT, whether an action is right or wrong ultimately depends on whether the action is directed in the appropriate ways toward what is good and whether it avoids what is evil. Notice how in this view, right and wrong are going to be defined in terms of what is good and evil—that is, the account of the good presumed by NLT in turn drives the account of the right offered by NLT. What this means, then, is that the concepts of good and evil are more fundamental than the concepts of right and wrong according to NLT.

The fourth element of NLT is what Aquinas labels the *first principle of practical reason*—the principle that what is good is to be done or pursued and what is evil is to be shunned or avoided. (Some translators render this principle in the active voice: We should do and pursue the good and shun that which is evil.) We will return to a fuller discussion of this principle below. For now, though, keep in mind that Aquinas thinks we can apprehend the truth of this principle simply by understanding the terms involved in it. In other words, Aquinas contends that the first principle of practical reason is a self-evident truth.

If what is good is to be done or pursued, then we obviously need to know what is, in fact, good for us as humans. And the fifth key element of NLT is the view that something is intrinsically good for humans if it perfects or completes us, given the kind of creatures we are by nature. This is what we might call a *perfectionist account of the good*. Following Aristotle, Aquinas assumes that we indeed have a certain nature as human beings. That nature, in turn, stakes out a teleological end that is appropriate for us to achieve. In other words, our nature is directed toward an ultimate goal or end state that is proper or fitting for us. In Aquinas's account, the highest teleological end for humanity is what he calls "bliss," or what we might think of as objective human flourishing. Admittedly, in one way, Aquinas holds that the most robust form of objective human flourishing—that is, perfect contemplation of the truth and complete and utter happiness—can only ever occur in communion with God in eternity. That communion with God is our *supernatural* end. But there is another variety of flourishing that is possible in *this* life on earth—the most robust form of objective human flourishing that we can achieve this side of eternity. That is our *natural* teleological end. Accordingly, what makes something good for us is that it contributes to the achievement of that end. That is, good things are good precisely because they perfect or complete us in the sense that they move us toward our natural teleological end. So one of way of summarizing the underlying account of the good in Thomistic NLT goes as follows: Something is intrinsically good for humans if and only if and because it perfects or completes us as the kind of creatures we are. Something is evil if and only if and because it impedes that perfection or completion. And something is value-neutral if and only if and because it neither perfects or complete us nor impedes our perfection or completion.

The sixth key affirmation of NLT is that there are *a variety of human goods* that are fitting objects of our pursuit. These goods provide us with reasons in favor of taking up this or that particular course of action. And NLT holds that we can discern what falls on this list of human goods through the proper use of reason. For example, NLT holds that, by consulting reason in the right way, we can discern that, say, life and knowledge (among other things) are human goods. We will return to this point below.

The final key thesis of NLT is that practical reason provides us with instruction on exactly how and when to pursue the human goods—and when to refrain and what to do in cases where there may be a conflict of human goods. That is, practical reason provides us with norms on how to pursue the human goods properly or most reasonably. We will return to a fuller discussion of these norms below.

8.2. Thomistic Natural Law Theory's Account of the Right

So far, we have mentioned several key theses of NLT, including its perfectionist account of the good. But what is NLT's account of the right? Under which conditions is an action morally obligatory, forbidden, or optional according to NLT? To see Aquinas's response to this question, we need to get a handle on the three essential components of his view about how moral obligations arise in the first place: (a) the first principle of practical reason; (b) how the first principle of practical reason stands in relation to the various things that are intrinsically good for humans; and (c) the norms of practical reason that help direct the proper pursuit of those goods.

The first principle of practical reason

To properly understand the first principle of practical reason, double back to the distinction between *theoretical* and *practical* reason. We can think of theoretical reason as that which seeks to understand the way things are; its aim is descriptive in nature. For example, when scientists try to discover things about the physical world, they are engaging in the theoretical reasoning process. By contrast, we can think of practical reason as that which seeks to understand the way things ought to be; its aim is normative in nature. Accordingly, the dictates of practical reason are effectively reason's way of prescribing what should happen if, say, we want to achieve some objective. Suppose, for example, that one wants to go to medical school. Practical reason issues a command: Develop good study habits, do well in college, and work on your application for medical school. So whereas theoretical reason is focused on getting the mind to map onto the world, practical reason endeavors to get the world to map onto the mind—that is, to chart out what things should be like or how they should become.[13]

Theoretical reason and practical reason both start with first principles, which we can think of as basic, underived, self-evident principles that guide the relevant reasoning processes moving forward. To see the point here, consider how the theoretical reasoning process unfolds at the most rudimentary level. According to Aquinas, the very first thing the mind grasps when engaging in the process of theoretical reasoning is *being*—and without grasping being, the mind cannot grasp anything else about the world.[14] After all, discerning the truth about anything requires a prior *apprehension* of the being or existence of the item in question. To apprehend something is simply to grasp a truth without the use of the intermediate steps of inference or reliance on some more fundamental premise. And when the mind apprehends being in this way, it becomes immediately apparent to the mind that we cannot simultaneously affirm *and* deny the being of something—to do so would be to fail to apprehend being in contrast to nonbeing. The mind thereby apprehends the *law of noncontradiction* as the first principle of theoretical reasoning; it is basic, underived, self-evident, and known through itself. In turn, this first principle provides the basis upon which all further theoretical reasoning can proceed.

Just as *being* is the first thing grasped by the mind in the process of theoretical reasoning, the *good* is the first thing apprehended in the process of practical reasoning, according to Aquinas. And here's why. When reasoning about how to attain some end, the mind is inevitably contemplating that end as something that is perfective or completive in some way, and hence as good. So just as when the minds grasps *being* and thereby sees that something cannot both be and not be, when the minds grasps the *good*, it immediately apprehends that the good is something to be sought (versus *not* sought). Thus, the mind apprehends as self-evident the following first principle of practical reason: "Good is to be done and pursued, and evil is to be avoided"[15]—a phrase that is sometimes translated from the Latin as "we should do and seek good, and shun evil."[16]

Human goods

Suppose the mind indeed apprehends that what is good is to be done and pursued and that what is evil is to be avoided. This is not an especially useful insight in itself, precisely because it is so general, and we can't actually pursue the good in abstraction. We need to know what is intrinsically good for *us* and how the good expresses itself in specific ways that we can actually sink our teeth into. In other words, we need to know what the good looks like concretely and not merely in abstract, formal terms. Once we are aware of how the good expresses itself in these concrete ways, we can then identify more particularized instantiations of the first principle of practical reason. To get to these particularizations, though, we need to identify the various things that are intrinsically good for humans—what we might simply call *human goods*. How might we discern these various particularized instantiations of the good?

Aquinas's approach to answering this question is by first taking stock of persistent human inclinations that are shared most widely in creation before homing in on the ones that are more unique to human beings in particular. These inclinations are tips or clues, as it were. Take, first, the inclination humans share with everything else in the creation. All substances, including humans, are inclined to preserve their own being. We can see, then, that *life*—the preservation of the being of a human substance—is good for us, given our nature as human beings. And discerning this particular manifestation of the good allows us to then identify an accompanying particularization of the first principle of practical reason (and hence one of the *other* general precepts of the natural law): *Life is to be preserved; death is to be avoided.*

Next, consider the natural inclinations that humans share in common with other animals, namely the inclination toward sexual unity of male and female, procreation, and the rearing of offspring. This inclination reflects another particularized instantiation of the good. Such an awareness, then, leads us to identify another general precept of the natural law: *Sexual union of male and female, procreation, and rearing of the young are to be sought.*

Finally, consider the inclination that is most distinctive to humans given our nature as rational creatures: to know the truth and to live in society with others. For Aquinas, "things that relate to such inclinations belong to the natural law (e.g., that human beings shun ignorance, that they not offend those with whom they ought to live sociably, and other such things regarding those inclinations)."[17] Also in this connection, Aquinas holds that "since the rational soul is the proper form of man, there is in every man a natural inclination to act according to reason."[18] Accordingly, he identifies rational conduct as a human good. Thus a general precept of the natural law is to act according to right reason.

So in Aquinas's account, life; procreation and education of the young; knowledge; sociability; and rational conduct can all be identified as intrinsically valuable human goods. Of course, it seems perfectly plausible that there are *additional* human goods that Aquinas could have named beyond those five, but he stops short of telling us what they might be. However, different contemporary proponents of NLT have argued that at least some of the items found in Figure 8.1 are intrinsically valuable human goods.[19]

Figure 8.1. Lists of Human Goods according to Different Contemporary Natural Law Theorists

THOMAS AQUINAS	GERMAIN GRISEZ[20]	T. D. CHAPPELL[21]	JOHN FINNIS[22]	MARK MURPHY[23]	ALFONSO GOMEZ-LOBO[24]
Life	Life and health	Physical and mental health and harmony	Life	Life	Life
Procreation					Family

THOMAS AQUINAS	GERMAIN GRISEZ	T. D. CHAPPELL	JOHN FINNIS	MARK MURPHY	ALFONSO GOMEZ-LOBO
Knowledge	Knowledge of truth	Truth and the knowledge of it	Knowledge	Knowledge	Theoretical knowledge
Social life				Community	
Rational conduct	Practical reasonableness	Reason, rationality, and reasonableness	Practical reasonableness	Excellence in agency	
	Appreciation of beauty	Aesthetic value	Appreciation of beauty	Aesthetic experience	Experience of beauty
	Playful activities		Play		Play
	Friendship	Friendship	Friendship	Friendship	Friendship
	Religion		Religion	Religion	
	Justice		Justice		
	Authenticity		Authenticity		
	Self-integration		Self-integration		Integrity
		Pleasure and avoidance of pain			
		Natural world			
		People			
		Fairness			
		Achievements		Excellence in work and play	Work
	Marital good		Marital good		
				Inner peace	
				Happiness	

For our purposes, we do not need to specify every possible particularization of the good to get the main point at hand: Our diachronically persistent human inclinations are somehow reflective of particularizations of what is intrinsically good for us as humans—of what perfects or completes us. In turn, those human goods entail particularizations of the first principle of practical reason, and these particularizations make up the most general precepts of the natural law.

Adjudicating norms of practical reason

Unfortunately, there are perfectly unreasonable and hence morally flawed ways to pursue the human goods. So the first principle of practical reason and the list of human goods aren't enough to generate a complete account of the right. We still need some principled way of specifying the conditions under which it is reasonable or appropriate, *all things considered*, to pursue life or sexual union or knowledge or sociability, or whatever else might be an intrinsically valuable human good.

To explain: Suppose we just grant that the principles "life is to be preserved," "sexual union of male and female is to be pursued," "sociability is to be pursued," and "ignorance is to be shunned" are all among the most general precepts of the natural law. Would a mother be permitted to lie in order to save the lives of her children (thereby acting on the precept that life is to be preserved)? Would a married man be permitted to pursue sexual union with a neighbor sunbathing on her patio (thereby acting on the precept that sexual union of male and female is to the pursued)? These kinds of questions make it clear that we need to specify the conditions under which it is actually appropriate to pursue the various human goods—especially when they come into conflict. Taken by themselves, the human goods (along with the accompanying particularizations of the first principle of practical reason) only provide us with reasons in favor of doing this or that. But those reasons are not yet *fully decisive* reasons since they might be defeated or overruled by other considerations we have to weigh in the balance. So we need to know what we should do once *all* those things have been considered. That is, we need some principled way of knowing when and under what circumstances we should act on this or that general precept. In other words, we need rational principles that help us adjudicate between the competing ways we might pursue the various human goods. Such principles will then enable us to identify what is obligatory, optional, or wrong for someone because they will specify the appropriate response to the human goods, all things considered. Call those principles the *adjudicating norms of practical reason.*

Aquinas stops short of giving us a neat list of these adjudicating norms, perhaps because they are so varied and context-dependent. However, he does offer a clue for what those adjudicating norms might be like. He contends, for example, that an action is evil precisely because it is flawed with respect to its object, circumstance, or end.[25] Mark C. Murphy offers a helpful elaboration of Aquinas's point:

> An act might be flawed through a mismatch of object and end—that is, between the immediate aim of the action and its more distant point. If one were, for example, to regulate one's pursuit of a greater good in light of a lesser good—if, for example, one were to seek friendship with God for the sake of mere bodily survival rather than vice versa—that would count as an unreasonable act. An act might be flawed through the circumstances: while one is bound to profess one's belief in God, there are certain circumstances in which it is inappropriate to do so (ST IIaIIae 3, 2). An act might be flawed merely through its intention: to direct oneself against a good—as in murder (ST IIaIIae 64, 6), and lying (ST IIaIIae 110, 3) and blasphemy (ST IIaIIae 13, 2)—is always to act in an unfitting way.[26]

Following Murphy's lead here, we might extract at least some of what is needed by reflecting on the different ways an act can be intrinsically flawed. For example, we might extract from Aquinas the following preliminary list of adjudicating norms of practical reason: one must not pursue a lesser good at the expense of a greater good; one must not pursue the human goods in the wrong contexts; and one must not intentionally damage or violate any of the human goods (see fig. 8.2.).

Figure 8.2. A (Preliminary) Thomistic List of Adjudicating Norms of Practical Reason

WITH RESPECT TO . . .	ADJUDICATING NORM OF PRACTICAL REASON
. . . an object	One must not pursue a lesser good at the expense of a greater good.
. . . a circumstance	One must not pursue the human goods in the wrong contexts.
. . . an end	One must not intentionally damage or violate any of the human goods—either directly or as a means to some end.

Now, consider how these norms might function, starting with the third one on the list. The norm that one must not intentionally damage or violate any of the human goods clearly helps to explain why murder, child abuse, harming others, bearing false witness, and various forms of antisocial behavior would be morally wrong according to NLT: When undertaken intentionally, such actions destroy, damage, violate, thwart, or otherwise prevent one of the human goods. This norm has been tremendously influential among proponents of NLT, especially with respect to sexual ethics in particular. Take, for example, the Roman Catholic position on birth control articulated by the papal encyclical mentioned at the outset of this chapter. One of the central ideas of that encyclical is that the use of artificial contraception is (in most cases, at least) intended to prevent a new life from resulting from an act designed to produce life in the first place. Given the adjudicating norm in question, one must not intend damage to any of the human goods, one of which (according to Aquinas) is procreation. It is not enough that one pursues a human good (say, marital unity); one must pursue that good in a way that does not intentionally damage some other good (say, procreation).

But what about cases wherein the reasonable pursuit of one human good unavoidably clashes with some other human good? It is worth noting here that proponents of NLT contend that it is sometimes morally permissible to act in ways that one foresees will damage a human good, but only if that damage is *unintended* and not out of proportion to the good effect the act is intended to have. The subsidiary norm at play here is the *doctrine of double effect*.

To illustrate how this doctrine is sometimes applied, imagine a pregnant woman has an aggressive form of uterine cancer and needs radiation treatment to save her life. Would she be morally permitted to get radiation if she knows the treatment could kill her unborn child? Given the doctrine of double effect, it *might* be permissible for a woman in this circumstance to accept the radiation treatment. Suppose, for example, the pregnant woman foresees that the radiation will likely kill her unborn baby, but she does not *intend* the treatment to do so—that is not *why* she is undergoing the treatment. Her intent is to simply prevent cancer from taking her own life. Moreover, the intended effect (saving her own life) is not out of proportion with the unintended evil effect (the death of the unborn baby). In this case, then, her action isn't ruled out as intrinsically flawed by the main adjudicating norm of practical reason in question (i.e., that one must never intend damage to a human good).

Part of the difficulty of applying the doctrine of double effect centers on the difficulty of determining what one's intention actually is in concrete situations. To illustrate the difficulty here, imagine a situation not unlike the tragic mass school shooting that occurred on the morning of March 27, 2023. Around 10:11 a.m., a twenty-eight-year-old individual named Audrey Elizabeth Hale used two assault-style rifles and a pistol to blast through the glass entryway to The Covenant School, a private Christian school in Nashville, Tennessee, connected to Covenant Presbyterian Church. In a premeditated attack on the elementary school Hale had attended as a child, the assailant fired off more than 150 rounds, killing three staff members and three young students, including the daughter of the pastor of the church on whose campus the school was located. Just sixteen minutes after the shooting began (only fourteen minutes after the initial call to 911), two police officers arrived on the scene and killed the assailant.

Now imagine *you* were present to a situation such as this. And suppose *you* have a clean shot at the back of the head of an assailant who is about to destroy the lives of innocent schoolchildren. Would it be morally permissible for you to pull the trigger? If so, is it possible that your intention is *solely* to save the life of a child—full stop—while killing the assailant is wholly *unintended*? Or is your intention actually to kill the assailant *for the sake of* saving the children? Aquinas seems to suggest that for such a killing to be morally permissible, the death of the assailant would need to be beyond one's intention.[27] Yet, so the critic might say, it is plausible that one might be intending to save the child *by means of* intentionally killing the assailant. Notice the contrast with the radiation case above: The pregnant woman is intending to save her own life by treating the cancer, *not* to kill her unborn baby. But, plausibly, the threatened schoolchild is saved *by means of the assailant's death*—or so the critic might contend. The point here is not to settle the score on these difficult cases in applied ethics. The point is merely to acknowledge the difficulty in parsing out intention and hence the difficulty in knowing exactly how to apply the doctrine of double effect—and other such adjudicating norms of practical reason—in every case.

For now, focus on another adjudicating norm of practical reason that is plausibly extracted from Aquinas: *One must not pursue a lesser good at the expense of a greater good.* Given such a norm, an action would be morally flawed if and when one pursues some good by forfeiting or foregoing some greater good. Such a norm can seem reminiscent of Augustine's famous depiction of sin as the disordered love of lesser goods over greater goods, and we know Aquinas was influenced by Augustine. Naturally enough, then, some of Aquinas's interpreters argue that there is an implicit hierarchy in Aquinas's list of human goods. If so, the rank-ordering of the goods could provide further guidance on how to pursue them. For example, if the good of *life* were to rank higher than, say, the good of *knowledge*, then in contexts where the pursuit of knowledge might conflict with the good of life, the latter would take precedent over the former.

The list of adjudicating norms we have mentioned so far is hardly exhaustive, and much of the ongoing work done by contemporary proponents of NLT centers on providing fuller articulation and defense of such adjudicating norms of practical reason. For example, one of the most important contemporary proponents of NLT, John Finnis, argues that there are at least nine such key norms of practical reason (see fig. 8.3).

Figure 8.3. John Finnis's List of Adjudicating Norms of Practical Reason

WITH RESPECT TO . . .	ADJUDICATING NORM OF PRACTICAL REASON
. . . one's life plan	One must have a *coherent* life plan; one's purposes must be harmonious.
. . . the variety of human goods	"There must be no leaving out of account, or arbitrary discounting or exaggeration, of any of the basic human values."[28]
. . . other humans	One must be impartial among human subjects who are or may be partakers of the basic goods.[29]
. . . detaching from limited projects	"One must have a certain detachment from all the specific and limited projects which one undertakes."[30]
. . . fidelity to one's commitments	"Having made one's general commitments, one must not abandon them lightly."[31]
. . . efficiency in pursuit of goods	One must "bring about good in the world . . . by actions that are efficient for their (reasonable) purpose(s)."[32]
. . . respect for all human goods	One must show respect for every basic good in every act.[33]
. . . common good	One must favor and foster the common good of one's communities.[34]
. . . one's conscience	One must follow one's conscience.[35]

NLT's account of the right, summarized

We are now in a position to reassemble Aquinas's full account of how moral obligations arise. In his view, the first principle of practical reason is encountered as a self-evident truth: We apprehend that what is good is to be done and pursued and that what is evil is to be shunned and avoided. From there, we discern particular instantiations of the good, which generate other general precepts of the natural law. At this point, though, we simply have initial reasons in favor of doing this or that. So we then must also discern and abide by the adjudicating norms of practical reason that further specify the conditions under which it is appropriate to pursue the various human goods at stake. Together, then, these three elements give rise to decisive or all-things-considered reasons to do this or that. That is, these three elements specify the appropriate way to respond to the human goods, which is to say that they specify what our moral obligations are. And according to Aquinas, all of this—that is, the natural law—is binding on us insofar as it captures God's perfect and eternal reason about the ordering of creation toward its proper end.

Finally, we can now summarize NLT's account of the right. An action is morally obligatory if and only if and because it is the only way one can pursue a human good in a manner that isn't ruled out by the adjudicating norms of practical reason. An action is wrong if and only if and because it either fails to pursue a human good or is ruled out by an adjudicating norm of practical reason. And an action is optional if and only if and because it pursues a human good in a way that isn't ruled out by an adjudicating norm of practical reason but yet the action in question isn't the only way to do so. Accordingly, we can depict NLT's moral decision procedure along the lines of the following flowchart (fig. 8.4).

Figure 8.4. NLT's Moral Decision Procedure

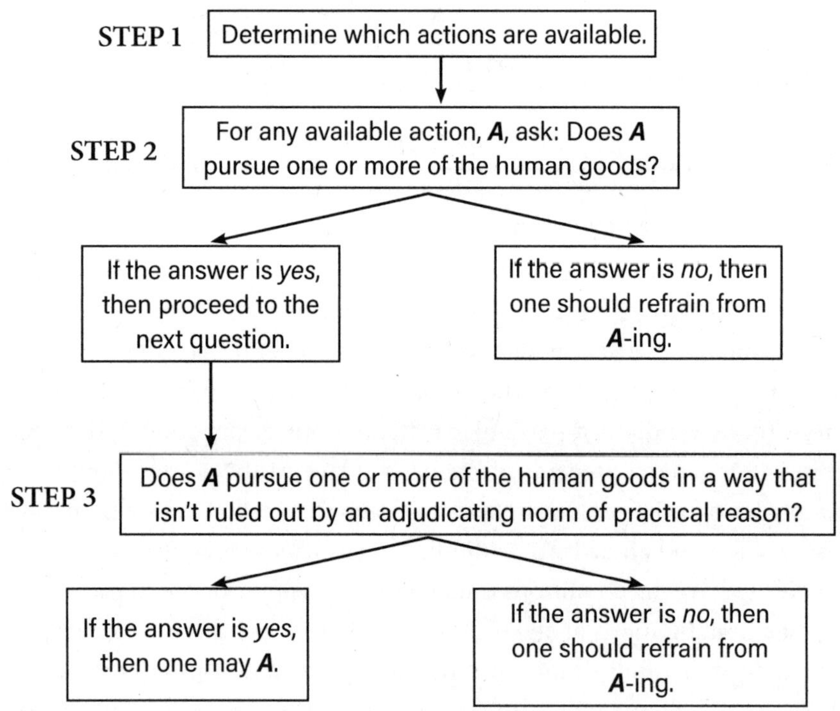

8.3. The Case for Natural Law Theory

There are three distinct sets of considerations in favor of NLT that we will highlight in this section. The first hinges on a defense of the three central elements of the Thomistic account of the right. The second highlights various sorts of advantages to NLT. The final argument stems from considerations of special significance from the perspective of the Christian religion. We will consider each in turn, but it is perhaps best to think of these three as working together to provide a cumulative case for NLT.

A Thomistic argument

If we have properly interpreted Thomistic NLT in the previous section of this chapter, then we might construe a summary argument for Thomistic NLT in the following manner:

(1) If the following propositions are true, then Thomistic NLT is the correct theory of morality:
  (a) The first principle of practical reason is self-evidently true.
  (b) Certain things are good for humans insofar as those things perfect or complete us.
  (c) There are adjudicating norms of practical reason that accurately specify how to properly pursue those human goods.

(2) Those three propositions (a–c) are true.

(3) Thus, Thomistic NLT is the correct theory of morality.

Whether this argument is successful pivots on just how defensible propositions (a), (b), and (c) are. Is it self-evidently true that what is good is to be done and pursued and what is evil is to be avoided? Is it true that certain things are intrinsically good for humans insofar as they perfect us or complete us? Are there indeed some norms of practical reason that specify how to properly pursue the human goods?

In some ways, the case for these three central claims of Thomistic NLT comes by way of the explanation of them in the preceding section. After all, if (upon explanation) these claims are at least initially plausible, and if they can ultimately withstand objections, then perhaps we have all we need in terms of an argument for NLT. But how might we critically evaluate those key claims?

For starters, one might reject proposition (b) because one simply rejects Aristotelian teleology. In other words, someone might reject the very idea that there is (are) some teleological end(s) appropriate to humans by dint of our nature as human beings. And if there is no teleological end toward which humans are appropriately directed, then there is no list of human goods that helps direct us to that end. Accordingly, a full defense of Thomistic NLT would require a defense of Aristotelian teleology too. (Admittedly, there is another version of NLT—what is commonly called *new* natural theory—that does not rely on Aristotelian teleology in the same way, and we will return to it below.)

Similarly, one might challenge proposition (c) by challenging the idea that there is some accurate list of norms issued by practical reason or by worrying that even if there is such a list, we do not have proper access to it. After all, says the critic, while there may be consistency among the proponents of NLT on what those norms are supposed to be, there isn't exactly uniformity. At any rate, notice that the extent to which one finds the Thomistic argument for NLT compelling will hinge on the degree to which one thinks NLT can withstand objections to propositions (a), (b), and (c).

The comparative advantages argument

A second type of case for NLT emphasizes its advantages in comparison to other moral theories. Consider six such advantages to which proponents of NLT might point. First, notice how NLT can provide a robust and coherent explanation for why certain actions that *seem* intuitively morally obligatory are, *in fact*, morally obligatory. For example, lots of people think it would be immoral to torture an innocent person *even if* doing so could deliver good consequences. Yet suppose that brutalizing a renowned terrorist's young daughter would cause the terrorist to cease and desist. While consequentialist theories of morality (and perhaps others) might struggle to explain the wrongness of torture in these cases, NLT does not: It is wrong because it clearly violates the adjudicating norm of practical reason according to which one must not intentionally damage one of the human goods (namely, life).

Second, NLT provides an objective basis for morality by locating that basis in human nature as opposed to cultural mores or individual preferences and desires or hypothetical agreements and so on. In short, empirical facts about actual human beings—as well as facts about the world around us—matter, morally speaking. Not only does this point allow NLT to avoid the vicious subjectivity of relativism or desire-satisfaction versions of utilitarianism, but it also allows facts about how humans actually operate to factor into our account of what we can know about morality. Admittedly, this doesn't exactly eliminate disagreement in cases of applied ethics, since there are still disagreements about human nature and about what is good for humans. But that should be expected because there are disagreements about all sorts of empirical matters. Importantly, though, there is widespread *agreement* about ethical questions, too. For example, almost everyone who has ever lived has known that it is wrong to kill other people just for fun. NLT can explain this widespread agreement: People know this because they have some sort of epistemic access to the fact that life is a human good and that goods ought to be protected.

This leads us to a third advantage of NLT. According to NLT, we have an admittedly imperfect but nonetheless widespread epistemic access to what we need to know in order to live a moral life. That is, according to proponents of NLT, virtually everyone has access to knowledge about the human goods and at least some awareness about how these goods are to be appropriately pursued. Consequentialist theories of morality encounter a problem in this vicinity. Since we are unable to predict the future (and hence whether some action will have the best consequences until the end of history), we are never positioned to know the moral status of an action. But this hardly squares with the data of our lived experience as moral agents because, in fact, we often *do* know that certain actions are either wrong or morally required without relying on consequential assessment. Indeed, there is widespread agreement across cultures about what many of our moral duties are, even in the face of narrow but persistent disagreements. NLT can explain this while some moral theories cannot.

A fourth advantage to NLT is that it offers a deep explanation of the metaphysical foundation of morality, and in a way that rival theories do not or cannot. For NLT, the account of the right is dependent on the account of the good. And the account of human goods centers on what is perfective or completive for humans given our nature. So what makes an action wrong or right according to NLT? The action either hinders or helps creatures with our nature; that is, it either hinders or helps the pursuit of human goods. Now, notice that a common complaint against other theories of morality is that they do not have a good answer to the question at hand. If virtue theorists were asked why some action is morally required, they might answer, "Because a virtuous person wouldn't refrain from doing it." Similarly, if social contract theorists were asked why some action is morally required, they might answer, "Because it conforms to rules that free, equal, rational, and self-interested individuals would agree to." In both cases, though, the answer seems get to things backward. And that's because it seems like a stretch to say that the fact that virtuous persons would do something is what *causes* the action to be required. Similarly, it seems bizarre to think that the fact that hypothetical deliberators would agree to something is what *causes* the action to be required. Instead, the fact that something is morally required seems to be the very reason virtuous persons would do it or ideal deliberators would agree to it. In other words, the order of causation seems to cut in the opposite direction.

While other theories of morality might not get the order of causation wrong in this way, their answers can seem less plausible than the answer provided by NLT. For example, if utilitarians were asked why an action is morally required, their answer would be, roughly, "Because it maximizes utility." Admittedly, utilitarians can insist that the simple fact that an action maximizes utility is also precisely what causes the action in question to be morally required. But the answer offered here seems less plausible than the one offered by NLT. After all, what feature of reality explains why utility maximization causes an action to become morally required? And why exactly should we assume morality tracks *only* consequences, especially in light of the many examples where morality appears to *not* track consequences exclusively? The account given by NLT seems deeper and thus can seem more plausible. A similar story can be told with respect to

Kantianism as well. Recall that the case for Kantian deontology pivots on the assumption that rationality makes a human person valuable beyond all price such that a person must be respected as an end in itself. Admittedly, this is an intuitively attractive assumption, but Kantian deontology doesn't tell us why this proposition is true beyond assuming it. By contrast, NLT can offer a more robust and thorough explanation of what makes the human goods good. In NLT, they are good precisely because they are perfective or completive of creatures with our nature. And according to *theistic* versions of NLT, we have the nature we have as human beings precisely because God created us in his image. Notice, then, how the explanation of the metaphysical foundations of morality offered by NLT goes further and runs deeper.

A fifth advantage to NLT is that it offers a nonreductive account of *multiple* goods, as opposed to saying there is just *one* such good. In this respect, NLT seems to have an advantage to rival theories. Recall that utilitarianism, at least in its initial formulation, holds that happiness (understood as pleasure and the privation of pain) is the only intrinsically good thing. A common complaint against utilitarianism is that such a reductive account of the good leads to troubling and counterintuitive implications like, for example, that one should choose a lobotomized life of happiness that is disconnected from reality over a less happy life in which one sees the truth—or that unconscious victims can be sacrificed for increased net happiness in society. One way to amend utilitarianism to help deal with these complaints is to accept value pluralism. Yet while accepting value pluralism might help utilitarianism circumvent the objection in question, the move can also seem ad hoc since there is nothing about utilitarianism itself to commend value pluralism, whereas value pluralism is built into the very explanatory fabric of NLT. And NLT enjoys a similar advantage vis-à-vis Kantian deontology as well. For Kant, there is only one thing that is intrinsically and unqualified good: a good will. NLT holds that there are multiple human goods in addition to the conditions for having a good will as Kant defines it.

Finally, NLT offers a compelling answer to the question of why someone should be moral. Given NLT, we should be moral because being moral means acting according to our nature as humans and doing that helps perfect or complete us in light of our proper teleological end(s). For NLT, this is not merely some idealized nature or ends; it is the *actual* nature given to us by the Author of our nature, and hence it is our *actual* function given to us by our creator. For many people, this is a more compelling answer to the question than utilitarianism or Kantian deontology or social contract theory can offer because those theories can only appeal to consequences or obeying the moral law for the sake of doing one's duty or following rules that free, equal, rational, and self-interested deliberators would agree to.

The fit between NLT and Christianity

A third type of case for NLT emphasizes the fit between NLT and Christian Scripture and tradition.[36] Consider first how some of the main outlines of NLT seem to square with Hebrew and Christian Scripture. For starters, the very notion that different kinds of creatures (such as human beings) have unique natures fits nicely with the creation account in the book of Genesis, which stresses that things were created according to *kinds* (Gen. 1:24). Admittedly, the Genesis account does not straightway entail that there is, say, a dog nature, a horse nature, an oak tree nature, and a human nature with certain teleological ends—but it indeed fits nicely with the idea that there are such natures.

Additionally, the thought that universally binding moral precepts can be deduced from the first principle of practical reason in conjunction with the list of human goods can seem to fit nicely with requirements of the Decalogue (Exod. 20:1–17). After all, if what is good is to be pursued and what is evil is to be avoided, and if life is an intrinsic human good, then *thou shall not murder.* If truth and knowledge are goods, then *thou shall not lie.* If sociability is a human good, then *thou shalt not steal or covet.* If family is a good, then *thou shall honor your father and mother* and *thou shall not commit adultery.* And so on. Notice how such general precepts would apply to all people and would hold in virtue of the fact that they reflect the posture we should take toward the human goods. Beyond the Decalogue, consider also the simple fact that, among the many moral teachings presented in the book of Leviticus, some instructions appear to pertain exclusively to the ancient Israelites, and others apply also to the foreigners living in Israel. The fact that some of the Levitical instructions would apply to all humans fits nicely with the idea that at least some of the general precepts of the moral law arise in virtue of facts of human nature.

Other elements of NLT can seem to fit with the presuppositions of the New Testament, perhaps most notably those in the apostle Paul's letter to the Romans. For example, Paul contends that the divine nature, while invisible, has been understood through what has been made, so people who fail to honor God are morally blameworthy (Rom. 1:20). The idea here seems to be that we have by nature the capacity to discern the moral law, at least insofar as it pertains to belief in God. Furthermore, Paul asserts that both the Jews and the Gentiles—in other words, *all* people—have epistemic access to other portions of the moral law insofar as that law is "written on their hearts" (Rom. 2:14–15). In sum then, while the biblical canon does not *explicitly* articulate some clear moral theory, it does seem to presuppose that we have certain moral obligations simply insofar as we are human and that we have some sort of epistemic access to what at least some of those obligations are. Those presuppositions fit with NLT.

Not only does NLT fit nicely with the affirmations and presuppositions of Scripture, but NLT has also enjoyed pride of place throughout two millennia of the vast Christian intellectual tradition since the close of the biblical canon. For example, following Cicero and Paul, the early church father Augustine of Hippo (354–430) argues that the eternal moral law is "stamped on the human mind" so that all people, at least in principle, have the ability to recognize its proper demands over us.[37] For Augustine, and for Aquinas whom he clearly influenced, the law that is stamped on our minds is unchanging, it can be recognized by people (precisely because it has been stamped on our minds), and it is subject to rational ordering. Augustine held not only that justice tracks a proper ordering of things, but that it is *necessarily the case* that justice tracks a proper ordering of things; it is necessarily the case that it is "just for everything to be properly ordered."[38] Augustine's views comport with NLT, and in fact his views heavily influenced Aquinas who (as we have seen) put forth what is widely regarded as *the* paradigmatic expression of NLT in and outside of the Christian tradition. And the prominence of NLT within the Christian tradition is not limited to the apostle Paul, Augustine, and Aquinas, as elements of

NLT can be seen in the works of early Christian writers such as Origen (ca. 185–253), Lactantius (ca. 250–325), and Ambrose (ca. 339–397) on up to such thinkers as John Dun Scotus (ca. 1265–1308), Francisco Suarez (1548–1617), and John Locke (1632–1704), among others. The simple fact is that the NLT tradition has overlapped in significant ways with the Christian intellectual tradition itself.

8.4. The Case against Natural Law Theory

Still, there are multiple objections to NLT, including some motivated from a purely secular philosophical perspective, and some motivated specifically from a Christian perspective.[39] We will discuss five such objections.

NLT commits the is-ought fallacy

Perhaps the most notorious objection to NLT centers on the charge that NLT commits the so-called *is-ought fallacy*, which is an accusation traceable back to David Hume (1711–1776). Hume contends, for example, that moral philosophers often argue from descriptive claims—claims like "human nature *is* such and such"—to normative claims—claims like "humans *ought* to do this or that." The problem, though, is that normative claims do not follow with logical necessity from purely descriptive claims. In other words, claims about what *is* the case and claims about what *ought* to be the case belong to two logically distinct categories, such that the claims of the one type simply cannot entail claims of the other type. But if this is the case, we cannot derive normative conclusions from nonnormative premises. And if it is logically illicit to derive normative claims from descriptive ones, then we cannot derive a list of normative precepts such as "We ought to pursue . . ." or "We ought to shun . . ." from a careful consideration of the descriptive facts about human nature alone. Accordingly, the central kernel of NLT is flawed—or so it seems.

One response available to proponents of NLT goes roughly as follows. Start by reflecting on the purposive nature of human action.[40] Everything we do seems to involve an implicit judgment that what we do is what we *ought* to do to achieve some desired end. Yet to desire some end is tacitly to judge it to be perfective or completive of oneself in some way, which is to say that one judges that the end is what one *ought* to desire. For example, if one desires to obtain a college degree, then one tacitly judges that a college degree *ought* to be sought. What difference does that make in relation to the objection on offer? Once we appreciate the teleological or perfective nature of desire itself—and, hence, the teleological or perfective nature of all purposive human action that is parasitic upon that desire—we can see that there is really no logical gap in the move from a descriptive claim about human nature (including facts about human inclinations and desires) to a normative claim about what one ought to pursue after all. If so, then there is no illicit move from the nonnormative to the normative because the premises, as it were, always already include normativity. Put differently, if facts about the sorts of creatures we are by nature always already contain within them a certain teleology, then facts about our nature are not wholly nonnormative in the first place.

In the face of the is-ought fallacy, another option for the proponent of NLT is simply to do an end-run around the putative problem by moving in the direction of what is sometimes called *new natural law theory* (hereafter, "new NLT"). Proponents of new NLT typically concede that traditional versions of NLT are indeed mistaken in trying to derive moral claims from descriptive observations about human nature. Yet proponents of new NLT nonetheless contend that there is still a list of human goods that we can discern, even though they do not think these goods are derivable from descriptive observations about human nature. Rather, proponents of new NLT argue that this list of basic human goods can be apprehended non-inferentially and in a self-evident fashion—that is, in a way that doesn't require us to *infer* a normative conclusion from any argument whatsoever. For example, according to proponents of new NLT, when we reflect on the nature of knowledge—as well as a life without knowledge—we can ascertain in a self-evident way that knowledge is a good to be sought. The same goes for other basic human goods such as life, procreation and education of the young, sociability, and so on. One need not *infer* from human nature to see as much.

Importantly, when proponents of new NLT claim that, say, knowledge is a good that ought to be sought, they insist that the "ought" in question here is merely a *premoral* ought. The list of basic, premoral human goods gets connected to a robust and demanding system of moral obligations only once we have the relevant specifications about the conditions under which it is appropriate to pursue those basic human goods. In other words, we would still need a list of adjudicating norms of practical reason to guide us in identifying the defective and the nondefective ways of pursuing the basic human goods. And without those norms, we would not yet have fully *moral* oughts. At any rate, proponents of new NLT can insist that they do not attempt to derive normative conclusions from descriptive premises. Rather, so the thought goes, they derive normative conclusions with the help of self-evidently true normative premises.

NLT conflicts with evolutionary theory

If one is slow to accept the defensive strategy of new NLT against the is-ought fallacy accusation above, then there is another problem facing proponents of *traditional* versions of NLT. As we have seen, traditional NLT relies on Aristotelian teleology to move from the descriptive to the normative. But what if we have reasons for rejecting teleology altogether? In other words, what if we have reasons for rejecting that there is some proper human function or teleological end or goal for humanity in the first place? If Darwinian evolutionary theory is true, then everything, including humans, is simply the product of millions upon millions of years of natural selection. Accordingly, there would have been no intelligent design plan, as it were, and hence no teleological end imprinted in things. To add to that problem, there wouldn't even have been a consistent human nature over time: As life on earth evolved, the natures of biological organisms changed over time too—albeit very, very slowly—and this would be true of *all* life on earth, including human life. What this means, then, is that if Darwinian evolutionary theory is true, our evolutionary ancestors simply lacked a stable human nature as such.

A proponent of NLT might respond to this worry in at least two ways. One way is simply to deny that humans have ancestors who lacked human nature. Yet even if we assume that the great weight of expert testimony from those working in evolutionary biology points to the truth, and even if we assume that humans do indeed have nonhuman evolutionary ancestors, there is still at least one available line of defense against the objection to NLT. A proponent of NLT might simply insist that, at some point in this evolutionary history, there emerged beings with the capacity for reasoning and enough agency to be morally responsible. Theistic defenders of NLT might even be comfortable allowing that God did something significant within *those* creatures—like inaugurating some kind of relationship with them, or miraculously granting them the gift of a soul, or whatever. If that were true, then at that particular point in the evolutionary timeline, human nature as such would have been inaugurated. It makes no difference to the argument if God used natural evolutionary processes over a vast stretch of time to create human nature. The function of a heart is to beat, no matter how God allowed the heart to be brought about. If this is true, then Darwinian evolutionary theory poses no fatal threat to Aristotelian teleology, and so the objection can thus be deflected.

NLT relies on unreliable human inclinations

A third objection to NLT stems from the fact that Thomistic NLT looks to diachronically persistent human inclinations as a convenient way of homing in on the human goods.[41] Unfortunately, humans throughout history seem to have been persistently inclined to do some pretty terrible things, so relying on diachronically persistent human inclinations to develop the list of human goods can seem problematic.

Recall how Aquinas attempts to develop the list of human goods in the first place. The thought is that we start by observing the world around us and then we take note of what we, as a kind, are persistently inclined toward—say, getting at the truth or experiencing beauty or having intimacy with other people or whatever. In turn, reflecting on these persistent human inclinations (in the proper way, at least) is supposed to tip us off to the goodness of various ends in question. Unfortunately, though, humans—both now and historically—seem to be naturally and persistently inclined toward all manner of things, not all of which are especially flattering.[42] Are humans any less inclined toward, say, selfishness, power-grabbing, violence, and sexual objectification of others than we are toward, say, knowledge or play or friendship? Sadly, it can often seem that humans are perhaps *even more* inclined toward the former than the latter. So if diachronically persistent human inclinations are bad tour guides in the moral life, then they ought not be consulted in drawing up a list of human goods—or so the objection runs.

One way around this problem is to, again, take a lesson from teleology. Some of our diachronically persistent human inclinations, when acted on, do in fact lead to human flourishing, while others do not. Only the inclinations that lead to flourishing should be used to home in on the human goods. So, for example, we find that the persistent human inclination to provide for one's loved ones does indeed tend to lead to flourishing, while the persistent human inclination to eat calorie-dense foods does not. As such, the first inclination, but not the second, would help us identify a human good. While this seems like a plausible enough response, the fact that the proponent of NLT needs to resort to it might indicate just how strongly NLT is tied to teleology.

NLT leaves God out of the picture

There are two more objections to NLT that are motivated primarily by theistic or Christian commitments. The first of these two objections is that, despite NLT's historical connection to theism and to the Christian intellectual tradition in particular, it ironically offers no *central* or even especially prominent role for God in its explanation of how moral obligations arise. After all, NLT can explain how moral obligations arise without making *any* explicit reference to God in the first place. However, if God actually exists, the disappearance of God into the background of the explanation of morality would seem to present a problem for NLT—or so the objection goes.

There are at least two ways that proponents of NLT can respond to this problem. First, the proponent of NLT can insist that God *does indeed* play a vital, albeit mediated, ontological role in how moral obligations arise: God creates the universe, and God creates humankind with a certain nature such that the natural law accords with the dictates of God's perfect reasoning about the ordering of the universe. So simply because we might be able to explain a certain feature of morality downstream from God's creative act without making any explicit reference to God does not entail that God plays no important role upstream from that explanation. After all, the theory of gravity makes no explicit reference to God. However, God can still factor into the explanation of gravity *upstream* from our explanation of it. In fact, many theories that explain the natural world around us make no explicit mention of God, yet those theories can still be understood as being built upon a theistic foundation such that God plays a vital explanatory background role in the development of the systems about which we offer theories.

One might worry that this line of defense against the objection isn't going to cut it from a theistic perspective because the role it affords to God in explaining moral obligation is simply *too* indirect and inadequately immediate.[43] As a remedy, one leading contemporary proponent of NLT, Mark C. Murphy, offers a second distinct way of responding to the objection—what he calls "moral concurrentism," according to which moral obligations are "immediately explained both by God and by human nature."[44] How so? In short, moral concurrentism holds that the human goods depend both on facts about the sorts of creatures we are *and* on facts about God's nature. More specifically in his view, the various human goods are good precisely because they resemble God—and hence participate in God's goodness—in ways that our natural kind *can* resemble God. Accordingly, both God's nature and human nature "jointly morally necessitate."[45] Thus, God factors *immediately* into the explanation of how moral obligations arise, and the objection at hand is thereby deflected.

NLT cannot explain all of our moral obligations

There is one final objection to NLT arising from a theistic perspective: Given theism—and Christian theism in particular—it seems plausible that at least some of our moral obligations are not, and cannot be, explained by NLT. That is, assuming Christian theism is true, it seems plausible that we have moral obligations that are not, and cannot be, explained by appealing to human goods or violations of adjudicating norms of practical reason.

To see why, we first need to double back to NLT's account of the right. Given NLT, the answer to the question, "Why is X morally obligatory?" would never terminate in something like, "Because God said so." Instead, the answer would terminate in the *reasons* God would have had in mind for saying so in the first place. But suppose there were a situation in which God were to command someone to do something but not because there were reasons that fully determined how God must command in that situation.

Suppose, in other words, that it were possible for a divine command to be *under*determined by all the relevant reasons at God's disposal. Call those commands *rationally underdetermined divine commands.* If rationally underdetermined divine commands are even possible, then it is possible for there to be moral obligations that are not, and cannot be, explained by NLT.

To explain: Theists can surely agree that God's sincerely commanding us to X entails that there is, in fact, a decisive reason for us to X—even if we do not or cannot know what that decisive reason is. After all, surely no theist would want to claim, for example, that both (a) God *sincerely* commands us to X, and (b) we do *not* have a decisive reason to X. Insofar as God is omniscient, God would surely know any and all reasons for someone to X. And because God is perfectly good, God would sincerely command someone to X only if there were, in fact, a decisive reason to X. But if it is possible for divine commands to be rationally underdetermined in the way we are imagining, then God could *sincerely* issue them. So suppose God were to issue a rationally underdetermined command. Insofar as God's sincerely commanding us to X entails that there is, in fact, a decisive reason for us to X, then God's commanding us to X in this case would *itself* constitute the decisive reason for us to X. So the answer to the question, "What makes X obligatory?" in this case would effectively be, "*Because God says so*." What this means, then, is that if rationally underdetermined divine commands are even possible, then it is also possible for there to be moral obligations that cannot be explained by NLT.

Why might we think rationally underdetermined divine commands are possible in the first place? The answer is, in part, because we can imagine unproblematic cases of rationally underdetermined *human* commands. Consider the following case from Janine Marie Idziak:

> John has been given the power to pardon one, and only one, of two persons placed under a death sentence. Suppose further that no relevant differences can be found between the two condemned persons. In such a case, there is no better reason for pardoning the one than for pardoning the other. However, John justly frees the one whom he chooses to pardon, although *reason*

> did not move his will to make this choice. And from the very fact that John *wills* to free this particular one, the act of freeing him is just.[46]

What makes the pardoned person's fate just is not John's reasons for selecting *this* man versus *that* man—reasons do not, because they cannot, determine the matter here. Rather, the thing that makes this person's fate just is "sheer will" on John's part.[47] So it seems that we can imagine unproblematic cases of rationally underdetermined human commands. Surely it is conceivable that at least one of God's commands is sufficiently similar to the decision John made in the example above such that prior *reason* does not determine how God commands but solely the divine *will.* And if such a predicament is even possible, then it is possible for there to be moral obligations that are not, and cannot be, explained by NLT.

But we can go further with this point. All three of the major Abrahamic religions appear to affirm that rationally underdetermined *divine* commands are not only possible but actual. Here is one such example affirmed by at least the Jewish and Christian traditions: God commanded the Israelites to rest *on the seventh day* (Exod. 20:8–10).[48] Accordingly, when God commanded the Israelites to rest on the seventh day, resting on the seventh day became morally obligatory for them. If God were to stop commanding them to rest on the seventh day, then it would no longer be morally obligatory for them to rest on the seventh day. And God's reasons for commanding the Israelites to rest on the *seventh* day (rather than on, say, the *third* day of the week) do not appear to be fully determinative. By that we simply mean that it does not seem that God's choice to command the *seventh* versus the *third* day was somehow fully necessitated by prior facts about human nature and/or facts about the divine nature and/or adjudicating norms of practical reason. So God's command here, like John's choice about whom to pardon, seems rationally *under*determined. But God's command to rest on the seventh day is not thereby somehow inefficacious or morally problematic.

If these very plausible assumptions are true, then at least some humans have had on at least some occasions some concrete moral obligations that are not, and cannot be, explained by NLT. Accordingly, in those cases, if we were to ask why those things are morally obligatory, the correct answer to that question would substantively terminate with "because God says so." Importantly, with respect to those actions, the connection between God's commanding X and the fact that X is morally obligatory is not one of mere correlation—that is, the divine command does not merely indicate or reiterate that there is a moral obligation. Rather, the divine command somehow ontologically grounds the moral obligation itself. If this is all true, then we have at least some moral obligations for which NLT does not, and in principle cannot, offer an explanation.

Fortunately, in any case, this objection need not be devastating for all versions of NLT. It is possible that some moral obligations *can* and *do* arise in one of the ways suggested by NLT, even if all our moral obligations cannot and do not arise in that way. So perhaps it is most fitting to conclude that, given the objection on offer, NLT isn't wrong as much as it is simply *incomplete* because there would be at least some reason to think moral obligations could arise in other ways too. So it makes sense, then, to think that NLT's explanation of morality will need to be supplemented.

chapter nine

DIVINE COMMAND THEORY

Consider the tale of two African American preachers. The first in our tale is Nat Turner, who was born into chattel slavery in Southampton, Virginia, on October 2, 1800.[1] He was an unusually intelligent child and, against all odds as a slave, he learned to read and write at a very young age. He dedicated himself to reading the Bible, fasting, and prayer, and he eventually came to see himself, and to be regarded by many within his community, as a latter-day prophet to whom God spoke directly through visions and voices, as well as through natural signs. Turner recounted toward the end of his life, for example, that at the age of three or four, "the Lord had shewn me things that happened before my birth" and he maintained that, over the years, the very same Holy Spirit that had spoken to the Old Testament prophets had appeared to him as well.[2] During his twenties, Turner managed to escape from slavery. But to everyone's astonishment, Turner voluntarily returned a month later because he had received a vision in which God chastised him for prioritizing the things of this world—namely, his own freedom—over the heavenly mission for which he was still being prepared among his fellow slaves.

After being traded several times, Turner was eventually enslaved by a man named Joseph Travis, whom Turner described as a "kind master" and Turner "had no cause to complain of his treatment to me."[3] Meanwhile, after receiving multiple revelations and signs in the years and months prior to living under Travis, Turner grew convinced that the divine command had finally come: He was to begin "the work of death" and slay his enemies "with their own weapons."[4] So on August 21, 1831, Turner and several other men broke into the Travis house under the cover of night and butchered the family in their sleep. No one was to be spared, so when they realized they had forgotten about the infant sleeping in the cradle, they doubled back to kill him, too. From there, Turner's posse marched from house to house, slaughtering every White person in their path. Before his insurrection was crushed two days later, about sixty enslaved and free Black people had joined Turner, and at least fifty-five White people were left slain, the majority of whom were unarmed women and children.

Turner's rebellion struck terror in the hearts of White Virginians—and it put the lie to the myth that Black folks were basically content with their station in a slave society. The backlash against Turner was no less bloody. Some estimates hold that more than one hundred enslaved and free Black people were killed, many of whom were also women and children. The Virginia legislature soon made it illegal for slaves to preach or receive an education. And although Turner himself had initially managed to outrun the militia sent to defeat him, he was captured about three months later, tried, and promptly hanged. In a confession recorded just prior to his execution, Turner acknowledged the gravity of his deeds, but he made it clear that his long-held conviction that God had ordained him for a special mission had been the impetus for what had "terminated so fatally to many, both white and black, and for which I am about to atone at the gallows."[5] In fact, Turner admitted that God's calling had been so compelling that "even now, sir, in this dungeon, helpless and forsaken as I am, I cannot divest myself of [it]."[6] Nat Turner, so it seems, sincerely believed two things: first, that God had commanded lethal retribution against the

White perpetrators of slavery; and, second, that he was morally obligated to obey that command.

The second preacher in our tale is Rev. James M. Lawson Jr. (1928–2024), who was born nearly a century after Turner died. A third-generation Methodist minister, Lawson grew up in a world marked by racial segregation and Jim Crow. While still an undergraduate at Baldwin Wallace College in Ohio, he was imprisoned for more than a year for refusing to participate in the draft during the Korean War. Upon his release in 1952, Lawson served as a missionary in India for several years, where he encountered the philosophy of nonviolent resistance connected to Mohandas Ghandi (1869–1948). Not long after returning to the United States to attend seminary, Lawson met a twenty-eight-year-old Baptist minister named Martin Luther King Jr. in 1957, who encouraged him to take his Ghandian principles of nonviolence to the main stage of the civil rights movement in the South. So Lawson transferred to Vanderbilt University to continue his graduate work in Nashville, where he led the workshops on nonviolence that launched the famous student sit-ins that eventually desegregated several downtown restaurants as well as established a model for other nonviolent protests throughout the Southeast—including the Freedom Rides—in the years to come. For his part in organizing the sit-ins, Lawson was expelled from Vanderbilt in 1960. King would go on to describe Lawson as "the mind of the movement" and "the leading theorist and strategist of nonviolence in the world."[7]

During an interview just months before he died in 2024, the ninety-five-year-old Lawson recounted a salient incident from his childhood that, to his mind, had animated his life's work in advancing civil rights.[8] One day when Lawson was in fourth grade, he had encountered a young White boy who hurled a racist epithet at him while he was out running an errand for his mother. Lawson smacked the boy in response. After returning home, he explained to his mother what had happened, and she in turn lectured him on the family's values in relation to the ways of Jesus, and she concluded that "there must be a better way." What Lawson described as his mother's "long soliloquy" had clearly triggered in him a "continuously transforming incident":

> It became a numinous experience for me, because I heard a voice, which came from what it seemed to me, a deep place in space, and then gradually I felt that it was coming from inside me, but from outside me, but it was coming to me and it was a voice deep within. That voice said, "Number one, you will never again fight anybody physically." . . . And then secondly, as she was talking, I heard the same voice saying, "and you will find the better way."[9]

Lawson pinpointed this numinous experience as the beginning of his lifelong commitment to nonviolence. James Lawson, so it seems, believed two things: first, that he was to obey the supernatural voice that had come to him; and, second, that he had been called to the way of nonviolence.

While this tale of two African American preachers is unique in many ways, Lawson and Turner are far from alone in the conviction that God sometimes issues commands about how we are to live and behave. In fact, many, if not most, people throughout the world today seem to believe something in this vicinity—even if they don't agree about the content of God's commands, or about how they are received, or about how they should be interpreted, or that they are so individualized in nature. After all, the overwhelming majority of Americans identify with one of the major Abrahamic religions—Christianity, Islam, and Judaism—as does more than half of the global population, and each of those religious traditions teaches that God issues commands.[10] So adherents of those religions are committed on some level to believing this as well. But notice, if one sincerely believes that the very same supremely powerful, wise, and good God who created the universe has commanded something, it can seem natural to suppose that one ought to obey that command.

So, minimally, it seems fair to say that a lot of people throughout the world today presuppose that morality is importantly connected to God's commands or some other prescriptive act of the divine will—and, more specifically, that we are morally obligated to do certain things *because* God commands (or wills or intends or prefers) them. That last view is, roughly, a view known as theological voluntarism or, as it is perhaps more commonly known, divine command theory (hereafter, "DCT"). Of course, the fact that a view is commonly held or widely presupposed hardly demonstrates its truth. But it does give us reason to consider the view seriously, which is the goal of this chapter.

9.1. What Divine Command Theory Says

Although some components of DCT date back to antiquity, the origin of DCT as a fully formed theory of ethics can be traced back to the high Middle Ages. Some scholars have tried to argue that Thomas Aquinas (1225–1275) was among the earliest proponents of DCT, though we think that attribution is pretty clearly mistaken.[11] More plausibly, other scholars regard John Duns Scotus (ca. 1265–1308) as one the first medieval architects of what would eventually morph into DCT.[12] At any rate, in the generations following Scotus, a long line of impressive thinkers stretching from William of Ockham (ca. 1287–1347) to John Locke (1632–1704) held that divine commands *can* and sometimes *do* give rise to moral obligations. Other figures, such as Andrew of Neufchateau (ca. 1340–1400), Pierre d'Alliy (1351–1420), Gabriel Biel (ca. 1420/5–1495), Martin Luther (1483–1546), and John Calvin (1509–1564), went even further to claim that *only* God's commands can give rise to moral obligations. At any rate, it is clear that by the dawn of the fifteenth century in the run up to the Protestant Reformation, the DCT position had crystallized as a distinctive theory of morality unto itself—and it would come to influence many who would follow in the Christian tradition for centuries thereafter.

In one way, DCT is a fairly straightforward theory of morality, which makes it easy enough to understand. In short, DCT holds that morality is wholly dependent upon God's commands (or God's expressed will or preferences). Perhaps more to the point, DCT holds that what makes an action right or wrong is the fact that God commands or forbids it. Accordingly, if God commands that we do something, then that action is morally obligatory; if God forbids something, then it is morally wrong.

To flesh out DCT more fully, we will highlight four key claims of the theory. DCT holds the following:

i. The good is prior to the right.
ii. The moral status of an action depends on divine commands.

iii. Divine commands hold only for those whom God has commanded.
iv. For a divine command to be binding, it must be promulgated.

First off, notice how DCT presumes the priority of the good to the right. In other words, for DCT, the proper account of what is good, bad, or value-neutral is explanatorily more fundamental than the proper account of the conditions under which an action is morally obligatory, optional, or wrong. In fact, the nature of what is good very much undergirds and even constrains DCT's account of the right. Afterall, DCT's account of the right affirms that what makes an action right is the fact that God commands it. But this account presupposes that God exists and that God is necessarily, intrinsically, and supremely good. So notice, then, how the account of the right banks on a prior understanding of what is good—namely, God. Thus, for proponents of DCT, the good (where "Good" is sometimes capitalized to highlight its personal or transcendent nature) is really the most basic category at play, at least to the extent that the nature of God's goodness limits the sort of things God might command in the first place precisely because God cannot command something contrary to God's nature as a good being.

A second key element of DCT is what we might label the *command-dependency thesis*, according to which the moral status of an action depends in a very important sense on divine commands. This is not to say merely that divine commands *indicate* what is obligatory, optional, or wrong. Rather, for DCT, divine commands are what *make* an action morally obligatory, optional, or wrong; and, in fact, God's command is effectively the *only* thing that does this heavy-lifting, so to speak. So according to DCT, a divine command is a necessary condition for the occurrence of a moral obligation. Notice the importance of this claim. Religious believers of all stripes might naturally believe they ought to do what God commands of them. But *that* belief alone is not enough to make one a proponent of DCT, since one can sincerely believe one should obey God's command while also denying that God's command is what *makes* the action morally obligatory. Yet DCT says God's command is what makes or grounds or causes or actualizes the obligation in question, and in that strong sense, morality is importantly dependent upon divine commands. This is a point to which we return below.

For now, consider the third key claim of DCT, which is what we might think of as the *scope-audience thesis*. In this view, a divine command actualizes a moral obligation for only those whom God has so commanded. And of course the scope of God's command could vary widely. Some commands could be given to all humans, while other commands could be directed to only one individual or to a specific subset of people. So notice how we might say that the scope of the moral obligation tracks the audience to whom a divine command is issued.

The fourth key claim of DCT is what we can think of as a *promulgation condition*. All proponents of DCT agree that in order for moral obligations to arise, God's commands must be promulgated, or made known. The basic idea here is that we surely cannot be obligated to do something if we have no way of knowing about that obligation in the first place. Suppose, for example, that a legislative body were to pass a new law in secret.[13] The problem, of course, is that a secret law is really no law at all; that law must be promulgated to become binding. The same goes for God's commands—that is, if they are to actualize moral obligations. And there are any number of possible means through which God's commands could be communicated. For example, God might promulgate his commands through (a) sacred texts such as the Bible; (b) the discernment processes of a church or ecclesial body; (c) human conscience; (d) direct supernatural revelations to specific individuals; or (e) other people (e.g., prophets) or social institutions. And so on. While proponents of DCT might differ on the precise mechanisms through which God might promulgate divine commands—as well as about how we can come to discover and rightly interpret them—all proponents of DCT agree that the divine command must be promulgated by some means in order to actualize moral obligations.

Before moving on, it is important to recognize that DCT gets depicted in a variety of ways depending on who is discussing it—and this can sometimes create confusion for those who are trying to understand DCT. For example, DCT sometimes gets depicted as *either* an account of the good *or* an account of the right or *both*. Notice that if DCT were contemplated as an account of the good, it would run roughly as follows: Something is good if and only if and just because God commands it. Something is bad if and only if and just because God forbids it. And something is value-neutral if and only if and just because God neither commands nor forbids it. We should point out, though, that almost no contemporary proponent of DCT contemplates DCT in this manner. That is, virtually no contemporary proponent of DCT holds that divine commands are what actually determine whether something is good, bad, or value-neutral. And for good reason. Theists take God to be a perfect being, and hence good. But if God's commands were what made something good, then how could we ever understand God as good? Because God commands himself? And what sense does that make? Frankly, it's not at all clear how that *would* make any sense. For that reason, among others, contemporary proponents of DCT are usually pretty quick to distance themselves from any effort to depict DCT as an account of the good. Accordingly, nearly all contemporary proponents of DCT readily acknowledge that something *other* than divine commands would need to provide the basis for an account of the good, though (unsurprisingly) their various accounts of the good remain patently theistic in nature. We, too, think it is best to understand DCT as strictly an account of the right and not as an account of the good. (Of course, that means any proponent of DCT needs to provide a supplementary and complimentary account of the good.)

So if we contemplate DCT as *strictly* an account of the right, how might that run? We can summarize it as follows. An action is morally obligatory if and only if and just because God commands it. An action is wrong if and only if and just because God forbids it. And an action is optional if and only if and just because God neither commands nor forbids it. In turn, such a DCT account of the right would naturally give rise to a fairly straightforward procedure for making moral decisions:

> STEP 1: Determine which actions are available.
> STEP 2: For each action, determine whether God commands it, forbids it, or neither commands nor forbids it.
> STEP 3: Obey the divine command.

The chief difficulty in following DCT's decision procedure centers on STEP 2. And proponents of DCT are in no way committed to saying the task of discerning or interpreting divine commands is an easy one—even, for example, among those who accept the divine inspiration of the Bible and regard it as a primary (or even exclusive) source of God's commands. For one thing, there are *lots* of commands articulated or implied within the biblical canon. Jewish tradition holds, for example, that there 613 divine commands expressed in the Torah alone (i.e., Genesis, Exodus, Leviticus, Numbers, and Deuteronomy), and one of the most famous versions of this particular list comes to us from the medieval Jewish philosopher and rabbi Maimonides (1138–1204). Keep in mind that Maimonides's list does not even attempt to catalog other commands contained within the remainder of the Old Testament—to say nothing of the New Testament. And some lists identify well over one thousand distinct divine commands found within the New Testament. So, in any case, it would take quite a bit of work to enumerate each and every divine command contained in Hebrew and Christian Scripture. Nonetheless, consider Figure 9.1 below, which is a (nonexhaustive) sampling of widely recognized divine commands conveyed in Hebrew and Christian Scripture.

Figure 9.1. Some Divine Commands Contained in Hebrew and Christian Scripture (NIV)

PASSAGE	DIVINE COMMAND	AUDIENCE
Gen. 1:28	"Be fruitful and increase in number; fill the earth and subdue it. Rule over the fish in the sea and the birds in the sky and over every living creature that moves on the ground."	Adam and Eve; humankind?
Gen. 3:3	"You must not eat fruit from the tree that is in the middle of the garden, and you must not touch it, or you will die."	Adam and Eve
Gen. 6-7	Specific commands on how to build the ark	Noah
Gen. 12:1	"Go from your country, your people and your father's household to the land I will show you."	Abram
Gen. 17	Circumcision	Abram; male descendants
Gen. 22:2	"Take your son, your only son, whom you love—Isaac—and go to the region of Moriah. Sacrifice him there as a burnt offering on a mountain I will show you."	Abraham
Gen. 22:12	"'Do not lay a hand on the boy,' he said. 'Do not do anything to him.'"	Abraham

PASSAGE	DIVINE COMMAND	AUDIENCE
Exod. 12	Instructions on the commemoration of Passover and the Festival of Unleavened Bread	Israelites; descendants
Exod. 20:3–17 **DECALOGUE**	"You shall have no other gods before me."	Israelites; descendants
	"You shall not make for yourself an image in the form of anything in heaven above or on the earth beneath or in the waters below. You shall not bow down to them or worship them."	
	"You shall not misuse the name of the LORD your God."	
	"Remember the Sabbath day by keeping it holy."	
	"Honor your father and your mother."	
	"You shall not murder."	
	"You shall not commit adultery."	
	"You shall not steal."	
	"You shall not give false testimony against your neighbor."	
	"You shall not covet."	
Exod. 21–40	Extensive set of civic and religious laws—from how to treat servants and parents to what should happen if one accidentally or intentionally destroys another's property, from how offerings and sacrifices should be made to how the tabernacle should be constructed and what priests should wear, among others	Israelites
Lev. 1-7	Various commands regarding different kinds of sacrifices	Israelites
Lev. 11	Various commands regarding clean and unclean foods	Israelites
Lev. 12–15	Various commands regarding sanitation practices among the Israelites	Israelites
Lev. 17	Various commands regarding sanitation practices—but not just for Israelites	Israelites; others in Israel
Lev. 18–20	Various commands regarding different dietary, sexual, sanitation, and civic practices	Israelites; others in Israel
Josh. 1:7-8	"Be strong and very courageous. Be careful to obey all the law my servant Moses gave you; do not turn from it to the right or to the left, that you may be successful wherever you go. Keep this Book of the Law always on your lips; meditate on it day and night, so that you may be careful to do everything written in it."	Joshua; Israelites

PASSAGE	DIVINE COMMAND	AUDIENCE
Josh. 6:3-5	"March around the city once with all the armed men. Do this for six days. Have seven priests carry trumpets of rams' horns in front of the ark. On the seventh day, march around the city seven times, with the priests blowing the trumpets. When you hear them sound a long blast on the trumpets, have the whole army give a loud shout; then the wall of the city will collapse and the army will go up, everyone straight in."	Joshua; Israelites
Matt. 3:2	"Repent, for the kingdom of heaven has come near."	Universal
Matt. 5-7 **SERMON ON THE MOUNT**	"You have heard that it was said to the people long ago, 'You shall not murder, and anyone who murders will be subject to judgment.' But I tell you that anyone who is angry with a brother or sister will be subject to judgment. Again, anyone who says to a brother or sister, 'Raca,' is answerable to the court. And anyone who says, 'You fool!' will be in danger of the fire of hell." (5:21–22)	Universal
	"You have heard that it was said, 'You shall not commit adultery.' But I tell you that anyone who looks at a woman lustfully has already committed adultery with her in his heart. If your right eye causes you to stumble, gouge it out and throw it away." (5:27–29)	
	"It has been said, 'Anyone who divorces his wife must give her a certificate of divorce.' But I tell you that anyone who divorces his wife, except for sexual immorality, makes her the victim of adultery, and anyone who marries a divorced woman commits adultery." (5:31–32)	
	"Again, you have heard that it was said to the people long ago, 'Do not break your oath, but fulfill to the Lord the vows you have made.' But I tell you, do not swear an oath at all." (5:33–34)	
	"You have heard that it was said, 'Eye for eye, and tooth for tooth.' But I tell you, do not resist an evil person. If anyone slaps you on the right cheek, turn to them the other cheek also. And if anyone wants to sue you and take your shirt, hand over your coat as well. If anyone forces you to go one mile, go with them two miles. Give to the one who asks you, and do not turn away from the one who wants to borrow from you." (5:38–42)	
	"You have heard that it was said, 'Love your neighbor and hate your enemy.' But I tell you, love your enemies and pray for those who persecute you." (5:43–44)	
	"Be careful not to practice your righteousness in front of others to be seen by them." (6:1)	

PASSAGE	DIVINE COMMAND	AUDIENCE
Matt. 5-7 **SERMON ON THE MOUNT**	"But when you fast, put oil on your head and wash your face, so that it will not be obvious to others that you are fasting." (6:17–18)	Universal
	"But store up for yourselves treasures in heaven, where moths and vermin do not destroy, and where thieves do not break in and steal." (6:20)	
	"Do not worry about your life, what you will eat or drink; or about your body, what you will wear." (6:25)	
	"Do not judge, or you too will be judged. For in the same way you judge others, you will be judged, and with the measure you use, it will be measured to you." (7:1–2)	
	"Do not give dogs what is sacred; do not throw your pearls to pigs." (7:6)	
	"Ask and it will be given to you; seek and you will find; knock and the door will be opened to you." (7:7)	
	"So in everything, do to others what you would have them do to you, for this sums up the Law and the Prophets." (7:12)	
	"Watch out for false prophets." (7:15)	
Matt. 22:34-40 **THE GREATEST COMMAND**	"Jesus replied: "'Love the Lord your God with all your heart and with all your soul and with all your mind." This is the first and greatest commandment. And the second is like it: "Love your neighbor as yourself." All the Law and the Prophets hang on these two commandments."'	Universal
Matt. 28:19-20 **THE GREAT COMMISSION**	"Therefore go and make disciples of all nations, baptizing them in the name of the Father and of the Son and of the Holy Spirit, and teaching them to obey everything I have commanded you."	Disciples; universal?
John 3:7	"You must be born again."	Nicodemus; universal
John 13:34-35	"A new command I give you: Love one another. As I have loved you, so you must love one another. By this everyone will know that you are my disciples, if you love one another."	Disciples; universal?
Rom. 13:8-10	"Let no debt remain outstanding, except the continuing debt to love one another, for whoever loves others has fulfilled the law. The commandments . . . are summed up in this one command: 'Love your neighbor as yourself.' Love does no harm to a neighbor. Therefore love is the fulfillment of the law."	Universal?

PASSAGE	DIVINE COMMAND	AUDIENCE
1 Pet. 1:14-16	"As obedient children, do not conform to the evil desires you had when you lived in ignorance. But just as he who called you is holy, so be holy in all you do; for it is written: 'Be holy, because I am holy.'"	Universal?
Eph. 4:25-5:4	Do: tell the truth, work to produce useful things, build one another up, love one another, share with one another, and imitate God Don't: steal, brawl, slander, and various other things	Universal

Even if one could chart out all the divine commands contained within the Bible, there would still remain several challenges related to discerning God's commands—challenges related to determining the scope of the target audience, the generality or specificity of the command in question, and the content of that command. First, notice how some of the commands listed in Figure 9.1 are narrow in audience (e.g., Adam and Eve or Abraham or Noah), while others are wider in scope (e.g., Israelites or the Israelites *and* those living in their land or even universal). And sometimes the scope of the audience remains unclear. In fact, one of the difficulties facing the early church centered on deciding the intended audience of the commandments originally promulgated to the Israelites through Moses. Were these commands meant to apply to Gentile converts to Christianity, for example? Second, notice how some of the biblical commands are specific behaviors (e.g., "abstain from *that* fruit," or "build a boat like *this*," or "go live over *there*"), while others are more general rules or principles ("be courageous," or "be holy"). In cases where the command is to follow a general rule or principle, interpreters still have to determine which actions would be consistent with the rule or principle in question. Third, it is sometimes unclear what the command in question is supposed to be—or even whether the teaching in question should be contemplated as a *command* in the first place or if it should be understood perhaps as something else altogether.

With respect to this last point, return to the Sermon on the Mount. There, Jesus says that to be a part of God's kingdom, one's righteousness must exceed that of the Pharisees and the teachers of the law. He then recites six ancient commands and follows up on each of these commands with an important twist. Focus on the fourth one for now:

> Again, you have heard that it was said to the people long ago, "Do not break your oath, but fulfill to the Lord the vows you have made." But I tell you, do not swear an oath at all: either by heaven, for it is God's throne; or by the earth, for it is his footstool; or by Jerusalem, for it is the city of the Great King. And do not swear by your head, for you cannot make even one hair white or black. All you need to say is simply "Yes" or "No"; anything beyond this comes from the evil one. (Matt. 5:33–37)

What exactly is going on here? Should we read this as Jesus issuing a *new* command for us to never swear or enter into a solemn vow about anything whatsoever? Some Christians, such as those in the Mennonite tradition, suggest as much. But perhaps what Jesus means to be teaching here isn't reducible to a command to abstain from specific outward behaviors or speech acts (though perhaps it might *include* that, too). Perhaps Jesus is instructing us to become the kind of people who don't need a system of oath-giving in the first place—precisely because we would be the sort of people who don't play tricks with our words. After all, if one is crafty enough, one could well devise an oath that one could fulfill in some literal or technical sense while still remaining perfectly deceptive and morally deficient. Perhaps Jesus is really saying: *Don't be like that guy. Be so trustworthy and full of integrity that your word is ironclad.* If this sort of interpretation is on target, then perhaps Jesus really means to be critiquing a reductive understanding of righteousness that is concerned only with mere behavioral compliance and rote rule-following. Perhaps Jesus means to be advancing a more holistic view of righteousness that is concerned *also* with the proper internal architecture of one's character. At any rate, our point here is simply that discerning divine commands in Scripture often requires serious intellectual work, which can make STEP 2 of DCT's decision procedure more complex than might meet the eye.

9.2. The Case for Divine Command Theory

The overall case for DCT can be organized into two subcategories: what we might think of as *secular* (or nonreligious) considerations versus decidedly *religious* arguments for DCT. In general, the secular case for DCT hinges on the thought that DCT provides a tidy explanation for certain things that might otherwise be difficult to explain. This sort of approach is secular in nature only insofar as it does not require that one antecedently buy into certain theological premises on the front end in order to motivate the considerations in question. Various religious arguments for DCT, by contrast, focus on what would seem to follow downstream from certain assumed theological assumptions, namely, that God exists and that God has a certain nature. Consider each approach in turn.

A secular case for DCT

One fairly cumulative secular case for DCT can be summarized as follows:

(1) DCT can explain certain things that can otherwise seem pretty difficult to explain, including most notably:
  (a) the fact that objective moral values and obligations exist;
  (b) salient features of moral obligations as we experience them; and
  (c) why we should be moral in the first place.

(2) Other moral theories do not or cannot explain (a), (b), and (c)—or at least not as well as DCT can.

(3) Thus, the fact that DCT can explain (a), (b), and (c) provides evidence for thinking DCT is the correct account of morality.

To get a better handle on how this secular case for DCT unfolds, we need to consider each of the claims made in premise 1.

Start with (a). One consideration in favor of DCT hinges on the thought that objective moral values and obligations are, well, pretty weird things. To see the point here, just imagine for a moment that God *doesn't* exist—and neither do angels, demons, spirits, and other such supernatural entities. In other words, just imagine that naturalism is true. Now, if naturalism *were* true, then as atheist philosopher J. L. Mackie points out, objective moral values and obligations "would be entities or qualities of a very strange sort, utterly different from anything else in the universe."[14] Why is that, exactly? Well, if there really were nothing beyond the natural world, then at the most basic level of explanation one would find only particles and the scientific laws of nature, like gravity. But scientific laws of nature would merely *describe* the workings of the world we inhabit, whereas objective moral laws (if there were any) would *prescribe* the way the world should be. So for Mackie and other atheist thinkers like him, the existence of objective moral values and obligations would present both a metaphysical and an epistemological conundrum. Where did these moral values and obligations come from in the first place? This can seem like a hard question to answer, especially since objective moral values and obligations would be such cosmic oddballs. And in light of that metaphysical mystery, there is an epistemological worry: How could we learn about these odd entities? This too seems like a tough question, especially since objective moral values and obligations wouldn't be knowable in the same way everything else appears to be knowable by us.

Notice how Mackie's point about the strangeness of objective moral values and obligations might be reconfigured into a consideration in favor of DCT. If facts about the natural world simply cannot provide an explanation for why objective moral values and obligations exist, then perhaps we really do need something *super*natural in the picture in order to explain how they exist. DCT, so it seems, can do the trick nicely here.

Now turn to (b). Another consideration in favor of DCT hinges on the thought that there are several key features of our experience of moral obligations that DCT seems well-suited to explain.[15] For example, our experience of moral obligations is such that we *care* about complying with them, failing to comply with them produces a sense of *guilt* or *blame*, we are interested in promoting *public compliance* with them, and we feel a sense of *urgency* about meeting those obligations. What is more, we experience moral obligations as being *indefeasible* in nature—that is, we experience full-blown moral obligations as things that cannot be trumped or defeated or overruled by other obligations or considerations we might have (e.g., familial, civic, legal, economic obligations, etc.).

How exactly does DCT explain these five salient features? Start by paying attention to how one's obligations often seem to arise within a framework of social relationships among and between multiple persons—within families, organizations and workplaces, communities, nations, and so on. More specifically, obligations seem to arise when claims or demands are made by one party upon another party within some social context. The *social* nature of obligations helps explain why we would care about our obligations, why we would feel guilt or blame when they aren't met, why we would desire for others to meet them, and why we would feel a sense of urgency about meeting them. We value our bonds within our social contexts and fear the sanctions of the communities of which we are a part. Importantly, though, the requirements that arise from the demands of others within strictly *human* communities are at most only premoral. Why is that? Admittedly, someone making a demand on us gives us a reason in favor of acting in such and such a way. But that reason does not in itself yet rise to the level of being a definitive, all-things-considered, and *indefeasible* reason to so act. If a parent or employer or police officer makes a demand of you, that gives you a reason to do the thing in question; but this reason can still be defeated (at least in principle) by other considerations that might come about. But suppose there were a God who commanded you to do something. Like parental, employer, or police commands, a divine command would of course give you a reason to act. But unlike demands made by other humans, the divine command would also give you a reason to act that could not be defeated by other considerations. So the divine command explains the *indefeasible* nature of moral obligations, in addition to the other salient features of moral obligations as we experience them.

To illustrate this last point, back up and notice that when we act, we not only have reasons for doing certain things, but we also sometimes have countervailing reasons for *not* doing those things. For example, you might have a perfectly good reason to show up at a certain location every day of the week at or before 8 a.m.: Your employer demands it. Of course, you could have even better reasons *not* to: Your sick child needs to be rushed to the hospital. So sometimes, your reasons can get *defeated* by other reasons you might encounter. Could there be any reasons that are so strong they simply couldn't be defeated by any other reasons? If so, those reasons would be *indefeasible*. The fact that you are *morally* obligated to do something seems to be an indefeasible reason for doing that thing. If, morally speaking, you ought to do something, then it ultimately does not matter if you do not want to do it, or if you would enjoy not doing it, or if other people are telling you not to do it. Actual full-blown moral obligations are indefeasible precisely because they cannot be defeated by preferences or other obligations or whatever else. And plausibly, divine commands would yield these peculiar indefeasible reasons. In other words, plausibly, God commanding you to do some act is so strong that it simply cannot be defeated by any other reasons you might come to have. After all, practically speaking, under what circumstances would it make sense to *not* do what an all-knowing, all-powerful, and perfectly good being tells you to do? Notice how, as a social theory of obligations, DCT can explain the indefeasibility of moral obligations particularly well—along with why we care about our moral obligations, why we feel a sense of guilt or blame when they aren't met, why we are interested in publicly inculcating those obligations, and why we feel a sense of urgency in meeting them. On the other hand, if there were no God in the picture, it is hard to see how morality could ever acquire this overriding, prescriptive quality, in addition to the other salient features of our experience of moral obligations.

Finally, consider (c) above. Why should we even care about being moral in the first place? Why should we be motivated to meet our moral obligations? One answer offered by proponents of virtue theory or utilitarianism is that doing so contributes to one's flourishing or happiness. A second answer at least some natural law theorists might offer is that doing so will help fulfill one's nature, given the kind of creature one is as a human. One might find both of these answers unsatisfying. Take the first answer: Some philosophers deny that fulfilling one's moral obligations *always* contributes to one's happiness. After all, sometimes meeting one's moral obligations makes one's life worse off and could even result in extreme pain or death. And consider the second answer: Some philosophers think that all the requirements of morality cannot be deduced from our human nature, since our nature as humans inclines us to evil as well as to good.[16] So if neither happiness nor entailments from our human nature are enough to answer the question of moral motivation, then DCT stands on final analysis as perhaps the only satisfactory answer to the question at hand. Why should we be moral? Because we should care about our relationship to God, and we should fear the sanctions of failing to care for that relationship in particular.

Of course, we are right to wonder how strong this cumulative secular case for DCT is. The answer to that question pivots on just how solid—and just how significant—each of the considerations (a)–(c) actually are. Return to (a), for example. Is it true that one would need to endorse some form of DCT to explain how there could be objective moral values and obligations in the first place? Even if God must be in the picture, would that alone entail that one's particular theistic account has to be DCT as opposed to, say, a theistic version of natural law theory or virtue theory or some other theistic version of morality? Regarding (b), even if we suppose DCT *can* explain the indefeasible nature of moral obligations, might there be other ways of explaining the indefeasibility of moral obligations that wouldn't require one to endorse DCT? Couldn't one perhaps follow natural law theory in appealing to facts about human goods, in combination with the adjudicating norms of practical reason, to explain why certain obligations cannot be overruled? And are moral obligations necessarily and always social in nature in the first place? A similar set of questions could be posed about (c) as well. Is it true that no moral theory beyond DCT can offer a compelling answer to the question of why we should be moral? At any rate, the strength of this cumulative secular case for DCT is going to pivot on whether premise 1 is true and upon an evaluation of just how forceful considerations (a)–(c) are. How much evidence would they actually provide?

Another approach to arguing for DCT focuses less on what DCT, if true, could explain and instead focuses on what would seem to follow downstream from the fact that God exists. This approach is what we might think of as a *religious* argument in the sense that it just starts with the assumption that God exists. From there, arguments of this sort proceed by taking stock of key implications on the nature of morality given God's nature as, say, a perfect being. The idea is roughly this: If God actually exists—and if God is who theists say God is—morality will have to be *this* way and not *that* way, consistent with what DCT asserts. Obviously, religious arguments for DCT will be compelling only if one accepts the underlying premise that there is a God; they won't be compelling to nontheists. (Of course, DCT itself will likely seem unmotivated to nontheists in the first place.) There are a variety of such religious arguments for DCT that have been offered throughout history.[17] Some proceed from the premise that God is the first cause of the universe, while others build on a claim about God's impeccability or God's omnipotence. In what follows, we will highlight two different but related religious arguments for DCT: One pivots on considerations about God's *sovereignty* over all things; the other pivots on a consideration of God's *authority* over the created order.

The argument from God's sovereignty

Consider, first, the argument from God's sovereignty. Start by reflecting on the nature of a perfect being—a being than which nothing greater can even be conceived. What must such a being be like? Well, one of the excellences that would belong to a truly perfect being is that it would be sovereign over all.[18] In other words, if a being isn't actually sovereign over all, then that being really isn't actually *perfect*; it lacks a key excellence or perfection that would otherwise make it better. So to be a perfect being, one must be sovereign over all. But what does it mean to be sovereign over all? Among other things, being sovereign over all includes being the *explanation* of all things. (If it doesn't explain all things, how could it be sovereign over all things?) Now, there are only two kinds of things that exist: things that are created, and things that are not created. Created things are explained by their creator. Things that are not created, by contrast, are explained by either being identical with the creator or by somehow being part of or an aspect of the creator. Now, one thing that exists—whether it is created or not—is the moral law. So if a perfect being actually exists, that perfect being would have to be the explanation of the moral law. And one clear way the perfect being could explain the moral law is by actualizing moral obligations by issuing commands in the way DCT asserts.[19] In fact, DCT is one of only a handful of historically influential theories that offers a tidy explanation of the manner by which God might explain the moral law—in fact, so the argument would go, DCT offers the best explanation of it. Thus, a proper reflection on the nature of God as a perfect being leads us in the direction of thinking that DCT is true. We can summarize the argument as follows:

(1) Assumption: God exists.
(2) By definition, God is a perfect being.
(3) To be perfect is to be sovereign over all.

(4) To be sovereign over all is to be the explanation of all things, including the moral law.
(5) Thus, God explains the moral law.
(6) One way the moral law is explained by God is the account offered by DCT: God actualizes moral obligations by issuing commands.
(7) DCT offers the best explanation of how God explains the moral law.
(8) Thus, probably, DCT is the correct theory of morality.

How successful is this argument? Of course, one way of challenging this argument is to question the perfect being theology it presumes—in other words, by questioning premise 2. This strategy is hardly available to a Christian who accepts the intellectual tradition handed down since at least the time of Anselm of Canterbury (1033/4–1109). But even a theist who (for whatever reason) rejects perfect being theology is probably going to accept the claim that God is sovereign over all. After all, most theists in the major Abrahamic traditions accept the claim that God's creative activity explains the existence of everything in the created order. Accepting this, the next question would simply focus on whether the inference in premises 5–8 is on solid enough footing. In any case, a serious worry facing this particular leg of the argument is that even if DCT provides *one* way of explaining how God explains the moral law, is DCT the *only* or *best* explanation for how God explains the moral law? How one answers that particular question will affect whether one judges premise 7 to be true or false, and hence whether one finds the whole argument of the sovereignty of DCT compelling in the first place.

The argument from God's authority

Consider a different religious argument for DCT, one that centers on a consideration about the kind of relationship that would occur between a creator (God) and his creatures (including us). Assuming that God exists and that God is the creator and sustainer of the universe and everything in it (including humans), it can seem that God doesn't just have the *ability* to compel our obedience (God is omnipotent, after all). God also has the legitimate *right* to compel our obedience. That is to say, God has not only *power* over us but also *authority*. And in virtue of this authority, God can obligate us (in the moral sense) simply by commanding us to do something.

What gives God this special kind of authority? Three points seem relevant here. First, following Richard Swinburne, we might say that since God is our creator and sustainer, we are in every way dependent on God, which entails that we have a moral obligation to please our benefactor—in much the same way that children might have moral obligations to please their parents (by obeying their wishes, for example) for taking care of them.[20] Second, following John Locke, we might say God is authoritative simply in virtue of the fact that, because God created the universe and everything in it (including us), we are God's *property*, as it were.[21] Since we *belong* to God, he retains the right to tell us what to do, which establishes God's authority to impose obligations on us simply by commanding us to do things. Or following John Duns Scotus, we might add yet a third consideration in favor of divine authority: God's authority stems from the fact that, assuming God exists, it is necessarily true that *God is to be loved*.[22] Suppose a perfect God exists—and exists necessarily. Because he is a perfect being, God is supremely good. The term "good" simply refers to what is to be loved. And assuming there exists such a thing as a *perfectly good* being, what or who else could possibly make more of a claim on our love than a perfectly lovable thing? So, necessarily, God is to be loved above all else. And, minimally, to love God involves obeying his commands. So, necessarily, we are obligated to love and obey God: The fact that we are obligated to obey his commands follows from the necessary truth that God exists as a perfect being who is to be loved above all else. So, if God exists, then his commands can morally obligate us.

To be clear, one doesn't need to be a theist to see the plausibility of the previous sentence. It is worth noting that this particular conditional claim—if God exists, then his commands can morally obligate us—is affirmed by even atheist critics of DCT. James Rachels, for example, captures the insight quite nicely:

> The point is not merely that it would be imprudent to defy God, since we certainly can't get away with it; rather there is a stronger, logical point involved—namely, that if we recognise

> any being *as God*, then we are committed, in virtue of that recognition, to obeying him. . . . To bear the title "God," then a being must have certain qualifications. He must, for example, be all-powerful and perfectly good in addition to being perfectly wise. And in the same vein, to apply the title "God" to a being is to recognise him as one to be obeyed. The same is true, to a lesser extent, of "King"—to recognise anyone as King is to acknowledge that he occupies a place of authority and has a claim on one's allegiance as his subject. And to recognise any being as God is to acknowledge that he has *unlimited* authority, and an unlimited claim on one's allegiance.[23]

Rachels denies that there is such a being as God who could lay claim to our obedience. But Rachels also rightly recognizes that *if there were such a being as God*, then he would be absolutely authoritative.

We are now in a position to bring the argument of God's authority for DCT full circle. One way of making the argument explicit runs as follows:

(1) Assumption: God exists.
(2) If God exists, then God is the creator and sustainer of the universe and everything in it, including humans.
(3) If God is the creator and sustainer of the universe and everything in it, including humans, then God has absolute governing authority over us; hence, God can legitimately require our obedience. God has this authority because:
    (a) We have an obligation to please our benefactors, and God created us. (Swinburne)
    (b) In virtue of creating us, we are God's property, and God retains property rights over us. (Locke)
    (c) It is necessarily true that God—a perfectly good being—is to be loved above all else. (Scotus)
(4) If God has absolute governing authority over us and, hence, God can legitimately require our obedience, then we have a moral obligation to obey God's commands.
(5) So, we have a moral obligation to obey God's commands.

(6) If humans have a moral obligation to obey God's commands, and *if* there is no other metaphysical ground for moral obligation, then DCT is the correct theory of morality.
(7) Aside from the commands of a governing authority that can legitimately claim human obedience, there is no other metaphysical ground for moral obligation.
(8) Thus, DCT is the correct theory of morality.

What can be said by way of critical evaluation of this argument? There are at least two points where critics might challenge it—namely, premise 3 and premise 7. Whether one takes premise 3 to be true will largely depend on how plausible and defensible propositions (a), (b), and (c) are. But even if we assume that the inference from premises 1–5 is sound, we might still wonder whether the remaining inference from premise 5 onward is sound. One could consistently accept premise 5, for example, while denying or simply remaining agnostic about premise 7, which is needed to get all the way to a purebred version of DCT.

The argument from Scripture

Another decidedly religious case for DCT proceeds by appealing directly to Hebrew and Christian Scripture. Here, in brief, is the basic structure of such an argument for DCT:

(1) If Hebrew and Christian Scripture presupposes, affirms, or implies X, then X is correct.
(2) Hebrew and Christian Scripture presupposes DCT.
(3) Thus, DCT is the correct account of morality.

Obviously enough, if one rejects the divine inspiration and authority of Hebrew and Christian Scripture, then this argument will seem dead on arrival because one would simply reject premise 1. But for those who affirm that Scripture contains the revelation of God to humanity, then premise 1 will seem compelling, and this sort of argument will be of rather serious consequence. So the question then becomes whether premise 2 is true.

Admittedly, one will not find in Scripture an explicit and direct assertion about whether the command-dependency thesis is true or false. (Recall, the command-dependency thesis holds that the moral status of an action depends on divine commands, which is the linchpin assertion of DCT.) But there are a variety of places throughout Hebrew and Christian Scripture in which the audience is given a set of commands and ordered to obey those commands—and in such a way that can seem to presume the command-dependency thesis. Take, for example, the so-called Holiness Code in Leviticus chapters 17–26. Chapter 19 begins as follows:

> The LORD said to Moses, "Speak to the entire assembly of Israel and say to them: 'Be holy because I, the LORD your God, am holy. Each of you must respect your mother and father, and you must observe my Sabbaths. I am the LORD your God. Do not turn to idols or make metal gods for yourselves. I am the LORD your God.'" (Lev. 19:1–4 NIV)

The remainder of this chapter of Leviticus continues in a similar fashion: Dozens of commands are issued by God to Moses, and the list is punctuated throughout by the repeated refrain, "*I am the LORD your God.*" In fact, some variation of this phrase is repeated fifteen times in Leviticus 19 alone. Similarly, the presentation of the Ten Commandments by God to the Israelites in Exodus 20 and Deuteronomy 5 is preceded by a reminder that "I am the LORD your God." One plausible way of interpreting the repetition of this refrain is that it reminds us that God's status relative to humans ("I am the LORD *your* God") positions God to actualize moral obligations simply by means of commanding things. In other words, God repeatedly reminds his audience about his authority relative to them—which is, or should be, sufficient to require their obedience. God is the Lord *your* God. God is *your* master. You are *not*. Thus, God can rightfully compel your obedience. Notice how this can seem to presuppose the command-dependency thesis.

There are also passages in the New Testament that seem to similarly presuppose something in the vicinity of DCT. In the book of Acts, for example, Luke recounts a speech given by the apostle Paul in Pisidian Antioch wherein Paul insinuates that, in order to be properly related to God, we should do what God says. Paul commented in his speech, "God testified concerning [King David of Israel]: 'I have found David son of Jesse, *a man after my own heart*; he will do everything I want him to do'" (Acts

13:22 NIV—emphasis added). One implication of this statement seems to be that one becomes a person "after God's own heart"—that is, a person who is morally excellent—precisely *because* one is willing to do whatever God wants one to do, that is, to obey God's will. If moral excellence is attached to obedience to God's command in this way, it is easy enough to see why: The moral status of actions depend on divine commands.

Finally, Jesus himself—whom Christians believe to be the second person of the Trinity, God Incarnate, the Son of God—makes it crystal clear that we should follow God's commands. Throughout the Gospels, Jesus clarifies what many of those commands are supposed to be, issues a variety of his own, and specifies which among God's commands are the most important (when he is asked in Mark 12, for example). So it is quite clear that Jesus is concerned about informing people about these divine commands and about getting people to obey them. Although Jesus does not explicitly affirm the command-dependency thesis per se, he does seem to connect the significance of obeying his commands with the fact that he (as God Incarnate) is authoritative over all. Consider the so-called Great Commission passage in Matthew 28 in which the resurrected Jesus gives his final word to the disciples in Galilee before his ascension:

> When they saw him, they worshiped him; but some doubted. Then Jesus came to them and said, "*All authority in heaven and on earth has been given to me*. Therefore go and make disciples of all nations, baptizing them in the name of the Father and of the Son and of the Holy Spirit, and teaching them to obey everything I have commanded you. And surely I am with you always, to the very end of the age." (Matt. 28:17–20 NIV—emphasis added)

Jesus seems to be insinuating here that we ("all nations") have a moral obligation to obey his commands *precisely because* he has all authority in heaven and on earth—which would include *moral* authority, too. In other words, he seems to be insinuating that his commands actualize moral obligations. And that seems squarely in the territory of the command-dependency thesis.

Admittedly, in John 15, Jesus tells his followers that they are his *friends* and not merely his servants or, say, soldiers or employees or whatever. But his remark here is coupled with an odd comment. Jesus says, "you are my friends *if you do what I command*" (John 15:14 NIV—emphasis added). This can seem like an odd comment because the commander–commandee relationship is not typically the kind of relationship seen between two friends but between servant and master, parent and child, soldier and officer, boss and employee, and so on. Nonetheless, Jesus says that his disciples are no longer his servants, "because a servant does not know his master's business" (John 15:15 NIV). Servants, children, soldiers, and employees might just do what they are told with no vision of the overall goals. Jesus says his disciples are not like this though. The idea seems to be that as we come to understand Jesus's business in the world, we come to take up his vision and goals, and we partner with him in that mission, whereupon we become his friends. Nonetheless, since Jesus has all authority whatsoever, friendship with him does seem to entail following his commands, even when they are followed from a sense of shared mission.

9.3. The Case against Divine Command Theory

Although DCT has enjoyed a long list of impressive proponents since the medieval period, it fell on hard times during much of the late nineteenth and twentieth centuries. For various reasons, the task of thinking about morality in terms of divine commands fell into disrepute among many professional philosophers, many of whom were nontheists. However, since the 1970s, DCT has been the focus of renewed interest—especially among Christian philosophers—and it has experienced something of a revival, as one commentator put it.[24] That revival has in turn led critics of DCT to articulate a variety of objections, the five most pressing of which we will discuss here.

DCT makes morality arbitrary

The most famous objection to DCT is inspired by Plato's dialogue the *Euthyphro*. In that dialogue, the titular character Euthyphro discusses the nature of piety with the character Socrates. After a few rounds of exchange about the nature of piety, Euthyphro asserts that piety can be defined as *what all the gods love*, while impiety can be defined as *what all the gods hate*. Socrates responds by posing the following dilemma: (a) Is something pious just because the gods love it? Or, (b) do the gods love something because it is already pious? Notice how the difference between option (a) and option (b) centers on the order of causation: In option (a), the fact that the gods love something causes it to be pious; in option (b), the fact that something is pious causes the gods to love it. Socrates's subsequent remarks in the dialogue can seem to suggest that, ultimately, he thinks the gods must have some sort of reason for loving what they love. After all, if the gods weren't motivated by some sort of reason, then their love would just be flat-out arbitrary, lacking in any rationale whatsoever. But if that's the case, the basis for piety (understood as what the gods love) would be arbitrary, which seems screwy. Surely piety isn't rooted in reasonless or arational whims! It seems, then, that the gods must have some sort of reason for loving what they love. So the answer to Euthyphro's dilemma must be option (b): Piety is loved by the gods precisely *because it is pious*. But that means poor Euthyphro has not yet explained the fundamental nature of piety with his proposed definition.

We can swap in the language of monotheism and morality for the references to the Greek gods and piety to recast Euthyphro's dilemma as an objection to DCT. Imagine a modern day Socrates were to pose the following dilemma to a proponent of DCT: (a) Is an action morally obligatory just because God commands it? Or, (b) does God command an action because it is morally obligatory? Notice how, for proponents of DCT, the answer is clearly option (a), since it seems to be entailed by the command-dependency thesis. But, unfortunately, DCT now seems vulnerable to the very same criticism facing Euthyphro's definition of piety above: DCT makes the basis of morality arbitrary.

To see the point here, just suppose option (a) is true: An action is morally obligatory just because God commands it. Furthermore, suppose God has not (yet) commanded us to abstain from theft (or murder, adultery, etc.), so theft (or anything else) is neither right nor wrong. On the basis of what reason, then, could God base his commands? It can seem that given option (a), there *could* be no such reason and thus the command would have to be arbitrary. Why? Well, suppose God had a perfectly good reason for commanding us to abstain from theft. Perhaps, for example, God knows that a prohibition on theft would help us respect persons or help maximize human happiness—or whatever. If there were any such reason on which God could base his command, then that reason would explain what makes the act morally obligatory—not the fact that God commands it. Accordingly, we would now be affirming option (b) and not option (a). So to avoid denying option (a) in favor of option (b), proponents of DCT appear to be forced into the corner of accepting the arbitrariness of God's commands—and hence the arbitrariness of morality. Or so goes the objection.

A fairly standard response to this arbitrariness objection is to return to a point we emphasized toward the opening of this chapter: that DCT should be understood as an account of the *right*, not as an account of the *good*. Additionally, a central affirmation of DCT is that the proper account of the good must precede and undergird the DCT account of the right.

Why do these two points matter in the face of the arbitrariness objection? Remember that Christian theists hold that God is a *perfect* being. And if God is perfect, then God is intrinsically and necessarily good. God is intrinsically good insofar as he is good in and of himself. In other words, God's goodness is not borrowed from anything external to God. And God is necessarily good—it is not possible for God to *not* be good. So God is intrinsically and necessarily good. And insofar as God is necessarily good, God's commands would have to be consistent with, or reflective of, God's intrinsically good nature, which ultimately means God's commands would have to be based on God's perfect reasoning about the intrinsic goodness of God's own nature. So, in fact, God's commands wouldn't be arbitrary at all. Why? DCT is strictly an account of the *right*, not an account of the *good*—and the good (God's nature) precedes the right (God's commands).

A new worry emerges at this juncture, though: If God's commands are always and necessarily limited by facts about God's own intrinsically good nature, then (so one might worry) it is not actually God's *command* on which the moral obligation depends but rather on facts about God's *nature*. In other words, if God has reasons for what he commands in such a way that shuts down the arbitrariness objection—reasons based on God's own intrinsically good nature—then *those reasons* are what determine the moral status of an action, not the fact that God commands it. And if this is correct, then in defending DCT against the arbitrariness objection, we seem to have toggled from option (a) over to option (b)—but that's just to forfeit DCT, isn't it?

In response to this worry, proponents of DCT hold that the divine command itself does something key to generating a moral obligation that it wouldn't otherwise obtain—and they think that's true *even if* all of God's commands follow necessarily from facts about God's own intrinsically good nature. The basic idea here is that God's command "raises the stakes," as C. Stephen Evans puts it, adding a kind of indefeasible reason for doing something that wouldn't be present in the absence of the divine command.[25] After all, so the story would go, facts about God's good nature would provide us with really good reasons for doing certain things. But facts about God's good nature cannot provide everything needed for there to be a full-blown moral obligation. Why? The fact that something is good provides us with a reason for doing that action—but other considerations might trump those reasons. But only God's command provides an *indefeasible* reason to do that action, and indefeasibility is the hallmark of moral obligation.

The problem of heinous commands

Another prominent objection to DCT starts by asking questions like this: What if God were to command us to steal or to commit adultery or—what is perhaps worst of all—to abuse children? The worry here is that the sheer possibility that God *might* or *could* issue such heinous commands is enough to be a fatal problem for DCT. After all, DCT entails that if God commands some action—*whatever it is*—then that action is morally obligatory. So if God were to command child abuse, for example, then child abuse would be morally obligatory. But surely child abuse would never be morally permissible, let alone obligatory! So DCT must be mistaken—or so goes the objection.

The most obvious response to this worry is to say that God would not and could not command something unfitting to God's nature, which is perfectly good. That is to say: God would not and could not command such things as theft, adultery, and child abuse precisely because those things are inconsistent with facts about God's nature as a supremely perfect being. After all, so the thought goes, God is necessarily and perfectly good, and the good is prior to the right. So God's nature limits the sorts of commands God can issue; heinous commands would and could never arise.

Unfortunately, this way of defending DCT faces a serious complication—at least for those who affirm the authority of Scripture: It can seem to clash with some of the apparent divine commands in the Hebrew Bible. Take, for example, the biblical narratives according to which God commands the Israelites to plunder the Egyptians (Exod. 12:36), or according to which God commands Hosea to marry the prostitute Gomer (Hosea 1:2), or according to which God commands Abraham to sacrifice his son Isaac (Gen. 22:2). In each account, God seems to command something that would ordinarily be regarded as morally wrong—theft, adultery, and child abuse—and in such a way that creates a problem for defenders of DCT who want to say that God would never and could never issue a heinous command.

How might proponents of DCT respond? For the sake of brevity, we will focus on the Abraham and Isaac case moving forward, but the general outline of our response to this case could serve also as a model for responding to the other cases as well. (Plus, the Abraham and Isaac case is clearly the most problematic one, so it deserves to be singled out.) To circumvent the problem facing DCT at this stage in the debate, a proponent of DCT would need to argue either (a) that the command given to Abraham was not actually heinous in the way it might seem; or, (b) that God did not really or sincerely command Abraham to sacrifice Isaac in the first place.

Concerning option (a), suppose one tries to argue that the command to sacrifice Isaac was not actually as heinous as it might seem on first pass. To be sure, this line of argument can seem like an especially bitter pill to swallow. After all, at least part of why God's commanding someone to kill a child seems heinous is that it seems perfectly outlandish to suppose that killing an innocent child could ever fail to be harmful to that child. But what if one actually had good reason to believe the child in question would indeed be raised (immediately?) from the dead, as the writer of the book of Hebrews suggests that Abraham believed at that time (Heb. 11:19)? Of course, it is quite difficult for us these days to imagine ever being in an epistemic situation where we confidently believed a child would be raised from the dead upon being killed. But such an epistemic situation is at least logically possible since being raised from the dead is at least *logically* possible. At any rate, notice how our own epistemic situation these days (by comparison to Abraham's) makes it far more difficult for us to see how such a command could ever fail to be anything but heinous. That's because we have access to information about God's nature and human nature—information provided in part by the Abraham and Isaac story itself—by which we can know that God did *not* actually desire child sacrifice, unlike the other regional gods worshiped in Abraham's day.[26] Accordingly, we would almost certainly never be justified in believing that God is commanding us to sacrifice a child, even if Abraham *was* so justified at the time.[27]

As for option (b), suppose one thinks that God did not actually or sincerely command Abraham to kill Isaac. The problem here is that one must either tear a pretty significant page out of the biblical cannon (which is a problem for those who affirm its authority) or offer a plausible interpretation of the Abraham and Isaac story according to which God was not *sincerely* doing what the text *appears* to be saying—namely, commanding Abraham to prepare to sacrifice Isaac. Regarding the latter tack, suppose one held that God's command to Abraham was simply insincere. That is, perhaps God merely allowed Abraham to *believe* for a while that God intended Abraham to do this (when, in fact, God never intended him to do so) so that God could in turn teach Abraham that God would not actually let him go through with the sacrifice[28]—precisely because *that* is the sort of thing God would never *actually* require of Abraham in the first place.[29] In this interpretation of the story, God's command to Abraham was insincerely issued, in part for the purpose of teaching Israel that God *does not*—and *would not* and indeed *could not*—require humans to engage in child sacrifice. Such an interpretation would seem to fit with another important narrative in the book of Jeremiah, wherein God condemns the worshipers of Baal for sacrificing their children as burnt offerings, which God repudiates specifically as "something I [God] did not command or mention, *nor did it enter my mind*" (Jer. 19:5 NIV—emphasis added).[30]

DCT has an epistemic problem

Critics of DCT often point to the fact that there are numerous, long-standing, and fundamental disagreements about what God has commanded. For starters, there is of course disagreement about whether God has commanded anything at all. Those who deny God's existence, for example, are committed to thinking that there couldn't be any genuine divine commands in the first place. And even among theists who readily accept that God commands (or has commanded) us to do various things, there is disagreement about the source and content of those commands. Whose book? Which interpretation? And so on. Whereas Christians believe the Bible is a source of God's commands, Muslims believe the Koran is. And even among Christians there are, of course, important disagreements about biblical interpretation, as well as other disputes about what God has commanded. After all, whereas Nat Turner believed God commanded violent retaliation against the perpetrators of slavery, James Lawson believed he was commanded to fight racial injustice through nonviolence. Notice, the basic worry is that even if DCT is true, we should despair of ever learning what our moral obligations are because we should despair of coming to know whether or what God has, in fact, commanded.

The worry can be extended even further. Russ Shafer-Landau insinuates that there are a host of obstacles facing religious believers "who seek divine guidance in trying to lead a moral life" precisely because there are at least seven key conditions that would need to be met before anyone could justifiably come to know whether or what God communicates about how we should live:

> It must be the case that (1) God exists, and that (2) we can be justified in believing this. (3) God must offer us moral advice, and (4) we must be able to defend the claim that He does so. Further, (5) theists must be justified in selecting a particular source of religious and moral wisdom, such as the Koran, the Book of Mormon, or the Christian Scriptures. Theists must also (6) defend specific interpretations of those sources. Finally,

> when an interpretation conflicts with tradition, religious believers must (7) successfully argue for the priority of one over the other.[31]

Notice the critical point here as it relates to DCT: If those seven key conditions go unmet, then DCT leaves the moral life virtually unnavigable. Why? We cannot really ever know what God commands us to do!

The first thing we note about this objection to DCT is that one's evaluation of it largely hinges on one's background beliefs about God's existence, as well as other salient religious claims. If one is antecedently confident that God does not exist, then of course one is going to conclude that we lack reliable epistemic access to God's commands. But if one is confident that God exists and has worked in the course of human history in some of the ways identified by the major theistic religions, then one would be far less impressed by this objection. Certainly, though, the religious believer needs to say *something* in light of widespread disagreement about what God has commanded. Shouldn't proponents of DCT be chastened by the fact that reasonable, intelligent people have, in good faith, attempted to ascertain what God expects of them—say, from the diligent study of Scripture—and have often come to conflicting judgments?

While it seems perfectly fitting for a proponent of DCT to be chastened by this fact, the proponent of DCT might also call our attention to another point: There is also widespread *agreement* (at least among many religious believers) about what God *has* commanded. For example, virtually every major monotheistic religion agrees that God has commanded us to refrain from murder and theft, for example. Surely it is no coincidence that the areas of widespread agreement among religious believers about God's commands match up with areas of widespread agreement about what our moral obligations are. In fact, *if* the level of agreement about God's commands failed to match up with the level of agreement about our moral obligations, then that disparity would indeed count *against* DCT. But if DCT is true, we should expect that our level of uncertainty and disagreement about God's commands would roughly match our level of uncertainty and disagreement about what our moral obligations are. And that seems to be roughly what we find. Yes, there are seemingly intractable disagreements over certain questions about what God's commands are, just as there are seemingly intractable disagreements about what our moral obligations are. But, for that matter, there are also seemingly intractable disagreements about certain astronomical phenomena, too. But it is not clear why facts of disagreement should make us despair of gaining any knowledge at all about God's commands, or any knowledge at all about what we are morally obligated to do, or any knowledge at all about astronomical phenomena. That said, we should all be prepared to acknowledge our fallibility with respect to what God has commanded, with respect to what our moral obligations are, and with respect to the facts of astronomy.

DCT renders natural facts morally inert

A fourth objection to DCT is that, by grounding morality in divine commands, DCT entails that natural facts about the actual world we live in are of no real moral significance. To illustrate the point here, start with a commonly held belief among Christians: God commands us to abstain from intoxication by means of alcohol. Call this situation *the present condition*. Now, imagine an alternative universe God could have created—call it the *alternative condition*. The alternative condition is exactly like the present condition with just one exception: Humans don't become inebriated through the consumption of alcohol but rather by drinking green tea. Would the exact same set of moral obligations in the present condition hold also in the alternative condition? On one level, it might seem intuitive to think the answer here would be *no*. That is, one might be tempted to think that drinking copious amounts of *green tea* would be morally problematic in the alternative condition, whereas drinking *alcohol* wouldn't be. Notice, however, that if DCT is true, nothing about our human nature (or facts about the natural world in which we exist) directly affects what our moral obligations are. Given DCT, the only things that make any moral difference are divine commands: *Natural facts are morally inert*. After all, we were supposing that God's commands in the alternative condition were identical to what they are in the present condition. If so, given DCT, folks in the alternative condition and the present condition would have an identical set of moral obligations, despite the important differences in human nature. In the alternative condition, humans would be morally blameworthy for drinking too much alcohol (even though, in that alternative condition, alcohol has no harmful effects on them), and they would be morally allowed to get smashed on as much green tea as they cared to drink.

Of course, a proponent of DCT might reply here by insisting that if God had created people so very differently, then God's commands would of course be different too. If drinking green tea to excess caused people to get drunk, then God would have commanded moderation in drinking green tea. But notice the peculiarity here. We seem to be saying that facts about the natural world (including human nature) might impose restrictions *on God* but that those same facts cannot possibly impose restrictions *on humans*. Mark C. Murphy contends that this a perverse result: "The notion that while created nature can of itself morally necessitate God's action [viz., God's will or command] it cannot of itself morally necessitate human action is paradoxical—that created nature has the power to bind God to action but lacks the power to bind us to action is a bizarre combination."[32]

One divine command theorist, John E. Hare, accepts this bizarre combination but argues that the worry about it is reduced when one realizes that, while facts about nature *constrain* what God might command, they do not *determine* what God commands. Further, Hare argues that humans and God are very different. So maybe it shouldn't be so surprising that God can be constrained by natural facts but that humans can be morally obligated only by God's commands.[33]

There is another way out of this particular conundrum, though: Contemplate DCT as only *part* of the full account of how moral obligations arise. What if DCT is correct to say that God's commands can and sometimes do actualize moral obligations but *wrong* to say that *only* God's commands can ground moral obligations? If at least some of our moral obligations could be fully grounded in something other than facts about God's commands—namely, facts about human nature and the natural world—then the inertness problem would be circumvented altogether. Why? Perhaps it is possible that some of our moral obligations arise because of divine commands, while some of our moral obligations arise in the manner described by, say, natural law theory. But if that is so, then we would need to look beyond the parameters of an unalloyed DCT to develop a more holistic theistic account of morality.

DCT is incomplete because it cannot explain how all moral obligations arise

A final objection further supports the thought that DCT needs to be supplemented by natural law theory in order to provide a complete account of morality. The complaint is that an unsupplemented DCT inevitably faces a pernicious *regress problem*. To see the force of this concern, consider how DCT holds that our most fundamental moral imperative is to obey God's commands. We might wonder, though, what makes the imperative "obey God's commands" *morally* imperative in the first place. Of course, it might be tempting to think the answer would just be, well, a *divine command*. But if the answer to the question is just, "God commands us to 'obey God's commands,'" notice how a new question would now emerge: What makes obeying that *prior* or *meta-level* divine command morally obligatory? Off to the races we go—a regress problem has arrived.

To provide a complete explanation of our moral obligations, proponents of DCT will need to answer the question of what makes the imperative to "obey God's commands" morally imperative in a way that cuts any such regress off at the pass. How might a proponent of DCT do this? There are several answers to this question that have been offered by different proponents of DCT throughout history. One might say, for example, that we should obey God's commands because, for example,

(a) we owe a debt of gratitude to God since he is the source of all good things, or
(b) obeying God's commands equips us to achieve our highest final end as humans, or
(c) we are God's property, or
(d) it is a necessary truth that we are morally obligated to obey God's command.

Perhaps *all four* of those answers are plausible enough. Notice that, in any case—and this point is vital—*none* of those accounts boil down to saying, "God commanded us to obey God's commands." In other words, none of those accounts try to answer the question by appealing to, say, some prior or meta-level divine command. And for good reason: Appealing to a prior or meta-level divine command to obey divine commands would simply invite the very same regress problem proponents of DCT need to avoid. After all, if one answers the question at hand with the response, "because God commanded us to obey his commands," then, naturally enough, one would wonder what made it the case that we ought to obey God's initial command that we obey God's commands. And for any version of DCT that holds that *all* of our moral obligations arise as a result of God's commanding, there seems to be no principled way out of this regress problem. What this means, then, is that there must be at least *one* moral obligation that is not and cannot be grounded in some fact about God's commanding—namely, the foundational moral obligation to obey God's commands.

It appears, then, that responding honestly to the regress problem on behalf of DCT exposes the fact that DCT is by itself inevitably incomplete and in need of supplementation to explain how we have at least *one* moral obligation that is *not* caused or constituted by or otherwise grounded in a divine command. Importantly, though, the point to take away here is not that DCT is false as much as it is that DCT is *incomplete*. And the root of the incompleteness of DCT stems from the presupposition that divine commands are necessary conditions for all moral obligations, which is entailed by the command-dependency thesis. Why not just say that divine commands are necessary for perhaps a *subset* of moral obligations? Could it be that some of our moral obligations arise because God commanded us to do something, while others (at least one, namely, the obligation to obey God's commands) arise in some other way?

chapter ten

TOWARD A NONREDUCTIVE COMBINATION THEORY

Almost all of the theories discussed in this book capture at least *something* pertinent to the nature of morality—if only a small part. But none of those theories gets *everything* right, though some come closer than others. So, naturally, we might wonder where we should go from here. In this final chapter, we want to explore the art of the possible for normative moral theory, especially for those who aspire to take the presuppositions, affirmations, and implications of the Christian faith seriously. To be clear, our goal here is not so much to develop or defend a full-blown moral theory as it is to sketch out a plausible path forward toward a principled combination of some of the more promising elements of the theories we have considered so far. We start by briefly surveying some of the key take-aways from the preceding chapters, and we conclude by recommending a few next steps in the direction of a plausible Christian combination theory of morality.

10.1. Looking Back

In light of the moral theories we have considered so far, we are right to reflect on two questions. What problems and shortcomings need to be avoided, circumvented, or overcome? What strengths and insights are worth hanging on to and further cultivating?

Cultural relativism

We started our investigation by considering different forms of relativism, particularly cultural relativism. Unfortunately, cultural relativism remains insufficiently motivated as a moral theory because there appears to be no cogent argument in its favor in the first place. Yet even if we overlook that shortcoming, cultural relativism faces a rather formidable case against it. For one thing, cultural relativism conflicts with our deep-seated convictions about the moral status of certain practices. For example, if cultural relativism is true, then it can be morally permissible, or even morally obligatory, for someone to torture members of a certain race or sex just for fun—as long as such a practice is endorsed by one's culture. But surely it is immoral to torture people for fun, no matter what their race or sex may be, and no matter whether one's own culture might approve. As it turns out, most of us would agree that any cultural group that endorses systematic racial or sexual oppression should be corrected. But the very idea that a culture even *could* be corrected—and hence morally improved upon—presents a conundrum for cultural relativism precisely because cultural relativism denies that there is any objective basis for such moral improvement to occur in the first place. To complicate matters, the pressures to morally improve a culture often hail from members of that very same culture. But as more and more people within a particular culture push for their culture's moral improvement, the moral code of that culture grows increasingly vague. So what *does* that culture actually endorse? Ultimately, there may simply be no principled way to resolve the vagueness in question, and when that is the case, cultural relativism inevitably produces contradictions about the moral status of contested practices.

There is a related problem facing cultural relativism: How do we specify, in precise terms, what counts as a cultural group in the first place? Cultural groups often overlap and intersect, and the lines between them are often blurry at best. That makes the effort to *clearly* identify the relevant boundaries and parameters nearly impossible.

Finally, even if we ignore all the other problems facing it, cultural relativism conflicts with some of the basic elements of the Hebrew and Christian Scriptures, which presuppose that there are culturally transcendent moral standards according to which certain practices are morally illicit—and sinful—for *everybody*, and not just for, say, the ancient Israelites or Christians. Accordingly, to esteem culture as the sole source of morality is to elevate culture to the level of a divinity, which is surely idolatrous. And idolatry is arguably chief among the sins according to the Jewish and Christian traditions.

Still, reflecting critically on cultural relativism can help bring into sharper focus a few items that are surely relevant to the moral life. For starters, the fact that there is serious disagreement among different individuals and societies about how we ought to behave should give us pause enough to reflect on whether *we* are the ones who could be wrong about this or that issue. But we do not need to give up on the thought that there is a culturally transcendent truth of the matter. Instead, we should endeavor to find out what that truth is, maintain an openness to correction, and continue to consider further reasons and arguments. In other words, we should adopt an attitude of fallibilism—that is, a kind of humility about our beliefs—since on any given occasion, *we* may be the ones who are wrong. *Humility* matters for the moral life. For one thing, humility and fallibilism can go a long way to abate dogmatism and ethnocentrism. And the very thing that initially attracts people to cultural relativism in the first place may be that cultural relativism seems like a fitting antidote to dogmatism and ethnocentrism. We are right to diagnose dogmatism and ethnocentrism as problems, but cultural relativism is simply the wrong prescription—as are subjectivism and emotivism.

Another lesson we can take away from our evaluation of cultural relativism is that our reasons for acting are not always strictly *moral* in nature. Sometimes, differences in cultural settings can provide us with reasons to act in this way or that way. For example, our reasons for eating certain foods may center on etiquette or tastes or cultural appropriateness in this or that setting. But those kinds of reasons do not always rise to the level of indefeasible *moral* reasons. So we are wise not to confuse or conflate *moral* reasons with reasons that have to do only with cultural conventions. Reflecting critically on cultural relativism can perhaps help us see this point more quickly. And the lessons we can learn from reflecting on subjectivism and emotivism are similar in nature, though the problems these two theories face are slightly different. Among other things, subjectivism entails that there can be no real moral disagreement, which is clearly false. And subjectivism also entails that each individual is infallible, which is surely out of sync with reality—*and* out of sync with the effort to practice humility in moral reasoning. Emotivism, for its part, clashes with the intuitive notion that moral language itself ought not be deceptive. After all, if emotivism were true, then when we take ourselves to be doing one thing (e.g., claiming that something is, in fact, wrong), we are really just doing something else altogether (e.g., expressing our own emotional states). Additionally, like cultural relativism, both subjectivism and emotivism squarely conflict with a central presupposition of the Christian faith: There is such a thing as a moral fact, not least of which is the reality of *sin*—and hence the *need* for a savior.

Ethical egoism

Like cultural relativism, ethical egoism as a theory remains in search of a good supporting argument. Ethical egoism says an individual should look out for one's own self-interests. In one way, this is not inconsistent with the affirmations of the Christian faith. After all, Jesus exhorts us to store up treasures for ourselves in heaven (Matt. 6:20). Admittedly, Jesus also sets the example of laying down his life for others—but only to take his life up again (John 10:17). So even from the perspective of the Christian faith, it can seem fair to say that one's self-interests do indeed matter. But ethical egoism goes to an extreme and says that one's own self-interests are *all* that matter and that one's sole obligation is to pursue one's own interests. In doing so, ethical egoism goes too far and, as a result, says much too little. Although one's self-interests are crucial, they still need to be balanced with the legitimate interests of others—and anything less is unjustifiably self-centered. Yes, we should indeed love *ourselves*. But we should love our neighbors, too. And if Jesus is right, we ought to love our neighbors *as we love ourselves* (Matt. 22:39).

One of the underlying problems of ethical egoism is that it contemplates individuals as isolated, atomistic, and unencumbered selves. Accordingly, ethical egoism fails to accommodate the fact that one's own genuine self-interests cannot always be divorced from some irreducibly *common* good. This puts ethical egoism at odds with an important presupposition of the Christian faith: What is genuinely good for a person—namely, the abundant life that one learns to lead under the tutelage of Christ and empowered by the Holy Spirit—becomes inextricably connected with the good of others such that one's own self-interest is not wholly separable from the interests of others. In fact, one's own ego is often at least partly bound up with the egos of others—perhaps most especially in the case of one's children or spouse or even one's closest neighbors and community members. If so, a person who contemplates one's own self-interests in the unencumbered way that ethical egoism envisions will, ironically, fail to obtain as rich of a life as one could otherwise enjoy. That's because the richest kind of life—the kind of life we were made for, according to Christ—allows one's own goals, interests, and sense of self to be bound up in the goals, interests, and selves of others, even to the point that one can take joy in sacrificing for them. Ultimately, the thought that one should pursue one's own isolated interests above all else conflicts with what Jesus identifies as the greatest command: to love God above all else (even more than oneself).

Utilitarianism

At first glance, utilitarianism can seem highly intuitive as a theory of morality. After all, how could it ever be wrong to do what would make the world as happy as possible? Still, the case for utilitarianism is not without problems. The chief argument that Mill offers pivots on the claim that happiness—understood as pleasure and privation of pain—is the *only* thing that is intrinsically good and desirable in and of itself. The key word here is "only." Such a bold claim is dubious precisely because we sometimes desire ends that *can* and, at times, *do* make us unhappy. We sometimes desire the truth, even though it will hurt. Sometimes, we desire fidelity or friendship despite knowing that it will bring far more pain than pleasure. And so on. As it turns out, then, one of the most questionable features of utilitarianism is its underlying hedonistic account of the good, which seems far too narrow and, hence, overly reductive. Mill claims that *everything* that is good is either instrumental to or part of happiness, where happiness is understood as pleasure and the absence of pain. But if there are *multiple* intrinsically valuable goods, as seems perfectly plausible, then the hedonism fundamental to Mill's utilitarianism is flatly false.

Hedonism is not the only source of problems for utilitarianism. Like ethical egoism, utilitarianism holds that the moral status of an action depends on its consequences. In one way, utilitarianism offers an improvement when compared to ethical egoism, which restricts the scope of consequences to those affecting an individual's own self-interests. Utilitarianism correctly advises us to attend to the consequences on *all* parties involved—not just those that affect oneself. In that sense at least, utilitarianism indeed meshes better with Christianity than ethical egoism does. But problems remain, in any case. While utilitarians are right to stress that the consequences of our actions indeed matter, those consequences are not the *only* things that matter. Motive and intention matter in some cases. And character matters, too. So the problem is that, yet again, utilitarianism seems far too reductive—not only in its account of the good but also in its account of the right.

A related problem is that utilitarianism presumes at its core that the ends justify the means. Yet some actions are surely beyond the pale—that is, certain actions should never be done—especially if we take the apostle Paul seriously when he teaches that we should do no evil that good may come about (Rom. 3:8). Finally, with respect to the blind impartiality required by utilitarianism: While it is true that in some cases we ought to act in ways that refuse to take into account our personal connections to the parties involved, it is also true that we sometimes have *special* obligations of loyalty to those closest to us—special obligations that extend beyond those we have to people in general or to those who are distant from us.

Kantian deontology

Kantian deontology enjoys significant appeal. One of the most salient features of Kantian deontology is its concern with universalizability. Although critics worry that Kantianism fails to provide enough guidance concerning how to properly articulate maxims—and hence that it fails to provide enough guidance in determining whether those maxims would pass the universalizability tests—surely Kant was correct to notice that, with respect to morality, *consistency* matters. If an action is morally wrong in this or that context, then it should also be wrong in relevantly similar contexts. In other words, we are surely right to expect consistency. The question, though, is whether we are right to expect that there are never *any* exceptions to what otherwise might seem to be very broad moral principles. This particular point remains tricky—even among those who endeavor to take Christianity seriously. While many influential figures in the Christian tradition have held, for example, that lying is always and everywhere wrong—thou shall not bear false witness, *period*—others have argued that there are sometimes exceptions to this prohibition when, say, greater goods or special divine dispensations are in play. Some appeal, for example, to the biblical narrative involving the Hebrew midwives (Exod. 1) or that of Rahab (Josh. 2), who appear to enjoy God's favor in the unique circumstances they faced. Of course, such an interpretation of those biblical narratives is hardly beyond dispute even among those Christians who affirm the divine inspiration of Scripture. But no matter how those exegetical issues are resolved, it remains true that consistency matters.

Another attractive and plausible feature of Kantianism is its emphasis on the value of human persons in relation to the whole enterprise of morality. Kant correctly contends that persons deserve respect and should never be treated as means only. Unfortunately, it is not always crystal clear what Kant's principle entails in this or that concrete situation. But even if we overlook that worry, there is a deeper curiosity that we eventually confront because Kant's own case for this principle leaves some important questions unanswered. His case is premised on the unconditional value of rational agents. Yet even if we are prepared to grant such a premise, we might still wonder: Why exactly does rationality make persons unconditionally valuable in the first place? Kantian deontology seems to simply assume that rationality indeed has this special power, but it would be nice to hear more as to why. The Christian faith can offer a deeper metaphysical backstory here: As rational beings, human persons are created in the image of a perfect and personal being—God—and bearing this divine image is precisely what makes human persons uniquely valuable beyond all price. Without such a metaphysical backstory, it is less obvious just how Kantian deontology makes the case in question, even if the conclusion is indeed correct. The Christian faith can help render this conclusion explicable.

At the root of his moral theory, Kant holds that the only intrinsically and unconditionally good thing is a good will, which he contemplates as a will that moves one to do one's duty for the sake of doing one's duty. It seems fair enough to say that, in many cases, one would indeed be morally praiseworthy for doing one's duty *for the sake of doing one's duty.* But in some cases, *other* motives seem morally fitting and even praiseworthy. For example, someone who sees that another person is suffering and is moved to help not out of respect for doing one's duty, per se, but out of compassion and love for the one suffering, surely exemplifies a praiseworthy character. In fact, in some cases, the person who is moved for such reasons (viz., compassion and love) seems *more* praiseworthy than someone who acts *merely* for the sake of doing one's duty. Accordingly, Kantianism seems too reductive in saying that the *only* action that has moral worth is a dutiful action that is done for the sake of doing one's duty. Yes, obedience to one's moral duty matters. But obedience to the moral law isn't the only thing that matters. Other motives can matter, too.

Perhaps the greatest strain between Christianity and Kantianism centers on the relationship between the good and the right. Insofar as Kant defines the good will as a will that moves one to do one's duty for the sake of doing one's duty, Kant regards the right to be explanatorily prior to the good. But if Christianity is true, the good must be explanatorily prior to the right—not the other way around. That's because, if a perfect being such as God exists, then God is both first and intrinsically and necessarily good. Moral obligations would, in turn, be explanatorily downstream from God. And if so, the good is prior to the right.

Social contract theory

When viewed in a certain light, SCT can seem like a promising and pragmatic approach to thinking about a theory of morality, especially given the facts of pluralism: The rules of morality emerge as the product of a fair initial agreement among free, equal, rational, and self-interested individuals seeking a way out of the nasty, brutish, and short state of nature. Unfortunately, though, SCT has a difficult time explaining what makes the terms of such a contract morally binding in the first place—especially if the contract wasn't hashed out by *us*, here and now, or even by our actual historical ancestors, but by idealized hypothetical parties. Even aside from that grounding problem, SCT faces a difficult dilemma: Either the hypothetical parties to the agreement have reasons for why they would agree to the rules, or they lack such reasons. If they have reasons, then those reasons would themselves seem to be what make the rules binding, not the fact that the rules were or would have been agreed to. Alternatively, if the parties to the agreement *lack* reasons for the rules to which they agreed, then their agreement would seem to be irredeemably arbitrary. Neither horn of the dilemma provides an especially satisfying account of morality.

Nonetheless, a lesson worth taking away from the discussion of SCT is that *agreement* matters—and so does honoring one's covenants. When we say we are going to do something, our word on the matter actualizes a moral reason to do what we said. Surely this point fits with the witness of the Christian tradition. After all, Christianity affirms God's covenant with Israel. Throughout the Hebrew Bible, God is repeatedly depicted as one who makes agreements with others. In fact, the very concept of faith is tied to trusting that God will keep his word. The New Testament writer of the book of Hebrews says, for example, that Abraham's wife Sarah exemplified faith insofar as she trusted God when he promised that she would bear children despite her old age (Heb. 11:11). In a similar vein, Jesus tells his disciples to abstain from swearing and making oaths but instead to simply let your yes be yes, and let your no be no (Matt. 5:36–37). Elaborate promises shouldn't be necessary for folks to trust that you will keep your agreements. Your word should be your bond.

But agreement is not and cannot be the root source of *all* moral obligations whatsoever. After all, we sometimes have moral obligations stemming from things *other* than agreements that we have entered or even agreements that we *would* have made. For example, if the Christian faith is true, we have moral obligations to do what God tells us to do. We also have obligations that arise because of certain encumbrances within, and connections we have to, certain communities, regardless of the agreements rational parties have made or would make. For example, we have at least some moral obligations to our natural families, and we have those obligations even in the absence of having entered into any formal or tacit agreements with them. And sometimes we have moral obligations to those who are incapable of rational agreement in the first place. After all, the moral community needs to include some things and persons who simply aren't capable of agreement—the unborn, infants, the disabled, the very elderly, the environment, nonhuman animals, and even future people. Lastly, if there is such a being as God, then the moral community cannot be limited to just those with whom *equality* can be plausibly claimed, unless we mean to exclude God.

Virtue theory

Virtue theory reminds us that a comprehensive theory of morality needs to do more than simply provide an account of which actions are morally required, forbidden, or optional. It also needs to say something about what makes a person *good* from the inside out and from the outside in, so to speak—and help us to see which internal traits enable or hamper our pursuit of living well. *Character* matters, in other words. Questions of character include questions about proper motivation, and one of the notable problems facing other moral theories is that they can seem to neglect this point. Classical utilitarianism, for example, focuses solely on consequences, thus ignoring the moral significance of motivation entirely. Kantian deontology, for its part, recognizes the significance of motivation, but it holds that acting solely for the sake of doing one's duty is the only morally praiseworthy motivation. But surely there are other praiseworthy reasons for acting, and virtue theory can countenance this point. A virtuous person doesn't visit her friend in the hospital simply for the sake of doing the dutiful act, for example. She acts compassionately out of love for the one who is suffering or, say, for the sake of friendship, or perhaps for the sake of serving Christ or bringing glory to God. Virtue theory, unlike Kant, doesn't have to do backflips to accommodate this point. After all, for virtue theorists, praiseworthy motivations can vary according to the particular good at stake in this or that particular circumstance. The courageous person, for example, doesn't just do the courageous act in a vacuum; the courageous person is compelled to do the courageous act for the right kind of motivation—that is, in the precise way that a courageous person would pursue *this* particular good in *that* particular situation. Ultimately, when we become internally constructed in such a way that morally valuable actions become second nature to us—together with the morally valuable motivations, desires, appetites, and perceptions—then our character becomes virtuous.

Such an approach to thinking about the moral life fits in a lot of ways with Christian Scripture and tradition. The concept of human flourishing plays a vital role in the Sermon on the Mount, for example. In it, Jesus has quite a bit to say about the kind of person one should become, and the character traits one should cultivate, if one wants to lead a blessed or flourishing life—that is, a life that can withstand times of trouble, a life that produces good fruit, so to speak. And the Gospel of John indicates that Jesus came for the purpose of helping people live an *abundant* life (John 10:10). Along similar lines, various lists of virtues and vices are peppered throughout the New Testament epistles as well. And throughout the Christian tradition, from the earliest stages on forward, there has been nearly continual reflection on the virtues and vices and how they enable or hamper living an abundant life.

Still, even if virtue theory squares with the Christian faith, neither is entailed by the other. After all, some virtue theorists propose a vision of the ultimate telos of humanity—and hence a list of virtues—that is perfectly inconsistent with the way of Christ. That's because one's list of virtues will ultimately depend on one's underlying account of the good. And if one's virtue theory is underwritten by an account of the good that is inconsistent with Christian teaching, then the schedule of virtues and vices that this theory proffers will be inconsistent with Christianity too. So the underlying account of the good matters quite a bit. And the fact that a given virtue theory is dependent on an underlying account of the good highlights an important limitation of virtue theory. Simply put, an account of virtues and vices does not by itself give us an account of the good, and thus, virtue theory cannot be a stand-alone account of morality.

Not only does virtue theory need a supplementary account of the good, but it also needs to explain what makes something obligatory, wrong, or optional—an account of the right. After all, pointing to the example of what the virtuous person would or wouldn't do really isn't going to cut it at the end of the day. If, for example, the fact that a virtuous person wouldn't do some action were the *full* causal explanation for why the action in question is wrong, then we would just run into the same sort of Euthyphro-styled problem that is thought to be fatal to other moral theories. After all, the same sort of dilemma would apply: Either the virtuous person has reasons for why she would refrain from doing the action in question, or she lacks such reasons. But if she *does* have reasons, then surely those *reasons* are what most fundamentally explain why the action is morally forbidden—not the fact that the virtuous person wouldn't do it. Alternatively, if the imaginary virtuous person lacks reasons for her actions, then her choices seem irredeemably arbitrary. Hence, while it might be true that we can discover what is wrong by imagining what the virtuous person wouldn't do in some relevantly similar circumstance, surely it is false to say that an action is wrong if and only if *and just because* the virtuous person wouldn't do it. In other words, the fact that a virtuous person would or wouldn't do something could only ever be right-indicative. It simply cannot be right-making.

Still, even though virtue theory cannot work as a stand-alone theory of morality, an account of the virtues and vices is nonetheless an indispensable component of a complete theory of morality. For one thing, a moral theory really needs to do more than just give us rules or merely state when an action is right or wrong. It also needs to offer practical guidance on *who* we ought to become, *which* internal traits we ought to cultivate, *how* we should live, *why* we should act in this or that way, and *what* kind of things we should care about and desire and feel good about. And an account of the virtues and vices can provide at least some of what is needed here. If it is true that some traits allow us to flourish while other traits wreck our lives, then a moral theory needs to help people recognize and understand those traits. After all, the point of moral theory isn't merely to reveal the fundamental structure of morality like, say, a model of a molecule would with respect to physics. It also needs to give us a map—or perhaps (even better) a *guide* to show us the way. We need practical help on living good lives and becoming good persons. If there are such things as vices and virtues, then a good understanding of those traits would go a long way to helping us cultivate the right traits, which should equip us to actually live good lives.

And it should matter to Christians that Jesus himself seems pretty clearly concerned about those internal features of one's character—not just one's outwardly behavior. Remember the Sermon on the Mount, for example, a large portion of which goes something like this: You have heard it said, "Thou shall not murder," but I tell you don't be an angry, contemptuous, and unforgiving person. You have heard it said, "Thou shall not commit adultery," but I say don't even lust in your heart. In fact, there are six different "you have heard it said" recitations in Matthew 5. In each case, Jesus recounts a well-known moral law, and then he instructs his disciples on how to honor the law in question while also letting it shape them on the inside. So, for example, if one isn't angry, contemptuous, and unforgiving, then one is less prone to murder. And it is worth noting that, immediately prior to this particular section of his sermon, Jesus told his disciples that their righteousness really ought to surpass that of the Pharisees, much of which seemed to be about rote rule-following and behavioral compliance without sufficient attention given to the internal architecture of their souls. So notice the basic nature of Jesus's response to their legalism: You have heard that you ought not do this or that, but you really need to cultivate appropriate perceptions, feelings, motives, and desires if you want to walk in the way of *abundant* life. Virtue theory squares with this sentiment.

Natural law theory

Despite all its upsides, virtue theory cannot work as a stand-alone theory of morality. And that's because any account of the virtues and vices is always going to be reliant upon an underlying account of the good. Furthermore, any account of the virtues and vices needs to be supplemented by an account of the right that can specify the right-making mechanism of morality, not merely the overarching right-indicating conditions. NLT endeavors to offer such an account of the good and the right, and like other theories we have considered, it enjoys some intuitive appeal. For starters, it can seem intuitive that facts about the kinds of creatures we are by nature make a bona fide moral difference. In other words, it can seem intuitive that *human nature* matters, morally speaking.

Another appealing feature of NLT is that it allows for a plurality of intrinsically valuable human goods as opposed to saying there is only one such good. Utilitarianism and Kantianism are ultimately too reductive on this front. For utilitarianism, happiness (understood as pleasure and the privation of pain) is the only intrinsically good thing. For Kant, the only intrinsically and unconditionally good thing is a will that moves one to do one's duty for the sake of doing one's duty. But, plausibly, there are intrinsically valuable goods beyond happiness or a good will. NLT holds that there are a variety of such goods—goods such as life, procreation and education of the young, knowledge, sociability, and rational conduct, among others.

NLT is attractive in other ways as well, in part because it provides an objective account of the good that is in some way grounded in empirically verifiable facts. For example, the fact that ingesting poison undermines one's health or the fact that amputating a healthy limb generally diminishes one's capacities—thereby damaging the good of life—gives one a morally salient reason to not ingest poison or amputate a healthy limb. Similarly, the fact that bearing false witness harms the good of knowledge (among other things) gives one a morally salient reason to not bear false witness. Since these are empirically observable facts about poison, amputation, and lying, the moral life takes on a certain empirical and objective dimension. And since the goods involved are grounded in facts about human nature, they are universal in scope—transcending culture, geography, personal preference, individual desire, and so on. For NLT, morality is not grounded in precarious features of subjectivity but (at least partly) in cold, hard facts about human nature and about what promotes human goods. Furthermore, this objective dimension of NLT is based on *human* nature, thereby allowing the things that distinguish humans from everything else to matter.

Additionally, consistent with the better angels of Kantian deontology, NLT recognizes the value of individual human persons and thus recognizes that they ought to be treated with respect—and not like mere *things*. In Kant's depiction, human dignity ultimately comes from our status as rational beings. For NLT, human dignity derives in part from the fact that we are capable of participating in unique ways in what is intrinsically good, or at least in the fact that we can participate in more of those goods than, say, nonhuman animals. Yet another way NLT recognizes the value of human persons is by reminding us that the empirical realities to which we should attend, if we are to attend to our moral obligations, are the realities about what human nature is like—facts about the sorts of creatures we are. Ultimately, this places human persons front and center in moral theorizing. Finally, for *theistic* versions of NLT, the fact that we humans were given our nature by God—together with the fact that we were given this nature with a special mission along with the rational agency that allows us to carry out that mission—partly explains human dignity. For Christians, this last point is crucial. We were created by a supremely good God who has given has us a rational nature and freedom, which allows us to take responsibility over a portion of the created order and, in some sense, to partner with God as cocreators. And there are other ways that NLT fits with Christian Scripture and tradition. Part of the overall arc of the biblical narrative is that humans were made according to their kind in the image of a loving God, given a special status and stewarding responsibilities, and are subject to a moral law that is applicable to all humans simply insofar as they are human. Accordingly, facts about the created order, including facts about humankind, seem to imply moral obligations for all people, consistent with the account offered by NLT. And, of course, key contributions to the natural law tradition have emerged from and coincided with the Christian tradition.

There are, however, drawbacks to NLT. One issue is that the account of the right found within NLT is ultimately dependent on a proper articulation of the adjudicating norms of practical reason. Put differently: Even if we grant the list of intrinsically valuable human goods at the heart of the NLT account of the good, we still need some way of specifying the appropriate (that is, moral and immoral) ways that those goods might be sought. So, ultimately, NLT's account of the right very much depends on the adjudicating norms of practical reason. However, the work done by natural law theorists to identify and explain the adjudicating norms and their internal relations to one another remains unfinished business. To the extent that NLT has only had limited success in articulating and defending these adjudicating norms, its success as a moral theory is to that same extent limited.

Even if we can overlook that particular concern, though, NLT still faces an incompleteness problem. If NLT offered a complete account of morality, then its account of the right should indeed be able explain *all* our moral obligations. But if it is possible that God sometimes issues rationally underdetermined commands, then it is possible for us to have at least some moral obligations that simply cannot be explained in the way that NLT describes. Suppose, for example, God has good reasons to command us to set aside a day of the week to rest and worship but no particular reason to identify *this* particular day of the week over *that* one. Suppose the third day of the week was as equally good as the seventh day, yet God picked the seventh all the same. It seems fair to say that, under those conditions, we would still have a moral obligation to observe the *seventh* day. But NLT does not itself explain why we would have such an obligation since, in the case of a rationally underdetermined divine command, it is God's command itself that gives rise to the fact that we have the specific moral obligation in question. So NLT appears to be incomplete—at least when viewed from the perspective of the Christian tradition.

Divine command theory

DCT holds that God's commands give rise to moral obligations. And despite the reticence of some modern moral philosophers to accept the idea that God's commands could do that, there remains an undeniable appeal to such a claim nonetheless—especially if we think there is such a being as God. After all, if there were indeed an all-knowing, all-powerful, supremely good and loving perfect being who created the universe, under what conditions would it ever make any practical sense *not* to do what such a being said to do? Surely, if under *any* conditions there were such a thing as legitimate authority, a perfect being would have authority in *all* conditions.

Another appealing feature of DCT is that it seems capable of explaining a number of salient features of our experience of moral obligations: Moral obligations are indefeasible; one who fails to meet one's moral obligations incurs guilt; we care about complying with moral obligations; we care about helping others comply with them; and those obligations are in some sense objective. If a perfect being tells us to do something, that gives us indefeasible reason to do it, which makes us incur guilt if we don't do it, which should motivate us to care about doing it and wanting others to care about doing it, which gives us reasons for doing it that override our subjective preferences on the matter. In other words, DCT plausibly explains several salient features of moral obligations.

Theists, and Christian theists in particular, have additional reasons to take DCT seriously. For one thing, the Bible can certainly seem to presume it at several junctures. For example, in the Holiness Code within the book of Leviticus, God offers a plethora of commands to the Israelites followed by the repeated refrain, "*for I am the LORD your God*." One plausible way of interpreting this matter is that God, simply by virtue of being Lord, can actualize obligations through the power of his command alone. Within the New Testament, Jesus emphasizes the importance of obeying divine commands when he says to his followers, "If you love me, keep my commands" (John 14:15 NIV). And in the so-called Great Commission passage, Jesus asserts that he has been given all authority in heaven and earth—which presumably includes moral authority—and he tells his disciples to teach others to obey his commands (Matt. 28:16–20). So it seems fair to say that DCT enjoys some apparent compatibility with the presuppositions and affirmations of Scripture. Additionally, DCT seems to either follow from, or fit nicely with, some common theological commitments. For example, DCT fits nicely with implications of the existence of a perfect being. If there exists a perfect being, then that perfect being is sovereign over all. Part of what that sovereignty entails is that God explains all things beyond himself. After all, only God is uncreated, whereas the existence of all else is ultimately explained by reference to God. But this means that moral obligations, too, are ultimately explained by reference to God. DCT fits this theological picture, especially in concert with the scriptural data above.

But there are limitations to DCT. It, too, needs to be supplemented with an account of the good precisely because any account of the good based exclusively on divine *commands* would create problems. After all, a theist will surely want to grant that God is good. But surely God's goodness isn't explained by the fact that God commanded that he exists. So a divine command account of the good isn't very plausible. Plus, if DCT's account of the right is going to stave off the charge of arbitrariness, it will need an account of the good that isn't based exclusively on divine commands. However, if the DCT account of the right is supplemented with some other theistic account of the good—perhaps an account of the good based on God's *nature*, for example—then this kind of objection can be avoided. And this is precisely what most contemporary proponents of DCT do: They generally bolster their DCT account of the right with an account of the good that contemplates the good as identical to God, or as a resemblance to God, or as an attraction to God, or something along those lines.

Nonetheless, DCT faces an incompleteness problem of its own, even when it gets depicted strictly as an account of the right. That's because at least one moral obligation cannot be explained by the appeal to divine commands. After all, why do we have a moral obligation to obey God's commands in the first place? For proponents of an unalloyed, purebred DCT, the only answer that could be given is "*because God said to do so*." But that sort of answer would, of course, invite a regress problem: Why do we have a moral obligation to obey that *prior* command to obey God's commands? One way out of the regress is to accept that the obligation to obey God's commands isn't fully explained by reference to God's commands but by something else—perhaps *necessity*. But the fact that we have one such moral obligation gives us reason to suspect we might have others, too. Ultimately, then, DCT lacks the resources to do all that we need a moral theory to do. So something else is needed. At the very least, it will need to be supplemented by some other account of what makes the divine command obligatory in the first place.

10.2. Looking Ahead

A pattern has emerged: Each theory we have examined highlights this or that salient element of the moral life and crafts an account of the good and/or an account of the right around that particular element—but at the expense of other important things. In doing so, those theories are reductive to one extent or another, which leaves them straining to account for those *other* important elements of the moral life. Utilitarianism, for example, reduces the moral life to the performance of actions that result in maximized happiness. Admittedly, consequences and happiness matter, but when one supposes that consequences and happiness are the *only* things that matter, troubling results ensue. Pretty soon one finds oneself defending the view that we could engage in all manner of evil so that good may come or that healthy people could be morally obligated to undergo a lobotomy—or worse. As it turns out, utilitarianism is certainly not alone in giving way to this reductive tendency. For ethical egoism, one's own self-interests are all that matter. For Kantian deontology, acting in conformity to, and for the sake of conforming to, a universalizable maxim is all that matters. For SCT, the rules that free, equal, rational, and self-interested people would agree to are all that matter. For virtue theory, developing the internal states that lead to flourishing is all that matters. For NLT, acting in ways that are reasonable given the intrinsically valuable human goods is all that matters. For DCT, obeying God's commands is all that matters. Notice the reductive turn in each case.

The reductive turn has at least two perverse effects. First, it obscures something relevant to the moral life. And second, it can lead us to double down in defense of an otherwise objectionable position. Consider the first problem with respect to ethical egoism, for example. Surely one's own self-interests matter. But to reduce morality to the pursuit of one's own self-interests obscures the truth that the interests of others matter too. The reductive tendency isn't just a problem for secular moral theories, by the way. Moral theories historically connected to the Christian tradition fall prey to this same reductive tendency as well. Take NLT, for example. Yes, facts about human nature and what is good for humans given that nature can sometimes explain our moral obligations; but they cannot explain *all* of them. Trying to use the NLT framework to explain *all* of our moral obligations subtly obscures the fact that God could issue rationally underdetermined commands, whereupon a moral obligation could arise in a way that isn't explained by NLT. Similarly, trying to explain *all* of our moral obligations by appeal to divine commands ultimately obscures the fact that we have an obligation to obey God that cannot stem from some prior divine command that we obey God.

Not only does the reductive turn obscure facts that are relevant to the moral life, it can also entrench us in defending morally bankrupt positions. If we hold that the moral life can be reduced to some singular proposition—for example, that one's sole obligation is to pursue one's own self-interest—then we are likely going to be quick, much *too* quick, to assume that even horrendous entailments of that singular proposition aren't so much objections to but simply implications of that same proposition. The result is that we may soon find ourselves defending morally insane positions that we should just surrender instead. Notice, for example, how defending ethical egoism would commit us to defending the crazy view that one is morally obligated to kill one's neighbor or mother or child if doing so served one's own genuine self-interest. Of course, not all the theories we have discussed would require one to embrace such barbaric conclusions, but all require their proponents to countenance some rather difficult views. Admittedly, the correct theory of morality might well lead us to hold some difficult views on final analysis, but we should get there only through fear and trembling, as it were. Our main point here is simply to underscore some of the collateral damage caused by the reductive turn.

Would a *nonreductive* approach offer a more promising way to theorize about morality? Is there a way to *combine* elements from some of the theories we have discussed so as to avoid the problems and hang on to the strengths? And is there a way to do that if we endeavor to take seriously the presuppositions, affirmations, and implications of the Christian faith?

Focus on the last question for now. Any theory of morality that is going to square neatly with the Christian faith needs to do several things: (a) It needs to offer an account of the good in which God factors centrally, and (b) it needs to affirm the priority of the good to the right. We should add another criterion, too: (c) It should enjoy some sort of support from Christian Scripture and tradition. Notice what the first two criteria eliminate. God plays either no role or no central role in the account of the good offered by cultural relativism, subjectivism, emotivism, ethical egoism, utilitarianism, or SCT. Now, while we might be able to imagine some version of Kantian deontology in which God could play a role in the account of the good, Kantianism still prioritizes the right over the good in such a way that God cannot play the proper kind of role. For Kant, the only intrinsically and unqualifiedly good thing is a good will—a will that moves one to do one's moral duty for the sake of doing one's duty. But if Christian theism is correct, then God—a perfect, supremely good being—precedes everything else, including any moral duties anyone might have. So if Christian theism is correct, then the correct account of the good would have to precede the correct account of the right, which is an order Kantian deontology reverses. This brings us back to the point we made above: Any theory of morality that is going to mesh with the Christian faith needs to start with an account of the good, and that account must assign God a central role.

Admittedly, there are competing theistic accounts of the good that might serve the purpose here. Robert M. Adams argues, for example, that God is essentially the Platonic form of the good and that everything else can be said to be good insofar as it faithfully *resembles* God in some way.[1] By contrast, Mark C. Murphy contends that every good is a divine likeness, but a likeness that is fitting and specific to the *kind* of thing to which it belongs.[2] And John E. Hare says something is good to the extent that it draws humans toward God.[3] There are other models, too. At any rate, while there are important differences among these theistic accounts of the good, they all share a crucial similarity: In each account, God plays a central role in the explanation of the good and hence in how we could come to understand what the various other goods are. Moreover, each of these theistic accounts of the good holds that God is intrinsically good, not merely extrinsically or instrumentally good. Furthermore, each of them contemplates God as having a *unique* relation to other things that are intrinsically good. Chiefly, God must causally explain why the other intrinsically good things are intrinsically good, and in a way that those other intrinsically good things could *not* causally explain why God is intrinsically good. In other words, God cannot be merely one among multiple intrinsically good things; God must be good in a way that is robustly and uniquely primary. At least some versions of virtue theory, NLT, and DCT could countenance such a theistic account of the good, as well as the idea that the good is prior to the proper account of the right. Furthermore, as we have seen, all three of these moral theories plausibly enjoy some level of support from Christian Scripture and tradition. So with reference to the three criteria mentioned above, virtue theory, NLT, and DCT survive as potential contenders in a way that the other moral theories considered in this book simply do not.

Nonetheless, each of these three contenders—virtue theory, NLT, and DCT—suffers from a common shortcoming: Taken on its own, each remains incomplete as a theory of morality and hence each stands in need of supplementation. Virtue theory is incomplete because it is parasitic on both an underlying account of the good and on a supplementary causal account of the right. That's because the fact that a virtuous person is virtuous is indexed to some underlying account of what is good, and the fact that a virtuous person would do something isn't what *causes* it to be the right thing to do. Little surprise, then, that the most influential Christian virtue theorist in history, Thomas Aquinas, is also the most influential Christian natural law theorist in history. And yet when taken by itself, NLT is also incomplete because it cannot account for the fact that God can, and sometimes does, issue rationally underdetermined commands. And DCT is incomplete because it cannot explain, by appeal to divine commands alone, why we morally ought to obey divine commands in the first place.

Is there a way to *combine* some version of all three of these theories that would overcome the incompleteness problems in question? There are really two questions we need to address here. First, we need to ask whether virtue theory, NLT, and DCT *can* be combined without giving rise to some logical incompatibility. Second, if such a combination is indeed logically possible, we need to ask whether such a combination would offer any resources to overcome the incompleteness problems in question.

Start with the first question. Obviously enough, any version of DCT that insists that a divine command is a necessary condition for *all* moral obligations would be incompatible with NLT. Likewise, any version of NLT that claims that *all* moral obligations can be explained by, say, facts about human nature in combination with the adjudicating norms of practical reason would be incompatible with DCT. This is a key point because we should neither seek nor accept *cheap* pluralism. For example, we couldn't (reasonably) endorse a combination of *both* utilitarianism and Kantian deontology. After all, utilitarianism says the moral status of an action turns on its consequences, but Kantianism says one's moral duty turns on whether the maxim of the action could be contemplated as universal law, without regard for eventual consequences. Those two theories are clearly incompatible with one another, and any pluralism that attempts to combine them would be a cheap pluralism indeed, one that merely turns a blind eye to internal contradictions.

Are there *nonreductive* versions of virtue theory, NLT, and DCT that are logically compatible with one another? By "nonreductive versions," we simply mean versions that do not insist that *all* moral obligations are explained in the same way. For example, a nonreductive version of DCT could hold that divine commands could indeed give rise to at least *some* of our moral obligations, though not necessarily *all* of our moral obligations. A nonreductive version of NLT could hold that facts about human nature in combination with the adjudicating norms of practical reason could give rise to at least *some* of our moral obligations, but not *all* of them. Happily, there is a relatively simple way that nonreductive versions of virtue theory, NLT, and DCT could all be compatible with one another. The idea is this: NLT explains *one* subset of our moral obligations, DCT explains *another* subset of our moral obligations, and virtue theory in turn provides us with the language and resources to move beyond a discussion of what makes something good or evil or what makes an action right or wrong and into a discussion about what makes a good *person* or character.

Our second question remains, however. Would combining some nonreductive version of NLT, DCT, and virtue theory do any real work for us? Would it help, for example, in eliminating the incompleteness problems mentioned above?

Happily, the answer here seems to be *yes*. Consider how such a combination approach would help address the objections facing reductive versions of each of these theories taken on its own. Virtue theory requires an underlying account of the good and a supplementary causal account of the right—precisely because it is untenable that an action is made obligatory by the simple fact that a virtuous person would do it. The virtuous person, after all, is acting on reasons. By supplementing virtue theory with

NLT and/or DCT, the combination approach can then provide those very reasons, thereby circumventing the worry that a reductive and unsupplemented virtue theory entails that virtuous people act arbitrarily.

Taken alone, reductive versions of NLT cannot explain how we have moral obligations relative to God's rationally underdetermined commands. That is, if God can issue a rationally underdetermined command, then there would be no way for reductive versions of NLT to explain the moral obligation that arises. But notice how adding in DCT's account of the right would help here. If God's commanding an action is *sufficient* for a corresponding moral obligation to occur—which nonreductive versions of DCT should be prepared to accept—then the human obligations that arise from God's rationally underdetermined commands become explicable. So the incompleteness of reductive NLT dissipates when combined with nonreductive DCT.

Along similar lines, notice how the incompleteness of reductive versions of DCT goes away when supplemented by a nonreductive version of NLT. When DCT is supplemented by NLT, it now becomes explicable why we have a moral obligation to obey God's commands in the first place: Given God's nature as a perfect being, and given facts about the kind of creatures we are by nature, it is necessarily true that our ultimate good is to be found in the love of God; and, minimally, love of God entails that we obey God's commands, which explains why we have a moral obligation to obey divine commands in the first place. But there's more. One problem facing reductive DCT is that it renders natural facts morally inert, and no facts about human nature have any bearing on our moral obligations. Instead, given reductive DCT, the *only* morally relevant factor is what God commands. But by allowing NLT to explain at least a subset of our moral obligations, the moral inertness problem simply evaporates into thin air. A combination of nonreductive versions of DCT and NLT can thus allow that facts about the kind of creatures we are as humans make a difference in the kinds of moral obligations we have.

In sum, then, we have good reason to think that nonreductive versions of virtue theory, NLT, and DCT are not logically incompatible with one another. Plus, we have good reason to think that real work can be done by combining them. In fact, the combination of these theories allows each of the component parts to overcome the incompleteness problem it faces when taken individually.

So where might we go from here? We are finally in a position to sketch a plausible, *nonreductive, combination account of the right*. Notice that if the combination approach to moral theorizing we have been imagining is on point, then there would be at least two subsets to the moral law. One subset includes the moral obligations we have because God commands some action. The other subset includes moral obligations that arise in the way that roughly accords with the account of the right provided by NLT. Accordingly, the nonreductive combination account of the right that we are imagining runs roughly as follows. An action is morally obligatory if and only if and because (a) it is commanded by God, and/or (b) it is the only way one can pursue a human good in a manner that isn't ruled out by the adjudicating norms of practical reason. An action is morally wrong if and only if and because (a) it is prohibited by God, and/or (b) it fails to pursue a human good or is ruled out by an adjudicating norm of practical reason. And an action is morally optional if and only if and because (a) it is neither commanded nor prohibited by God and (b) it pursues a human good in a way that isn't ruled out by an adjudicating norm of practical reason but yet the action in question isn't the only way to do so.

Now, in order to capture a comprehensive theory of morality, we would still need to add to this combination theory an account of the virtues and vices. Such an account of the virtues and vices would need to align with the underlying theistic account of the good on which the NLT and DCT components of the combination theory rely. In fact, we can think of that account of the virtues and vices as a practical fleshing out of the underlying account of the good in terms of a person's character—that is, in terms of *who* we should become. Consider the simple fact that in any plausible theistic account of the good, human life is recognized as a good. Temperance and courage are virtues at least in part because they enable a person to pursue, preserve, protect, and respect the good of life. After all, temperance is exhibited by someone whose appetites are shaped and controlled in a way that promotes one's overall well-being, including the healthy functioning of one's body. Similarly, courage is exhibited in one's confidence in wisely enduring obstacles or dangerous circumstances to preserve some good—especially life. And so on.

Of course, the conceptualization and application of the virtues and vices can be done well or poorly. But when it is done well, it can indeed help us become better people. Rebecca DeYoung shares a helpful illustration of a particular moment in her own life. She recalls how during the first year of graduate school, she felt intimidated by and inferior to those around her—like she was an inadequate imposter who simply didn't belong among her peers. As a result, she was slow to speak up in her classes, despite the fact that she knew and understood the material well. However, DeYoung explains that after she encountered Thomas Aquinas's account of the vice of *pusillanimity* (smallness of the soul), she was able "to see [herself] in the mirror for the first time."[4] The awareness paid dividends: In being able to name, understand, and diagnose this vice in herself, she was eventually able to gain power over it in her life. Our point here is simply that reflection on the virtues and vices can indeed equip us to become better people, and we are right to expect that a comprehensive theory of morality should help us do that.

An account of the virtues and vices can assist a combination theory of morality in another way, too—by providing resources for thinking about internal traits that make the pursuit of the good life, and hence right behavior, easier and more natural. After all, human flourishing concerns more than simply discharging our moral duties; it is also about becoming persons for whom doing the right thing is *second nature*. Recall Jesus's point in the Sermon on the Mount: True righteousness is about more than mere behavioral compliance to the moral law; it is also about *who* we allow ourselves to become. And we walk in the way of abundant life, in part, by becoming virtuous. A comprehensive account of the moral life doesn't merely tell us what is good and right but also about how we ought to go after those things and about the kinds of people we should strive to become. So an account of the virtues and vices is surely an indispensable component in the combination theory of morality that we have in mind.

We thus conclude our inquiry by citing some of the advantages of combining nonreductive versions of NLT, DCT, and virtue theory. First, such a combination theory of morality represents a decidedly realist theory of morality, and hence it can simply avoid many of the problems facing cultural relativism, subjectivism, and emotivism. And yet, in keeping with an important insight that accompanies a critical evaluation of those theories, the combination theory we have in mind remains fully compatible with the need to practice humility with respect to one's moral judgments and cultural background. In keeping with ethical egoism, the nonreductive combination theory of morality can allow that the pursuit of one's own self-interests is, at times, permissible. However, contrary to ethical egoism, the combination theory requires the pursuit of one's own self-interests to be balanced against the interests of others and ultimately subjugated to the love of God above all else. As with utilitarianism, a combination theory can affirm that the consequences of one's actions matter and need to be taken into account—and that we need to consider how those consequences affect *all* parties involved. In contrast to classical utilitarianism, however, the combination theory we have in mind can allow that there is more than one intrinsically good thing. In fact, it affirms not only that God is intrinsically good but that there are multiple intrinsically valuable human goods, too—life, procreation, knowledge, sociability, rational conduct, and so on. Accordingly, the combination theory can avoid some of the reductive tendencies and pitfalls associated with both utilitarianism and Kantian deontology. After all, because this combination theory allows for multiple adjudicating norms of practical reason, it can avoid some of the pitfalls of claiming that there is only *one* dictate of practical reason, whether that be "maximize value (happiness, which is pleasure)" or "act only on maxims that you can will to become universal law." That's because the combination theory holds that there are multiples norms of practical reason that can help govern the pursuit of human goods and hence the moral life. Meanwhile, with SCT, the combination theory can affirm the importance of agreement among free, equal, rational, and self-interested persons and the significance of covenant-making, while avoiding the host of difficulties facing SCT. And a combination of nonreductive versions of virtue theory, NLT, and DCT allows each of the component parts to overcome the incompleteness problem it faces when it is taken individually.

What is more, the combination theory of morality has the distinct advantage of looking not just to human reason as the guide to the moral life but also to divine revelation. In that sense, it provides space for both faith *and* reason to work in tandem. And a final advantage of this combination theory of morality is that it can help explain why each of its component parts—virtue theory, NLT, and DCT—can lay legitimate claim to at least some scriptural support and explain why each has also enjoyed at least some pride of place within different segments of the vast Christian intellectual tradition. And it can do this in a way that doesn't require biblical or denominational gerrymandering and, hence, in a way that seeks to be ecumenical in outlook. In other words, this combination theory of morality is, we hope, a *mere* Christian moral philosophy.

BIBLIOGRAPHY

2 Clement. Translated by Alexander Roberts and James Donaldson. Available on Peter Kirby's *Early Christian Writings*. https://www.earlychristianwritings.com/text/2clement-roberts.html.

Adams, Robert. *Finite and Infinite Goods: A Framework for Ethics*. Oxford University Press, 1999.

American Museum of Natural History. "The Immortal Jellyfish." May 4, 2015. Accessed July 13, 2022. https://www.amnh.org/explore/news-blogs/on-exhibit-posts/the-immortal-jellyfish.

Amnesty International. "Iran: Abusive Forced Veiling Laws Police Women's Lives." May 28, 2019. https://www.amnesty.org/en/latest/campaigns/2019/05/iran-abusive-forced-veiling-laws-police-womens-lives/.

Anderson, R. Lanier. "Friedrich Nietzsche." In *Stanford Encyclopedia of Philosophy*. Stanford University, 1997–. Article published March 17, 2017; last modified May 19, 2022. https://plato.stanford.edu/entries/nietzsche/.

Anscombe, G. E. M. "Modern Moral Philosophy." *Philosophy* 33, no. 124 (1958): 1–19.

Aquinas, Thomas. *On Law, Morality, and Politics*. 2nd ed. Translated by Richard J. Regan. Edited by William P. Baumgarth and Richard J. Regan. Hackett, 2002.

———. *Summa Theologica*. Translated by Fathers of the English Dominican Province. Christian Classics, 1948.

Aristotle. *Nicomachean Ethics*. Translated by C. D. C. Reeve. Hackett, 2014.

Associated Press. "British Woman Marries Dolphin." *Fox News*, January 13, 2015, accessed July 27, 2022. https://www.foxnews.com/story/british-woman-marries-dolphin.

Augustine. *The Essential Augustine*. Edited by Vernon J. Bourke. Hackett, 1974.

———. *On the Free Choice of the Will*. Translated by Thomas Williams. Hackett, 1993.

Aune, David E. *The New Testament in Its Literary Environment*. Westminster Press, 1987.

Bakewell, Sarah. "Clang Went the Trolley." *New York Times*, November 22, 2013, accessed February 26, 2025. https://www.nytimes.com/2013/11/24/books/review/would-you-kill-the-fat-man-and-the-trolley-problem.html?smid=tw-share&_r=0.

Benedict, Ruth. "Anthropology and the Abnormal." *Journal of General Psychology* 10 (1934): 59–84.

Bennett, William J. *The Death of Outrage: Bill Clinton and the Assault on American Ideals*. Simon and Schuster, 1998.

Bentham, Jeremy. *Principles of Morals and Legislation*. In *The Classical Utilitarians: Bentham and Mill*. Edited by John Troyer. Hackett, 2003.

Blevins, Gregory A., and Terrance Murphy. "Feeling Good and Helping: Further Phonebooth Findings." *Psychological Reports* 34, no. 1 (1974): 326.

Blom, Rianne M., Raoul C. Hennekam, and Damiaan Denys. "Body Integrity Identity Disorder." *PLoS One* 7, no. 4 (Apr. 2012): 1–6. https://doi.org/10.1371/journal.pone.0034702.

Boissoneault, Lourraine. "How the 1867 Medicine Lodge Treaty Changed the Plains Indian Tribes Forever." *Smithsonian Magazine*, October 23, 2017. https://www.smithsonianmag.com/history/how-1867-medicine-lodge-treaty-changed-plains-indian-tribes-forever-180965357/.

Bourke, Joanna. "Bestiality, Zoophilia, and Human-Animal Sexual Interactions." *Paragraph* 42, no. 1 (2019): 91–115.

Boyd, Craig A., and Don Thorsen. *Christian Ethics and Moral Philosophy: An Introduction to Issues and Approaches*. Baker Academic, 2018.

Breen, Patrick. "Understanding the Gospel of Nat Turner." *Smithsonian Magazine*, October 7, 2016. https://www.smithsonianmag.com/history/understanding-gospel-nat-turner-180960714/.

Brill, Steven, John Gregory, Anicka Slachta, Kendrick McDonald, and Gabby Deutch. "Robert F. Kennedy Jr. on Vaccines, COVID and Dr. Fauci: 'I Read the Science.'" *Newsweek*, March 1, 2021. https://www.newsweek.com/robert-f-kennedy-jr-vaccines-covid-dr-fauci-i-read-science-1572688.

Brown, Donald. *Human Universals*. McGraw-Hill, 1991.

Cascone, Sarah. "'The Pain Is Part of the Process': Why Two Artists Are Pushing Body Modification to the Extreme." *artnet*, April 7, 2022. https://news.artnet.com/market/tiamat-legion-medusa-carlos-motta-2093003.

Centers for Disease Control. "The Tuskegee Timeline." Accessed May 17, 2022. https://www.cdc.gov/tuskegee/timeline.htm.

Chappell, T. D. J. *Understanding Human Goods*. Edinburgh University Press, 1995.

Clanton, J. Caleb, and Kraig Martin, eds. *Nature and Command: On the Metaphysical Foundations of Morality*. The University of Tennessee Press, 2022.

Clark, C. Blue. "*Lone Wolf v. Hitchcock*." In *Encyclopedia of the Great Plains*, edited by David J. Wishart. University of Nebraska–Lincoln, 2011. https://plainshumanities.unl.edu/encyclopedia/doc/egp.law.027.html.

Clemens, Aurelius Prudentius. *Prudentius*. Translated by H. J. Thomson. Harvard University Press, 1949.

Clement of Alexandria. *Paedagogus*. 3 volumes. Compiled by Peter Kirby. https://www.earlychristianwritings.com/clement.html.

———. *Stromata*. 8 volumes. Compiled by Peter Kirby. https://www.earlychristianwritings.com/clement.html.

Clinton, William J. "Remarks on the After-School Child Care Initiative in the Roosevelt Room in the White House on January 26, 1998." The American Presidency Project. https://www.presidency.ucsb.edu/node/225911.

Crisp, Roger. *Mill on Utilitarianism*. Routledge, 1997.

Daily Mail. "'Top of My Priorities Is to Say Goodbye to Mr. Bojangles, My Penis': Former Banker, 58, Spends $75,000 on 18 Horn Implants, Castration, and Ear Removal to Become a 'Transspecies Reptilian.'" Daily Mail. August 15, 2019, accessed July 25, 2022. https://www.dailymail.co.uk/femail/article-7361427/Former-banker-spends-75-000-surgery-transspecies-reptilian.html.

Dancy, Jonathan. "Moral Particularism." In *Stanford Encyclopedia of Philosophy*. Stanford University, 1997–. Article published June 6, 2001; last modified September 22, 2017. https://plato.stanford.edu/archives/win2017/entries/moral-particularism/.

DeYoung, Rebecca Konyndyk. *Glittering Vices: A New Look at the Seven Deadly Sins and Their Remedies*. 2nd ed. Brazos Press, 2020.

Dickson, E. J. "Death of a TikTok Cosplay Star." *Rolling Stone*, October 21, 2021. https://www.rollingstone.com/culture/culture-features/cosplay-tiktok-manslaughter-yandere-snow-helen-hastings-1234452/.

Didache. Translated by Alexander Roberts and James Donaldson. Available on Peter Kirby's *Early Christian Writings*. https://www.earlychristianwritings.com/text/didache-roberts.html.

Doris, John M. *Lack of Character: Personality and Moral Behavior*. Cambridge University Press, 2002.

———. "Persons, Situations, and Virtue Ethics." *Nous* 32, no. 4 (1998): 504–30.

Dougherty, M. V. "Thomas Aquinas and Divine Command Theory." *Proceedings of the American Catholic Philosophical Association* 76 (2002): 153–64.

Driver, Julia. *Ethics: The Fundamentals*. Blackwell, 2007.
Duns Scotus, John. *Ordinatio, Book 3*. Supplemental, distinction 37. In *Duns Scotus on the Will and Morality*. Translated by Allan B. Wolter. Edited by William A. Frank. Catholic University of America Press, 1997.
Durston, Kirk. "The Consequential Complexity of History and Gratuitous Evil." *Religious Studies* 36 (2000): 65–80.
Easley, Jonathan. "Democrats Accused of Double Standard on Biden, Kavanaugh." *The Hill*, May 2, 2020. https://thehill.com/homenews/campaign/495757-democrats-accused-of-double-standard-on-biden-kavanaugh/.
Evagrius of Pontus. "On the Eight Thoughts." In *Evagrius of Pontus: The Greek Ascetic Corpus*. Translated by Robert E. Sinkewicz. Oxford University Press, 2003.
Evans, C. Stephen. *God and Moral Obligation*. Oxford University Press, 2013.
"Felicity Huffman Sentenced to 14 Days in Jail, First Parent Sentenced in College Admissions Scandal." NPR's *All Things Considered*, September 13, 2019, accessed May 17, 2022. https://www.npr.org/2019/09/13/760642060/felicity-huffman-sentenced-to-14-days-in-jail-first-parent-sentenced-in-college-.
Fienberg, Joel. "Psychological Egoism." In *Ethics: History, Theory and Contemporary Issues*, edited by Steven M. Cahn and Peter Markie, 527–34. 3rd ed. Oxford University Press, 2006.
Finnis, John. "Is Natural Law Compatible with Limited Government." In *Natural Law, Liberalism, and Morality*, edited by Robert P. George. Oxford University Press, 1996.
———. *Natural Law and Natural Rights*. Clarendon Press, 1980.
"Florida Man Who Consumed Dog Flesh Avoids Prison." *Orlando Sentinel*, December 23, 2013. https://www.orlandosentinel.com/2013/12/23/florida-man-who-consumed-dog-flesh-avoids-prison/.
Foot, Philippa. *Natural Goodness*. Oxford University Press, 2001.
———. "The Problem of Abortion and the Doctrine of Double Effect." In *Virtues and Vices and Other Essays in Moral Philosophy*, 19–32. Oxford University Press, 1978.
Fraga, Kaleena. "The Inspiring Story of Corrie ten Boom, the Dutch Watchmaker Who Saved 800 Jews from the Holocaust." *All That's Interesting*, July 1, 2021. https://allthatsinteresting.com/corrie-ten-boom.
Fraser, Chris. "Mohism." In *Stanford Encyclopedia of Philosophy*. Stanford University, 1997–. Article published October 21, 2002; last modified September 22, 2020. https://plato.stanford.edu/archives/win2020/entries/mohism/.
Gauthier, David. *Morals by Agreement*. Oxford University Press, 1987.
Geach, Peter. *God and the Soul*. Routledge & Kegan Paul, 1969.

George, Robert P. *In Defense of Natural Law*. Oxford University Press, 1999.

Goldstein, Joseph. "U.S. Soldiers Told to Ignore Sexual Abuse of Boys by Afghan Allies." *New York Times*, September 20, 2015, accessed May 5, 2022. https://www.nytimes.com/2015/09/21/world/asia/us-soldiers-told-to-ignore-afghan-allies-abuse-of-boys.html.

Gomez-Lobo, Alfonso. *Morality and the Human Goods: An Introduction to Natural Law Ethics*. Georgetown University Press, 2002.

Grenz, Stanley J. *The Moral Quest: Foundations of Christian Ethics*. InterVarsity Press, 1997.

Grisez, Germain G. "The First Principle of Practical Reason: A Commentary on the *Summa Theologiae*, 1–2, Question 94, Article 2." *Natural Law Forum* 10, no. 1 (1965): 168–201.

———. "The True Ultimate End of Human Beings: The Kingdom, Not God Alone." *Theological Studies* 69 (2008): 38–61.

———. *The Way of the Lord Jesus*. Volume 1: *Christian Moral Principles*. Franciscan Herald Press, 1983.

Grudem, Wayne. *Christian Ethics: An Introduction to Biblical Moral Reasoning*. Crossway, 2018.

Gushee, David P. *Introducing Christian Ethics: Core Convictions for Christians Today*. Front Edge Publishing, 2022.

Harding, Luke. "Victim of Cannibal Agreed to be Eaten." *The Guardian*, December 3, 2003. https://www.theguardian.com/world/2003/dec/04/germany.lukeharding.

Hare, John E. *God and Morality: A Philosophical History*. Wiley-Blackwell, 2009.

———. *God's Call: Moral Realism, God's Commands, and Human Autonomy*. William B. Eerdmans, 2001.

———. *God's Command*. Oxford University, 2015.

Hauerwas, Stanley. *Approaching the End: Eschatological Reflections on Church, Politics, and Life*. William B. Eerdmans, 2013.

Hayashi/Panos, Noriko. "Grab and Run: Kyrgyzstan's Bride Kidnappings." *Newsweek*, November 3, 2013, accessed May 5, 2022. https://www.newsweek.com/grab-and-run-1634.

Henderson, Donald A. "The Eradication of Smallpox—An Overview of the Past, Present, and Future." *Vaccine* 29, no. 4 (2011): D7–D9.

History Channel editors. "September 11 Attacks." History Channel. February 17, 2010, accessed May 12, 2022. https://www.history.com/topics/21st-century/9-11-attacks.

Hobbes, Thomas. *Hobbes's Leviathan, Reprinted from the Edition of 1651, with an Essay by the Late W. G. Pogson Smith*. Clarendon Press, 1909.

Hollinger, Dennis. *Choosing the Good: Christian Ethics in a Complex World.* Baker Academic, 2002.

Holmes, Arthur F. *Ethics: Approaching Moral Decisions.* 2nd ed. IVP Academic, 2007.

Humane World for Animals. "Asia's Dog Meat Trade: FAQs." Accessed June 23, 2025. https://www.humaneworld.org/asia/en/about-asias-dog-meat-trade-faqs.

Hunt, Morton M. *Sexual Behavior in the 1970s.* Playboy Press, 1974.

Idziak, Janine Marie. "Divine Commands Are the Foundation of Morality." In *Contemporary Debates in Philosophy of Religion*, edited by Michael L. Peterson and Raymond J. VanArragon, 290–99. Blackwell, 2004.

———. "In Search of 'Good Positive Reasons' in Favor of an Ethics of Divine Command: A Catalogue of Arguments." *Faith and Philosophy* 6, no. 1 (1989): 47–64.

———. Introduction to *Questions on an Ethics of Divine Commands*, by Andrew of Neufchateau, xi–xliii. Translated and edited by Janine Marie Idziak. University of Notre Dame Press, 1997.

Isen, A. M., and P. F. Levin. "Effect of Feeling Good on Helping: Cookies and Kindness." *Journal of Personality and Social Psychology* 21, no. 3 (1972): 384–88.

Joyce, Richard. "Moral Anti-Realism." In *Stanford Encyclopedia of Philosophy.* Stanford University, 1997–. Article published July 30, 2007; last modified February 11, 2015. http://plato.stanford.edu/archives/win2016/entries/moral-anti-realism/.

Justin Martyr. *Dialogue with Trypho.* Translated by Alexander Roberts and James Donaldson. Available on Peter Kirby's *Early Christian Writings.* Accessed March 6, 2025. https://www.earlychristianwritings.com/text/justinmartyr-dialoguetrypho.html.

———. *First Apology.* Translated by Alexander Roberts and James Donaldson. Available on Peter Kirby's *Early Christian Writings.* Accessed March 6, 2025. https://www.earlychristianwritings.com/text/justinmartyr-firstapology.html.

———. *Second Apology.* Translated by Alexander Roberts and James Donaldson. Available on Peter Kirby's *Early Christian Writings.* Accessed March 6, 2025. https://www.earlychristianwritings.com/text/justinmartyr-secondapology.html.

Kane, Gregory. "Clinton Not Solely to Blame for U.S. Moral Breakdown." *The Baltimore Sun*, July 17, 1999, accessed May 12, 2022. https://www.baltimoresun.com/news/bs-xpm-1999-07-18-9907180187-story.html.

Kant, Immanuel. *Grounding for the Metaphysics of Morals, with On the Supposed Right to Lie Because of Philanthropic Concerns.* 3rd ed. Translated by James W. Ellington. Hackett, 1993.

———. *Lectures on Ethics*. Translated by Louis Infield. Hackett, 1963.
———. *The Conflict of the Faculties*. Translated by Mary J. Gregor. University of Nebraska Press, 1992.
———. *The Metaphysics of Morals*. In *Ethical Philosophy*. 2nd ed. Translated by James W. Ellington. Hackett, 1994.
———. "On a Supposed Right to Lie Because of Philanthropic Concerns." In *Grounding for the Metaphysics of Morals, with On the Supposed Right to Lie Because of Philanthropic Concerns*. 3rd ed. Translated by James W. Ellington. Hackett, 1993.
King, Martin Luther, Jr. "Letter from a Birmingham Jail." In *The Atlantic*. Originally published May 19, 1963. https://www.theatlantic.com/magazine/archive/2018/02/letter-from-a-birmingham-jail/552461/.
Kinsey, Alfred C., Wardell B. Pomeroy, and Clyde E. Martin. *Sexual Behavior in the Human Male*. W. B. Saunders, 1948.
Klein, Dan. "Widow Not Allowed to Say Goodbye to Dying Husband at Hospital." WishTV. May 8, 2021. https://www.wishtv.com/news/coronavirus/widow-not-allowed-to-say-goodbye-to-dying-husband-at-hospital/.
Kramer, Stephanie. "Polygamy Is Rare around the World and Mostly Confined to a Few Regions." Pew Research Center. December 7, 2020. https://www.pewresearch.org/fact-tank/2020/12/07/polygamy-is-rare-around-the-world-and-mostly-confined-to-a-few-regions/.
Latane, Bibb, and John M. Rodin. *The Unresponsive Bystander: Why Doesn't He Help?* Appleton Century Crofts, 1970.
Latane, Bibb, and Judith Rodin. "A Lady in Distress: Inhibiting Effects of Friends and Strangers on Bystander Intervention." *Journal of Experimental Social Psychology* 5, no. 2 (1969): 189–202.
Lawson, James. "James Lawson: The Architect of the United States Civil Rights Movement (Best of NSE)." Interview with Lee C. Camp. *No Small Endeavor* (podcast), July 11, 2024. Audio 6:00–11:00. Transcript available online at https://www.nosmallendeavor.com/james-lawson-best-of-nse.
Lejay, Paul. "Aurelius Clemens Prudentius." In *The Catholic Encyclopedia*. Vol. 12. Robert Appleton, 1911. http://www.newadvent.org/cathen/12517c.htm.
Lewis, C. S. "Appendix: Illustrations of the *Tao*." In *The Abolition of Man*, 83–102. HarperOne, 2001.
Locke, John. *An Essay concerning Human Understanding*. In *The Works of John Locke in Nine Volumes*. 12th ed. C. and J. Rivington and Partners, 1823 [1689].
———. *Second Treatise of Government*. In *Locke: Two Treatises of Government*. Edited by Peter Laslett. Cambridge University Press, 2017.
———. *Two Treatises of Civil Government*. Edited by Thomas Hollis. A. Millar, et. al. 1689.

Lone Wolf v. Hitchcock. 187 U.S. 553 (1903).

Lucado, Max. "Decency for President." *Max Lucado* (blog). February 26, 2016. https://maxlucado.com/decency-for-president/.

MacIntyre, Alasdair. *After Virtue: A Study in Moral Theory*. 2nd ed. University of Notre Dame Press, 1984.

Mackie, J. L. *Ethics: Inventing Right and Wrong*. Penguin, 1990.

The Martin Luther King Jr. Research and Education Institute. "The Reverend James M. Lawson, Jr." Stanford University. Last updated February 1, 2024. https://kinginstitute.stanford.edu/reverend-james-m-lawson-jr.

McCarthy, Colman. "A Matter of Death and Life: Review of *Circumstantial Evidence: Death, Life, and Justice in a Southern Town* by Pete Earley Bantam." *Washington Post*, October 10, 1995, accessed July 18, 2022. https://www.washingtonpost.com/archive/lifestyle/1995/10/10/a-matter-of-death-and-life/b7af4803-56aa-4f0f-addd-e048a76a3d19/.

McDonald, John. "Bill Bennett Is Too Harsh on Bill Clinton." *Hartford Courant*, August 29, 1998. https://www.courant.com/news/connecticut/hc-xpm-1998-08-29-9808290064-story.html.

McInerny, Ralph. *Ethica Thomistica: The Moral Philosophy of Thomas Aquinas*. Rev. ed. The Catholic University of America Press, 1997.

———. "The Principles of the Natural Law." *American Journal of Jurisprudence* 25 (1980): 1–15.

Mill, John Stuart. *Utilitarianism*. In *The Classical Utilitarians: Bentham and Mill*. Edited by John Troyer. Hackett, 2003.

Morales, Mark, and Dakin Adone. "Felicity Huffman Gets 14 Days in Prison in Connection with College Admission Scandal." CNN, September 13, 2019. https://www.cnn.com/2019/09/13/us/felicity-huffman-sentencing/index.html.

Mosebach, Martin. *The 21: A Journey into the Land of Coptic Martyrs*. Plough Publishing, 2019.

Murphy, Mark C. *An Essay on Divine Authority*. Cornell University Press, 2002.

———. *God and Moral Law: On the Theistic Explanation of Morality*. Oxford University Press, 2011.

———. *Natural Law and Practical Rationality*. Cambridge University Press, 2001.

———. "The Natural Law Tradition in Ethics." In *Stanford Encyclopedia of Philosophy*. Stanford University, 1997–. Article published September 23, 2002; last modified May 26, 2019. https://plato.stanford.edu/archives/sum2019/entries/natural-law-ethics/, §2.3.

National Geographic. *9/11: One Day in America*. Season 1, episode 2: "The South Tower." Accessed May 12, 2022. https://www.nationalgeographic.com/tv/shows

/911-one-day-in-america/episode-guide/season-01/episode-02-the-south-tower/vdka24572289.

National Public Radio. "Frequently Asked Questions about Lobotomies." *NPR*, November 16, 2005, accessed July 16, 2022. https://www.npr.org/templates/story/story.php?storyId=5014565.

"Nat Turner's Rebellion." National Museum of African American History and Culture. Accessed March 6, 2025. https://nmaahc.si.edu/explore/stories/nat-turners-rebellion.

"Nat Turner's Rebellion: To Rebel and Make Insurrection." Library of Virginia. Accessed March 6, 2025. https://www.lva.virginia.gov/exhibits/DeathLiberty/natturner/index.htm.

Niebuhr, Reinhold. *Moral Man and Immoral Society: A Study in Ethics and Politics*. Charles Scribner's Sons, 1932.

Nozick, Robert. *Anarchy, State, and Utopia*. Basic Books, 1974.

Pence, Gregory E. *Classic Cases in Medical Ethics: Accounts of Cases That Have Shaped Medical Ethics, with Philosophical, Legal, and Historical Backgrounds*. 3rd ed. McGraw Hill, 2000.

Pennington, Jonathan T. *The Sermon on the Mount and Human Flourishing: A Theological Commentary*. Baker Academic, 2017.

Pew Research Center. "Religious Composition by Country, 2010–2050." December 21, 2022, accessed March 26, 2024. https://www.pewresearch.org/religion/interactives/religious-composition-by-country-2010-2050/.

Pinckaers Servais. *Morality: The Catholic View*. Translated by Michael Sherwin. St Augustine's Press, 2001.

Pinker, Steven. *The Blank Slate: The Modern Denial of Human Nature*. Penguin Book, 2002.

Pojman, Louis, and James Fieser. *Ethics: Discovering Right and Wrong*. 7th ed. Wadsworth/Cengage, 2012.

"Police: Tampa Man Killed, Cooked Family Dog." *Spectrum News 13*, June 28, 2013. https://mynews13.com/fl/orlando/news/2013/6/28/police_tampa_man_kil?cid=rss.

Pope Paul VI. *Encyclical Letter "Humanae Vitae" of the Supreme Pontiff Paul VI* (1968). Accessed July 25, 2022. https://www.vatican.va/content/paul-vi/en/encyclicals/documents/hf_p-vi_enc_25071968_humanae-vitae.html.

Porter, Jean. *Natural and Divine Law: Reclaiming the Tradition for Christian Ethics*. Novalis, 1999.

Quinn, Philip L. *Divine Commands and Moral Requirements*. Clarendon Press, 1978.

———. "The Recent Revival of Divine Command Ethics." *Philosophy and Phenomenological Research*, supplement (1990): 345–65.

Rachels, James. "God and Human Attitudes." *Religious Studies* 7, no. 4 (1971): 325–37.

Rachels, James, and Stuart Rachels. *The Elements of Moral Philosophy*. 9th ed. McGraw-Hill, 2019.

Rae, Scott B. *Moral Choices: An Introduction to Ethics*. 4th ed. Zondervan, 2018.

Raffaele, Paul. "Sleeping with Cannibals." *Smithsonian Magazine*, September 2006, accessed May 5, 2022. https://www.smithsonianmag.com/travel/sleeping-with-cannibals-128958913/.

Rand, Ayn. *Anthem*. Cassell, 1937.

———. *The Virtue of Selfishness: A New Concept of Egoism*. Signet, 1964.

Rand, Jacki Thompson. "Medicine Lodge Treaty." In *The Encyclopedia of Oklahoma History and Culture*. Oklahoma Historical Society. Article published January 15, 2010. https://www.okhistory.org/publications/enc/entry?entry=ME005.

Rawls, John. *A Theory of Justice*. Belknap Press, 2003.

Rettew, David. "The TikTok Inspired Surge of Dissociative Identity Disorder." *Psychology Today*, March 17, 2022. https://www.psychologytoday.com/us/blog/abcs-child-psychiatry/202203/the-tiktok-inspired-surge-dissociative-identity-disorder.

Richardson, Robert. *Memoirs of Alexander Campbell, Embracing a View of the Origin, Progress and Principles of the Religious Reformation which He Advocated*. 2 volumes. Standard Publishing, 1897.

Roberts, Amber. "Otherkin Are People Too; They Just Identify as Nonhuman." *Vice*, July 16, 2015, accessed July 25, 2022. https://www.vice.com/en/article/mvxgwa/from-dragons-to-foxes-the-otherkin-community-believes-you-can-be-whatever-you-want-to-be.

Roberts, Robert C. "Situationism and the New Testament Psychology of the Heart." In *The Bible and the University*, edited by David Lyle Jeffrey and C. Stephen Evans, 139–60. Zondervan, 2007.

Ross, W. D. *The Right and the Good*. Edited by Philip Stratton-Lake. Clarendon Press, 2002 [1930].

Sandel, Michael. *Democracy's Discontent: America in Search of a Public Philosophy*. Belknap Press, 1996.

———. *Justice: What's the Right Thing to Do*. Farrar, Straus and Giroux, 2009.

Schmidt, Susan, Peter Baker, and Toni Locy. "Clinton Accused of Urging Aide to Lie." *Washington Post*, January 21, 1998. https://www.washingtonpost.com/wp-srv/politics/special/whitewater/stories/wwtr980121.htm.

Shafer-Landau, Russ. *The Fundamentals of Ethics*. 5th ed. Oxford University Press, 2021.

Siker, Jeffrey S. *Jesus, Sin, and Perfection in Early Christianity*. Cambridge University Press, 2015.

Smith, Adam. *An Inquiry into the Nature and Causes of the Wealth of Nations*. Volume 1. Edited by Edwin Cannan. Methuen, 1904.

Stevenson, Bryan. *Just Mercy: A Story of Justice and Redemption*. Spiegel & Grau, 2014.

Stocker, Michael. "The Schizophrenia of Modern Ethical Theories." *Journal of Philosophy* 73, no. 14 (1976): 453–66.

Stout, Lynn A. "Taking Conscience Seriously." In *Moral Markets: The Critical Role of Values in the Economy*, edited by Paul J. Zak, 157–72. Princeton University Press, 2007.

Stump, Elenore. *Aquinas*. Routledge, 2003.

Sullivan, Jennifer. "Man in Infamous Enumclaw Horse-Sex Case Faces New Charges in Tennessee." *Seattle Times*, October 20, 2009, accessed September 9, 2022. https://www.seattletimes.com/seattle-news/man-in-infamous-enumclaw-horse-sex-case-faces-new-charges-in-tennessee/.

Swinburne, Richard. "Duty and the Will of God." *Canadian Journal of Philosophy* 4, no. 2 (1974): 213–27.

———. *Revelation: From Metaphor to Analogy*. 2nd ed. Oxford University Press, 2007.

———. "What Difference Does God Make to Morality?" In *Is Goodness with God Good Enough? A Debate on Faith, Secularism, and Ethics*, edited by Robert K. Garcia and Nathan L. King, 151–63. Rowman & Littlefield, 2009.

Tertullian. *De Spectaculis, or The Shows*. Translated by the Rev. S. Thelwall. Available on Peter Kirby's *Early Christian Writings*. Accessed March 6, 2025. https://www.earlychristianwritings.com/text/tertullian03.html.

———. *A Treatise on the Soul*. Translated by Peter Holmes. Available on Peter Kirby's *Early Christian Writings*. Accessed March 6, 2025. https://www.early-christianwritings.com/text/tertullian10.html.

———. *Of Patience*. Translated by the Rev. S. Thelwall. Available on Peter Kirby's *Early Christian Writings*. Accessed March 6, 2025. https://www.earlychristianwritings.com/text/tertullian25.html.

Thomson, Judith Jarvis. "The Trolley Problem." *The Yale Law Journal* 94, no. 6 (1985): 1395–415.

Timmons, Mark. *Moral Theory: An Introduction*. 2nd ed. Rowman & Littlefield, 2013.

Turner, Nat. *The Confessions of Nat Turner*. Edited by Thomas R. Gray. Lucas & Deaver, 1831. https://digitalcommons.unl.edu/cgi/viewcontent.cgi?article=1014&context=etas.

Valens, Ana. "Otherkin Are the Internet's Punchline. They're Also Our Future." *Daily Dot*, September 15, 2020. https://web.archive.org/web/20250313005409/https://www.dailydot.com/irl/otherkin/.

Vašečková, B., M. Patarák, V. Petrušová, and Ľ. Forgáčová. "Self-Amputation in Patient with Body Integrity Dysphoria in Comorbidity with Gender Dysphoria: A Case Report." *Psychopathology* 55, no. 5 (Mar. 2022): 310–16. https://doi.org/10.1159/000522596.

Vigdor, Neil. "Tennessee Brothers Who Hoarded Hand Sanitizer Settle to Avoid Price-Gouging Fine." *New York Times*, June 22, 2020. https://www.nytimes.com/2020/04/22/us/hand-sanitizer-matt-colvin-noah-coronavirus.html.

Wilkens, Steve. *Beyond Bumper Sticker Ethics: An Introduction to Theories of Right and Wrong*. 2nd ed. IVP Academic, 2011.

Wong, Herman, and Cleve R. Wootson Jr. "Police Seeking DNA of Male Staff at Health-Care Facility Where Woman in Vegetative State Gave Birth." *Washington Post*, January 8, 2019, accessed July 16, 2022. https://www.washingtonpost.com/health/2019/01/09/police-seeking-dna-male-staff-health-care-facility-where-woman-vegetative-state-gave-birth/.

World Health Organization. "Female Genital Mutilation." WHO. Accessed June 26, 2024. https://www.who.int/news-room/fact-sheets/detail/female-genital-mutilation.

Yoder, John Howard. *The Politics of Jesus*. Eerdmans, 1972.

NOTES

Chapter One Introduction

[1]Moral philosophy is not helpfully distinguished from the study of ethics. For this reason, we will use the terms *ethics* and *morality* interchangeably in this book, and that is intentional. We recognize that sometimes different writers will draw or stipulate distinctions between these terms. But those distinctions are unstable, and they are not especially helpful.

[2]John Locke, *An Essay concerning Human Understanding*, in *The Works of John Locke in Nine Volumes*, 12th ed. (C. and J. Rivington and Partners, 1823 [1689]), 1.3:4.

[3]The most noteworthy of the books we have in mind here include: Craig A. Boyd and Don Thorsen, *Christian Ethics and Moral Philosophy: An Introduction to Issues and Approaches* (Baker Academic, 2018); Steve Wilkens, *Beyond Bumper Sticker Ethics: An Introduction to Theories of Right and Wrong*, 2nd ed. (IVP Academic, 2011); and Arthur F. Holmes, *Ethics: Approaching Moral Decisions*, 2nd ed. (IVP Academic, 2007).

[4]John Rawls has been very influential in defending this kind of argument. See, for example, John Rawls, *A Theory of Justice* (Belknap Press, 2003), 392–96.

[5]To see our point, consider nearly any section of Thomas Aquinas's *Summa Theologica*. Aquinas cites not only Scripture but an array of prior Christian thinkers. Similarly, Augustine cites (among other authorities) the twenty-seven books of the Christian New Testament, and in his *On Christian Doctrine* (2.8.13), he clearly recognizes the authority of Scripture for the moral life.

[6]Among contemporary authors, there are quite a few influential Christian scholars who work in moral philosophy. Among the many we could cite, we note Robert Adams, *Finite and Infinite Goods: A Framework for Ethics* (Oxford University Press, 1999); G. E. M. Anscombe, "Modern Moral Philosophy," *Philosophy* 33, no. 124 (1958): 1–19; Stephen Evans, *God & Moral Obligation* (Oxford University Press, 2013); John Finnis, *Natural Law and Natural Rights* (Clarendon Press, 1980); Peter Geach, *God and the Soul* (Routledge, 1969); Robert George, *In Defense of Natural Law* (Oxford University Press,

1999); John Hare, *God's Command* (Oxford University, 2015); Mark Murphy, *God & Moral Law: On the Theistic Explanation of Morality* (Oxford University Press, 2011); Jean Porter, *Natural & Divine Law: Reclaiming the Tradition for Christian Ethics* (Novalis, 1999); Philip L. Quinn, *Divine Commands and Moral Requirements* (Clarendon Press, 1978); Elenore Stump, *Aquinas* (Routledge, 2003); and Richard Swinburne, "What Difference Does God Make to Morality?," in *Is Goodness with God Good Enough*, ed. Robert K. Garcia and Nathan L. King, 151–63 (Rowman & Littlefield, 2009).

[7]Three particularly influential texts in the field of Christian ethics include Reinhold Niebuhr, *Moral Man and Immoral Society: A Study in Ethics and Politics* (Charles Scribner's Sons, 1932); John Howard Yoder, *The Politics of Jesus* (William B. Eerdmans, 1972); and Stanley Hauerwas, *Approaching the End: Eschatological Reflections on Church, Politics, and Life* (William B. Eerdmans, 2013). See also David P. Gushee, *Introducing Christian Ethics: Core Convictions for Christians Today* (Front Edge Publishing, 2022); Wayne Grudem, *Christian Ethics: An Introduction to Biblical Moral Reasoning* (Crossway, 2018); Scott B. Rae, *Moral Choices: An Introduction to Ethics*, 4th ed. (Zondervan, 2018); Dennis Hollinger, *Choosing the Good: Christian Ethics in a Complex World* (Baker Academic, 2002); Stanley J. Grenz, *The Moral Quest: Foundations of Christian Ethics* (InterVarsity Press, 1997).

[8]See note 3 above.

[9]The following list draws from Holmes, *Ethics*, 14–17.

[10]Locke, *Essay concerning Human Understanding*, 4.19:14.

Chapter Two Relativism

[1]The facts of this story are relayed in "Florida Man Who Consumed Dog Flesh Avoids Prison," *Orlando Sentinel*, December 23, 2013, https://www.orlandosentinel.com/2013/12/23/florida-man-who-consumed-dog-flesh-avoids-prison/. See also "Police: Tampa Man Killed, Cooked Family Dog," *Spectrum News 13*, June 28, 2013, https://mynews13.com/fl/orlando/news/2013/6/28/police_tampa_man_kil?cid=rss.

[2]See Humane World for Animals, "Asia's Dog Meat Trade: FAQs," accessed June 23, 2025, https://www.humaneworld.org/asia/en/about-asias-dog-meat-trade-faqs.

[3]See Amnesty International, "Iran: Abusive Forced Veiling Laws Police Women's Lives," May 28, 2019, https://www.amnesty.org/en/latest/campaigns/2019/05/iran-abusive-forced-veiling-laws-police-womens-lives/.

[4]See, for example, Noriko Hayashi/Panos, "Grab and Run: Kyrgyzstan's Bride Kidnappings," *Newsweek*, November 3, 2013, https://www.newsweek.com/grab-and-run-1634.

[5]See Stephanie Kramer, "Polygamy Is Rare around the World and Mostly Confined to a Few Regions," Pew Research Center, December 7, 2020, https://www.pewresearch.org/fact-tank/2020/12/07/polygamy-is-rare-around-the-world-and-mostly-confined-to-a-few-regions/.

[6]See the World Health Organization's factsheet on "Female Genital Mutilation," https://www.who.int/news-room/fact-sheets/detail/female-genital-mutilation.

[7]See Paul Raffaele, "Sleeping with Cannibals," *Smithsonian Magazine*, September 2006, https://www.smithsonianmag.com/travel/sleeping-with-cannibals-128958913/

[8]Our presentation of a theory's account of the good and the corresponding account of the right in this chapter and throughout the book mimics the strategy of presentation on offer in Mark Timmons, *Moral Theory: An Introduction*, 2nd ed. (Rowman & Littlefield,

2013). Timmons distinguishes between the theory of value and the theory of right conduct.

[9]See "Appendix: Illustrations of the *Tao*," in C. S. Lewis, *The Abolition of Man* (HarperOne, 2001), 83–102.

[10]See Brown's list as presented in the appendix of Steven Pinker, *The Blank Slate: The Modern Denial of Human Nature* (Penguin Book, 2002), 435–39. See also Donald Brown, *Human Universals* (McGraw-Hill, 1991), 13–15.

[11]Ruth Benedict, "Anthropology and the Abnormal," *Journal of General Psychology* 10 (1934): 73.

[12]Joseph Goldstein, "U.S. Soldiers Told to Ignore Sexual Abuse of Boys by Afghan Allies," *New York Times*, September 20, 2015, emphasis added, https://www.nytimes.com/2015/09/21/world/asia/us-soldiers-told-to-ignore-afghan-allies-abuse-of-boys.html.

[13]A similar point is made by Steve Wilkens, *Beyond Bumper Sticker Ethics: An Introduction to Theories of Right and Wrong*, 2nd ed. (InterVarsity Press, 2011), 36.

[14]For the inspiration of this particular example, see Steven Brill, et al., "Robert F. Kennedy Jr. on Vaccines, COVID and Dr. Fauci: 'I Read the Science,'" *Newsweek*, March 1, 2021, https://www.newsweek.com/robert-f-kennedy-jr-vaccines-covid-dr-fauci-i-read-science-1572688.

[15]See Martin Mosebach, *The 21: A Journey into the Land of Coptic Martyrs* (Plough Publishing House, 2019).

[16]Alasdair MacIntyre, *After Virtue*, 2nd ed. (University of Notre Dame Press, 1984), 19.

[17]It is hard to overstate the theological centrality of sin throughout the Bible. From Genesis 3, where humans first behave in a way that is morally wrong, to Genesis 4, where the first murder caused the blood of Abel to "cry out from the ground" against Cain, to the flood account, where the reality of widespread sin caused God to have to start over with mankind, to Joseph's brothers to David having Uriah murdered to the repeated idolatry of the Israelites, and over and over again, the narrative of the Bible is driven by the reality of sin. The theological centrality of sin is continued in the New Testament, where Jesus dies as a way of dealing with the problem of sin. Jesus himself regularly taught in ways that assumed moral realism. For example, he regularly taught about forgiveness, which assumes there is an objectively morally blameworthy act that needs to be forgiven. He taught about how the sheep will be divided from the goats (Matt. 25), and how the guilty will be punished (Matt. 5–7). The apostle Paul indicates that the morally upright will be rewarded and the morally guilty (in some sense) will be punished (Rom. 2), while also acknowledging that, in another sense, we are all morally guilty (Rom. 5). The point here is just that it is impossible to overstate the centrality of the concept of sin throughout the Christian narrative.

Chapter Three Ethical Egoism

[1]For an especially powerful recollection of the events of the day, including a discussion of Rick Rescorla, see the National Geographic documentary, *9/11: One Day in America*, season 1, episode 2, "The South Tower," https://www.nationalgeographic.com/tv/shows/911-one-day-in-america/episode-guide/season-01/episode-02-the-south-tower/vdka24572289. We draw also from History Channel editors, "September 11 Attacks," History Channel, February 17, 2010, https://www.history.com/topics/21st-century/9-11-attacks; as well as the Wikipedia entry on Rick Rescorla.

[2] See Neil Vigdor, "Tennessee Brothers Who Hoarded Hand Sanitizer Settle to Avoid Price-Gouging Fine," *New York Times*, June 22, 2020, https://www.nytimes.com/2020/04/22/us/hand-sanitizer-matt-colvin-noah-coronavirus.html.

[3] Here we are following Joel Fienberg, "Psychological Egoism," in *Ethics: History, Theory and Contemporary Issues*, ed. Steven M. Cahn and Peter Markie, 3rd ed. (Oxford University Press, 2006), 529–31.

[4] For a discussion of experiments that appear to confirm the reality of altruism, see Lynn A. Stout, "Taking Conscience Seriously," in *Moral Markets: The Critical Role of Values in the Economy*, ed. Paul J. Zak, 157–72 (Princeton University Press, 2007).

[5] See, for example, Louis Pojman and James Fieser, *Ethics: Discovering Right and Wrong*, 7th ed. (Wadsworth/Cengage, 2012), 89–90.

[6] Adam Smith, *An Inquiry into the Nature and Causes of the Wealth of Nations*, ed. Edwin Cannan, vol. 1 (Methuen, 1904), 421—emphasis added.

[7] Smith, *Inquiry into the Nature*, 421.

[8] Ayn Rand, *The Virtue of Selfishness: A New Concept of Egoism* (Signet, 1964), ix.

[9] For a dramatized presentation of this position in Rand's work, see chapter 11 of Ayn Rand, *Anthem* (Cassell, 1937).

[10] Of course, following Jesus, the Christian could also point out that those folks *weren't actually acting in their own long-term best interest*, though perhaps they thought they were.

[11] We are following Pojman and Fieser, *Ethics*, 92.

[12] James Rachels and Stuart Rachels, *The Elements of Moral Philosophy*, 9th ed. (McGraw-Hill, 2019), 79–82.

[13] See, for example, Russ Shafer-Landau, *The Fundamentals of Ethics*, 5th ed. (Oxford University Press, 2021), 119–20.

[14] Aristotle, *Nicomachean Ethics*, trans. C. D. C. Reeve (Hackett, 2014), 138 [1155b30].

[15] See, for example, the order for marriage in the Book of Common Prayer (Anglican), as well as in the Roman Catholic Order for Celebrating Matrimony. Though some of the language varies, the underlying point remains the same: The traditional marriage vow is that A will be faithful to B, regardless of whether doing so is in A's self-interest.

[16] See, for example, John Duns Scotus, *Ordinatio*, bk. 3, suppl., dist. 37, in *Duns Scotus on the Will & Morality*, ed. William A. Frank, trans. Allan B. Wolter (Catholic University of America Press, 1997), 202.

Chapter Four Utilitarianism

[1] As reported by Channel 8 News in Indianapolis, Indiana. See Dan Klein, "Widow Not Allowed to Say Goodbye to Dying Husband at Hospital," WishTV, May 8, 2021, https://www.wishtv.com/news/coronavirus/widow-not-allowed-to-say-goodbye-to-dying-husband-at-hospital/.

[2] See, for example, Chris Fraser, "Mohism," in *Stanford Encyclopedia of Philosophy*, sect. 7, https://plato.stanford.edu/archives/win2020/entries/mohism/. See also Julia Driver, *Ethics: The Fundamentals* (Blackwell, 2007), 41.

[3] Jeremy Bentham, *Principles of Morals and Legislation*, in *The Classical Utilitarians: Bentham and Mill*, ed. John Troyer (Hackett, 2003), 21 [VI.v.5–6]—emphasis added.

[4] Our thought experiment closely mimics the example given in Roger Crisp, *Mill on Utilitarianism* (Routledge, 1997), 24.

[5] American Museum of Natural History, "The Immortal Jellyfish," May 4, 2015, accessed July 13, 2022, https://www.amnh.org/explore/news-blogs/on-exhibit-posts /the-immortal-jellyfish.

[6] John Stuart Mill, *Utilitarianism*, in *The Classical Utilitarians*, 99 [chap. II.2]—emphasis added.

[7] Bentham, *Principles of Morals and Legislation*, 10 [I.xi].

[8] Bentham, *Principles of Morals and Legislation*, 11 [I.xiii]—emphasis original.

[9] Mill, *Utilitarianism*, 122 [IV.2–3].

[10] Our interpretation and evaluation of Mill's argument draws partly on Mark Timmons, *Moral Theory: An Introduction*, 2nd ed. (Rowman & Littlefield, 2013), 127–28.

[11] Mill, *Utilitarianism*, 111 [II.22].

[12] Mill, *Utilitarianism*, 108 [II.18].

[13] See, for example, Augustine, *The Essential Augustine*, ed. Vernon J. Bourke (Hackett, 1974), 159–60.

[14] Our examples are inspired by Kirk Durston, "The Consequential Complexity of History and Gratuitous Evil," *Religious Studies* 36 (2000): 65–80, at 66.

[15] As reported by National Public Radio, "Frequently Asked Questions about Lobotomies," *NPR*, November 16, 2005, https://www.npr.org/templates/story/story .php?storyId=5014565.

[16] This example originates with Philippa Foot and is developed more fully by Russ Shafer-Landau. See Philippa Foot, *Natural Goodness* (Oxford University Press, 2001), 85; Russ Shafer-Landau, *The Fundamentals of Ethics*, 5th ed. (Oxford University Press, 2021), 30.

[17] Herman Wong and Cleve R. Wootson Jr., "Police Seeking DNA of Male Staff at Health-Care Facility Where Woman in Vegetative State Gave Birth," *Washington Post*, January 8, 2019, https://www.washingtonpost.com/health/2019/01/09/police-seeking -dna-male-staff-health-care-facility-where-woman-vegetative-state-gave-birth/.

[18] See Robert Nozick, *Anarchy, State, and Utopia* (Basic Books, 1974), 42–45.

[19] Michael Sandel, *Justice: What's the Right Thing to Do* (Farrar, Straus and Giroux, 2009), 55–56.

[20] This point originates in Shafer-Landau, *Fundamentals of Ethics*, 51.

[21] Sandel, *Justice*, 73–74. See also Luke Harding, "Victim of Cannibal Agreed to be Eaten," *The Guardian*, December 3, 2003, https://www.theguardian.com/world/2003 /dec/04/germany.lukeharding.

[22] For more information, see the account given by McMillian's own defense attorney in Bryan Stevenson, *Just Mercy: A Story of Justice and Redemption* (Spiegel & Grau, 2014).

[23] Quoted in Colman McCarthy, "A Matter of Death and Life: Review of *Circumstantial Evidence: Death, Life, and Justice in a Southern Town* by Pete Earley Bantam," *Washington Post*, October 10, 1995, https://www.washingtonpost.com/archive/lifestyle /1995/10/10/a-matter-of-death-and-life/b7af4803-56aa-4f0f-addd-e048a76a3d19/.

[24] Basil, quoted in Rebecca Konyndyk DeYoung, *Glittering Vices: A New Look at the Seven Deadly Sins and Their Remedies*, 2nd ed. (Brazos Press, 2020), 123—emphasis added.

[25] Sandel, *Justice*, 225.

Chapter Five Kantian Deontology

[1]See Mark Morales and Dakin Adone, "Felicity Huffman Gets 14 Days in Prison in Connection with College Admission Scandal," CNN, September 13, 2019, https://www.cnn.com/2019/09/13/us/felicity-huffman-sentencing/index.html.

[2]Tony Jack, quoted in "Felicity Huffman Sentenced to 14 Days in Jail, First Parent Sentenced in College Admissions Scandal," NPR's *All Things Considered*, September 13, 2019, https://www.npr.org/2019/09/13/760642060/felicity-huffman-sentenced-to-14-days-in-jail-first-parent-sentenced-in-college-.

[3]See Centers for Disease Control, "The Tuskegee Timeline," https://www.cdc.gov/tuskegee/timeline.htm. See also Gregory E. Pence, *Classic Cases in Medical Ethics: Accounts of Cases that Have Shaped Medical Ethics, with Philosophical, Legal, and Historical Backgrounds*, 3rd ed. (McGraw Hill, 2000), 253–76.

[4]Immanuel Kant, *Grounding for the Metaphysics of Morals, with On the Supposed Right to Lie Because of Philanthropic Concerns*, 3rd ed., trans. James W. Ellington (Hackett, 1993), 7 [393]—emphasis in the original.

[5]Kant, *Grounding for the Metaphysics of Morals*, 7 [393].

[6]Our interpretation of Kant on this point borrows from Mark Timmons, *Moral Theory: An Introduction*, 2nd ed. (Rowman & Littlefield, 2013), 214–15 and 221–25.

[7]Kant, *Grounding for the Metaphysics of Morals*, 30 [422].

[8]Julia Driver, *Ethics: The Fundamentals* (Blackwell, 2007), 90.

[9]See, for example, Kant, *Grounding for the Metaphysics of Morals*, as reprinted in book 2 of Immanuel Kant, *Ethical Philosophy*, 2nd ed., trans. James W. Ellington (Hackett, 1994). See also, Timmons, *Moral Theory*, 213–18.

[10]Kant, *Grounding for the Metaphysics of Morals*, 36 [429].

[11]Kant, *Grounding for the Metaphysics of Morals*, 35 [428].

[12]Our reconstruction of Kant's argument, as well as the critique of it, follows Louis P. Pojman and James Fieser, *Ethics: Discovering Right and Wrong* (Wadsworth, 2012), 135–36.

[13]We borrow this point from Russ Shafer-Landau, *The Fundamentals of Ethics* (Oxford University Press, 2021), 185–86.

[14]Steve Wilkens, *Beyond Bumper Sticker Ethics: An Introduction to Theories of Right and Wrong*, 2nd ed. (InterVarsity, 2011), 123.

[15]Our discussion of the Golden Rule, as well as the example used here, follows Michael J. Sandel, *Justice: What's the Right Thing to Do* (Farrar, Straus and Giroux, 2009), 124–25.

[16]See Immanuel Kant, "On a Supposed Right to Lie Because of Philanthropic Concerns," in *Grounding for the Metaphysics of Morals*, 63–67, at 65 [427]—emphasis added.

[17]Kaleena Fraga, "The Inspiring Story of Corrie ten Boom, the Dutch Watchmaker Who Saved 800 Jews from the Holocaust," *All That's Interesting*, July 1, 2021, https://allthatsinteresting.com/corrie-ten-boom.

[18]W. D. Ross, *The Right and the Good*, ed. Philip Stratton-Lake (Clarendon Press, 2002 [1930]), 21.

[19]Ross, *Right and the Good*, 29.

[20]Ross, *Right and the Good*, 31.

[21]Michael Stocker, "The Schizophrenia of Modern Ethical Theories," *Journal of Philosophy* 73, no. 14 (1976): 462.

[22]Stocker, "Schizophrenia of Modern Ethical Theories," 462.

[23]Stocker, "Schizophrenia of Modern Ethical Theories," 462.

[24]Our discussion of this objection follows Craig A. Boyd and Don Thorsen, *Christian Ethics and Moral Philosophy: An Introduction to Issues and Approaches* (Baker Academic, 2018), 114–15, as well as nn11–12.

[25]Immanuel Kant, *Lectures on Ethics*, trans. Louis Infield (Hackett, 1963), 24.

[26]Kant, quoted in Robert Merrihew Adams, *Finite and Infinite Goods: A Framework for Ethics* (Oxford University Press, 1999), 284—emphasis added. See also Immanuel Kant, *The Conflict of the Faculties* [AK VII, 63].

Chapter Six Social Contract Theory

[1]Our introduction pulls heavily from Lourraine Boissoneault, "How the 1867 Medicine Lodge Treaty Changed the Plains Indian Tribes Forever," *Smithsonian Magazine*, October 23, 2017, https://www.smithsonianmag.com/history/how-1867-medicine-lodge-treaty-changed-plains-indian-tribes-forever-180965357/. See also Jacki Thompson Rand, "Medicine Lodge Treaty," in *The Encyclopedia of Oklahoma History and Culture*, ed. David J. Wishart (University of Nebraska–Lincoln, 2011), https://www.okhistory.org/publications/enc/entry?entry=ME005; C. Blue Clark, "*Lone Wolf v. Hitchcock*," in Wishart, ed., *Encyclopedia of the Great Plains*, https://plainshumanities.unl.edu/encyclopedia/doc/egp.law.027.html; and *Lone Wolf v. Hitchcock*, 187 U.S. 553 (1903).

[2]Thomas Hobbes, *Hobbes's Leviathan, Reprinted from the Edition of 1651, with an Essay by the Late W. G. Pogson Smith* (Clarendon Press, 1909), 96–97.

[3]John Locke, *Two Treatises of Civil Government*, ed. Thomas Hollis (A. Millar, 1689), 305–6 [II.ix.123]—emphasis in the original.

[4]For the following points, we draw from Russ Shafer-Landau, *The Fundamentals of Ethics*, 5th ed. (Oxford University Press, 2021), 210–16; and James Rachels and Stuart Rachels, *The Elements of Moral Philosophy*, 9th ed. (McGraw-Hill, 2019), 91–93.

[5]Martin Luther King Jr., "Letter from a Birmingham Jail," *The Atlantic*, emphasis added, https://www.theatlantic.com/magazine/archive/2018/02/letter-from-a-birmingham-jail/552461/.

[6]Louis Pojman and James Fieser, *Ethics: Discovering Right and Wrong*, 7th ed. (Wadsworth/Cengage, 2012), 69.

[7]For a rich discussion of situated or encumbered selves, see Michael J. Sandel, *Democracy's Discontent: America in Search of a Public Philosophy* (Belknap Press, 1996), 111–19.

[8]On this objection, we follow Julia Driver, *Ethics: The Fundamentals* (Blackwell, 2007), 108–9.

[9]C. Stephen Evans, *God and Moral Obligation* (Oxford University Press, 2013), 136–40.

[10]See Donald A. Henderson, "The Eradication of Smallpox—An Overview of the Past, Present, and Future," *Vaccine* 29, no. 4 (2011): D7–D9.

[11]Driver, *Ethics*, 119.

[12]David Gauthier, *Morals by Agreement* (Oxford University Press, 1987), 268.

[13]Gauthier, *Morals by Agreement*, 268—emphasis added.

Chapter Seven Virtue Theory

[1]Susan Schmidt, Peter Baker, and Toni Locy, "Clinton Accused of Urging Aide to Lie," *Washington Post*, January 21, 1998, https://www.washingtonpost.com/wp-srv/politics/special/whitewater/stories/wwtr980121.htm.

[2]See William J. Clinton, "Remarks on the After-School Child Care Initiative in the Roosevelt Room in the White House on January 26, 1998," The American Presidency Project, emphasis added, https://www.presidency.ucsb.edu/node/225911.

[3]Bennett, cited in John McDonald, "Bill Bennett Is Too Harsh on Bill Clinton," *Hartford Courant*, August 28, 1998, https://www.courant.com/news/connecticut/hc-xpm-1998-08-29-9808290064-story.html. See also William J. Bennett, *The Death of Outrage: Bill Clinton and the Assault on American Ideals* (Simon and Schuster, 1998).

[4]See Gregory Kane, "Clinton Not Solely to Blame for U.S. Moral Breakdown," *The Baltimore Sun*, July 17, 1999, https://www.baltimoresun.com/news/bs-xpm-1999-07-18-9907180187-story.html.

[5]Max Lucado, "Decency for President," February 24, 2016, https://maxlucado.com/decency-for-president/.

[6]See, for example, Jonathan Easley, "Democrats Accused of Double Standard on Biden, Kavanaugh," *The Hill*, May 2, 2020, https://thehill.com/homenews/campaign/495757-democrats-accused-of-double-standard-on-biden-kavanaugh/.

[7]Aristotle, *Nicomachean Ethics*, trans. C. D. C. Reeve (Hackett, 2014), 8–9 [1097a20–1097b15].

[8]Mark Timmons claims that virtue theory is committed to the virtue-dependency thesis. See Mark Timmons, *Moral Theory: An Introduction*, 2nd ed. (Rowman & Littlefield, 2013), 278–79. One simple reason why we disagree with Timmons on this point is that Thomas Aquinas was not committed to the virtue-dependency thesis. After all, for Aquinas, virtue theory rests on, and plays a complementary role with, his natural law theory.

[9]Admittedly, one could plausibly conceive of virtue theory in a way that affirms the priority of the right to the good. For example, one could be a *Kantian* virtue theorist. But that is fairly atypical among proponents of virtue theory.

[10]See, for example, Germain Grisez, "The True Ultimate End of Human Beings: The Kingdom, Not God Alone," *Theological Studies* 69 (2008): 38–61.

[11]See, for example, John Finnis, *Natural Law and Natural Rights* (Clarendon Press, 1980), 33–36.

[12]Thomas Aquinas, *Summa Theologica*, trans. Fathers of the English Dominican Province (Christian Classics), pt. IIa–IIae, q. 55, a. 1.

[13]One such place includes Proverbs 6:16–19, which presents a list of seven character traits that are detested or hated by God. See also Joshua 1 (which contains several refrains calling the Israelites to courage), or Micah 6:8 (which calls people to justice, kindness, and humility), or any number of passages that extol wisdom (such as Prov. 1) or faith (such as Gen. 11) or mercy (Lam. 3).

[14]See Wisdom 8:7 (RSV): "And if any one loves righteousness, her labors are virtues; for she teaches self-control and prudence, justice and courage; nothing in life is more profitable for men than these." This point is noted in Rebecca Konyndyk DeYoung, *Glittering Vices*, 2nd ed. (Brazos Press, 2020), 26.

[15]The *Didache* is not particularly long, and a variety of translations can be found online. See, in particular, the Roberts-Donaldson translation (Alexander Roberts and James Donaldson) available on Peter Kirby's *Early Christian Writings*, https://www.earlychristianwritings.com/text/didache-roberts.html.

[16]See 2 *Clement*, trans. Alexander Roberts and James Donaldson, on Peter Kirby's *Early Christian Writings*, https://www.earlychristianwritings.com/text/2clement-roberts.html.

[17]See, for example, Justin Martyr's *First Apology*, *Second Apology*, and *Dialogue with Trypho*, available at https://www.earlychristianwritings.com/justin.html.

[18]See, for example, Tertullian, *Of Patience*, *A Treatise on the Soul*, and *De Spectaculis* (esp. chapter XXIX), which are all available at https://www.earlychristianwritings.com/tertullian.html.

[19]See, for example, Clement of Alexandria, *Paedagogus* and *Stromata*, available online at https://www.earlychristianwritings.com/clement.html.

[20]Paul Lejay, "Aurelius Clemens Prudentius," *The Catholic Encyclopedia*, vol. 12 (Robert Appleton Company, 1911), http://www.newadvent.org/cathen/12517c.htm.

[21]See, for example, *Prudentius*, translated by H. J. Thomson (Harvard University Press, 1949), 274–343.

[22]DeYoung, *Glittering Vices*, 23.

[23]Augustine, quoted in DeYoung, *Glittering Vices*, 23. See also, Augustine, *On the Morals of the Catholic Church against the Manichees* 15.25, as quoted in Servais Pinckaers, *Morality: The Catholic View*, trans. Michael Sherwin (St Augustine's Press, 2001).

[24]Our discussion of Evagrius, and of the capital vices tradition in general, is indebted to chapter 2 of DeYoung, *Glittering Vices*.

[25]See Evagrius of Pontus, "On the Eight Thoughts," in *Evagrius of Pontus: The Greek Ascetic Corpus*, trans. Robert E. Sinkewicz (Oxford University Press, 2003), 66–90.

[26]This chart borrows heavily, with only minor revisions, from DeYoung, *Glittering Vices*, 25. DeYoung notes that Cassian's list mimics Evagrius's list, though Cassian's is ordered from carnal vices to spiritual vices. Since Cassian thought wrath was more of a carnal sin than sadness, he switched the two in the ordering.

[27]See Jeffrey S. Siker, *Jesus, Sin, and Perfection in Early Christianity* (Cambridge University Press, 2015), 46.

[28]See Jonathan T. Pennington, *The Sermon on the Mount and Human Flourishing* (Baker Academic, 2017), 41–67.

[29]Our presentation here draws mostly from the language of the NIV. This chart is partially indebted to David E. Aune, *The New Testament in Its Literary Environment* (Westminster Press, 1987), 194–196.

[30]See Philippa Foot, "The Problem of Abortion and the Doctrine of Double Effect," in *Virtues and Vices and Other Essays in Moral Philosophy* (Oxford University Press, 1978), 19–32.

[31]Sarah Bakewell, "Clang Went the Trolley," *New York Times*, November 22, 2013, https://www.nytimes.com/2013/11/24/books/review/would-you-kill-the-fat-man-and-the-trolley-problem.html?smid=tw-share&_r=0.

[32]Here we follow the so-called "fat man" version of the trolley problem developed by Judith Jarvis Thomson in "The Trolley Problem," *The Yale Law Journal* 94, no. 6 (1985): 1395–415.

[33]Bakewell, "Clang Went the Trolley."

[34] See, for example, Jonathan Dancy, "Moral Particularism," in *Stanford Encyclopedia of Philosophy*, Stanford University, 1997–, article published June 6, 2001, https://plato.stanford.edu/archives/win2017/entries/moral-particularism/.

[35] Aristotle, *Nicomachean Ethics*, 1098a25–29.

[36] Timmons, *Moral Theory*, 276.

[37] In what follows, we draw from Louis Pojman and James Fieser, *Ethics: Discovering Right and Wrong*, 6th ed. (Wadsworth, 2009), 147–52.

[38] See R. Lanier Anderson, "Friedrich Nietzsche," in *The Stanford Encyclopedia of Philosophy*, Stanford University, 1997–, article published March 17, 2017, https://plato.stanford.edu/entries/nietzsche/.

[39] Our example mimics Russ Shafer Landau, *The Fundamentals of Ethics*, 5th ed. (Oxford University Press, 2021), 289.

[40] See, for example, John M. Doris, *Lack of Character: Personality and Moral Behavior* (Cambridge University Press, 2002), and John M. Doris, "Persons, Situations, and Virtue Ethics," *Nous* 32, no. 4 (1998): 504–30.

[41] A. M. Isen and P. F. Levin, "Effect of Feeling Good on Helping: Cookies and Kindness," *Journal of Personality and Social Psychology* 21, no. 3 (1972): 384–88.

[42] Gregory A. Blevins and Terrance Murphy, "Feeling Good and Helping: Further Phonebooth Findings," *Psychological Reports* 34, no. 1 (1974): 326.

[43] See Bibb Latane and John M. Rodin, *The Unresponsive Bystander: Why Doesn't He Help?* (Appleton Century Crofts, 1970). See also Bibb Latane and Judith Rodin, "A Lady in Distress: Inhibiting Effects of Friends and Strangers on Bystander Intervention," *Journal of Experimental Social Psychology* 5, no. 2 (1969): 189–202.

[44] See Robert Roberts, "Situationism and the New Testament Psychology of the Heart," in *The Bible and the University*, ed. David Lyle Jeffrey and C. Stephen Evans (Zondervan, 2007), 139–60.

[45] Robert Richardson, *Memoirs of Alexander Campbell, Embracing a View of the Origin, Progress and Principles of the Religious Reformation which He Advocated*, 2 vols. (Standard Publishing, 1897), 1:406–7—emphasis added.

[46] Plausibly, Jesus not only teaches us that merely following the command to refrain from murder is insufficient to establish righteousness and that the deeper problem of wrath is what generally precedes murder; he also teaches us something about where wrath itself comes from. "Raca" is an Aramaic word of deep contempt, expressing the worthlessness of the object of the curse. If one is in the habit of expressing contempt for others by cursing them, then one is likely to become a wrathful person. Contempt itself has a preceding condition of the soul, too. If one develops the habit of viewing others as complete idiots or worthless morons, then one is in danger of the fires of hell! For one thing, you would be in danger of developing contempt toward others, which might develop into wrath, which might lead to murder. So if you want to be morally upright, it's not enough to act in compliance with the prohibition on murder. If you want to be a citizen of God's kingdom, you need to become the kind of person who doesn't habitually feel and express contempt for others, and you even need to become someone who doesn't go around thinking about what big idiots and morons other people are. This sort of interpretation of Jesus's teaching is strengthened by the peculiar fact that the judgment in each of the three examples follows a sequence of increased authority. Not only are you subject to judgment if you murder someone, but you could be liable to the *court* for wrath of the sort that motivated Cain. In fact, you could be brought to the Sanhedrin (a *high* court) for expressing deep contempt. In fact, just thinking of someone as a

complete idiot or a moron could make you liable to the *divine* court! Plausibly, Jesus escalates the authority of the court in each case as a way of making the point that one who goes about one's everyday life regularly thinking, *What a moron!*, is already moving one's internal life in the direction of the very kind of brokenness that ultimately terminates in murder, and one has in fact already damaged oneself and one's relationships in the process. The citizen of the kingdom of God refrains from murder quite naturally because one isn't the kind of person who is given to wrath or contempt or even just routine and casual disregard of others. It is not enough to comply with the command against murder. One's righteousness must go beyond the righteousness of the mere rule-keepers. The citizens of God's kingdom keep the rules for the right kinds of motivations, and those motivations include *more than mere compliance with a behavioral command.*

Chapter Eight Natural Law Theory

[1]B. Vašečková, M. Patarák, V. Petrušová, and Ľ. Forgáčová, "Self-Amputation in Patient with Body Integrity Dysphoria in Comorbidity with Gender Dysphoria: A Case Report," *Psychopathology* 55, no. 5 (Mar. 2022): 310–16, https://doi.org/10.1159/000522596.

[2]Rianne M. Blom, Raoul C. Hennekam, and Damiaan Denys, "Body Integrity Identity Disorder," *PLoS One* 7, no. 4 (Apr. 2012): 1–6, https://doi.org/10.1371/journal.pone.0034702.

[3]See, for example, the characters reported on in E. J. Dickson, "Death of a TikTok Cosplay Star," *Rolling Stone*, October 21, 2021, https://www.rollingstone.com/culture/culture-features/cosplay-tiktok-manslaughter-yandere-snow-helen-hastings-1234452/.

[4]David Rettew, "The TikTok Inspired Surge of Dissociative Identity Disorder," *Psychology Today*, March 17, 2022, https://www.psychologytoday.com/us/blog/abcs-child-psychiatry/202203/the-tiktok-inspired-surge-dissociative-identity-disorder.

[5]See Amber Roberts, "Otherkin Are People Too; They Just Identify as Nonhuman," *Vice*, July 16, 2015, accessed July 25, 2022, https://www.vice.com/en/article/mvxgwa/from-dragons-to-foxes-the-otherkin-community-believes-you-can-be-whatever-you-want-to-be. See also Ana Valens, "Otherkin Are the Internet's Punchline. They're Also Our Future," *Daily Dot*, September 15, 2020, https://web.archive.org/web/20250313005409/https://www.dailydot.com/irl/otherkin/.

[6]Sarah Cascone, "'The Pain Is Part of the Process': Why Two Artists Are Pushing Body Modification to the Extreme," *artnet*, April 7, 2022, https://news.artnet.com/market/tiamat-legion-medusa-carlos-motta-2093003. See also Daily Mail, "'Top of My Priorities Is to Say Goodbye to Mr. Bojangles, My Penis': Former Banker, 58, Spends $75,000 on 18 Horn Implants, Castration, and Ear Removal to Become a 'Transspecies Reptilian,'" Daily Mail, August 15, 2019, https://www.dailymail.co.uk/femail/article-7361427/Former-banker-spends-75-000-surgery-transspecies-reptilian.html.

[7]Our discussion of Boreman in what follows pulls entirely from Joanna Bourke, "Bestiality, Zoophilia, and Human-Animal Sexual Interactions," *Paragraph* 42, no. 1 (2019): 91–115.

[8]Linda Susan Boreman, quoted in Bourke, "Bestiality, Zoophilia," 92.

[9]See Alfred C. Kinsey, Wardell B. Pomeroy, and Clyde E. Martin, *Sexual Behavior in the Human Male* (W. B. Saunders, 1948), 670–76; and Morton M. Hunt, *Sexual Behavior in the 1970s* (Playboy Press, 1974). Both of these studies are older and potentially

methodologically flawed, but they are apparently still the best-known data on the matter. See Bourke, "Bestiality, Zoophilia," 95–100.

[10] See, for example, Associated Press, "British Woman Marries Dolphin," *Fox News*, January 13, 2015, https://www.foxnews.com/story/british-woman-marries-dolphin.

[11] Jennifer Sullivan, "Man in Infamous Enumclaw Horse-Sex Case Faces New Charges in Tennessee," *Seattle Times*, October 20, 2009, https://www.seattletimes.com/seattle-news/man-in-infamous-enumclaw-horse-sex-case-faces-new-charges-in-tennessee/.

[12] Pope Paul VI, *Encyclical Letter "Humanae Vitae" of the Supreme Pontiff Paul VI* (1968), § II, a. 13. Accessed online July 25, 2022, at https://www.vatican.va/content/paul-vi/en/encyclicals/documents/hf_p-vi_enc_25071968_humanae-vitae.html.

[13] Germain G. Grisez, "The First Principle of Practical Reason: A Commentary on the *Summa Theologiae*, 1–2, Question 94, Article 2," *Natural Law Forum* 10, no. 1 (1965): 175–76.

[14] Our discussion in this section follows Ralph McInerny, "The Principles of the Natural Law," *American Journal of Jurisprudence* 25 (1980): 3–5.

[15] See, for example, Grisez, "First Principle of Practical Reason," 170. See also, McInerny, "Principles of Natural Law," 3.

[16] Aquinas's *Summa Theologiae* as excerpted in Thomas Aquinas, *On Law, Morality, and Politics*, 2nd ed., trans. Richard J. Regan, ed. William P. Baumgarth and Richard J. Regan (Hackett, 2002), 43 [ST Ia–IIae, q. 94, a. 2]. All subsequent references to Aquinas's *Summa Theologiae* will follow the conventional citation format [ST #, q. #, a. #] and will refer to the Regan translation mentioned here, unless otherwise noted.

[17] Aquinas, ST Ia–IIae, q. 94, a. 2.

[18] Aquinas, ST Ia–IIae, q. 94, a. 3.

[19] The content of this chart, including the citations to the different natural law theorists, draws from Mark C. Murphy, "The Natural Law Tradition in Ethics," in *The Stanford Encyclopedia of Philosophy*, Stanford University, 1997–, article published September 23, 2002, https://plato.stanford.edu/archives/sum2019/entries/natural-law-ethics/, §2.3.

[20] Germain Grisez, *The Way of the Lord Jesus*, vol. 1: *Christian Moral Principles* (Franciscan Herald Press, 1983), 121–22.

[21] T. D. J. Chappell, *Understanding Human Goods* (Edinburgh University Press, 1995), 43.

[22] John Finnis, "Is Natural Law Compatible with Limited Government," in *Natural Law, Liberalism, and Morality*, ed. Robert P. George (Oxford University Press, 1996), 5.

[23] Mark C. Murphy, *Natural Law and Practical Rationality* (Cambridge University Press, 2001), 96.

[24] Alfonso Gomez-Lobo, *Morality and the Human Goods: An Introduction to Natural Law Ethics* (Georgetown University Press, 2002), 10–23.

[25] Aquinas, ST Ia–IIae, q. 18, a. 1.

[26] Murphy, "Natural Law Tradition in Ethics," §1.3.

[27] Aquinas, ST IIa–IIae, q. 64, a. 7. We should note that Aquinas's position is more complicated than we have depicted it since he believes it would be permissible for a *public* official (e.g., a police officer) to shoot to kill—that is, to intend death—because that public official is acting on behalf of the state. Aquinas held that the state could intend such a death without violating the adjudicating norms of practical reason.

[28] John Finnis, *Natural Law and Natural Rights* (Oxford University Press, 1980), 105–6.

[29] Finnis, *Natural Law and Natural Rights*, 106–7.

[30] Finnis, *Natural Law and Natural Rights*, 110.

[31] Finnis, *Natural Law and Natural Rights*, 110.

[32] Finnis, *Natural Law and Natural Rights*, 111–18.

[33] Finnis, *Natural Law and Natural Rights*, 118–25.

[34] Finnis, *Natural Law and Natural Rights*, 125.

[35] Finnis, *Natural Law and Natural Rights*, 125–26.

[36] Our discussion in this section follows Craig A. Boyd and Don Thorsen, *Christian Ethics and Moral Philosophy* (Baker Academic, 2018), 77–81.

[37] See Augustine, *On the Free Choice of the Will*, trans. Thomas Williams (Hackett, 1993), sect. 1.6. Cited also in Boyd and Thorsen, *Christian Ethics and Moral Philosophy*, 78n9.

[38] Augustine, *On the Free Choice of the Will*, sect. 1.6.

[39] Some of the material in this section derives in part from our chapter on natural law theory in J. Caleb Clanton and Kraig Martin, eds., *Nature and Command: On the Metaphysical Foundations of Morality* (The University of Tennessee Press, 2022).

[40] Our response follows Ralph McInerny, *Ethica Thomistica: The Moral Philosophy of Thomas Aquinas*, rev. ed. (The Catholic University of America Press, 1997), 37.

[41] Murphy, "Natural Law Tradition in Ethics," §2.2—emphasis added. We should point out that this objection may not apply to newer versions of NLT that do not attempt to identify human goods by attending to descriptive facts about human inclinations.

[42] Murphy, "Natural Law Tradition in Ethics," §2.2; see also Mark Timmons, *Moral Theory: An Introduction*, 2nd ed. (Rowman & Littlefield, 2013), 95.

[43] See Mark C. Murphy, *God and Moral Law: On the Theistic Explanation of Morality* (Oxford University Press, 2011), 74–99, esp. 80–90.

[44] Murphy, *God and Moral Law*, 148.

[45] Murphy, *God and Moral Law*, 148.

[46] Janine Marie Idziak, "Divine Commands Are the Foundation of Morality," in *Contemporary Debates in Philosophy of Religion*, ed. Michael L. Peterson and Raymond J. VanArragon (Blackwell, 2004), 298—emphasis added. See also Janine Marie Idziak, Introduction to *Questions on an Ethics of Divine Commands*, by Andrew of Neufchateau, xi–xliii, trans. and ed. Janine Marie Idziak (University of Notre Dame Press, 1997), xvii.

[47] Idziak, "Divine Commands Are the Foundation," 298.

[48] Mutatis mutandi for Islam, which holds that God commands congregational prayer and rest on the *sixth* day of the week.

Chapter Nine Divine Command Theory

[1] Our gloss on Nat Turner draws from several sources. See, for example, Patrick Breen, "Understanding the Gospel of Nat Turner," *Smithsonian Magazine*, October 7, 2016, https://www.smithsonianmag.com/history/understanding-gospel-nat-turner-180960714/. See also "Nat Turner's Rebellion," National Museum of African American History and Culture, https://nmaahc.si.edu/explore/stories/nat-turners-rebellion; and "Nat Turner's Rebellion: To Rebel and Make Insurrection," Library of Virginia, https://www.lva.virginia.gov/exhibits/DeathLiberty/natturner/index.htm. Finally, see Nat Turner's final confession in Nat Turner, *The Confessions of Nat Turner*, ed. Thomas R. Gray (Lucas & Deaver, 1831), https://digitalcommons.unl.edu/cgi/viewcontent.cgi?article=1014&context=etas.

[2] Turner, *Confessions of Nat Turner*, 7.

[3] Turner, *Confessions of Nat Turner*, 11–12.

[4] Turner, *Confessions of Nat Turner*, 11.
[5] Turner, *Confessions of Nat Turner*, 7.
[6] Turner, *Confessions of Nat Turner*, 7.
[7] See, for example, Stanford University's Martin Luther King Jr. Research and Education Institute's introduction to Reverend James M. Lawson Jr., available online at https://kinginstitute.stanford.edu/reverend-james-m-lawson-jr.
[8] See James Lawson, "James Lawson: The Architect of the United States Civil Rights Movement (Best of NSE)," interview with Lee C. Camp, *No Small Endeavor* (podcast), July 11, 2024, audio 6:00–11:00. Transcript available online at https://www.nosmallendeavor.com/james-lawson-best-of-nse.
[9] Lawson, "James Lawson."
[10] See, for example, the Pew Research Center, "Religious Composition by Country, 2010–2050," December 21, 2022, https://www.pewresearch.org/religion/interactives/religious-composition-by-country-2010-2050/.
[11] See, for example, M. V. Dougherty, "Thomas Aquinas and Divine Command Theory," *Proceedings of the American Catholic Philosophical Association* 76 (2002): 153–64.
[12] John E. Hare contends, for example, that Scotus's moral philosophy represents "the best version we have of a divine command theory." See Hare, *God's Call: Moral Realism, God's Commands, and Human Autonomy* (Wm. B. Eerdmans, 2001), 50. In our view, such an attribution stands in need of significant qualification. However, it is true that Scotus affirms that—in some cases—God's commands give rise to moral obligations.
[13] We borrow this example from C. Stephen Evans, *God and Moral Obligation* (Oxford University Press, 2013), 37.
[14] J. L. Mackie, *Ethics: Inventing Right and Wrong* (Penguin, 1990), 38. See also the supplement "Mackie's Arguments for the Moral Error Theory" in section 4 of Richard Joyce, "Moral Anti-Realism," *The Stanford Encyclopedia of Philosophy*, Stanford University, 1997–, article published July 30, 2007, https://plato.stanford.edu/archives/win2016/entries/moral-anti-realism/.
[15] See, for example, Evans, *God and Moral Obligation*, 15, 29–32, and 118. Also see Robert Merrihew Adams, *Finite and Infinite Goods* (Oxford University Press, 1999), 235–38.
[16] John E. Hare, *God's Command* (Oxford University, 2015), 141.
[17] See especially Janine Idziak, "In Search of 'Good Positive Reasons' in Favor of an Ethics of Divine Command: A Catalogue of Arguments," *Faith and Philosophy* 6, no. 1 (1989): 47–64.
[18] This argument draws from Mark C. Murphy, *God and Moral Law: On the Theistic Explanation of Morality* (Oxford University Press, 2011), 6–12.
[19] To be clear, Murphy does *not* endorse this last move. While he argues that, given theism, morality must have a theistic explanation, he does not think that this is enough to entail divine command theory. See Murphy, *God and Moral Law*, 12–13.
[20] This kind of argument can be seen in Richard Swinburne, "Duty and the Will of God," *Canadian Journal of Philosophy* 4, no. 2 (1974): 213–27. See also Swinburne, "What Difference Does God Make to Morality?," in *Is Goodness with God Good Enough*, ed. Robert K. Garcia and Nathan L. King (Rowman & Littlefield, 2009), 155–56; Richard Swinburne, *Revelation: From Metaphor to Analogy*, 2nd ed. (Oxford University Press, 2007), 90; Adams, *Finite and Infinite Goods*, 252–53; and Mark C. Murphy, *An Essay on Divine Authority*, (Cornell University Press, 2002), 94–104.

[21] John Locke, *Second Treatise of Government*, in *Locke: Two Treatises of Government*, ed. Peter Laslett (Cambridge University Press, 2017), 271 [II.ii.§6].

[22] For more on this sort of argument, see Hare, *God's Command*, 17–18; see also Hare's *God and Morality: A Philosophical History* (Wiley-Blackwell, 2009), 97.

[23] James Rachels, "God and Human Attitudes," *Religious Studies* 7, no. 4 (1971): 332–33—emphasis in the original.

[24] Philip L. Quinn, "The Recent Revival of Divine Command Ethics," *Philosophy and Phenomenological Research*, supplement (1990): 345–51. Quinn attributes this revival to the work of Robert M. Adams, Philip L. Quinn, Janine Marie Idziak, Edward R. Wierenga, and Richard J. Mouw.

[25] Evans, *God and Moral Obligation*, 35.

[26] See Hare, *God's Command*, 298.

[27] We say that we would *almost* certainly never be justified in believing that God has commanded us to sacrifice a child (instead of saying that we would never be so justified) precisely because it remains logically possible that God could raise the sacrificed child from the dead. Admittedly, we cannot imagine the circumstances in which we would be epistemically justified in believing of some given child that God would raise the child from the dead and that God would want us to sacrifice the child to show God's power in doing so. But such circumstances seem logically possible, if immensely improbable. Perhaps if we lived at a time and in a culture where it was widely accepted that the gods desired child sacrifice, and perhaps if God had communicated to us in the past in veridical ways, it would seem different to us.

[28] And thus, by the ought-implies-can principle, God nullifies any would-be obligation to sacrifice Isaac. Because Abraham simply *cannot* kill Isaac (by God's power to prevent him), there is no sense in which he *ought* to kill Isaac.

[29] See Hare, *God's Command*, 173–75. Of course, as Hare notes, we might wonder why God did not just tell Abraham forthrightly without going through this routine. Hare speculates that "perhaps Abraham had to form the intention to do the act himself in order to see fully what was wrong with his ancestral practice [of child sacrifice]" (175n121). See also Hare, *God and Morality*, 269–70.

[30] See Adams, *Finite and Infinite Goods*, 279.

[31] Russ Shafer-Landau, *The Fundamentals of Ethics*, 5th ed. (Oxford University Press, 2021), 75.

[32] Murphy, *God and Moral Law*, 124.

[33] Hare, *God's Command*, 112.

Chapter Ten Toward a Nonreductive Combination Theory

[1] Robert Merrihew Adams, *Finite and Infinite Goods: A Framework for Ethics* (Oxford University Press, 1999), 31–33.

[2] Mark C. Murphy, *God and Moral Law: On the Theistic Explanation of Morality* (Oxford University Press, 2011), 160.

[3] John E. Hare, *God and Morality: A Philosophical History* (Wiley-Blackwell, 2009), 253.

[4] Rebecca Konyndyk DeYoung, *Glittering Vices: A New Look at the Seven Deadly Sins and Their Remedies*, 2nd ed. (Brazos Press, 2020), 2.

INDEX